THE
BIRTH OF
EMPIRE

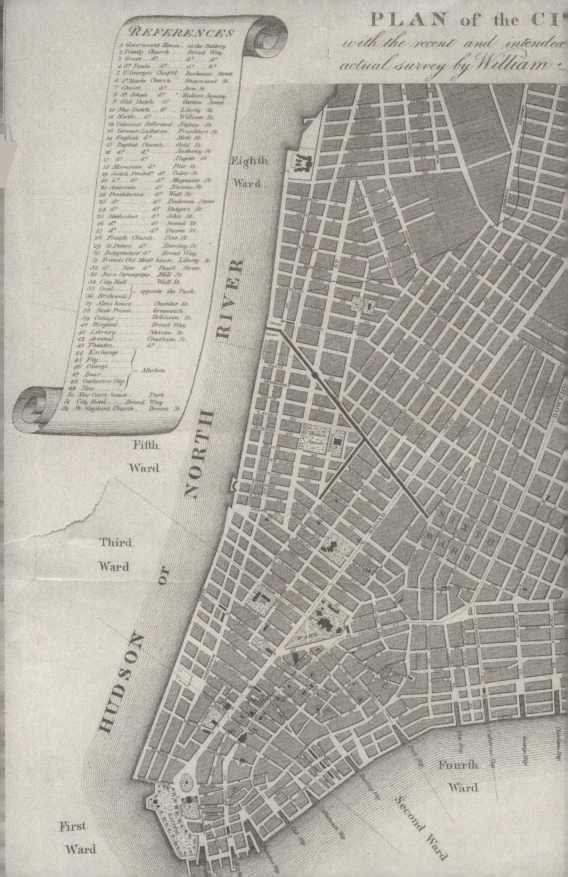

CONTENTS

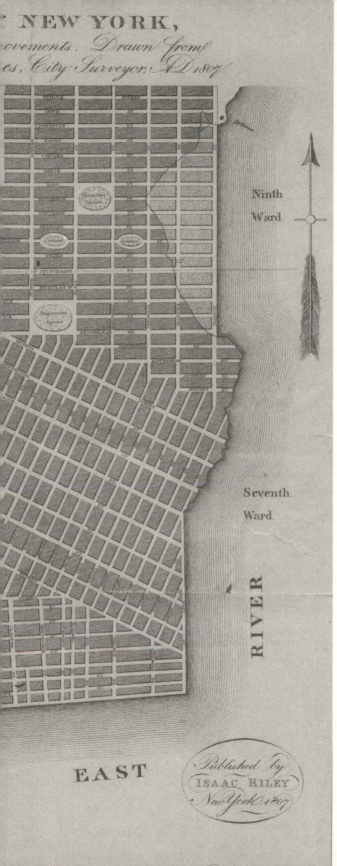

THE
BIRTH OF
EMPIRE

o o o

*De Witt Clinton
and the
American
Experience,
1769–1828*

EVAN CORNOG

New York o Oxford

Oxford University Press

1998

Oxford University Press

Oxford   New York

Athens   Auckland   Bangkok   Bogotá   Buenos Aires   Calcutta
Cape Town   Chennai   Dar es Salaam   Delhi   Florence   Hong Kong   Istanbul
Karachi   Kuala Lumpur   Madrid   Melbourne   Mexico City   Mumbai
Nairobi   Paris   São Paulo   Singapore   Taipei   Tokyo   Toronto   Warsaw

and associated companies in
Berlin   Ibadan

Published by Oxford University Press, Inc.
198 Madison Avenue, New York, New York 10016

Oxford is a registered trademark of Oxford University Press

Library of Congress Cataloging-in-Publication Data
Cornog, Evan.
The birth of empire : DeWitt Clinton and the American experience,
1769–1828 / Evan Cornog.
p.   cm.
Includes bibliographical references and index.
ISBN 0-19-511949-5
1. Clinton, DeWitt, 1769–1828.   2. Legislators—United States—
Biography.   3. United States.   Congress.   Senate—Biography.
4. Governors—New York (State)—Biography.   5. Mayors—New York
(State)—New York—Biography.   6. Erie Canal (N.Y.)—History.
7. New York (State)—Politics and government—1775–1865.   8. United
States—Politics and government—1783–1865.   I. Title.
E340.C65C74   1998
974.7′03′092—dc21   97–53112
[B]

A portion of this work originally appeared in *The American Scholar.*

1 3 5 7 9 8 6 4 2

Printed in the United States of America
on acid-free paper

For

my parents,

and for Ann

o   o   o

ACKNOWLEDGMENTS

IN OFFERING MY THANKS to those who helped in the production of this book, it seems logical to start with the librarians. The debt historians owe to librarians is immeasurable, but seldom has this been brought so clearly home to me as when I was doing this book. Part of my work was done while the New-York Historical Society was in imminent danger of closing, in the spring of 1993, a time when frantic historians were packed into the library's reading room, racing to fill in gaps in their research before the society's holdings became unreachable, perhaps for years, or were dispersed through sale. The library staff worked feverishly under the most depressing conditions, and to them in particular I extend my thanks. The great majority of DeWitt Clinton's papers are in the collection of Columbia University, and the librarians in the Rare Book and Manuscript Library there were efficient, courteous, and helpful. I would also like to thank the staffs of the New York State Library and the New York Public Library.

At Columbia University, where this book took its original form as a doctoral dissertation, I received invaluable guidance and encouragement from Richard Bushman, Ann Douglas, Eric Foner, and Herbert Sloan. Elizabeth Blackmar generously spent hours discussing my topic with me as I was beginning my research, and alerted me early on to several fruitful lines of approach. My adivsor, Kenneth T. Jackson, provided calm direction and acute suggestions, and served as a constant reminder of the author's obligations to his readers. Eric McKitrick, although he had retired by the time my thesis was under way, was involved in every step of the research and writing, sharing his profound knowledge of the politics and culture of the period, and sharing as well occasional plates of oysters and pints of Guinness. He read the entire manuscript with an active pen, saving me from errors and suggesting improvements on nearly every page.

Several friends were also kind enough to read and critique my work. Lex Kaplen read an early version with minute attention and contributed greatly to improving both the shape and the sound of my arguments, and John Bennet read the final version and clarified some remaining obscurities. Other helpful comments came from Clifton Hood, Sarah Henry, and the members of the George Washington Plunkitt Benevolent Society.

At Oxford University Press, I wish to thank Sheldon Meyer, to whom I sent the manuscript, and Thomas LeBien, who edited it with care, sensitivity, and efficiency. Also at Oxford, Susan Ferber, Robert Milks, and Jack Rummel oversaw the transition from manuscript to book with uncommon care and courtesy.

Three writers and friends—Richard Whelan, Shirley Hazzard, and the late Francis Steegmuller—have encouraged my work by word and, more important, by example, and to them I owe more than I can say.

Finally I want to thank Ann, my love, for every kind of support.

THE
BIRTH OF
EMPIRE

INTRODUCTION

Gentlemen of New York

B Y THE TIME OF DeWitt Clinton's birth, on March 2, 1769, the Clinton family had been in New York for nearly four decades. By DeWitt's tenth birthday, his father had become a major general in the Continental Army, and his uncle George was governor of the new state of New York. At twenty-one, he had graduated from Columbia College, was completing his study of the law, had published well-received political articles in a New York City newspaper, and had started learning his duties as secretary to the governor. By his thirty-fifth birthday, he had served as a state assemblyman, state senator, and United States senator, and had become New York City's mayor.

The success of DeWitt's father and uncle had paved the way for this charmed ascent. His upbringing instilled in him a set of qualities that help account for both his triumphs as an architect of innovative government policies and his failures as a politician. Raised in comfort, educated at the best schools, welcome in the most exclusive homes in New York, the young politician had many advantages. Growing up amid the ferment of revolution and nation-building, he had a sense of fitness to command that was wedded to a seriousness of purpose, a cognizance of the high stakes involved in the nation's early politics. But along with these good qualities he possessed a self-importance, haughty bearing, and hostility to criticism that eventually alienated many of his closest allies. As his friend James Renwick put it, "There was hardly any distinguished individual of our state who has not at one time been opposed to Clinton, and at another united with him in pursuit of the same political object."[1]

For Clinton, as for Renwick, the politics that mattered was that conducted by "distinguished individuals," and he achieved his greatest successes when he managed to work amicably with other leaders in the state of New York. At no other time in his career did he succeed as fully as he did in promoting the construction of the Erie Canal, the great state project that transformed New York and the nation in the early decades of the nineteenth century.

On December 30, 1815, a public meeting was held at the City Hotel at Broadway and Cedar Street, in lower Manhattan, to solicit support for a proposed canal that would link Lake Erie with the Hudson River. A notice of the meeting had been published in the *New York Evening Post* that afternoon, and doubtless some citizens came as a result of that announcement. But the organizers of the meeting wanted an influential audience, and so, as one of them later recalled, "cards of invitation [were] addressed to about one hundred gentlemen of that city, to meet at the City Hotel." The organizers were part of the city's recognized elite; all were prominent professionally and were active in a variety of political, fraternal, cultural, and charitable organizations. They were as compact and cozy-seeming a ruling class as one could imagine.[2]

William Bayard, who was chairman of the gathering, was one of the town's leading merchants and had strong Federalist credentials. Bayard's father and the rest of his family had left New York with the British troops at the end of the Revolutionary War, but the son remained and in 1786 started a shipping firm that grew and thrived through the uncertainties of the Napoleonic wars, securing profits robust enough to offset the depredations of the British admiralty courts and other hazards. The firm won the trust of bankers in Holland, gaining access to that scarcest of commodities in the United States—capital. In 1815 Bayard was also the president of the Bank of America, where such prominent New Yorkers as Archibald Gracie and Philip Hone served as directors.[3]

Another prominent Federalist present was Cadwallader D. Colden, an attorney and philanthropist. Colden's paternal grandfather, also named Cadwallader, had served as a colonial lieutenant governor of New York and was perhaps the first person to advocate improving navigation to the west to exploit the break in the Appalachian Mountains carved by the Mohawk River. The younger Colden's activities were not limited to his law practice. In 1815 he was the president of the Manumission Society, a director of the American Academy of Arts, a "counsellor" of the Literary and Philosophical Society, a trustee of the New-York Hospital, and one of the grand officers of the Sovereign Grand Consistory of the Masons.[4]

Thomas Eddy was certainly the man at the meeting most knowledgeable about the potential of the canal and the problems involved in realizing that potential. Eddy was a founder of the Western Inland Lock Navigation Company, a private corporation chartered in the 1790s with a view toward constructing canals for profit. But the company, undercapitalized and lacking the power of eminent domain, had become mired in debt, in engineering difficulties, and, indeed, in mire. A state takeover could save the project. Eddy had displayed a remarkable aptitude for turning private energies to the public good. His greatest efforts had been directed toward prison reform, but he was also instrumental in the founding of the Bloomingdale Asylum for the insane, and he was treasurer of the Literary and Philosophical Society and of the New-York Hospital, a trustee of the New-York Free School Society, and a director of the Humane Society, which aided the city's destitute.[5]

The secretary of the City Hotel gathering was John Pintard, who had been one of New York's most successful businessmen after the revolution. He was among the city's first stockbrokers, married a well-connected and celebrated beauty, Eliza Brashear, and by 1789 had been elected to the post of assistant alderman for the Second Ward. But in 1792 the stock speculator William Duer was ruined when some of his speculations went bad, and Pintard, who had endorsed a note for Duer, was ruined with him. Pintard moved to Newark, but his creditors pursued him, and he spent a year in prison there for debt. He returned to New York, serving as city inspector beginning in 1804 and as clerk of the Common Council until 1809, when he resigned to become secretary of the Mutual Insurance Company. He was recording secretary of the New-York Historical Society, secretary of the American Academy of Arts, a trustee of the Society Library, and a founder of the General Theological Seminary and the American Bible Society. He had been a sachem of the Tammany Society and was a Mason, a member of the Holland Lodge.[6]

The only person among the organizers not from New York City was Jonas Platt, the Federalist leader of Oneida County and a judge on the New York Supreme Court.[7] He had attended Columbia College in the 1780s, and there had joined a debating group called the Uranian Society. A pioneering settler of central New York, he had won election to the state senate and was the Federalist candidate for governor in 1810. He had broached the subject of making the canal a state project in a conversation with Thomas Eddy in the spring of 1810. The City Hotel meeting of 1815, intended to revive the plan, was hatched by Eddy and Platt that fall when Platt arrived in New York in the course of his judicial duties.[8]

Support for the canal was not limited to Federalists, however. An important faction of the Jeffersonian, or Republican, party was represented at the meeting by John Swartwout, who had been one of Aaron Burr's chief lieutenants when Burr was vice president. Swartwout and his brothers had moved to New York City from Dutchess County and built a successful business as importers and merchants. Swartwout was a director of the City Bank and, like Pintard, had been a Tammany sachem.[9]

The last of the organizers was DeWitt Clinton. Forty-six years old, he had held important positions in the city, state, and national governments for twenty-five years. By the time he was thirty-one, he was the leader of the Republican party in the state, and in that role pioneered the use of a "spoils system" of patronage that granted state offices to supporters and denied them to opponents. He had served briefly as a United States senator, introducing legislation that led to the passage of the Twelfth Amendment, which clarified the procedure for electing the president so that no intended vice president could scheme to take the prize in the Electoral College or the House of Representatives, as Burr was thought to have tried to do in 1801. The amendment embedded political parties in the very fabric of the Constitution. Clinton had resigned from the Senate in 1803 to return to New York City as mayor and had relinquished that office only nine months before the City Hotel meeting. If the other canal boosters were diligent in their pursuit of the public good through voluntary organizations, Clinton was fanatical. In 1815 he was president of the Literary and Philosophical Society, the American Academy of Arts, and the Free School Society, and second vice president of the Historical Society. He was a director of the Humane Society and a trustee of the New-York Lying-In Hospital. He was a leading Freemason and, like Pintard and Colden, a member of the Holland Lodge, which he had entered in 1790, along with a German immigrant named John Jacob Astor.[10]

Clinton had a serious interest in the natural sciences and archaeology, and his endeavors had won him membership in the Linnaean Society of London and the Wernerian Society of Edinburgh, as well as the Academy of Natural Sciences in Philadelphia. His *Introductory Discourse Before the Literary and Philosophical Society,* delivered in May 1814, was admired for the capable summary it gave of the progress of the sciences in America.[11]

Clinton had also made a mark for himself as a political propagandist, beginning in 1787 with a series of letters opposing the federal Constitution and including a pamphlet during the 1800 election defending Thomas Jefferson against charges of godlessness. He had also written numerous articles attacking political foes in New York and defending himself from their sallies. For most of the previous decade he had been one of the controlling figures in the Manhattan Company and had used the company's banking powers to support both his political and his philanthropic activities.

His appearance was as impressive as his career had been accomplished. He was six feet three inches tall, still slender, with brown hair combed back from his face to reveal the high, broad forehead that at the time was held to signify deep intelligence. His eyes were dark hazel and endowed with a penetrating gaze that some found unnerving. His lips were thin, and his mouth was set in a grim line that betrayed a personality more attached to dignity than to mirth. As Clinton aged, he put on weight, particularly after his health was compromised in a riding accident in 1818, and later portraits show a more jowly statesman, but the glint of the eyes and set of the mouth remain unchanged. One traveler who observed him in the early 1820s commented that "there is something in his countenance, which, to a stranger seems to denote a little haughtiness and reserve, tho he is said to be very amiable in the society of his friends." This combination of high achievement, formidable appearance, and palpable self-regard led Clinton's enemies to dub him the "Magnus Apollo." Although the City Hotel meeting was attended by many prominent figures, DeWitt Clinton was unquestionably the leading man present.[12]

The connections among these men may have been close, but they were not always comfortable. Consider the relationship between the meeting's chairman, William Bayard, and its secretary, John Pintard. When Pintard was languishing in jail in Newark, he made this notation in his diary: "Newark in carcere, Wednesday, 24th May, 1798. . . . Mrs Pintard went to town this morning at 6 o'clock, to use her oratory with Messrs Leroy & Bayard & Mr Cornelius Bogart, to withdraw their actions in the Federal Court." Her oratory must have worked, for the next day Pintard's diary notes that his creditor Bayard had "relented," and he was soon released.[13]

A more serious dispute marred the history of DeWitt Clinton's relations with John Swartwout. In 1802 Clinton was directing the assault against Aaron Burr in a political pamphlet war that exceeded even the customary squalid tone of such battles. Hearing reports of allegations made against him by Swartwout, Burr's right-hand man, Clinton called Swartwout "a liar, a scoundrel, and a villain." After an exchange of unrepentant letters, a duel was arranged, in which Swartwout was wounded twice before Clinton broke it off and refused to fire again. (There are other connections here as well: When Swartwout's chief shot Alexander Hamilton in 1804, the dying Federalist was taken to the house of William Bayard and was attended by Dr. David Hosack, who served as a director or trustee of many of the organizations named above, and who wrote the first biography of his good friend DeWitt Clinton.) The canal project, however, was judged sufficiently important for its advocates to put aside past (and present) differences and work together for its realization.[14]

Most of these men lived and worked within a few blocks of Wall Street, where the city's banks were spread out along two blocks. New York was truly a "walking city" then—homes and businesses were intermixed on the same blocks, and even the wealthy lived close to where they worked—but one had to be careful whom one might run into.[15]

One also had to be careful where one stepped. Visitors to New York often remarked on the cows and pigs that wandered through the streets, and the dead animals left to decay where they fell. New York was a dirty city, and a growing one. In 1815 it had perhaps 100,000 inhabitants, and the built-up area extended as far north as Houston Street and Greenwich Village.[16]

The physical compactness of the city, characteristic of its time, was about to disappear forever, as was another aspect of New York life that was displayed in this remarkable group of men, and even in a single individual, DeWitt Clinton—a combination of political eminence, reform activism, business leadership, cultural engagement, and scientific distinction. These men can be seen as a kind of culmination of the virtues of the eighteenth century, but the project they had gathered to launch would hurl New York, and the nation, headlong into the nineteenth.

Of all these men, the one to whom the canal meant most was Clinton, and that December night in 1815 was the critical moment in his career. His tenure as mayor had ended in March, when his political adversaries on the state Council of Appointment (which controlled most state offices, including the mayoralty) had replaced him with John Ferguson, the grand sachem of the Tammany Society. Only three years before, in 1812, Clinton had run for president, losing narrowly to James Madison. (Had Pennsylvania gone for Clinton, he would have been elected.) The defeat had undercut his power in New York. Although he was a lifelong member of the Republican party, his presidential candidacy had been waged with the cooperation of leading Federalists who hoped to defeat Madison by backing another Republican, one more palatable to northeastern interests. The conflicting messages Clinton's supporters conveyed to different audiences in that campaign had sullied his political reputation.

So in 1815 Clinton was out of office, with the Federalist party disintegrating and the New York Republican party dominated by Governor Daniel D. Tompkins and a rising political tactician named Martin Van Buren, who would make party loyalty the glue of American politics. Clinton's uncle George, who as governor had launched DeWitt's career and as vice president under Jefferson and Madison had furthered it, was dead, and Clinton's own uncompromising manner and his hauteur had alienated many former supporters. His political career, most thought, was over. He needed a cause to rebuild his reputation, and in the proposed Erie Canal he saw his chance.

The timing of the meeting was opportune for the canal's chances as well. The 1810 meeting between Platt and Eddy had resulted in a bill appointing commissioners (including Clinton) to survey possible canal routes, and their recommendations had led to a bill authorizing construction. But the War of 1812 had diverted attention and money, and in 1814 the authorization had been repealed. Interest in the canal had revived with the end of the war, in 1815.

That year marked the beginning of an expansive new era. The victory of Andrew Jackson at the Battle of New Orleans in January, although irrelevant to the outcome of the war, provoked an outpouring of nationalistic sentiment and brought a sense of new possibilities. Across the Atlantic, the end of the Napoleonic wars presented new opportunities (and challenges) for American commerce. And European immigration, negligible for a quarter century, was growing, providing more workers for American businesses and increasing the demand for farmland; thus the pace of westward expansion accelerated, and with it the need for transportation to bring the products of those farms to domestic and foreign markets.

The time was right for bringing the issue of the canal forward. The issue was right for moving Clinton's career forward again. The meeting at the City Hotel was called not to gauge opinion but to mold it. The purpose was to secure an endorsement of a proposed "memorial," or petition, to the state legislature, calling on it to authorize the construction of a canal. Clinton was the author of that memorial. When the results of the meeting were published in the *Evening Post* on January 2, the text was essentially a verbatim copy of Clinton's minutes. His own contribution was stressed: "De Witt Clinton, Esq., from the committee appointed for that purpose at a former meeting, reported, that . . . it would be proper to present a memorial to the Legislature in favor of a Canal from Lake Erie to the Hudson." The meeting voted to print a thousand copies of Clinton's memorial and to gather signatures for an appeal to the state legislature. Most of the desired legislation was passed in April 1816. But Tompkins and Van Buren, loath to see a project so closely associated with Clinton succeed, managed to limit the authorization for that year to further surveys. The following year, after Tompkins left Albany to become James Monroe's vice president, the legislature gave final authority to build the canal, and the state's voters elected Clinton to succeed Tompkins by a vote sufficiently lopsided that the great chronicler of (and participant in) New York's early political battles, Jabez D. Hammond, termed it "unanimous."[17]

Clinton took a chance in associating himself so closely with the planned canal. Had the project suffered the fate of the Western Inland Lock Navigation Company's attempt, his political resurrection would have been brief. But it did not, and Clinton remained a prominent figure in national as well as state politics until his death, in 1828.

The world the Erie Canal created would leave little room for the compact elite that had managed the meeting at the City Hotel. Seldom in the future would business, government, culture, and reform march so closely together. DeWitt Clinton was the exemplar of the public-spirited polymath, and through him we can see both the possibilities of this kind of leadership and the causes of its downfall. It is one of the many ironies of his career that few things contributed as much to this change as the canal he brought into being.

The Erie Canal was the grandest public works project of the nineteenth century, and it hastened the economic changes that were reshaping the country. By developing western New York and then funneling migrants to the new states beyond, it fostered greater migration to the west. It greatly lowered the cost of transporting bulky goods like grain, linking new settlements to domestic and foreign markets. The financing of the project promoted the growth of American capital markets and honed the financial skills of New York's bankers. The canal insured New York City's position as the nation's leading metropolis, and the Port of New York soon dwarfed its rivals. This economic link to the west forged political links that would prove crucial in the sectional crisis that climaxed in the Civil War.

Clinton saw the canal's success as confirmation of his belief that the state's proper role in the economy is an active one. Such direct participation by government in economic matters was far more common at the beginning of the nineteenth century than it was at its end. The Erie Canal was the most successful of these activist efforts, but that success carried the seed of ultimate failure. For the canal spawned many imitators, and it was the troubles they fell into with the Panic of 1837 that discredited state activism and led to the embrace of the laissez-faire policies that would prevail from the 1850s into the twentieth century.

Change was occurring in political practices as well. For George Clinton and his nephew DeWitt, governing New York had been a family business. (A few other families, notably the innumerable Livingstons, also played prominent roles.) In the half-century between the revolution and DeWitt's death, the two Clintons sat in the governor's chair for a total of thirty years. Strength of personality, recognized achievements, and family connections were initially sufficient to the task. But the spread of settlers across New York meant that the state's affairs could no longer be casually managed by a small and coherent elite, particularly when geographical expansion was accompanied by population growth throughout the state and by more liberal voting requirements (for white males) contained in the New York State Constitution of 1821.[18] Although the spread of democracy certainly did not eliminate the power of prominent families, it did change the terms under which those families could exercise their power and allowed new sources of political might to emerge. Here, too, Clinton was an innovator, helping to develop two crucial pieces of American political machinery, the spoils system and party conventions. But (unlike Van Buren) he was not able to carry his innovations to their logical conclusions. Clinton was born in a time of elite governance, but he died at the dawn of the age of mass politics. And in politics, as with the canal, the world that was coming to have no place for Clinton was one he had done much to create.

The meeting at the City Hotel in 1815 straddled these eras, and its form displayed the contradictory logic of the transitional politics of the time. Clinton's own manuscript minutes of the gathering describe it as a "numerous & respectable meeting of the citizens of New York." The "respectable" side was clear—the distinguished supporters of the canal and the invitations sent to the prominent men of the city. But by

1815 the rising democratic spirit (and the practicalities of the legislative process) demanded that the support for such measures be "numerous" as well—hence the ad in the *Evening Post*.[19]

The new world no longer held an honored place for the patrician politician, the amateur scientist, or the scholar-statesman. The building of the canal gave Clinton his greatest victory, and was his greatest achievement, but the world it helped hurry into being would soon discard the amateurs for a new breed of professional politicians. Public service was ceasing to be a duty and was becoming a career.

Living at the end of the twentieth century, we sometimes find it hard to remember how rapidly the pace of change accelerated around the end of the eighteenth century. DeWitt Clinton was born a subject of King George III in a province whose inhabitants were concentrated along the Hudson River and the shores of Long Island. New York was only the sixth most populous of the thirteen British colonies, with a third the population of Virginia, and fifteen thousand fewer inhabitants than Connecticut.[20] Its largest city, New York, was less important than Philadelphia. In New York City, the Church of England was the established church and was supported by local taxes. Slavery was widespread (James Clinton, DeWitt's father, was a slaveholder), and society's various orders were clearly differentiated. What manufacturing there was took place in small shops, with master, journeymen, and apprentices all understanding (if not always accepting) their customary rights and obligations.

In Europe, 1769 was the year Richard Arkwright received a patent for his first cotton-spinning machine. Haydn was at the beginning of his career, Samuel Johnson was at the peak of his, and Tiepolo was at the end of his. With the exception of Benjamin Franklin's experiments and the paintings of Benjamin West and John Singleton Copley, the cultural life of the British colonies in North America had produced almost nothing deemed worthy of European notice.

By the time of Clinton's death, New York, no longer a colony, was the most populous state and had emerged from Virginia's shadow to become the most important state in national politics. Furthermore, it had developed the political party system that became the model for America. New York City was the commercial and financial capital of the Western Hemisphere. Nearly half the nation's imports, and almost a third of its exports, passed through the Port of New York.[21] Settlers were streaming west along the Erie Canal. The religious ferment of the Second Great Awakening was sweeping the "burned-over district" in western New York. Slavery had been abolished in the state. The franchise had been greatly extended. The social bonds that tied master, journeyman, and apprentice together were loosened as businesses, some in the form of corporations, began paying wages to their workers and eroding the social traditions of the precapitalist era.

Cultural life had changed as well, with the neoclassical, aristocratic culture of the eighteenth century giving way to the romantic, bourgeois culture of the nineteenth. In Europe, by 1828 Chopin and Liszt were already prominent, Corot had shown his first important work at the Paris Salon, and Tennyson had published his first book of poems. In the United States, Samuel F. B. Morse was nearing the end of his career as a painter and the beginning of one as an inventor, and the innovations of Eli Whitney and Robert Fulton had already transformed America. American painters, musicians, and writers still received little acclaim from Europe, but that year saw the publication of Nathaniel Hawthorne's first novel, *Fanshawe,* and the first edition of Noah Webster's *American Dictionary of the English Language*.

Webster's work is emblematic of a more collective enterprise of invention that was well under way: Americans were inventing their own nation, different from England, with its own history, symbols, and beliefs. The most potent of these symbols was George Washington, and the "creation myth" of the American people was the story of the revolution. The ideology that suffused the revolution, republicanism, provided the accepted vocabulary of politics, and this remained so well into the nineteenth century, even as the social foundations of republican beliefs were dissolving.

The ultimate sources of that republicanism were the ancient republics of Greece and Rome. But while many Americans idealized the bucolic side of the ancient world and embraced the model of the virtuous husbandman (like the Roman Cincinnatus), for Clinton the model was the expansionist Athens of Pericles, pouring the nation's wealth into great public buildings and financing the works of playwrights and sculptors. If Clinton's proud bearing and cultural pretensions caused his opponents to mock him as the Magnus Apollo, what he really wanted to be was an American Pericles. Clinton never gained that eminence, and his failure to do so can tell us as much about America as it does about him.

One

o   o   o

POLITICAL APPRENTICE

Dewitt clinton's early success in politics owed much to the prominence of his family, but his family's distinction was of recent date and owed much to two qualities that would prove central to DeWitt's career—the skillful cultivation of political connections and the earnest pursuit of professional skills. Education and patronage were the twin stars under which the family's fortunes grew.

FAMILY AND CHILDHOOD

The Clinton family's arrival in America was anything but auspicious. They had emigrated from Ireland to America forty years before DeWitt's birth. Their presence in Ireland was the result of the decision of one William Clinton to support King Charles I against Cromwell a century earlier. Fleeing England after Charles's defeat, he lived on the Continent, then settled in Scotland and joined the Presbyterian Church. He later moved to Northern Ireland, where Presbyterians were disliked by both local Catholics and imported Anglicans. Perhaps for this reason, perhaps owing to rising rents in Ulster, in 1729 William's grandson Charles (DeWitt's grandfather) decided to emigrate. The emigrants were unfortunate in their choice of a vessel: The captain of the *George and Anne* was a murderer and an extortionist. He prolonged the journey until his passengers were starving and many had died, and then demanded a bribe to set them ashore. Charles Clinton lost a son and a daughter on the voyage. The captain landed on Cape Cod rather than at the original destination, Philadelphia, in order to avoid prosecution, which might have befallen him in a properly officered port. Charles Clinton and his wife and remaining daughter lived in Massachusetts until 1731, when they moved to Ulster (now Orange) County, New York. (Both names recall the Scots-Irish backgrounds of many early residents.)[1]

Charles Clinton and two other veterans of the hellish voyage bought adjacent farm sites near the Hudson and named their compound Little Britain. He and his wife, Elizabeth, had four sons in America—Alexander, Charles, James, and George. The first two became doctors, James entered the military, and George studied law and began a political career.[2]

In the four decades after Charles Clinton's arrival in New York, the family established itself as an influential force in the province. Charles Clinton served as a justice of the peace and a judge of the Court of Common Pleas, and held the rank of colonel in the French and Indian War. In 1743, when a distant relation named George Clinton was appointed royal governor of New York, the family's fortunes advanced. Charles Clinton had worked for the provincial government as a surveyor beginning the year he arrived in New York, and it was his employer, Surveyor General Cadwallader Colden, who brought him to the notice of the governor. Charles was offered the post of high sheriff of New York City, but he preferred to remain in private life. His son George, however, was pleased to accept an appointment as clerk of the Court of Common Pleas in Ulster—a post he held from 1759 until his death, in 1812.[3]

Charles Clinton's two oldest sons, Alexander and Charles, both studied medicine in New York City, and both returned to the vicinity of Little Britain to practice. The family's medical tradition may have encouraged DeWitt's interest in the natural sciences and his association with various endeavors that were intended to advance the state of medical knowledge and practice in America.

DeWitt's father, James Clinton, combined military duties with the life of a farmer and land speculator. He entered military service in 1756 as a junior officer in the state militia, and by 1774 he was a lieutenant colonel. At the same time, George, Charles's youngest son, was enlarging his legal and political experience. He became the local district attorney in 1765, and in 1768 won election to the provincial assembly. There he joined the struggle against the Anglican, mercantile, and royalist forces led by the DeLanceys and became closely allied with the large and influential Livingston family.[4]

According to Clinton family accounts, a dying Charles Clinton urged his sons, "Preserve your country's freedom," and as the dispute between Britain and its North American colonies ripened into rebellion and then revolution, the Clintons played prominent roles. James joined the patriot militia in 1775 as a colonel, and became a brigadier general in the Continental Army the following year. George Clinton had been a radical from his early days in the assembly, and his opposition to the Anglican merchant interests matured into opposition to the Crown. On December 19, 1775, the Committee of Safety in New York appointed George Clinton a brigadier general, and his military service was apparently decisive in his election as the first governor of the state of New York, in 1777. One of the losing candidates, Philip Schuyler, wrote to another, John Jay, that although he intended to support Clinton, he felt that Clinton's "family and connections do not entitle him to so distinguished a predominance."[5]

Schuyler's view probably reflected the opinion of a significant portion of the colonial ruling class in 1777. But the war changed things. By 1783, George Clinton was not only the new state's governor but a figure of national political importance. James Clinton was a major general—a war hero—and the lands he received in payment for his military service added to his holdings. Although the Clintons were not wealthy like the Schuylers and the Livingstons, George and James Clinton had secured the family a high station in a society where old distinctions were undercut by the war, the departure of many Loyalists, and the country's new republican spirit. George Clinton's rise epitomized the emergence of a new standard of fitness for office under which those who had fought in the revolution were especially favored.

In 1765, James Clinton married Mary DeWitt, and they had four sons and three daughters. DeWitt was their third son and fifth child. The site of his birth is unclear, but the generally accepted version holds that he was born in the family's house at Little Britain, now part of the town of New Windsor, on the west bank of the Hudson about fifty miles north of New York City.[6]

In any case, DeWitt spent his early years in his father's house in New Windsor. The 1770s provided an unusually dramatic environment in which to grow up, but we know little about DeWitt's childhood. A family story recounts that when word came in 1775 that James Clinton had been wounded at Quebec, DeWitt (age six) asked for a gun. Two years later, General Clinton was writing to his wife asking her to tell DeWitt to "prevent the Negroes from becoming Intirely idle." The imperious manner that was later to alienate Clinton's allies and enrage his opponents was perhaps shaped by this early opportunity to impose his will on others. In spite of the war, the Clintons saw to it that DeWitt received an education. He studied with a local Presbyterian minister for a time and in 1782 was sent to Kingston to study at a private academy. There he joined a debating society whose topics combined issues drawn from ancient history and literature—"Did Brutus do right in killing Cesar?" and "Whether was Ajax or Ilissees most advantage to the Grecians"—with issues of more immediate significance: "Whether it is upon the whole advantageous for these States to restore their revolted Subjects [Tories] to their former Rights and Privileges[?]" and "Whether large Estates and extensive manors are inconsistent with the nature and principles of a Republic?"[7]

The debating society included the children of many prominent New York families—Livingston and Roosevelt and LeRoy and Ten Broeck. The question concerning Brutus's ethics was suggested by Edward Livingston, DeWitt's predecessor as mayor of New York, who resigned after allegations of financial impropriety, reestablished himself in New Orleans, and later served as President Andrew Jackson's secretary of state. The presence of so many sons of wealthy and influential families was a tribute more to the academy's uniqueness than to its excellence. Clinton later wrote that in the early 1780s the Kingston academy was "the only seminary in the State, and almost all the young men desirous of classical education resorted to that useful institution."[8]

By then, of course, the Clintons were themselves among the state's influential families. On Evacuation Day—November 25, 1783, when the British garrison surrendered New York City—DeWitt came to New York City for the first time to see his father ride just behind Washington in the victory parade. His uncle George rode beside Washington.[9]

COLUMBIA AND THE LAW

Six months later, DeWitt was back in New York City, on his way to Princeton to en-
roll in the College of New Jersey, which his uncle Alexander had attended (Aaron
Burr's father had headed it at the time). The fate of King's College was then uncertain. The building that had housed it stood dilapidated after years of use as a British
military hospital; DeWitt had seen that for himself while watching the Evacuation
Day parade. Mayor James Duane had proposed legislation to revive the college, and
the legislature had passed an act for reconstituting (and renaming) it. But no appointments had been made, and nothing much was happening to move this forward.
The arrival of the governor's nephew, bound for an out-of-state college, proved a
catalyst. The humiliating prospect of DeWitt's having to attend the College of New
Jersey galvanized Duane and his allies, and King's College was reborn as Columbia,
with DeWitt enrolled in its first class. Speaking at his alma mater the year before his
death, Clinton recalled the circumstances: "On the 17th of May of that year, the first
student was admitted into Columbia College. . . . The Regents of the University
attended the examination in person, so important did the Fathers of the Republic
consider it, to countenance the incipient efforts in favor of intellectual improvement.
I may say, I trust without the imputation of egotism, that I was the first student and
among the first graduates of this our Alma Mater on its revival."[10]

The Columbia faculty included William Cochrane, a graduate of Trinity College
Dublin, whose field was classical literature; John Kemp, who had studied mathematics at the University of Aberdeen; and Dr. John Daniel Gross, a German immigrant
who taught his native language and geography and moral philosophy. James Renwick, who later taught at Columbia, pointed to Kemp as a great influence on Clinton's career. Renwick wrote that Kemp in his mathematics classes expounded on the
dangers of public debt, "urging the necessity of providing for every debt contracted a
sum sufficient not only to defray the interest, but to pay off the principal by an an-
nuity. In his lectures in illustration of the mechanical part of natural philosophy
. . . the principles and history of canal navigation formed a favorite theme." While
suspicion of public debt was widespread and there were many other partisans of canal
navigation, it seems reasonable to accept Renwick's assessment that Kemp's views
helped shape Clinton's on these topics.[11]

Kemp and Cochrane were the only full-time professors. Kemp also chaperoned
the students, and did so with sufficient vigor that the young Clinton wrote a protest
to the regents complaining of Kemp's relentless surveillance. (The regents sustained
Kemp.) But Clinton was clearly no hell-raiser. After Clinton's death, Cochrane
praised his former student in lavish terms: "He did everything well: upon the whole,
he seemed likely to me to prove, as he did prove, a highly useful and practical man;
what the Romans call 'civilis,' and the Greeks πολιτικος, a useful citizen, and qualified to counsel and direct his citizens to honour and happiness."[12]

This encomium is couched in the vocabulary and assumptions of the Enlightenment, from the Latin and Greek references to the concern with practicality, the idea

that the virtuous citizen must be as well a "useful" citizen. The Enlightenment came in many flavors, but the one that DeWitt Clinton most consistently tasted in his youth emanated from Scotland. The faculty of Columbia included scholars trained in Scotland (like Kemp) or greatly influenced by Hume and Kames (like Gross). And the minister who had helped educate DeWitt's father and his uncle George, Daniel Thain, was, like Kemp, educated at Aberdeen. The influence of Scottish philosophers in America was helped along by a variety of similarities between the nations, including a common language, a similar provincial pride and jealousy of London, and a cultural life rooted in the upper middle classes and among professionals. As Henry May put it, "The only completely acceptable European teachers, for the early builders of nineteenth-century official culture, were the Common Sense philosophers of Scotland." Clearly, Clinton's love of and involvement with empirical science, his promotion of public education, his attempts to render the administration of New York City and State more efficient—all these owe something to the influence of Scottish thinkers as translated by Columbia.[13]

At Columbia, as at the Kingston academy, DeWitt sought self-improvement outside the classroom. He joined the Uranian Society, which had been formed with the aim of improving student writing and pubic speaking. Perhaps the best insight into his values and ambitions at this stage in his life comes from a "dream" he wrote down on January 6, 1789. In the dream, Clinton is "suddenly transported into the Republic of Urania," a "region of delight and the abode of enjoyment" where the principal pleasures are friendship and knowledge. The citizens there seem "desirous to please and promote each other's good." He discerns "to my astonishment that they are Polytheists" and that "they worshipped high beings styled in the dialect of men friendship and literature." He comes upon a temple of gold "starred with Diamonds" on which are "written with letters of Gold" the words "sacred to friendship and literature." Inside he finds Friendship and Literature together on an emerald throne. Friendship (a woman) is in a "Robe of White" and under her feet are the "spoils of malignity." Literature is in a gown and slippers, "his forehead was furrowed with deep thinking and hard study," and "Genius & Application were his prime ministers." But discord enters the temple. One young man, called the Alderman, who is in love with Good Nature (one of Friendship's attendants), was "making interest and soliciting votes for some of his friends" for the upcoming election of priests. His electioneering efforts are opposed by another young man, this one in love with Wit (a handmaiden of Literature). Wit's lover "cut off the flaps of the Alderman's Small Clothes" and a fracas follows. Literature is "enraged at the fight—Friendship gnashed her teeth," and the citizens make "dismal lamentations." At this unsettled moment, the narrator awakens.[14]

Like all utopian visions, this literary effort, however conventional for its time, provides a clear expression of the author's values, and much of Clinton's career may be seen as an attempt to plant the Republic of Urania in New York State. Clinton's ideal republic is certainly grounded in virtue—as is shown by the desire of citizens to do good for one another. If the presence of gold and diamonds in the temple strikes an unrepublican note of luxury, that note is typically Clintonian, in that the resources have been devoted to the common good and to the aggrandizement of the state. Individual luxury might be corrupting, but collective ostentation was evidence of society's success. Perhaps the most prophetic part of the dream is that the aims of Literature and Friendship are thwarted by tawdry electioneering.

If literature was best served by Genius and Application, DeWitt tried to make up for his shortcomings in the first department by zeal in the second. He was such a hardworking student that his family sometimes worried about him. Early in February 1785, his brother Alexander wrote home to their parents about how the three Clinton boys were doing in New York. Alexander said that his own job, as secretary to the governor, was giving him "just enough business to keep me employed all Day," and that he saw his brother Charles often, but that "as DeWitt is in College and more confined I do not see him so often." Charles looked after his younger brother, letting his parents know that "I got [DeWitt] a suit of Cloaths from Brooks which he wanted very much." Back in Little Britain such communications were welcome, but DeWitt himself was a most deficient correspondent. A few weeks after Alexander's letter, Mrs. Clinton wrote to DeWitt to scold him for not writing and to "beg that in future you will not miss one opportunity of informing me . . . of your welfare and other matters which however trifling they may be you may be sure cannot fail being agreeable to me." She wanted to know specifically "what progress you make in your studies, whether your present situation is agreeable, & what manner yourself & your brothers spend your leisure hours." Her admonition was not successful. Eighteen months later she wrote Alexander, "Is my son Dewitt Dead or is he alive or has he forgot he has a mother in being as I have not had one line from him since he left home."[15]

However lacking DeWitt may have been as a son and correspondent, he was scrupulous in his schoolwork. He graduated first in his class in 1786—the first class to graduate from Columbia College. New York was then the nation's capital, and as the *New York Journal and Weekly Register* reported in April 1786, "The Honorable the Continental Congress, and both Houses of the Legislature, suspended the public business, to support the important interests of Education by their countenance, and grace the ceremony by their august presence." As the premier student, DeWitt was given the honor of delivering the Latin oration, choosing as his topic *De utilitate et necessitate studiorum artium liberalium,* and he concluded, according to the paper, with a "polite and well-adapted salutation, in the same language, to the Members of the Legislature, to the Regents and Professors, and to the audience at large."[16]

What effect must all this success and acclaim have had on DeWitt? At barely seventeen, he was lecturing—in Latin, no less—to the leading men of the nation. His family's prominence had increased as he had grown, and he must have felt that he would be entitled to a large role in his country's future affairs. Certainly he gave every sign in later life of viewing his successes as somehow owed to him and seeing his disappointments as tricks of fate or the result of the plots of churlish rivals. Why not? Behold a boy who at age eight is expected to keep the family slaves in line, whose family is conspicuous in arms and politics at a time when those are the two skills valued most in the society, who provides the occasion for the revival of the college in

New York City, and graduates first in his class two years later. Looking out on the dignitaries of the city, state, and nation, DeWitt Clinton would have had to be a young man of exceptional humility not to have been carried away by a sense of his own importance. Events would check that considerable pride many times over the next forty years, but each time a subsequent success would inflate it again.

The next step after graduation was to prepare for a career. The law was the inevitable choice, and DeWitt read for the bar in the office of Samuel Jones. Jones had studied law (along with George Clinton) under William Smith, whose other students included Gouverneur Morris and Robert R. Livingston. (Morris and Livingston had, along with John Jay, drafted the state constitution of 1777, and both men would later serve with distinction as minister to France.) Jones had pursued a vacillating course during the revolution, first opposing British rule and later electing to stay in New York City under British occupation. Nevertheless he was sufficiently popular in the new state to win election to the assembly in 1786, the year DeWitt began his legal studies. According to David Hosack, DeWitt "ever cherished for Mr. Jones the warmest filial affection," but after just a year with Jones, he was contemplating moving on. The immediate impetus for this desire for change may have come from the death of his brother Alexander, who drowned in the Hudson in March 1787. DeWitt does not reveal how his eldest brother's death affected him, but it must have hit him hard. It may have spurred the desire for new surroundings that surfaced at the same time. DeWitt also may have felt pinched for cash and thought he could earn more by setting himself up to practice law in the lower courts. In June 1787, DeWitt's father wrote his son that he had no objection to his plan to practice in the county courts, but thought "if you have to stay the three years with Mr. Jones it will be no loss to you if you behave with Prudence and Oeconomy and adhere to the Principles of virtue which I hope will be the case. I will endeavor to support you with credit while in town if it be in my power."[17]

Although money would be a worry for DeWitt all his life, it was not yet a major one, and he seems not to have indulged in the vices with which New York City, even then, was so ready to tempt a young man on his own. In fact, his family seemed to worry not about his falling prey to licentiousness but about his health's suffering from a too intense pursuit of his studies. His uncle Charles, the doctor, wrote to him in November 1787, urging him not to make himself sick by studying too hard. There is, Charles advised, "Improvement to be obtained from Men as well as Books; and blending them properly, the one will serve as an agreeable Relaxation to the other; when I say Men, I do not exclude Women if they are your Choice also, but I leave that matter solely to yourself, as you appear to be circumspect in your Conduct about them."[18]

In 1790, when DeWitt had passed the bar and was preparing to begin his professional life in earnest, James Clinton urged him to return to Little Britain and suggested that DeWitt's younger brother, George Clinton, Jr., ought to join him there for his own legal training. Governor Clinton wrote his brother James to say that he opposed this course. DeWitt, he said, should "settle in this city," particularly because he "has attended more to books than men and manners, and should he settle in the country, he will instead of acquiring those accomplishments which he has hitherto neglected . . . become more rusticated and have less chance of distinguishing himself as a man of eminence in his profession."[19]

Already, though, the law had ceased to be DeWitt's intended profession. For several years his uncle George had been introducing him to the charged world of New York and national politics. The law was to be only a means to an end.

POLITICAL BAPTISM

DeWitt graduated from college as the great debate over the proper form of government for the United States was heating up. In January 1786, the Virginia legislature called for a meeting of all the states to seek solutions to problems that had arisen under the Articles of Confederation. The meeting took place that September in Annapolis and a measure (proposed by Alexander Hamilton) was passed calling for a convention to consider changes in the Articles. This proposal was backed by Congress, and on May 25, 1787, the Federal Convention opened in Philadelphia. By September 17 the Constitution—a replacement for, rather than a modification of, the Articles of Confederation—was signed and forwarded to the states for ratification.

New York was to be a crucial state for ratification, in part because George Clinton had made clear his opposition to the new constitution. As governor, he had felt what he took to be the meddling hand of the Continental Congress on many occasions— in resolving land claims and other matters related to Vermont statehood; in Indian policies; and over revenues from the Port of New York. A stronger national government would, the governor thought, simply worsen matters for the state. Now DeWitt took up his pen and put to use in the defense of his uncle's views the rhetorical skills he had been cultivating at Kingston and at Columbia's Uranian Society.[20]

Beginning on December 6, 1787, and continuing into early 1788, letters signed "A Countryman" appeared in Thomas Greenleaf's *New York Journal and Weekly Register*. On December 22, DeWitt's younger brother, George, wrote that the letters "are very good and I think better adapted to the understanding of the common people than any piece in the newspapers." Unfortunately for DeWitt Clinton's literary reputation, a contrasting series of arguments, in favor of the Constitution, had begun appearing in New York papers late in October 1787 over the name "Publius." This series was, of course, *The Federalist*, written by Alexander Hamilton, John Jay, and James Madison.[21]

Clinton adopts the pose of a humble and ill-educated but virtuous "Countryman," whose sincere questions about the Constitution are meant to expose the mendacity and power-grabbing tendencies of those favoring a stronger central government. He presents himself in the first letter as an honest farmer who has sold some cattle to the army and received "Morris's Notes" (paper money) in return. Soon, a man from Philadelphia comes along and tells him such notes are not worth their face value, but offers to buy them at a discount. After selling them, the naive Countryman is told by his neighbor that this is all a scheme to benefit the "great men."

Clinton—stepping out of his Countryman's character—then cites the Italian jurist and legal philosopher Cesare Beccaria on the tendency of governments to concentrate power in the hands of the few, to the detriment of the many, and says he fears that "this is the case with the new constitution men," who have given such great power to the "president-general" and the Senate. He was unable to resist displaying his erudition.[22]

The views advanced in some of the "Countryman" letters, moreover, were decidedly more egalitarian than Clinton's own. He accused the Federalists of endeavoring to make a place in government for "the better sort of people to sit in, so that they might not be troubled with the common people, or rabble as they feigned to call them." Yet while Clinton's political principles may have had abstractly egalitarian overtones, his subsequent career would demonstrate little desire to share his place at the high table with that same "rabble."[23]

Although the biographer might wish that his subject's writings on these issues could be treated as worthy rivals of *The Federalist,* they are in fact a rather pat set of republican clichés. Out of the constitutional provision for setting the places and times for elections to the House and Senate—it is left to the states' discretion, although "Congress may at any time by Law make or alter such Regulations"—Clinton the Countryman concocts a fanciful scene in which the election is held only in New York City, where the "great folks" will divide the spoils among themselves, and "not one in a hundred of us country people" will be able to make it there to vote. Clinton even raises the specter of a true aristocracy's being created in the United States: Despite the constitutional prohibition on titles of nobility, he warns, it would take only an amendment to give Congress the ability to bestow such titles.[24]

In his stand on the Constitution, Clinton was both aping the views and advancing the interests of his powerful uncle George. Governor Clinton's opposition to a stronger national government may have been rooted in sincere suspicion of the danger to liberty such a government would pose. But it was also an act of self-interest: As governor of New York, George Clinton had been fighting with Congress for years over the national government's claim on the duties collected at the Port of New York. New York, Clinton and others felt, needed these revenues for itself. The governor himself has been credited[25] with writing a number of essays in opposition to the Constitution under the properly republican pen-name "Cato." These writings sought to preserve the status quo by elucidating various shortcomings of the Constitution. Whoever wrote the "Cato" letters, George Clinton certainly endorsed the views expressed in them, being content with things as they were. The governor and others conducted a negative campaign against the Constitution and refrained from offering proposals of their own, because the anti-Federalist coalition was united only in its dislike of the Constitution. Any attempt to propose a rival program would invariably have divided the ranks of those opposing ratification.[26]

"Cato" and the "Countryman" at first appeared to have won the battle of the essayists—the Clintonians secured two-thirds of the seats at the ratifying convention, which opened for business in Poughkeepsie on June 17 by choosing George Clinton as its president. With the governor in Poughkeepsie was DeWitt, who wrote to

Thomas Greenleaf, offering to send "an account of the proceedings here—as particular and accurate as a weak memory will allow." Clinton's dispatches to the *Journal* continued the battle waged in the "Countryman" letters. Those taking the anti-Federalist side were praised, those favoring the Constitution mocked. But the election of the delegates in April proved to be the high-water mark of the anti-Federalist tide in New York. During the first eight days of the Poughkeepsie convention, as Clinton was reporting to Greenleaf that "the Republican members are . . . united as one man," New Hampshire (on June 21) and Virginia (on June 25) ratified the Constitution. New Hampshire's vote meant that nine states had ratified, and the Constitution was now legally in force. Ratification by Virginia, then the largest state, added practical weight to the legal force of the document. In Poughkeepsie, Alexander Hamilton was relentless in his arguments for ratification. His repertoire of persuasion ranged from high-minded arguments drawn from *The Federalist* to menacing hints that, if the state were not to ratify, New York City and the surrounding counties (which had elected pro-Constitution delegates) would secede.[27]

New York's ponderous deliberations were beginning to seem moot, although the consequences of an outright rejection by New York were not something the Federalists wished to contemplate. The debate in Poughkeepsie eventually turned away from that central question toward amendments that would make the document more protective of individual and states' rights. The tone of Clinton's reports grew more tentative, until on July 18 he wrote apologetically to Greenleaf's associate Charles Tillinghast, "I would have written to you oftener were it not that the political sky is so frequently overcast and so variable to appearance that I am oftentimes at a loss what to think or what to say." By this point the Clintonian forces were arguing for making ratification conditional on passage of the amendments they felt were necessary to protect liberty. The convention endorsed thirty-two proposed amendments; some of them were eventually reflected in the Bill of Rights. (If all thirty-two had passed there would not have been much left of the federal government.) Five days after Clinton's weather report to Tillinghast the storm broke, as Clinton's own teacher and employer, Samuel Jones, moved to change the wording of New York's ratification from making acceptance of New York's amendments a condition of ratification to ratifying "in full confidence" that they would be accepted. The final vote in favor was 30 to 27—the closest vote of any of the ratifying states. A New York City mob (with a member of the Livingston family at its head) celebrating ratification looted Greenleaf's shop and carried off his type.[28]

DeWitt Clinton, not yet twenty, had tasted political defeat for the first time.

Two

o   o   o

POLITICAL JOURNEYMAN

To THIS DAY, the post of secretary to the governor of the state of New York is the second most powerful position in the executive branch. Under George Clinton, the office was subject to the most literal-minded kind of nepotism—the governor appointed his nephews. Not long after Alexander Clinton died, in 1787, he was replaced by DeWitt, who held the post until 1795, when his uncle declined to run for reelection.[1] Although the post of governor was sharply circumscribed in New York's 1777 constitution, and government generally was of very limited scope compared with its twentieth-century form, secretary to the governor was still a powerful post for a nineteen-year-old apprentice lawyer.

With the state and national capitals in New York City, the teenage Clinton was at the center of a rapidly changing political world. The unanimity of opinion that lay behind the election of George Washington, and that Washington tried to further by appointing to his administration leading figures of assorted political opinions, was dissolving as differences of ideology, and disgruntlement over the distribution of government jobs and favors, began parsing the national government into two camps, whose presiding figures, then and in the shorthand of generations of historians, were Thomas Jefferson and Alexander Hamilton. At the outset of the new national government, many in the North thought that George Clinton, the symbol of anti-Federalist reservations about the Constitution, should have been chosen vice president as an earnest of the government's intention to enact various amendments that New York and other states had proposed. Patrick Henry advanced the case for Clinton in Virginia, and when a New York committee sought to do the same it pointed to Clinton's Virginia support as evidence of the governor's appeal. This was the first appearance on the national ticket of the Virginia-New York link that was to characterize the first quarter of the following century. Hamilton, who had frustrated George Clinton's hopes at Poughkeepsie, also helped thwart this design.[2]

Clinton's tenure as secretary nearly ended in 1789, when Hamilton directed an effective Federalist campaign in New York State, winning the assembly, increasing the Federalist majority in the senate, and coming within a few hundred votes of electing Robert Yates governor.[3] It was another event of 1789, however, that was to shape both national and New York politics over the next decade. The French Revolution and its consequences—the British response, the Terror, and the Napoleonic era—became reference points for American politics in the years after Washington's inauguration. It would help decide the result of presidential and gubernatorial elections, alter the vocabulary of American politics, and even change the composition of the Clinton family. For the American government in 1789, sympathy for fellow-revolutionaries in France was tempered by the chastisement of a king who had lent decisive assistance to America in the struggle for independence.

There were divisive domestic issues as well. In his first "Countryman" letter, DeWitt had posed as a farmer cheated by a speculator from Philadelphia who traded him hard money for scrip that, according to Clinton's virtuous yeoman, could be redeemed in Philadelphia at face value. Funding the obligations of the national government, and assuming those of the states, was one of the most serious problems to confront the new republic. The solution to the problem demonstrated the seriousness of the divisions, and also illustrated that the schism between supporters and critics of the Constitution was not the only important source of friction. Hamilton, as secretary of the treasury, wanted above all to establish the public credit of the United States. He proposed to have the national government fund both its outstanding debt (about $54 million) and the debts of the states (another $25 million). The creation of such a large funded debt would, Hamilton hoped, provide investment capital for the new nation, tie the country's richest men to the national government, and strengthen the federal government at the expense of the states. The most controversial part of Hamilton's plan was the assumption of state debts, and opposition to it (as well as to other aspects of the plan) was led by Virginia representative James Madison. On April 12, 1790, Madison won a victory in the House of Representatives, defeating assumption by a vote of 31–29. Hamilton's plan for assumption remained unfulfilled and appeared doomed to remain so until June, when a meeting between Jefferson, Madison, and Hamilton resulted in a deal whereby the Virginians would help secure passage of Hamilton's plan in return for Hamilton's support for situating the nation's capital on the banks of the Potomac. The deal was struck at a dinner in New York on or about June 20, and by the end of July both the act moving the capital to the South and the act for the funding of state debts had been passed by Congress. The nation's government headed south for a ten-year residence in Philadelphia while the eventual federal city was being erected on the Potomac.[4]

New Yorkers were incensed, although the object of their disgust was Philadelphia more than Virginia. Newspapers pointed to the previous inhospitable behavior of Philadelphians—a disturbance there in 1783 had caused Congress to move out of Philadelphia—and enumerated the trouble and expense New York had undergone to prepare the city (and the old City Hall, which had been renovated at great cost by Pierre Charles L'Enfant) to be the nation's future capital. This anger was doubtless sharpened by interurban jealousy (Philadelphia was still the nation's most populous and cultivated city) and an intensifying commercial rivalry (New York would soon surpass Philadelphia as a port).[5]

For DeWitt Clinton, the departure of the president and Congress was clearly a bitter disappointment. In a long letter to his uncle Charles, he denounced those who he felt were responsible for the loss of the capital and drew a dismal portrait of the effect it would have on New York City. He anticipated that the state legislature would soon move to Albany (as it did in 1797), whereupon "this devoted City will never be the residence of foreign powers," and that in place of exalted officials like senators and ambassadors the city would have merely aldermen and constables. "In short," he wrote, "the little will be great—ambition will be gratified."[6]

ALTHOUGH NEW YORK CITY WAS now a smaller pond, DeWitt Clinton was becoming a bigger fish. And in that pond the political currents were shifting. If the anti-Federalists had been united only in their opposition to the Constitution, it was similarly true that once the Constitution was ratified there was less coherence among those who had supported it. And when the new government made its appointments, there were too few high offices to go around to the many who felt they deserved them. One of the most aggrieved was Robert R. Livingston, chancellor of New York State, who had given the oath of office to Washington but had received no office from him. (The chancellor was the chief judge of the Court of Chancery, an equity court similar to today's civil courts.) In the early 1790s, three families presided over New York State politics—the Schuylers, the Clintons, and the Livingstons. In the epigrammatic summary of the nineteenth-century writer James Parton, "The Clintons had *power,* the Livingstons had *numbers,* the Schuylers had *Hamilton.*" Philip Schuyler, George Clinton's gubernatorial rival in 1777, who had dismissed Clinton's family as being insufficiently elevated to provide the state with a governor, was now United States senator, and his son-in-law Alexander Hamilton was treasury secretary and a leading force in Washington's government. As governor, George Clinton did have power, but the Federalists controlled the legislature. The Livingstons were less well situated, and when Washington and Hamilton did not grant them what they saw as their due, they joined forces with the Clintonians in an alliance that was to help shape New York and national politics for the next decade. The first major beneficiary of this new alliance was Aaron Burr, whose career would over the next dozen years first rise along a steep trajectory and then fall even more precipitously. Burr would be an important ally of DeWitt Clinton's and, in turn, a deadly enemy.[7]

When the New York legislature chose the state's United States senators in 1789, Schuyler had been elected to a two-year term. The other seat had gone to a recent arrival from Massachusetts, Rufus King, who had received Hamilton's backing and had taken the seat that was understood by the Livingstons to be slated for James Duane, a relation of theirs by marriage. After this and other disappointments had driven the Livingstons into the Clintonian ranks, Schuyler's post was in jeopardy, and in 1791, when his term expired, Burr was elected with the support of the Clinton-Livingston faction (in spite of the fact that he had actively supported Robert Yates for governor against George Clinton in 1789). One attraction of this arrangement for the Livingstons was that Burr, who had been attorney general of New York, would have to vacate that office, which Governor Clinton agreed to bestow on Morgan Lewis, another Livingston-by-marriage. The historian Jabez Hammond attributed Schuyler's defeat in part to his manners, which, "having been formed in camps"—Schuyler was a general in the Revolutionary War—"and not in courts or among the people, were austere and aristocratic, and rendered him personally unpopular." Hammond would make similar observations about the political consequences of DeWitt Clinton's demeanor.[8]

Schuyler's defeat was an alarm bell for Federalists in New York. With the Livingstons now firmly allied with Governor Clinton, and Burr in league with them, Hamilton decided to play the Federalists' trump card in New York, John Jay, who was then chief justice of the United States Supreme Court. "There had never been a time," DeAlva S. Alexander wrote in 1906, "since John Jay entered public life that he was not the most popular man in the city of New York." If Jay could wrest the governorship away from George Clinton, then Hamilton would have access to the vast patronage of the state government to strengthen the Federalist cause. In those days, the offices in the gift of the national administration were few—in 1801 there were about three thousand, including nearly nine hundred deputy postmasters and many other low-level appointees. By contrast, the New York Council of Appointment had recorded more than eight hundred appointments the year before, and by the time of the council's elimination, in 1821, it would control more than fifteen thousand offices. In addition to Jay's great prestige, Hamilton had other forces working in his favor. For one thing, a close friend of George Clinton's, Alexander Macomb, was implicated in a scandal concerning the sale of state lands, and the governor was tarnished by association (the governor was one of the commissioners of the land office who had allowed Macomb to buy more than 3.6 million acres of state lands for 8 pence an acre). Clinton's opposition to the Constitution was also used against him. But Jay had liabilities, too, many of them associated with Hamilton. The Clintonian forces harped on the Hamiltonian financial system and the Bank of the United States as emblems of a continuing subjugation of the people by a corrupt aristocracy—now homegrown rather than British. The charges were given added weight by the spectacular collapse of the fortunes of William Duer, the New York speculator (and Hamilton protégé), whose ruin carried a number of other New Yorkers down with him. (Burr, incidentally, hoped to get the Federalist nomination and oppose the governor who had just a year earlier secured his election to the United States Senate, but Hamilton's success in enlisting Jay quashed that idea.)[9]

George Clinton's cause was significantly advanced by the absence of state taxes; the governor's sincerely republican belief in small government, combined with the state's revenues from land sales and from government securities it held, appeared to obviate any need for them. (There were various licensing and other fees collected by the state.) Yet despite such advantages and Clinton's fifteen years in office, Jay's popularity and stature had won the day. Or, rather, would have, if technical objections had not been raised to the votes from Tioga, Clinton, and Otsego counties. The first two were thought to have gone narrowly for the governor, but Otsego was believed to have delivered a large majority for Jay; if those votes were allowed, Jay would win the election. The dispute was referred to a joint committee of the legislature that was controlled by the Clintonians: The votes from the three disputed counties were thrown out, and Clinton was declared reelected. Although George Clinton himself seems not to have taken an active personal hand in this maneuver, his reputation was ever after clouded because of it. Thomas Jefferson wrote to James Madison, "It does not seem possible to defend Clinton," and "the cause of republicanism will suffer." Although there was some political intimidation in Otsego County—Judge William Cooper, the imperious Federalist leader there, bullied some voters into supporting Jay—such tactics were common to both sides, and the grounds for tossing out the Jay votes were hardly more than pretexts. For instance, the ballots of Otsego County were disallowed because the term of office of the sheriff who delivered them had just expired. Both sides tried to make political capital out of the election in the next session of the legislature, the Clintonians over Cooper's behavior in Otsego County, and the Federalists over the canvassers' action in voiding the votes. The only person who behaved impeccably in the affair was Jay, who, once the decision had been made, refrained from prolonging the dispute.[10]

If George Clinton's cause was helped by the frugality of his administration, that same characteristic (and the republican small-government principles that lay behind it) contributed to a minimum of tangible achievement by the state government under his stewardship. (To opponents of large government, of course, this was itself an achievement.) Still, it was under George Clinton in 1792 that the first legislative steps toward the construction of a great canal were taken, with the founding of the Western Inland Lock Navigation Company. This move received the governor's support, although the leadership of the effort was distinctly Federalist, with Philip Schuyler leading the way and serving as president of the company.

But if state government was moving slowly, state politics were becoming more intense. The arrival in April 1793 of Edmond Charles Genet, the new minister from the French Republic, elicited demonstrations of republican sympathy for the revolutionaries in France and Federalist counterdemonstrations in support of neutrality. Genet's attempts to oppose and subvert Washington's neutrality policy and enlist Americans in the war against Britain embittered his official relations, and when Washington's government eventually told the French government that Genet's activities were obnoxious, and that his recall would be welcome, Genet, fearful of what might happen to him if he returned to France (where the Jacobins had just come to power), decided to remain in America. He married Governor Clinton's daughter Cornelia, and the couple took up residence on a Long Island farm, the title of which was initially held by DeWitt Clinton, since state law then forbade the acquisition of property by foreigners. Later, DeWitt Clinton served as Genet's translator—for example, in a 1797 letter to Jefferson in which Genet blamed Jefferson for all his public misfortunes.[11]

Genet's appointment had followed two events of greater weight in France—the proclamation of the French Republic and the declaration of war with Britain. With fellow republicans at war against an old foe, American sympathies were placed at odds with American interests, which required both strict neutrality and economic links with Britain (at least to keep the government solvent). America was certainly not prepared for war, but the war between Britain and France placed strains on America—particularly because of the harsh treatment of neutral shipping by both sides—that would continue to vex relations for two decades, leading to the quasi-war with France in 1798 and to the War of 1812 with Britain. At this point, the strains were threatening to fracture Washington's cabinet, as Hamilton argued for suspension of the country's 1778 treaty with France, which could involve America in her ally's defense, and Jefferson argued for the rights of France under the treaty (although he did not urge hostilities). DeWitt Clinton was among those who sympathized with the French position. Early in 1794 a correspondent described to him the celebration of a French victory at the Tontine Coffee House in Manhattan, followed by a "special meeting of the Democratic Society."[12]

Although Democratic-Republican enthusiasm was widespread in New York, Federalism was still robust, and the Federalists gained control of the legislature in the state elections in April 1793. Early in 1794, Federalist legislators challenged George Clinton's power directly. They wished to secure the appointment of Egbert Benson to the state supreme court, but knew that the Council of Appointment, elected by the state senate the year before and dominated by Republicans, would oppose him. The resurgent Federalists elected their own council (although the one-year term of the sitting council had not expired) and appointed Benson to the bench on January 29, 1794. Up to that point the power of nomination had always rested with the governor, with the Council of Appointment exercising merely the power to approve or disapprove. The Federalists, led by Philip Schuyler, now claimed that the council possessed a concurrent power to nominate. Clinton at first categorically rejected this interpretation of the state constitution, but he later acquiesced and Benson's appointment stood. The Federalist council then proceeded to exercise its appointive powers with highly partisan results.[13]

The conclusion of this story was postponed for a half dozen years by the results of the election of 1795. Aging and weary after eighteen years in office, and stung by the widespread denunciation of his tainted victory over Jay in 1792, George Clinton declined to run for reelection (as he had declined to fight strenuously Benson's appointment), and Jay was elected with a substantial Federalist majority in the legislature. DeWitt had lost his job.

DERUSTICATING DEWITT CLINTON

George Clinton's desire that his talented nephew remain in New York and learn from men as well as from books was clearly satisfied. If DeWitt Clinton did not join the Democratic Society in 1794, it was one of the few such organizations he didn't join. These groups brought him into contact with leading figures of the city and state—contact independent of his influential role as his uncle's secretary.

The first group he joined was New York's Society of St. Tammany, which had been founded in 1787 but sputtered until 1789, when John Pintard (then a thriving business-man and a political force, whose life had not yet been blighted by Duer's ruin) ener-gized it, hoping that the society would "serve in some part to correct the aristocracy of our city." President Washington and George Clinton were given honorary titles, Pintard was made its sagamore, and DeWitt Clinton, then just twenty, was its scribe. Although political motives may have actuated Pintard to some degree, in its early years the Tammany Society was not the political organization it was to become, to DeWitt Clinton's detriment, twenty years later. Cultural betterment of its members and of the city was among its goals, and in 1790 the society opened the city's first mu-seum. As political divisions emerged in the 1790s, the Tammanyites became more par-tisan as well, and a number of the society's members joined the Democratic Society in 1794. By 1797 the followers of Aaron Burr were the guiding faction of Tammany.[14]

A year after becoming scribe of the Tammany Society, Clinton joined another or-ganization that was to have lasting influence on his career. On September 3, 1790, he became a Mason and a member of New York's Holland Lodge. In 1792 he became secre-tary to the Holland Lodge, and the following year he became a warden. Clinton even-tually became the nation's Masonic leader, with consequences for his political career, as we shall see. In 1793 he was installed as worshipful master of the Holland Lodge, and he delivered an address in which he interpreted to the members the importance and nature of their order. Clinton was not yet twenty-five, and he felt called on to stress his unworthiness for his new office: "Sensible I am, brethren, that neither my age, ex-perience, nor abilities entitle me to fill this place, to which your partiality, not my merit, has called me." Masonry, he said, was first and foremost a "moral institution," one that tried to embody the "important truth" of the *"natural equality of mankind."* So powerful was this truth that "the glare of wealth, the pride of birth, the ostentation of intellect and the hauteur of office hide their diminished heads before it." Clinton even extended this spirit to a religious tolerance that seems extraordinary for its time, noting that, just as the Holland Lodge contained a Bible, "in like manner the follow-ers of Moses, Mahomet, and Brama, may introduce into their Masonic assemblies, their Pentateuch, their Alcoran, and their Vedam." This was very good for an organi-zation that was so obsessively hierarchical, and whose membership remained largely restricted to the political and business elite in the state. (Indeed, its exclusiveness would lead to the eruption of the anti-Masonic movement in the 1820s[15]).

Other organizations claimed Clinton as a member. Among them were the Black Friars, a benevolent organization, and the Humane Society of the City of New York, which helped the destitute by providing medical care and assisting them to regain their livelihoods. In a speech to the Black Friars, DeWitt spelled out a reform pro-gram that foreshadowed some of the actual measures he enacted, or sought to enact, when in office. Lamenting the still powerful presence of the "prison, the house of madness, the retreat of poverty, the horrid gibbet, and the blood streaming scaffold," he advocated education, charity, and reform to change human society. He called for schools in which one would find "agriculture, commerce, and manufactures encouraged—the polite arts and the useful sciences patronized—and the rights of nature and the rights of religion respected." To defeat disease, poverty, and famine, there should be established "hospitals, almshouses and public granaries." Instead of adhering to accepted notions of criminal justice, society should attempt to employ "proper correctives" to combat "the moral evils which prevail. The shackles of slavery will then fall to the ground and the horrid instruments of capital punishment be only seen on the descriptive canvas" depicting the past. In place of restrictive navigation rules, tariffs, and duties, "a free commerce will be universally established." As a beacon for all these changes, a "university, for the illumination of the world, will also be founded." The Earth itself would be transformed: "The hand of art will change the face of the Universe, Mountains, deserts, and oceans will feel its mighty force." A high-flown and high-minded program indeed. And yet in all these areas—penal reform and education, emancipation of slaves and transformation of the landscape—DeWitt Clinton would make some real contributions.[16]

But might there not have been a divergence between Clinton's view of a moral, egalitarian society and his view of his own place in New York society? One of the other organizations he joined was the militia; he secured a commission from his uncle as a lieutenant. By 1794 he was a captain, and he set forth regulations for his company that included required attendance and fines for missing a drill. Like the boy who wore a uniform as his father was off fighting the British and their Indian allies, DeWitt Clinton in his mid-twenties seems to have relished the paraphernalia of military life. In 1795 a friend wrote from London, "I have ordered a very handsome regimental sword for you, & except Ludlows & Roosevelts I am sure will not be equalled in the United States for Beauty, strength and order."[17]

One reason he wanted a uniform and a sword may have been to impress women. Clinton's papers reveal little about his romantic interests and activities as a young man about the city. His family's concerns about his excessive studiousness, and his uncle's mention of "Women if they are your choice," and his comment that DeWitt was "circumspect in [his] Conduct about them," suggest that Clinton at least was not a wastrel. His close college friend Francis Silvester wrote him in 1788, "Have you engaged in the mazy study of the Law, or have you become a *Galant?"* Mazy studies would seem to have been the answer. But perhaps not for long. As DeWitt was coming into his own, establishing his own identity in New York separate from that of his uncle (he moved into his own lodgings at 34 Liberty Street in 1795), he seems to have assumed the role of eligible New York bachelor. His friend in London who ordered the regimental sword for him, John Speyer, also reported on the ladies of that city in a way that he must have believed his correspondent would find interesting. "The girls are very pretty here and as complaisant as one cou'd wish it," Speyer wrote. "As to filles de joie, except Paris this is the first town in Europe for them, but they are dangerous fire ships. Tho' I have been very fortunate in my rambles—as some of my American friends have been sadly taken in." Whether DeWitt took similar rambles in New York we cannot know. In 1806, the proprietors of a house of prostitution declared that Mayor Clinton had granted them a license to run it, but the charge seems unlikely and was not taken up by his political opponents.[18]

By the mid-1790s, DeWitt's romantic inclinations were coming to concentrate on one Maria Franklin, who combined beauty with a significant estate inherited from her recently deceased father, the Quaker merchant Walter Franklin. The Franklin house on Cherry Street was sufficiently grand to have been chosen as a residence for George Washington when he arrived in the city in 1789. In a letter to DeWitt in January 1794, his cousin Cornelia, who was soon to marry Genet, wrote with news from New York (DeWitt was then in Albany with his uncle George) and closed with the information, "I saw the Franklins at the Concert last evening [&] Maria desired me to remember her to you and Sally hoped you would be here before the next Assembly—Peg DePeyster sends you a kiss." In reply, on March 9, DeWitt sent his love to all his friends, "female particularly." Maria Franklin's wealth undoubtedly went well with her beauty: She had inherited a house in Newtown (now part of Queens), other lands upstate, cash assets of twenty-four thousand pounds, and assorted possessions. And DeWitt Clinton was certainly an eligible bachelor. His impressive appearance and influential family doubtless made him a desirable match. A substantial private fortune would provide the kind of cushion that a rising young man needed—particularly if, like DeWitt, he came from a family rich in honors but modest in wealth. The wedding was held early in 1796, attended by a few members of each participant's family. The new Mrs. Clinton was of "retiring and domestic habits," according to James Renwick; she could hardly have been otherwise, since she bore ten children before she died in 1818.[19]

YOUNG POLITICO

The retirement of his uncle George from politics, although only temporary, made it imperative that DeWitt Clinton develop his own political following, in the same way that he was building his own social ties and starting his own family. He first appeared as a candidate for office in the spring of 1795, one of seven Republicans running for New York City's seats in the state assembly. Only one of the Republicans got enough votes to win; Clinton had the third-highest total among the group but was defeated. It was the misfortune of New York's Republicans that John Jay's election preceded the publication of the details of the treaty he had negotiated with the British concerning a variety of matters left over from the revolution and exacerbated by the war between Britain and France. Republican sympathy for France and lingering resentment against Britain (which was suspected of encouraging Indian raids against American settlements) had stimulated various military activities in New York early in 1794, well before Jay was sent to Britain to negotiate a peaceful settlement. George Clinton, in his address to the legislature on January 7, 1794, asked for appropriations to fortify New York harbor as well as other defenses along the state's frontiers. DeWitt Clinton appears to have written to his friend Edward Livingston about this, for early in March, Livingston responded by lamenting the poor state of the city's fortifications and complained that so much "attention is paid to the interests of party, so little to that of the State," which he found a "very alarming feature in our Legislative Character." A largely unsympathetic Federalist legislature finally appropriated forty-two thousand pounds for strengthening the state's defenses. To augment this, the commissioners of fortifications asked for volunteers to help strengthen the city's defenses, whereupon militia regiments, the Tammany Society, the Democratic Society, and various other organizations lent their aid.[20]

The Federalist attitude toward Great Britain seemed almost treasonous to Republicans like Livingston and Clinton, and on July 2, 1795, the charge seemed confirmed, when the text of the treaty Jay had secured first appeared in the American press—a day after Jay's inauguration. The many advantages for America of the Jay treaty appeared at first sight to be overbalanced by the concessions Jay had made to the British version of the rights of neutrals in wartime.[21]

The initial response was a wholesale repudiation of Jay and the treaty. Jay was hanged in effigy in New York City, and when Hamilton spoke there publicly in defense of the treaty he was jeered by a hostile crowd and hit in the head by a rock. Sensing an opportunity, DeWitt Clinton corresponded during the summer with John Beckley, clerk of the House of Representatives and an active Jeffersonian partisan, to attempt a coordinated response to the treaty. Beckley wrote to Clinton on July 24 describing the Republican plan to circulate a petition opposing the treaty throughout Philadelphia, "by which," he concluded in a rather sinister tone, "we shall discover the names and numbers of the British adherents, Old tories, and Aristocrats, who modestly assume the title of federalists and stile themselves the best friends of our beloved president." For Beckley, President Washington was the victim of advisers who were serving British interests. In September, stressing the secrecy that had attended the Philadelphia committee's efforts, Beckley wrote to Clinton that his advice on how to proceed had been "communicated at our select meeting."[22]

Perhaps hoping to capitalize on lingering resentment of the Jay treaty, in 1796 Clinton made another run for the assembly. But however virulently some New Yorkers opposed the Jay treaty, it still had considerable support. For one thing, it avoided war; for another, it secured the return of seven frontier forts that the British had held since 1783, four of which were in New York State. As a result, the Federalist candidates did better than expected, and DeWitt Clinton lost again. The next year, the Republicans tightened their campaign organization, appealed to a growing population of poor voters (who could vote for assembly candidates if they paid at least 40 shillings a year in rent), and publicized several local disputes that were portrayed, fairly, as examples of Federalist high-handedness. This last issue had begun to pick up steam the year before, when a state assemblyman, William Keteltas, was jailed for protesting the imprisonment of two Irish ferrymen and the whipping of one of them for refusing to give preferential treatment to a city magistrate. By 1797, protest was coalescing around a law, enacted by the Federalist-controlled legislature in February, that sought to reduce the risk of yellow fever by ordering businesses that gave off rank odors—soapmakers, glue factories—to move to the city's periphery. The bill was branded by Republicans as a class measure, taking work away from those who collected the ashes used in soap manufacturing because (it was alleged) John Jay lived close to a tallow-chandler and objected to the smell. When Samuel Latham Mitchill, a chemistry professor at Columbia, agreed to represent the tradesmen affected, the Federalists revised the law and Mitchill was promptly given a place on the Republican ticket. It seems probable that Clinton played some role in this maneuver; after leaving his uncle's employ as secretary, he had resumed the scientific pursuits he had enjoyed at Columbia by studying botany with David Hosack and chemistry and zoology with Dr. Mitchill. Both men would remain close to Clinton for the balance of his career. In April 1797, Clinton won election handily, and the following January he took his seat in the assembly.[23]

ATTORNEY AND SPECULATOR

While Clinton was engaged in these political races, he earned a living as a lawyer and began speculating in real estate. He was a tough bargainer, quick to pursue derelict debtors and delinquent correspondents, although his hectoring was usually veiled in the courtly locutions of the eighteenth century. One regular recipient of his letters was Oliver Phelps, from whom he and three other investors had purchased a large tract of land in western New York. Writing to Phelps of certain shortcomings on Phelps's side in their transactions, Clinton states that he is "cordially inclined to accommodate" Phelps, so far as is "consistent with the trust reposed in me" by the other investors. (Clinton's negotiating style is reminiscent of Melville's Captain Bildad, who tries to get Ishmael to accept a tiny share of the potential profits of the *Pequod*'s voyage by invoking the widows and orphans who have their money invested in the ship.) A month later, seeking clarification of Phelps's title to fifty thousand acres west of the Genesee, he writes that he himself is not concerned about it but needs to satisfy "persons with whom I am negotiating." Early in 1797, he writes Phelps that when he expressed "astonishment that you had made no provision whatever for the payment of your note, I had no intention to convey any reproach. My pressing for payment is no more than my duty as a trustee." In a society in which duelling still flourished, a certain courtesy when making accusations was sensible. It seems clear, however, that Clinton was a tenacious protector of his own interests as well as those of his partners.[24]

Even relatives were not immune from his sharply worded missives. Recipients included his wife's uncles, who held her property in trust until her majority, which came nine months after their marriage. Maria's uncle John Franklin was curtly instructed, "I will thank you to account with me for the rent you have received on her behalf and to pay the balance." But others received gentler treatment—for instance, Peter B. Porter, who purchased land from Clinton and his partners in western New York. Clinton treated Porter, who had just been appointed clerk of Ontario County, with care. Porter was apparently late in paying a creditor, who was pressing Clinton to "prosecute upon it," but Clinton promised that Porter would be given "full notice." Whether or not Porter harbored any resentment over their dealings, he was to become a major political opponent in western New York and would fight Clinton tenaciously over the choice of the western terminus of the Erie Canal.[25]

Clinton's legal practice brought him into contact with important business and political leaders throughout the state, but these contacts, as in the case of Porter, were sometimes adversarial. A more tranquil way of forming connections arose from his important place in the state's Masonic organization. In the spring of 1799, he was traveling in upstate New York on Grand Lodge business, delivering warrants for lodges and collecting money for the Grand Lodge charity fund. He lists a string of lodges and notes that "a great proportion of the above lodges were constituted by me in person—this was by no means a pleasant task, as the distance of some of them from Albany was considerable—I however thought it my indispensable duty to do it wherever it could be done without interfering with my public avocations." He was happy to report that Masonry was thriving in the west, and that "the Grand Lodge is greatly respected & its authority almost universally acknowledged." It can have done no harm to Clinton's career to meet the leading figures of the growing towns of the state, particularly since he was bringing the blessing of the Grand Lodge.[26]

REPUBLICANISM TRIUMPHANT

If Jay's treaty helped avert war with England, it nearly precipitated one with France. France's advocacy of the rights of neutral ships, of course, stemmed not from any Gallic sense of fair play but from the fact that France's navy and merchant fleet were vastly inferior to Britain's, so France depended on neutral shipping to keep the country itself and its colonies supplied. When the United States capitulated to Britain's restrictions on neutral shipping, France retaliated. President John Adams sent emissaries to France to explain the American position and secure more favorable treatment from the French, but when emissaries from Talleyrand, the French foreign minister, tried to extort a bribe for his cooperation, the Americans indignantly refused. The publication of the reports from the commissioners in France, in April 1798, caused a new flood of bellicose feeling in America, this time directed against France. (Talleyrand's agents were referred to in the reports as Messrs. X, Y, and Z, from which this matter came to be known as the XYZ Affair.) A Federalist effort to strengthen the army and navy was begun, which included calling Washington out of retirement to command the forces. Although many Republican friends of France denounced the new belligerence, in New York, which as a port was both dependent on commerce and vulnerable to attack, there was considerable support for improving the city's defenses. In the state assembly, Clinton broke with his party and supported the state taxes needed to improve and enlarge fortifications, and he even volunteered his labor, as he had four years earlier, to dig trenches and build walls. So did his uncle George, who was now almost sixty.[27]

Clinton's break with his party over war taxes did not develop into a serious rupture. For one thing, other Republicans were also caught up in the war fever, either on their own or because they sensed the mood of their constituents. And, more important, he refused to acquiesce in the Alien and Sedition Acts passed by the Federalists to stifle dissent—and to stifle the Republicans. The Alien and Sedition Acts produced a number of martyrs, none more widely known than Congressman Matthew

Lyon of Vermont. To his Federalist adversaries he was known as the "Spitting Lyon" (he had once responded to an insult from a Federalist colleague by spitting in his eye on the floor of the House; the victim later attacked Lyon there with a cane). Lyon narrowly escaped expulsion from the House for his expectoration, but in 1798 he was convicted under the Sedition Act of libeling President Adams. (Lyon had suggested in print and in public speeches that Adams was power-mad and maybe just plain crazy.) He was fined a thousand dollars and sentenced to four months in prison. Lyon was re-elected to his House seat while in jail, and in January 1799, Clinton was asked to help secure Lyon's release. Clinton's earlier correspondence with John Beckley had confirmed his place in the growing national organization that was coalescing around the figure of Thomas Jefferson. Albert Gallatin, the Republican leader in the House of Representatives and one of Jefferson's closest allies, wrote from Philadelphia to ask Clinton to assist a messenger who was taking seven hundred dollars to Vermont to help pay Lyon's fine. Gallatin also asked him to try to raise another four hundred dollars to pay the fine (and perhaps some travel expenses, since the fine was only a thousand dollars).[28]

Although Lyon was popular in his Vermont district, the surge of anti-French feeling in 1798 brought John Adams to the peak of his never-sought popularity, and set the last high-water mark of Federalism. That year John Jay easily won reelection as governor, even though his opponent was the leader of the Livingston clan, Chancellor Robert R. Livingston. But also in the same election, Clinton advanced from the assembly to the state senate. Soon the gradual lessening of the likelihood of war with France, combined with hostility to the Alien and Sedition Acts, strengthened the Republican interest in New York and the nation.

DeWitt Clinton was emerging as a powerful force in New York independent of his uncle's popularity, but there was another young man of great political talent and even sharper ambition who was now clearly the leading figure in New York Republicanism—Aaron Burr. Since the 1780s Burr had sailed an independent (and haphazard) course in politics—a course determined by his assessment of what could best advance his own career at any particular moment. Yet so talented and charming was he that for a decade he had pursued this course without provoking any serious enmity. When he masterminded the founding of the Manhattan Company, in 1799—the water company for New York City that served as cover for the chartering of a bank to serve Republican interests as the Bank of New York served the Federalists—he was able to enlist even Alexander Hamilton as a backer. To be the leading Republican in the state as 1799 turned into 1800 was to hold an important position. The mathematics of the Electoral College had made it clear that the pivotal state in the 1800 presidential election would be New York. Neither solidly Federalist, like the states to its north and east, nor firmly Jeffersonian, like the states south and west of Maryland, it had made the difference for Adams in 1796. To elect a Virginian president, it was decided, there must be a New Yorker for vice president (a formula that was to be followed for five of the next six presidential elections). When Albert Gallatin wrote to his father-in-law, James Nicholson, a New Yorker and a Revolutionary War veteran, to sound out local sentiment, he was informed that Burr would be a more popular choice than the other two men being considered, George Clinton and Robert Livingston. Gallatin himself may have been inclined toward Burr, since Burr had championed Gallatin's cause when the Genevan émigré was denied a seat in the United States Senate in 1794 because he had not been an American citizen for a sufficient time. Gallatin also sought the opinion of Matthew Davis, Burr's lieutenant and later his biographer, who, not surprisingly, informed Gallatin that Burr was "the most eligible character."[29]

It is one of the curiosities of the electoral process in 1800 that the selection of the ticket came after the race was decided. Presidential electors were then chosen in New York by the legislature, not directly by the people, so the key contest was for control of the state legislature in the April elections. Burr engineered the nomination of a Republican slate that was designed with an exquisite sense of the factionalism of the party in New York, and needed all his persuasive powers to come into being—for example, such august figures as George Clinton and Horatio Gates, the hero of Saratoga, had to stand for assembly seats. Jabez Hammond wrote in 1842 that those who had attempted to deny Burr credit for the victory were, in his gentle term, "uncandid" and stressed that prospects for a Republican success in New York had seemed dim just a few months earlier, and that Burr, by putting together his distinguished slate of candidates, had made the victory possible.[30]

DeWitt Clinton did not play a prominent part in the 1800 race. His oldest son, Franklin (like DeWitt, he had been given his mother's family name as his first name), was seriously ill, and a surviving letter recalls the hideous ministrations of the medical profession of the time. Franklin was subjected to "a mercurial purge" and given "small doses of nitre," then a "decoction of the bark with E. Vitriol," which successfully restored the boy's appetite. Medical wisdom then decided he was getting too plump, and when he appeared to have jaundice, he was given a "calomel purge." The last treatment mentioned was "Sydenham's beer of Rhoi & absynth." To survive such treatment is a testimony to the hardiness of young Franklin. In spite of his son's troubles, Clinton found time to lend his rhetorical skills to the electoral battle. One of the accusations commonly leveled against Jefferson by the Federalists was that he was "an atheist in religion," as Hamilton put it. Clinton, writing as "Grotius," took up Jefferson's side in a pamphlet entitled "A Vindication of Thomas Jefferson." Probably his most persuasive argument was that "in the hour of adversity, like most other sinners, the leaders of the aristocratic faction call upon that religion for assistance and support, which in the full tide of prosperity they either neglected or despised." Recalling that Hamilton, when asked why there was no mention of God in the Constitution, replied, "We forgot," one recognizes some justice in Clinton's jibe. However, Clinton's efforts to clear Jefferson of godlessness by a lawyerly recasting of Jefferson's expressed doubts about Noah's flood probably swayed few voters.[31]

Clinton may well have resented the fact that Burr received so much credit for the New York victory, and hence for the election of the Republican ticket. He certainly did not welcome the presence in state politics of a challenger for preeminence. For the next four years, he would fight to curtail Burr's power in the state, and in this effort his greatest ally would be Burr's own ambition. Although Burr would make several colossal errors over the next half-dozen years, he certainly made none greater than appearing to court Federalist support when a tie in the electoral vote between him and Jefferson—the result of a constitutional defect that failed to require electors to specify whether votes cast were for president or vice president—threw the election of 1800 into the House of Representatives. The story of the election has been told in detail many times, and Clinton's role in the deliberations in Washington was insignificant, but the matter must be mentioned briefly here, because he would play an important part in ending the conditions under which a similar deadlock could take place.

Modern students of this period have been struck by the extreme rhetoric of the politics of the Federal era—the charges of monarchism made against Washington, Adams, Hamilton, and others; the scurrilous journalism practiced by Jefferson's protégé Philip Freneau and by Hamilton's ally John Fenno. Charges of treason—that Jay had sold out the United States in his treaty, that Jefferson and Madison were agents of the French government—were as common in politics then as negative television commercials are today. The skies of classical republicanism were clouded by plots and conspiracies, all threatening the historically demonstrated fragility of republics. Federalist opposition to Jefferson was fundamental; his election was seen as a calamity from which the country could never recover. The two great dangers to republics were held to be oligarchy and mob rule; after twelve years of being accused of the first by Jefferson's allies, the Federalists were equally sure that Jefferson's anointment would result in the second.[32]

Hamilton tried to take practical steps to prevent Jefferson's election. After the result of the New York legislative elections in April, he wrote Governor Jay to urge that the method of choosing presidential electors be changed to direct election of electors—a proposal advanced by Burr and Clinton in the legislature the previous year, only to be thwarted by Federalist opposition. Jay's response demonstrates why he was so highly regarded by his colleagues: "This is a measure for party purposes which I think it would not become me to adopt." Hamilton had personally worked the New York City wards to get out the Federalist vote in the legislative elections, and he viewed the elevation of Jefferson as a disaster—but not as great a disaster as the election of Burr, "who, on all hands, is acknowledged to be a complete Catiline." Others in the party nevertheless conspired, when the House met to resolve the tie, to bring in Burr ahead of Jefferson, on the theory that his election would sever him from the Jeffersonians, who would then repudiate him, so that he would have to turn to the Federalists for support. The plot, of course, failed. Burr's own role in the matter remains murky, although his recent biographer, Milton Lomask, absolves him of actively plotting to displace Jefferson. It is clear, however, that Burr could have prevented the crisis simply by breaking his own silence and disavowing any claim to the presidency for himself; when Jefferson and Burr stood before Congress at the inauguration in 1801, as Henry Adams noted a century ago, the audience saw two men who "profoundly disliked and distrusted each other." No wonder, then, that Burr's power quickly started to diminish in New York.[33]

REACHING FOR NEW YORK'S SPOILS

The New York legislative elections of 1800 had not only brought in the Republican ticket but deprived the Federalists of control of the state government. Jay's term as governor had another year to run, but a Republican legislature was eager to exercise the power that the voters had conferred on the party. The leader in this effort was DeWitt Clinton.

The Council of Appointment had its origins in the revolutionary-era fear of a powerful executive, and provided a strong legislative voice in government appointments. While in some ways analogous to the power of the United States Senate to advise and consent on such matters as nominations of Supreme Court justices, the Council of Appointment's powers reached far down into the government. "Not only the state officers," wrote the historian Howard Lee McBain, "not only the whole judiciary from the Chancellor down to the pettiest justice of the peace; but every district attorney, the mayor and recorder of every city, every county clerk, surrogate and sheriff, together with a whole army of auctioneers, coroners, masters, and examiners in chancery, inspectors of turnpike roads, various commercial and mercantile inspectors, commissioners for sundry purposes and even public notaries, held their commissions from this council." The lack of clarity in the 1777 state constitution over who, exactly, held the power of nomination had been exploited once before, as we have seen. In 1794 the Federalists had challenged George Clinton's power and claimed a concurrent power of nomination for the other members of the council, which was composed of the governor and four senators—one from each of the state's four major geographical divisions under existing electoral law. In that year, George Clinton had capitulated to the Federalists and allowed their nominations to proceed.[34]

Returned to power in the legislature, the Republicans were in no mood to allow Governor Jay to have his way with appointments. In December 1800, Marinus Willett, a revolutionary soldier and supporter of George Clinton, wrote DeWitt Clinton, "I think it would justly merit the appellation of Dastardly weakness if the republicans when they have it in their power should not remove the gentlemen called federalists from offices of honor and profit and endeavour to fill them with honest virtuous republicans."[35]

His wishes were granted. On February 11, 1801, Governor Jay met the new Council of Appointment. Like the one George Clinton had faced in 1794, it had replaced a council that still had half a year left in its term. Like the one George Clinton had faced, it was dominated by the opposition—there were three Republican members (DeWitt Clinton, Ambrose Spencer, and Robert Roseboom), and one Federalist (John Sanders). But, unlike George Clinton, John Jay refused to acquiesce. After the council had vetoed several of Jay's nominations, DeWitt Clinton offered a nomination of his own. Jay ignored it, and presented further nominees of *his* choosing, which the council would not even vote on. The meeting adjourned, and Jay dealt with the problem by simply not calling the council into session again. He then sent a message to the legislature on February 26 presenting his side of the argument. Denouncing the precedent set by the appointment of Egbert Benson to the state supreme court in 1794, Jay wrote that he had always assumed that the state constitution "vested the right of nomination exclusively in the Governor" and went on to needle DeWitt Clinton with the news that "it gave me pleasure to find, on conferring with my predecessor, that this opinion was strengthened by his informing me that he had always claimed this right, and never yielded or conceded it to be in the council." George Clinton was torn between his own earlier struggle over this issue and his desire to support his nephew and his party, and in March he wrote to DeWitt Clinton that although the dispute was disturbing to public confidence, he felt sure that "a majority disapprove the conduct of the Governor."[36]

Efforts to resolve the question in the legislature or by judicial opinion were fruitless, and in April the legislature passed an act recommending a constitutional convention to clarify the matter. In October of that year the convention met and revised the constitution so as to make clear that the power of nomination was held by both the governor and the other members of the council. DeWitt Clinton was ill and was not present at the convention. He was doubtless irritated that the convention had chosen as its president Aaron Burr, whose strength in New York remained formidable.[37]

And Clinton would soon be assailing Burr's power in New York, because the elections in the spring of 1801 had consolidated Republican control of the state. John Jay ended his public career and entered a long and quiet retirement. George Clinton emerged from a brief and fitful retirement to run for governor again, facing Stephen Van Rensselaer, the patroon, whose vast holdings along the Hudson were both the source of his political power and a significant handicap to winning an election in the age of Jefferson. George Clinton won handily, and by the end of 1801 DeWitt Clinton was using his influence with his uncle and his place on the Council of Appointment to emerge as the most powerful political figure in the state of New York.

Three

o   o   o

CLINTONIANS AND BURRITES

T HE REPUBLICAN VICTORIES OF 1800 and 1801 had greatly weakened the power of the Federalists, and that weakness allowed existing rivalries within the Republican ranks to sharpen into public discord and even bloodshed. If the politics of New York a decade earlier could be described as being divided among the Schuylers, the Clintons, and the Livingstons, by 1801 Aaron Burr and his associates had created a new force. The founding of the Manhattan Company had given Burr a powerful tool to win influential people to his side, and his skillful conduct of the state campaign for Jefferson in 1800 had won him admirers and made clear his skill in the developing art of popular politics. Burr's questionable conduct during the confused months between the elections of 1800 and Jefferson's eventual triumph in the House of Representatives on February 17, 1801, had squandered much of his political capital, particularly with the Virginia leadership in Washington. But he remained an important and popular figure in New York, as was shown by his election to the presidency of the 1801 state constitutional convention.[1]

The animosity of the Clintons toward Burr arose from several sources. There was, of course, the reluctance of George and DeWitt Clinton to share power in the state with others. An alliance with the Livingstons had been necessary, but more partners—or a formidable rival—would be undesirable. And Burr had revealed himself to be at best an inconstant ally. He had, it should be recalled, supported Robert Yates's candidacy against George Clinton for governor in 1789, but had nonetheless received the governor's support for the United States Senate in 1791. And the following year, he had sought ways to supplant Clinton as the Republican candidate for governor. By 1801, however, Burr's ambitions were not of much concern to George Clinton. Clinton's wife had died the year before, and he had little interest in moving to Washington and becoming vice president. His desire to retire from politics was apparently sincere, and the offices he held over the next decade, until his death, in 1812, were accepted more out of a sense of obligation (and vanity) than out of ambition. Although George Clinton had said that he was not interested in the vice presidency when he was approached by James Nicholson (on behalf of Albert Gallatin) in 1800, he still resented the elevation of Burr to the office. Burr had his own reservations about accepting the vice presidency—he worried that the promise of the office on the part of the Virginians and their southern allies "could not be relied on," according to Nicholson. Only when Burr's friends told him it was his duty to run, Nicholson wrote, did he accept the vice presidential nomination. While such avowals of disinterestedness are mere boilerplate in the politics of the period, in this case there may be some truth to the story. Burr's real ambition had been to run for governor of New York in 1801. He had had designs on the office in 1795, when George Clinton had declined to run, but the nomination had gone to Robert Yates. Burr blamed Clinton for denying him the nomination and planned to seek the office again.[2]

For George Clinton, Burr's presence was only an irritant, but for DeWitt Clinton, Burr was a real threat. DeWitt Clinton was thirty-two in 1801, but Burr was just forty-five, and promised to be a power in state and national politics for some years to come. Between DeWitt Clinton and the Burrites, the rivalry would develop into rhetorical excess and, finally, physical violence.

Burr's exact actions in the congressional drama that eventually led to the election of Jefferson will never be known, but in New York what mattered was the way things seemed. Many felt that Burr had tried to steal the election from the great champion of republicanism by remaining silent when he could have settled it in one stroke, and that his self-interested inaction had nearly delivered the nation into the hands of the Federalists again. Even before Congress assembled to decide, Republicans had suspected a Federalist plot. George Clinton had written DeWitt Clinton in January 1801 that the "equality of votes for Jefferson and Burr" would be exploited by "a faction destitute of Principle & rendered desperate by Disappointment." But at that time George Clinton had still been confident that Burr would do the right thing: "Indeed I have reason to believe from Burr's explicit Declaration to me that he will not countenance a Competition for the Presidency with Mr Jefferson & especially as he must be sensible that such Competition would end in his Ruin."[3]

The perception that Burr encouraged (or at least failed to discourage) efforts to make himself rather than Jefferson president did prove ruinous to Burr's political future. But this downfall was hastened and abetted by the Clintonian party in New York. The struggle took shape in an exchange of pamphlets in which Clintonians and Burrites accused each other of whatever crimes seemed most likely to offend the largest segment of the electorate. The opening salvo came in 1802 from James Cheetham, writing as "A Citizen of New York," in *A Narrative of the Suppression by Colonel Burr of the History of the Administration of John Adams.* Cheetham had arrived in the United States in the late 1790s, and first, apparently, had come under the patronship of Aaron Burr; soon, however, he joined with DeWitt Clinton's cousin David Denniston to found the *American Citizen,* the principal Clintonian paper of the early 1800s. (An important Republican printer of the time, Denniston had published DeWitt Clinton's defense of Jefferson in 1800.) Cheetham corresponded with Jefferson about the activities of New York's Burrites and their enemies, and Jefferson, as Milton Lomask suggests in his biography of Burr, may have known that Cheetham's *Narrative* was in the works.[4]

The crux of Cheetham's argument was that Aaron Burr had encouraged John Wood to write a critical account of the Adams presidency and then tried to suppress it when he sought Federalist support against Jefferson in the House of Representatives. Cheetham accused Burr of plotting to steal the election from Jefferson, to which end "he had agents in the different states during the Presidential election." The difficulty of providing positive proof of Burr's actions, with regard either to the suppression of Wood's history or to the election of 1800, was explained by the fact that Burr was exceedingly cunning, refusing to commit his plans to writing, and avoiding even speaking of them "in the presense of more than one man!" Other attacks from Cheetham came in *A View of the Political Conduct of Aaron Burr, Esq.,* and *A Letter to a Friend on the Conduct of the Adherents to Mr. Burr,* published in 1803, which paid greater attention to Burr's ambitions in New York State politics. He included the accusation that New Jersey Senator Jonathan Dayton, a leading Burrite, had "visited the western parts of the Union to see what could be effected" in the way of military action in the West. The action contemplated would supposedly have been in response to the movements of the Spanish intendant at New Orleans, but the specter of Burrite freebooting in the West was already a threat in the minds of Cheetham and other Clintonians.[5]

Other pamphleteers joined in on each side, and the level of invective was intense. Perhaps the most extravagant charges were made by John Wood in his *A Full Exposition of the Clintonian Faction, and the Society of the Columbian Illuminati,* in which DeWitt Clinton, his uncle George and his allies, and James Cheetham were all implicated in monstrous conspiratorial designs. Wood claimed that there was a secret society, called Theistical but better understood as the Columbian Illuminati, composed entirely of Clintonians. He linked it vaguely with a European movement founded on May Day 1776, by Adam Weishaupt, a former Jesuit, who called his group the Perfectabilists; connected with the Freemasons, they were rumored to have been "the real agents and conspirators of the French revolution." The Columbian Illuminati, presumably an American offshoot, was, according to Wood, "a society fraught with the blackest intentions, to overturn the divine revelation, and to raise the hand of opposition against the opinion of every christian." Although he did not say that DeWitt Clinton was a member, he claimed that he had seen a list of its members, ninety-five in all, and that every one was a Clintonian. And Clinton was clearly doing the society's bidding with his appointments: "Mr. Clinton has afforded his patronage to several who were avowed deists, and he has been the means of displacing christians, to make room for deists." Beyond that,

> he bestows in bountiful measure, all his patronage to support their political paper, the *American Citizen.* Nothing can prove more distinctly the mutual affection and sympathy which exist between Mr. Clinton and the Columbian Illuminati, than these acts of kindness. The link which connects the infidels of New-York with the Clinton family, must now be obvious, and the ardent zeal which is displayed to promote the greatness of that family.[6]

Besides picturing the Illuminati as embracing the nefarious principles of Thomas Paine (who, with the publication of *The Age of Reason,* had now been cast as the champion of atheism), Wood insinuates that they condoned even incest and that Clinton may have taken advantage of the supplicant women who "throw themselves at the feet of De Witt to shield their husbands from beggary." As for his brother George Clinton, Jr., "perhaps a greater simpleton is not to be found in the whole city of New-York, if his cousin, the Governor's son, be excepted."[7]

The Clintons found a more formidable tormentor in "Aristides," the pseudonym of William P. Van Ness, a New York City Burrite. "Aristides" attacked the Clintonians with considerable effect in *An Examination of the Various Charges Exhibited Against Aaron Burr, Esq., Vice-President of the United States.* As Dixon Ryan Fox notes, "[I]t circulated more widely through the country than any earlier pamphlet except *Common Sense."* Van Ness was a gifted pamphleteer, and Cheetham was badly outclassed. Although the identity of "Aristides" was not known until much later, Burr's hand was clearly discernible in his work. DeWitt Clinton himself detected as much. Complaining to Thomas Tillotson (a doctor and a Livingston-by-marriage who was then New York's secretary of state), he wrote:

> The abuse I have received is so general and so brutal that I can scarcely work myself up to a very high pitch of irritation—but viewing it as I do as an exhibition of the cloven foot of Burr, I have learnt it is possible to entertain a worse opinion of him than I had before. The little band mean to run him for Govr—and are very active here—We are determined to meet them with correspondent exertions and trust that you will not be idle in your quarter.[8]

Clinton was particularly annoyed by the success of "Aristides" in keeping his identity secret. In the same letter, he told Tillotson he wanted to confront the author and bring him before the "proper forum" to "answer for his misconduct." Unable to unmask his tormentor, he decided to sue the printers of the pamphlet, the firm of Ward & Gould. When the publishers heard of this plan, they wrote Clinton to say that they

> sincerely regret that you have determined to prosecute in case we do not disclose the name of the author of the pamphlet alluded to, which is wholly incompatible with engagements which we think proper not to violate though at the hazard of pecuniary distress. We are no party in the thing—we adventured in the publication from a presumption that as the friends of Mr. Burr had not prosecuted for the reiterated attacks on them, that a like clemency would be observed by the opposite side.[9]

But the fury of the Clintonians would admit no clemency. George Clinton, too, was enraged by the accusations of "Aristides," in particular his allegation that the former governor had desired the vice presidency in 1800, and that he had "dwindled into the mere instrument of an ambitious relative." The publishers grew less willing to hazard "pecuniary distress" following Burr's murder of Alexander Hamilton in July 1804 and the subsequent rapid decline of his influence in New York. By December of that year, Ward & Gould were capitulating to Clinton's pressure; indeed, the Burrites had been powerless to help when a judgment had been entered against the firm in favor of Ambrose Spencer and Thomas Tillotson. (Spencer, "Aristides" claimed, had left the Federalist party only because Governor Jay had refused to appoint him comptroller, while Tillotson, it was charged, had accepted the office of secretary of state as part of a deal with the Clintonians to advance DeWitt Clinton.) Ward & Gould offered Clinton the following terms: They would reveal the identity of "Aristides," "provided he will not be prosecuted"; they would disclose the names of his backers; and they would fully disclose the circumstances behind the publication of the pamphlet. In Clinton's papers for 1805 there is a letter from Ward & Gould thanking him for his assistance in securing a settlement. Clearly aware of where power now resided in New York, they avowed that the experience had taught them that their original assessment of his character had been wrong. "We had an idea," they wrote him, "that your temper was haughty & imperious; that you was difficult of access, & disposed to prosecute to the utmost those that power might place in your hands, or those whose political sentiments & conduct were opposed to your own." Now they realized that he was "always ready & willing to lean as far as strict honor would permit to the side of humanity."[10]

"Strict honor" entered into the battle of Clintonians against Burrites in more sanguinary ways. Burr's 1804 duel with Hamilton was only the last of the affairs of honor the Burrites took part in beginning in 1802. The first of these duels, and the most important for this work, took place in July 1802 between DeWitt Clinton and John Swartwout, one of Burr's closest allies. Swartwout had advised Burr on his pursuit of the vice presidency in 1800, and on the possibility of challenging Jefferson for the presidency in the House in 1801. When the Clintons and Livingstons ousted Burr as a director of the Manhattan Company, Swartwout lost his post there as well. After Cheetham's attacks on Burr began, Swartwout declared that Clinton's opposition to Burr was basely motivated and founded on his own ambitions. DeWitt Clinton promptly called Swartwout "a liar, a scoundrel, and a villain." Such words could not, under the code then prevailing among gentlemen, pass unchallenged. When Swartwout asked for an explanation, Clinton admitted using the first two words but denied the third. Swartwout demanded either an apology or "satisfaction," but when a mild apology was drawn up by the deputy state attorney general, Richard Riker, and approved by Clinton, Swartwout rejected it. So the affair had to be settled by combat, and on July 31 the two men proceeded to the dueling ground at Weehawken, New Jersey.[11]

The rules were drawn up with the fastidious exactitude that characterized the code of dueling. The seconds agreed on the distance between the duelists (ten yards), the length of the gun barrels (not to exceed eleven inches), and other details. In spite of the short distance between them, neither combatant managed to hit his opponent on the first three tries. After the first exchange, Clinton's second, Riker, conveyed his principal's feeling that the matter should end there, with honor satisfied, but Swartwout refused. This happened again after the second and third exchanges, at which point Swartwout declared he would not be satisfied until Clinton signed an apology that had been drawn up by Swartwout's side. Clinton refused, the duel continued, and on the fourth exchange, he wounded Swartwout in the left leg. After Swartwout's doctor removed the bullet, Swartwout insisted that they continue, and on the next shot Clinton again hit him in the leg. Still John Swartwout was not satisfied, and wanted to go on, but Clinton had had enough. According to Riker, Clinton turned to him and to Swartwout's second, Colonel William Stephens Smith, and said, "I don't want to hurt him; but I wish I had the *principal* here. I will meet him when he pleases." The wounded Swartwout was taken to the house of the "principal" (Burr) and both sides busied themselves with portraying the duel in the best possible light. The Clintonians claimed their man had acted honorably and had broken it off from a sense of basic humanity. The Burrites intimated that Clinton had stopped out of fear, though without explaining how he could have endured five exchanges of fire before his fear overwhelmed him.[12]

SENATOR CLINTON

One of the facts that gave some pungency to Burrite attacks on the Clintons was that the state legislature, controlled by DeWitt Clinton, had elected him to the United States Senate in 1802 after John Armstrong had resigned to tend his ailing wife. Burr and his supporters charged that Armstrong had been moved aside to satisfy DeWitt Clinton's ambition, and that as part of the deal Thomas Tillotson had been appointed secretary of state of New York, thus providing a Livingston relation with public office to compensate for the one Armstrong was vacating. (General Armstrong had married Alida Livingston, and Tillotson was the husband of the former Margaret Livingston, both sisters of Chancellor Robert R. Livingston.) Jabez Hammond dismissed the Burrite account as being "void of any shadow of proof." And, indeed, a letter from General Armstrong to Tillotson shows that although Armstrong had originally intended to return to Washington that winter, his wife's worsening health required that he resign immediately. A subsequent letter to Tillotson, after DeWitt Clinton had become the favorite to replace Armstrong, affords some pleasant insights into the scurryings for offices, particularly about the appointment of a new naval officer for the port of New York. Theodorus Bailey wanted the post, and Armstrong urged that DeWitt Clinton be brought into Bailey's camp. (Bailey was apparently a supple politician. He was an ally of Burr's who was on the list of five Republicans Burr recommended to Jefferson to replace Federalist appointees. But Burr had recommended him for a different job, that of city supervisor, and was pushing Matthew L. Davis for naval officer. Bailey, however, had Livingstonian support for that post, and we shall meet him later as a Clintonian emissary to the Burrites.) "If D. W. [Clinton] should go to the Senate," Armstrong wrote, "he should be previously brought to support B[ailey]. I don't mean that this should be stipulated & reduced to a bargain—but everything that might be said for its justice as it applies to B. & its policy as it applies to the party, should be urged upon him, with freedom & with force." As for a Clinton-Armstrong bargain for the latter's Senate seat, as alleged by the Burrites, it seems doubtful that there was one. Jabez Hammond likely has things right when he states that such a deal would have been beneath Armstrong's dignity, and when he asks, "Who would have been more likely, without factitious aid, to receive the support of the majority of the republican members of the legislature than De Witt Clinton?"[13]

Clinton's short term as a senator began in February 1802, when he went to Washington to present himself to President Jefferson with a letter of introduction from his uncle George Clinton. Governor Clinton mentioned DeWitt Clinton's services to him as secretary, but stressed that his elevation to the Senate stemmed entirely from his own abilities and the recognition of those gifts by the citizens of New York. And he went on, "His political principles are pure, and he has too much dignity ever to deviate from them; nor will you find him destitute of talents and information." The president had reason to look with favor on the junior senator from New York. For one thing, DeWitt Clinton's "Grotius" pamphlet, defending Jefferson against the charge of being unchristian, substantiated George Clinton's assessment of DeWitt's republican principles. Moreover, as Dixon Ryan Fox wrote, it was always the policy of the Virginia Dynasty to oppose whoever was most powerful in the state of New York, and early in 1802 that person was still Aaron Burr.[14]

Clinton left little record of his feelings about the town of Washington, or the experience of being in the Senate. He was a senator for less than two years, but managed in that time to influence three major areas of policy. They were immigration reform, American policy toward Spanish administration of the port of New Orleans, and the constitutional provision for the election of president and vice president. In the first instance, he championed legislation that reduced the waiting period for immigrants wishing American citizenship from fourteen years to five. One effect of this action was to strengthen Clinton's popularity among New York's Irish immigrants, who, while not yet arriving at the flood rates of later decades, were already a visible force in the city's political and economic life. Clinton's own family ties to Ireland also helped line up Irish voters behind him, as would other actions he would take that were favorable to the liberties of American Catholics.[15]

The controversy over New Orleans gave Clinton the chance to make his only important speech on the Senate floor. When the Spanish intendant at New Orleans revoked the right of American citizens to deposit goods there (which had been granted in the Pinckney treaty with Spain of 1795), some Federalist senators urged military action and scolded the Jefferson administration for not protecting American interests in Louisiana. Clinton chided the hotheads, expressing faith in the king of Spain's desire to preserve American rights along the Mississippi, and argued against any military steps, studding his speech with citations from prominent jurists like Vattel and Burlamaqui. He reviewed the actions of other nations with respect to Spanish abrogations of accepted rights and emphasized that even Great Britain, mighty as it was, usually resorted to negotiation rather than force. He cited violations of the 1795 treaty by the Spanish during the Washington and Adams administrations and asked whether the Federalists at that time had proposed "to seize New Orleans with an armed force," as they were now doing. He pointed out the cost of a war with Spain and the consequences for the republic of the heavy taxation that would be needed to support it. The best policy, he said, echoing Washington's Farewell Address, "would be to avoid European connections and wars. The time must arrive when we will have to contend with some of the great powers of Europe; but let that period be put off as long as possible." He urged against expansionist designs, not only toward Canada and the West Indies but even toward "those vast countries to the west, as far as where the Pacific rolls its waves." In its mixture of partisan sniping, learned bombast, and general good sense, the speech was typical of Clinton's public utterances. While it may not have been needed to prevent a military adventure against New Orleans, it must have ratified DeWitt Clinton's orthodoxy in the eyes of the Jefferson administration.[16]

The president's ability to provide federal patronage in New York made him a potentially useful figure to Clinton in the midst of his struggles with Burr. But Jefferson's use of patronage in New York seems to have been more in accord with the principle of divide and rule than with that of rewarding loyal service. Burr's biographer Milton Lomask rejects the notion that Jefferson froze Burr out of the process completely, pointing out that of Burr's five recommendations to Jefferson in the spring of 1801 two were soon appointed—John Swartwout as United States marshal and Edward Livingston as federal district attorney. (Burr's support, however, was hardly the only thing these men had going for them in New York. The Swartwouts were an influential Republican family in the city, and the Livingstons, of course, were the preeminent Republican family in the state.) Jefferson, too, was unwilling to act as ruthlessly in dismissing Federalists as DeWitt Clinton had when he got control of the Council of Appointment, and the president did not replace the Federalist holding the lucrative office of collector of the port of New York until 1803. When he did so, the office went to Samuel Osgood, the second husband of DeWitt Clinton's mother-in-law, Maria Bowne Franklin.[17]

By far the most important legislation that Clinton as a senator played a role in was the Twelfth Amendment to the Constitution. The Twelfth Amendment was, as Richard Hofstadter put it, the "decisive step . . . toward constitutional recognition of the role played by parties in the federal government." The immediate catalyst for passage of the amendment was the deadlocked election of 1800, but the deficiencies of the constitutional provisions for the election of president and vice president had become apparent eight years earlier. In 1792 the emerging division of American politics into Federalist and Republican parties was still in its earliest stages, but not so early as to prevent maneuvering over the second spot on the ticket. (Once George Washington yielded to entreaties to accept a second term, there was no possibility of opposition for the presidency.) Vice President John Adams offered a target for the opposition faction that was forming around Thomas Jefferson and his Virginia allies. As they would for most of the next three decades, the Virginians looked toward New York for a candidate who could bring that state's support to the Jeffersonians and would have appeal elsewhere in the North. The obvious choice was George Clinton, who had just been reelected governor, although the circumstances of that 1792 election had tainted Clinton so much that Jefferson himself thought Clinton should have declined the governorship. (Aaron Burr's supporters sought to have Burr, rather than Clinton, made the vice presidential candidate, but the move failed.) With what Richard P. McCormick has called "the presidential game" still confined to a small number of elite political leaders, enough support was gained for Clinton so that if Pennsylvania had voted for him rather than for Adams he would have been elected.[18]

In the 1796 election, it was the Federalists led by Hamilton, not the Republicans, who intrigued, and this time the intention was to place Thomas Pinckney in the president's chair. The closeness of the election between Adams and Jefferson offered the possibility that Jefferson might somehow be chosen, and one scheme was to line up Federalist support behind Pinckney, a South Carolinian who could count on gaining greater support in the South than Adams. Burr again made a play of his own, as his ally Jonathan Dayton, a senator from New Jersey, sought to persuade the Federalists that Adams had no chance and the party's only hope of preventing Jefferson's election was to support Burr. Hamilton's detestation of Burr helped squelch this scheme, while the effort to elect Pinckney foundered on New England's refusal to abandon Adams. Enough New England votes were discarded to cost Pinckney the vice presidency, and Adams and Jefferson were elected.[19]

The tie in the number of electoral votes for Jefferson and Burr in the 1800 presidential election, and the confusion and uncertainty that preceded Jefferson's eventual election, was the final proof that the authors of the Constitution had been careless in their provisions for the election of the national executive. The election of 1796, which left the Federalist Adams with Jefferson as his vice president, stimulated some Federalist interest in reforming electoral procedure, and the Jefferson-Burr confusion four years later broadened the support for a change. In 1802, the legislatures of New York, Vermont, and North Carolina passed resolutions calling on Congress to amend the Constitution to require that each elector specify which of his votes was for president and which for vice president. When the matter was taken up in Washington, however, it became a partisan issue, supported by the Republicans and opposed by the Federalists. In 1803, when the measure was passed by Congress and sent to the states for ratification, the debate had begun in the House, but the resulting House bill was ignored by the Senate, which passed its own bill, which was eventually approved by the House. The Senate version was introduced on October 21, 1803, by DeWitt Clinton, "in very nearly the wording eventually adopted," according to the historian Lolabel House. Clinton's bill left blank the number of candidates who should be considered by the House of Representatives if the Electoral College could not elect a president. (The number eventually selected, three, had a significant effect on the outcome of the next election decided in the House, that of 1824.)[20]

Since the bill proposed a constitutional amendment, it required a two-thirds majority in the House and the Senate. Clinton was in a hurry to gain Senate consideration of the bill, because the Republicans had barely enough votes for passage, and one Republican senator was about to resign to take his new appointment as mayor of New York. That senator, of course, was DeWitt Clinton. In the event, action on the bill was postponed until early December. It passed the Senate by 22 votes to 10, and on December 9 it passed the House by 84 to 42, but the vote of the Speaker was required to secure the needed two-thirds majority. Ratification by the states followed swiftly, and the amendment was declared in force on September 25, 1804, in time for that year's presidential election.[21]

Clinton's departure from Washington was complicated by another matter as well. Jonathan Dayton had opposed the Twelfth Amendment as a Clintonian attack on his friend Burr. On October 24, arguing that under Clinton's bill the best man for the office would lose simply because the presidential candidate with whom he was paired had lost, Dayton offered an amendment to Clinton's bill to delete all mention of selection of the vice president. Clinton not unreasonably accused Dayton of stalling, and Dayton retorted that Clinton was indulging his tendency to "arraign motives instead of meeting arguments." When Senator Wilson Cary Nicholas of Virginia moved the passage of Clinton's bill as it stood, Dayton again complained that Clinton had used "such rudeness and such indecency of language" as to require "a fitter time and a fitter place" to respond. That evening, in a note to Clinton, he made it clear that he wished for an apology or a duel. Clinton, who was to leave for New York the next day, wrote an apology, stating that any words "which fell from my lips in debate" were not intended to "impeach his [Dayton's] veracity," and if they were taken that way it was "contrary to my intention."[22]

Senator Nicholas, for one, was clearly concerned about the danger to Clinton, even after he left Washington. Three days after Dayton's challenge, Nicholas wrote to Clinton, "I most sincerely hope [you] will reach New York without injury to your health, your *life* is too valuable to your friends and to your country to be risked upon common occasions." Nicholas also assured Clinton that his friends all approved of his conduct in the affair. A month later, two friends of Clinton felt it necessary (or were perhaps asked by Clinton) to sign a brief statement describing the quarrel and defending Clinton's conduct. The two, Robert Wright and General Samuel Smith (both senators from Maryland), insisted that Clinton had sought an amicable settlement and that Dayton had been the more belligerent of the two. They said it was well known that Clinton had been scheduled to leave town to return to New York City and this urgency to leave was not, as some of the Burrites suggested, evidence of Clinton's cowardice in the face of a challenge.[23]

Nor were the duel with John Swartwout and the near duel with Jonathan Dayton the only violent consequences of the Burr-Clinton rivalry. Not long after the Clinton-Swartwout duel, Richard Riker, Clinton's second, fought (and was severely wounded by) Robert Swartwout, John's brother. And in 1803 William Coleman, the editor of the *Evening Post* (and a former business partner of Burr's), was sufficiently angered by Cheetham's conduct toward Burr to challenge Cheetham to a duel (which the latter somehow evaded) and to fight Captain Thompson, the city's harbor master, who was a loud defender of Cheetham. Coleman killed Thompson. And, independently of the quarrel with Clinton, in 1804 Burr fought his fatal duel with Alexander Hamilton. Hamilton's son and biographer, John C. Hamilton, suggested the possibility of a plot to kill his father, one in which challenges would be issued until a successful duelist ended his life. Jabez Hammond notes a similar accusation against the Burrites in the case of Clinton, supported by the examples of the Clinton-John Swartwout, Riker-Robert Swartwout, and Coleman-Thompson duels. Hammond was apparently unaware of the Dayton challenge in Washington, but concludes that "no man who is acquainted with the frank and open hearted John Swartwout can for one moment tolerate the idea that he was a party to such a combination. I am certain Mr. Clinton did not." It may be, however, that such a combination could have existed without Swartwout's participation, or that the idea of such an effort arose only as a consequence of Swart-wout's duel with Clinton. In Clinton's exchanges with John Swartwout and Jonathan Dayton it is always Clinton who is trying to be conciliatory and the Burrites who are in-transigent. Encomiums to the sterling character of John Swartwout do not quite put the matter to rest. And the Burrites continued their provocations until the end of the decade. The letters of "Philo-Cato," published in book form in 1810, continued to bait DeWitt Clinton, saying that "Aristides" had not concealed his identity, and that "if your object was an *honourable* satisfaction" it might have been had, but that your "*nerves* would not permit you to make him *personally* responsible."[24]

Whether or not there was a plot against Clinton (or against Hamilton), the erup-tion of such violence illustrates not only the political passions of the period but also the intensely personal character of political rivalry during the early development of political parties. The spoils system, with its rewards for party loyalty, had only just begun to acquire even a tinge of legitimacy, and the organization of parties was still determined to a significant extent by networks of personal loyalty—particularly in New York State. If the development of the party system took some of the passion out of politics, perhaps that was not such a bad thing.

THE STRUGGLE WITH BURR

Why would anyone, we might ask today, surrender a Senate seat to take the office of mayor of New York City? It must be remembered that in 1803 the federal government was small, headed by a president who was making it smaller, and quartered in a town whose rude accommodations and pestilential climate were already proverbial and would remain so for decades. Certainly for a person of the cultural attainments and aspirations of DeWitt Clinton, the nation's capital was an unattractive alternative to living in New York City. While weighing the step that fall, Clinton wrote to his uncle George that he found living apart from his family for six months at a time "insup-portable." In December 1803, back in New York City, Clinton wrote a friend, "I find my situation here very pleasant as I enjoy the society of my family which I was deprived of at Washington." But it seems unlikely that personal reasons alone would suffice to cause Clinton to leave the Senate. Two other reasons, one financial, one political, probably provoked the step.[25]

Supporting a growing family, he must have welcomed the substantial income of the mayor's office—worth more than ten thousand dollars a year, although there were also considerable expenses that a mayor had to absorb. A senator received far less, and had to pay the cost of a Washington boardinghouse as well as of a home in his own state. Although Maria Clinton had brought a handsome dowry with her, Clinton doubtless felt the need to bring in a substantial income of his own, and his contributions to charitable and cultural organizations put a drain on his finances as well as on his time. Also, according to Jabez Hammond, Clinton was a generous lender to, and endorser of notes for, Republican businessmen who were eager to start new enterprises.[26]

But along with financial and personal considerations for leaving the Senate there was the need to deal conclusively with the threat of Aaron Burr in New York. By the fall of 1803, Burr's followers were preparing for the next year's gubernatorial race. Already by mid-November George Clinton had told his nephew that he would not run for reelection, because "the Cause of Republicanism is now so well established as not to require any new sacrifice on my part." He pledged that he would keep his intentions to himself until after the legislature met. Thus it is curious that, the same day George Clinton wrote to DeWitt, the *Albany Register* began echoing the accusations that Cheetham had been publishing for more than a year. The state Republican papers were following the city's lead in the condemnation of Burr.[27]

By not standing for reelection, George Clinton created two problems for DeWitt: It would be easier for Burr to run, since he would not have to oppose the revolutionary hero who had such a long record of service to the state; and it meant that DeWitt had to find a candidate capable of beating Burr. DeWitt first tried to persuade his uncle to run again. He even sought to enlist Thomas Jefferson's aid, suggesting that if Jefferson wrote to Governor Clinton the latter might agree to run, but Jefferson declined to use his influence, writing delphically that he could "only brood in silence over my secret wishes." As for Burr, with George Clinton withdrawing he saw an opportunity to escape the vice presidency and rebuild his political career. His first move, too, was to turn to Jefferson, who recorded Burr's approach in his memoranda known as the *Anas*. On January 26, Burr came to the president and opened the conversation with a review of his career in New York, saying that "he had come to N.Y. a stranger some years ago, that he found the country in the possn of two rich families, (the Livingstons & Clintons) that his pursuits were not political & he meddled not." Burr's rendition of events stressed his loyalty to Jefferson, and he asserted that he had agreed to take the office of vice president, Jefferson recorded, "with a view to promote my fame & advancement." Following this imaginative recasting of his career, Burr came to the reason for his visit:

> He observed he believed it would be for the interest of the republican cause for him to retire; that a disadvantageous schism would otherwise take place; but that were he to retire, it would be said he shrunk from the public sentence, which he never would do; that his enemies were using my name to destroy him, and something was necessary from me to prevent and deprive them of that weapon, some mark of favor from me, which would declare to the world that he retired with my confidence.

Jefferson was cordial but cool, saying that he thought it would be inappropriate to appoint his vice president to another office and disclaiming any connection to attacks on Burr. Reflecting on the conversation, Jefferson was not charitable toward Burr: "Burr must have thot that I could swallow strong things in my favor, when he founded his acquiescence in the nominn as V.P. to his desire of promoting my honor." Jefferson related that, once the two had met, Burr's "conduct very soon inspired me with distrust," and that Burr had received the vice presidential nomination only as a reward for his labors in the New York State elections of 1800. Two weeks after this conversation, Burr was in New York City, setting in motion his campaign for governor.[28]

Crucial to that campaign would be Federalist support, and Burr had already received encouragement from Federalist leaders whose goals were more extensive than merely winning the governorship in New York. Some Federalists in New England, worried about the decline of their party and resentful of the power of Virginia and its slave-state allies, began exploring the possibility of secession. One fruit of their efforts was a motion, passed by the Massachusetts legislature, calling for a repeal of the three-fifths rule in the Constitution, which gave disproportionate influence to voters in slave states by counting three-fifths of the voteless slave population in apportioning representation (and therefore presidential electors). Led by Senator Timothy Pickering of Massachusetts, they intrigued (in an inept way) with Anthony Merry, the British minister to the United States, and explored the possibility of backing Burr in the 1804 race for governor, hoping that he might bring New York into the northern confederacy. David Hackett Fischer has argued convincingly that the plots of the so-called Essex Junto were not much of a threat to the union, and that the Hartford Convention a decade later posed an "infinitely more serious" one. In any case, for Burr the notion of Federalist support was welcome, and if he could obtain it without committing himself to any particular plan of action, so much the better. Senator William Plumer of New Hampshire, who attended a Washington meeting with Burr early in 1804 to discuss the matter, came away convinced that Burr supported secession. But, as he reflected on Burr's statement, he concluded that "perhaps no man's language was ever more apparently explicit, & at the same time so covert & indefinite." Burr was willing to accept the Federalists' support, but without any specific commitments to them.[29]

The alliance of Clintonians and Livingstons that controlled the state Republican party selected John Lansing, the chancellor, as its candidate. (Robert R. Livingston had resigned as chancellor in 1801 after being appointed minister to France by Jefferson.) But Lansing withdrew when, he later claimed, it was made clear to him by George Clinton that, while Lansing would be governor in name, he would be expected to attend to the wishes of DeWitt Clinton and his allies, and that he should name DeWitt Clinton chancellor in his place. With Lansing's withdrawal, the Clinton-Livingston faction needed another candidate. DeWitt Clinton was felt to be too young for the post, and he had just left his Senate seat to become mayor. A third major office in less than a year might have seemed excessive. The candidate chosen was Morgan Lewis, who had sought to be appointed mayor when Edward Livingston resigned, and who, having married a Livingston, could satisfy that part of the coalition. Clinton felt that Lewis could be controlled and would not be a serious rival for power. In the first of these assumptions he was soon proved to be wrong, but the second was confirmed. Lewis had risen, like DeWitt Clinton, via appointments. He had seen service in the Revolutionary War, served as state attorney general in 1791–92, and had then been appointed to the state supreme court, of which he became chief justice in 1801. Neither in intelligence nor in the enthusiasm of his supporters was Lewis a match for Burr. Alexander Hamilton, who had thought Lansing stood a good chance against Burr, felt that after the emergence of Lewis as the candidate "the probability [of victory], in my judgment, inclines to Burr."[30]

On February 18, in Albany, Burr was nominated for governor by a small group of legislators. Burr's hopes for success stood on two pillars. The first was his own faction of the Republican party, which was centered in New York City but was also strong in other parts of the state, where it could rely on such prominent supporters as Erastus Root of Delaware County; John Van Ness Yates of Albany; and Peter B. Porter, the Ontario County clerk. But the second pillar was even more vital to Burr's success: strong support from the state's Federalists. Some of them saw Burr as their chance to retake the governorship that they had relinquished just three years before. Others, in league with the Essex Junto or with similar notions of their own, sought to make Burr part of their secessionist plans. On February 16—two days before the meeting of Burrite Republicans—Federalists met at Lewis's City Tavern in Albany to discuss the race for governor. Although Alexander Hamilton urged his fellow-Federalists to support John Lansing rather than Burr (Lansing's withdrawal from the race would not become known for a week), the meeting backed Burr. The campaign that followed was vituperative. Cheetham's *American Citizen,* with Clinton's blessing, recapitulated the accusations that had already been aired during the pamphlet war (of which the 1804 governor's race was the final and decisive battle). Burrites published lists of Clintonians and Livingstons in office, and enumerated their substantial salaries, while claiming that Burr was free of such costly allies. Clinton's side published its own lists of Burrites and the state offices they had been promised if Burr should be victorious. Hamilton's opposition to Burr had become known the day after the meeting in Albany, and it cut deeply into Burr's Federalist support.[31]

Throughout the spring, Clinton's correspondents were sending him their assessments of the campaign's progress. On March 7, Brockholst Livingston wrote from Albany that the election was proceeding well: "Swartwout is certainly out of spirit. Lewis will get in by ten thousand votes." A later letter from an anonymous "Clintonian" was more concerned: "The old Govr. *ought not* to have *declined*. Little Aaron will undoubtedly get in." Morgan Lewis described a Federalist friend who considered himself bound by party ties to go with Burr as the Federalist candidate. From Washington, Gideon Granger, the postmaster general, wrote on March 27 that he was worried that the New Englanders who were then settling in western New York would bring their Federalist sympathies with them and throw the election to Burr. The "old Govr." himself wrote from Albany a week later that Republican "apostates" and Federalists "together will make a formidable diversion in favour of Burr." But at the end of April the vote was held, and on April 27 at 5:00 P.M. George Clinton wrote from Albany that Burr had carried that city by only 92 votes, a much smaller margin than was expected. So the election of Lewis seemed secure, as it proved to be. For every Republican who supported Burr, a Federalist (perhaps swayed by Hamilton's position) came out for Lewis, who won by a majority of more than eight thousand votes out of just under fifty-three thousand cast.[32]

The final stage of Burr's political destruction in New York came, of course, by his own hand, when he fatally wounded Alexander Hamilton in their duel in Weehawken, on the same dueling ground where Clinton had exchanged shots with John Swartwout two years earlier. Swartwout was among a group of Burr's friends who saw him off the morning of the duel, and William P. Van Ness, "Aristides" himself, was Burr's second. The doctor attending the duel was David Hosack, later to be Clinton's first biographer. Burr's career as a politician was at an end, and Clinton appeared to have New York firmly in his grip. John Lansing had declined to run for office to be governor in name only, a puppet of the Clintons. Morgan Lewis's acceptance of the post was felt by DeWitt Clinton to be an acknowledgment of his acceptance of the condition that Lansing had rejected. And Clinton himself, as mayor, now had large responsibilities, as well as a large income, of his own.[33]

Four

o   o   o

MAYOR CLINTON

T HE CITY CLINTON CAME back to lead in 1803 was a flourishing port whose population would grow during that decade from 60,000 to nearly 100,000. Although in 1803 Philadelphia was still the nation's largest city, by 1815, when Clinton left the mayoralty for good, New York would be firmly in the lead. One obvious difference between the mayoralty then and now was that the office was appointive, one of the thousands of posts, large and small, disposed of by the Council of Appointment in Albany. But other differences are even more striking. The city had a population in 1800 that was less than a hundredth the size of the present metropolis. The scope of city government was much smaller: police protection was minimal, fire protection was the responsibility of volunteers, there was no public education, and "social services" were provided at a rudimentary level by the public almshouse and by private charity. But if the scope of the mayor's office was narrower, his involvement in the running of the city was much more direct. Although the mayor today retains the title of magistrate, in Clinton's time the mayor presided in Mayor's Court (which heard civil cases) and the Court of General Sessions (which sat in criminal matters), and was a member of the Court of Oyer and Terminer (before which the most serious cases were usually heard). In fact, this judicial function was one of the mayor's principal occupations. For Clinton, the other main areas of concern were police matters, issues pertaining to public health, regulation of the city's economic life (through inspections, licenses, taxes, and various forms of encouragement of commerce and manufacturing), fostering the intellectual growth of the city and supporting institutions designed to facilitate that growth, and acting as a diplomat when the Napoleonic wars blew into New York's waters, as they did periodically. When the United States declared war on Britain in 1812, the mayor's responsibility with regard to the city's defenses expanded greatly. And Clinton, while he was carrying out his mayoral duties, also continued to lead his party, or his faction of the party, in New York State.[1]

Being mayor is vastly different from sitting in a legislature. The appointive powers of the mayor, and his executive responsibilities, presented Clinton with both opportunities and problems. Jabez Hammond believed that Clinton made a critical error when he left the United States Senate, and the national forum it provided, to return to New York City as mayor. Hammond was a friend and political ally of Clinton's, and thought that as early as 1803 Clinton was already aspiring to the presidency. "If then, such were his views," Hammond wrote, "he was guilty of an error; and so far as I can perceive, his first error in respect to his own political fortunes, in resigning his seat in the senate of the United States." His Senate seat, or, if he preferred, a cabinet post or diplomatic assignment (which his uncle's influence could easily have secured) would have kept him constantly "before the American people" and thus prepared a path to the presidency. Hammond continues:

> All these advantages he gave up in order to come back to the city of New-York, thereby becoming a party in the controversies of the bar-room politicians of that city, and to the petty quarrels of the city and state of New-York. . . . True, he might have the momentary pleasure of disposing of those appointments and enjoying the flattery which those small and successful office-seekers might lavish upon him; but did it not occur to him that the unsuccessful candidates for office would be more numerous than the successful ones, and that the disappointed would remember the injury they imagined done to them, longer than the appointed would the favor conferred on them, by the person who procured their appointment?[2]

Hammond's observations are interesting for several reasons. His mention of the "momentary pleasure" of controlling appointments, and of "enjoying the flattery" that would follow, suggests that Clinton savored the power he had, even when it was applied to such "pitiful offices" as clerks and sheriffs. And Hammond's view of the long memories of the disappointed is an acute assessment of the dangers of dispensing patronage. But how many political figures of Clinton's generation (or after) prospered without rewarding followers with jobs? And, while ideology helped draw some distinctions, in each party there were certainly many men whose ideological appeal was similar but whose victory or disappointment would rest not on republican orthodoxy but on the strength of a political organization that could, and did, reward supporters with offices, government contracts, and other preferences. Cabinet rank and foreign service might have given a figure prominence, but without the support of a strong organization (whether loosely controlled by a few elite figures, like the Virginia Dynasty, or a more organized political engine, such as the one Van Buren would build in New York) such eminence could easily remain impotent. The pleasures and pains of controlling patronage would be Clinton's whether he was mayor or senator. In both cases, the bulk of the appointments Clinton controlled had nothing to do with the office but flowed from his position in the state Republican party, and from his power in the state Council of Appointment. As Hammond himself says elsewhere, the major obstacle to Clinton's success was not the amount of power he possessed but the abrasive way he exercised it.

While Clinton was a man of great political ambition, he had other ambitions as well. He craved the approval of the learned for his intellectual efforts as much as, or even more than, he desired the electoral approval of his fellow citizens. But he also had a sincere wish to make New York, and the nation, a better place. Clinton's early biographers described his intellectual goals in reverent tones, while some recent historians have derided them. His educational reforms have been labeled "social control," and his cultural organizations dismissed as productive of little of lasting value. He created no path, it has been said, by which any product of the public schools he founded could advance to membership in the Literary and Philosophical Society.[3] These issues will be considered at length in the following chapter. It is easy to portray even Clinton's most admirable positions as being governed by expediency: his concern with the condition of Irish immigrants can be cast as a cynical effort to win their votes, his opposition to slavery portrayed as a means to become the leader of a northern party, and so forth. But it is too simple to discount moral positions because the values they defend have now become commonly accepted. Even the cleverest politician cannot always figure out what course will be the most self-serving, particularly in an era when opinion polls were nonexistent. For DeWitt Clinton, heir to a family tradition of Revolutionary War patriotism and a leading figure in the effort to draw the political and economic outlines of a new nation, personal ambition is only part of the picture. Clinton's hopes for a better world may have been founded partly on his desire to be given credit for the improvement, but we should recognize that more altruistic aims played a role.

That artful politician Thomas Jefferson has been granted secular sainthood for his high aims, while the less skillful Clinton's cultural efforts have been pegged as window-dressing for his political goals. With a figure like Clinton, motivation is particularly difficult to assess, because his letters and diaries are so lacking in introspection or any statement of guiding principles, while his public utterances are both stilted and—because public is what they were—under suspicion as being mere rhetoric. Perhaps it is safer to gauge Clinton's place by his actual achievements rather than by the rhetoric attached to them.

When Clinton took office, New York City was on the threshold of a political revolution. Although the Jeffersonians had swept all before them in the nation and now controlled the government of the State of New York, the city nevertheless remained a Federalist bastion. Federalist control was maintained by a strict interpretation of the Montgomerie Charter of 1730, which barred those without property from voting for the members of the Common Council and allowed men with property in more than one ward to vote in each ward where they owned property. Republican efforts to evade the charter limits by putting together groups of Republicans to buy lots in crucial wards and thus qualify them as voters were largely unsuccessful because the Federalist-dominated council threw out most of their votes. The key to changing the system lay in the state legislature, which could alter the suffrage requirements for all city offices. An effort to secure a change in Albany had failed in 1802 because the legislature wanted the request to come directly from the Common Council. In the state legislative sessions of 1803 and 1804, however, the Republicans won the day. In the first, they secured passage of a bill redrawing ward boundaries (the old ones had favored the Federalists) and creating two more wards, to include the increasingly populous (and Republican) northern fringes of the city. Nevertheless, in the city elections of November 1803, the Federalists took six of nine wards. Clintonians and Burrites were in agreement about the need for suffrage reform, but with DeWitt Clinton as mayor the Burrites offered other kinds of proposals as well—annual popular election of the mayor and replacing his income from various fees with an annual salary. (The creation of a salary would wait until 1813, and the first direct election for mayor did not occur until 1834.) Although the proposals clearly had merit, the motive was to embarrass the incumbent. The Clintonians easily squelched the Burrites' suggestions, and the more limited suffrage-reform proposals became law in April 1804. As enacted, the bill extended the franchise to those male resident taxpayers of legal age paying rent of twenty-five dollars or more a year. It also limited each voter to casting only one vote, no matter how many wards he might own property in, and established the secret ballot (city elections had been conducted by voice voting until this time). That November, the Republicans won seven of the nine wards, losing only the First and Second wards on the southern tip of the island.[4]

The mayor's involvement in the life of the city was nowhere more direct than in the exercise of police powers. The mayor was the functional as well as the nominal head of the city police. On occasion, Clinton had to lead forces into the streets to suppress riots of one sort or another. In one incident, the city watch was on the losing end of a fracas with some seamen, and Clinton assembled a group of civilians to come to the aid of the watch. On the way to the riot he encountered a group of militia officers, who thereupon accompanied him. The appearance of the mayor and uniformed officers was sufficient to end the rioting. A more serious kind of violence erupted on December 25, 1806, outside St. Peter's Church. On Christmas Eve, a small crowd had gathered outside the church, "with a view," as Clinton later described it, "of insulting the Congregation of the Roman Catholic Church of this City." The following night an anti-Catholic mob again assembled outside the church, and this time the taunts grew into violence. Several members of the watch were wounded, and one, Christopher Newslanger, was stabbed to death. Clinton went to the scene with reinforcements to help quell the riot, and the next day issued a proclamation offering a $250 reward for "the discovery of the leaders of the disturbances."[5]

Matters of life and death also occupied Clinton as the ex officio head of the city's board of health, particularly when one of the periodic epidemics of yellow fever struck the city. Clinton's letters and diaries are filled with mentions of meetings of the board of health, and of deliberations over proper quarantine measures, sanitation problems, and facilities to aid the victims of epidemics. Pestilence discouraged visitors and often prevented citizens from traveling to other towns. Yellow fever was treated as an infectious disease by the authorities of the time (the disease, carried by mosquitoes and not contagious, was not understood until the work of Walter Reed and others a century later). Sometimes the presence of a disease could have a positive consequence, as in the fall of 1804, when fear of yellow fever caused the British fleet then haunting New York Harbor to sail to Nova Scotia in search of more salubrious waters.[6]

The departure of the fleet eased tensions at a time when the mayor was mediating between French and British forces in the harbor and trying to preserve American neutral rights and avoid bloodshed. A good deal of Clinton's correspondence be-tween 1803 and 1807 is taken up with remonstrances to foreign captains, letters to Washington seeking guidance, and testimony to the purely American origins of men the British had seized as deserters. The port of New York provided safe harbor and was a source of supplies for the ships of the belligerents, but maintaining the peace while crews from Britain and France were in port was difficult. Even more difficult was the task of making it possible for a French ship, for example, to leave port without being immediately pounced on by the Royal Navy. Such concerns greeted Clinton on his return to New York in 1803 and were present to some degree until he finally left office in 1815, some months after the end of the War of 1812.

Clinton initially tried to avoid difficulties with the British. In December 1803, he arranged for certain vagrants in the city jail who were British deserters (now repen-tant) to return to their vessels. But such convenient prisoners were not plentiful, and the tensions of trying to protect the city's and the nation's neutral rights increased. Efforts to get the warships of one nation to observe a twenty-four-hour quarantine when those of a hostile power left port were frequently unavailing. Clinton, of course, had no way to enforce his desires, and the national government was also inca-pable of getting the great powers of Europe to abide by the rights claimed by a minor power. When Clinton wrote to Secretary of State James Madison in June 1804 to relate further British violations of neutral rights, the best Madison could promise in his reply was that the British actions would be made the subject of "every proper repre-sentation and requisition to the British Government."[7]

The lack of adequate federal protection for New York became a pressing issue in April 1806, when the HMS *Leander* fired too close to the bow of an American vessel in the waters off New York, killing a seaman named John Pierce. The *Leander* had already made itself unpopular around the city with its high-handed methods of forcing American vessels to submit to searches. Clinton's political ally James Fairlie voiced his concern about this ship on March 6, and the philanthropist Henry Rutgers wrote him the following day that the *Leander*'s conduct "offers ample matter for traducing the Administration." After Pierce's death, demonstrations against the British erupted in the city, and Pierce's body became a symbol in a political tussle between Clinton and the Federalists. Clinton had called for the Common Council to defray the cost of Pierce's funeral, but the Federalists then offered to pay for it themselves. John Pintard recorded in his diary that Pierce's brother was entreated by both sides to let them bury Pierce and finally was "persuaded that more respect wd be paid to his brother by public authority, than individuals, gave an order . . . to deliver the Corpse to the Committee." On the day of Pierce's funeral, demonstrators seized supplies purchased for British vessels and delivered them to the Almshouse.[8]

The mayor used the public outcry over Pierce's death to press for a greater federal presence in New York, and obtained a Common Council resolution calling for the dispatch of United States frigates to New York for the port's protection. The reply from James Madison was typically proper, the action taken typically ineffectual. President Jefferson closed the port of New York to the *Leander* and the two ships sailing with her, the *Cambrian* and the *Driver,* and ordered the arrest of the *Leander*'s captain,

Henry Whitby—an order impossible to carry out. The *Leander*'s captain, meanwhile, had written Clinton to place the blame for the incident and its aftermath on the city government because it had not prevented violence between New Yorkers and the ship's crew. When an attack on an American vessel in Virginia waters the following year brought a stronger response from the Virginians running the government in Washington, some New Yorkers perceived a double standard and denounced the administration. Although the Virginia incident was more serious, since it involved an actual attack by a British ship, HMS *Leopard,* on a United States warship, the *Chesapeake,* in which more than a score of sailors were killed or wounded, the New Yorkers' grievance was founded on the correct perception that Jefferson and Madison cared less about New York than they did about Virginia. The widespread outrage over the *Chesapeake* incident threatened to carry the nation to war with Britain, but so ill-prepared was the United States for war in the summer of 1807 that after the British rebuffed American remonstrances over the matter and ignored the accompanying demands for the end of impressment, the Jefferson administration had few palatable choices. In November and December 1807, the combination of new British orders in council and then Napoleon's Milan Decree put neutral shipping in a vise: to obey the rules laid down by one belligerent left one open to seizure by the other. Lacking the power to respond militarily, and with the oceans a free-fire zone, Jefferson and Madison tried to put into practice their theories about commercial warfare. The result was the Embargo, the idea of which was to bring Britain to her knees by closing American ports, thus depriving Britain of a major market for her exports and denying her West Indian colonies the supplies needed to sustain their sugar-based economies. Over the next two years, the Embargo would have a crushing effect on the economy of New York City and altered the political balance in New York State.[9]

In the meantime, though, British and French interference with shipping around the port of New York was not just an affront to American honor but also a threat to the city's livelihood. Maintaining the economic health of the port was one of Mayor Clinton's concerns, and the municipal government had responsibilities for insuring that ships had decent wharves to tie up at, that their crews were treated fairly, and that the goods exported from New York should meet standards of quality that would give the city's merchants a good commercial reputation. As the principal point of entry for goods from Europe, the port of New York was the major source of revenue for the federal government. In 1828, the fees collected in the port were sufficient to cover *all* the expenses of the national government except the service on the debt. Indeed, the office of collector was one of the great patronage plums that could be bestowed by the president. In 1829, when Andrew Jackson appointed Samuel Swartwout collector, this former Burrite and the brother of Clinton's dueling opponent managed to collect more than a million dollars for himself, and took up residence abroad.[10]

Two important concerns of city government were managing the city's growth and regulating its businesses to insure that the commercial reputation of the town would not suffer because of poor merchandise. We know little about Clinton's involvement in the day-to-day workings of city markets, inspections, and licensings, but his efforts to expand the city's economy are evident in a number of areas. For instance, he was willing to assist rising young businessmen, often from his own pocket and—as Jabez Hammond points out—to his own detriment. Those Clinton lent to were generally "vigorous and energetic supporters of the democratic party," and since the mayor was also a director of the Manhattan Bank, those he recommended were certain to get loans. "Anxious to patronise young men, and liberal to a fault, Mr. Clinton lent his influence and name to all republican young men in whose capacity he had good confidence, and whose habits he supposed to be good." Unfortunately, some failed to repay their loans, through bad luck or "downright knavery," and Clinton was left encumbered with debt, "which embarrassed and harassed him during his life."[11]

This habit of lending to worthy Republicans who were hoping to go into business illustrates Clinton's straddling of the old and new political eras. If his intention was to bind these men to him politically, it is curious that he risked his family's welfare to do so when the city and state governments offered ample patronage, lucrative contracts, and other financial opportunities under his influence. Although he understood the use of patronage better than those who came before him, he tried to sustain a notion of noblesse oblige that had been common among the elite of his father's generation but was becoming rare in American politics.

One kind of political ambition seeks to use politics to remake the world, another wants to use it as a means to rise in the existing world. One seeks to eliminate privilege, the other to obtain it. Clinton had plenty of both kinds of ambition. Although he helped create the spoils system and the patronage chieftains who rose with it, he remained more attached to an earlier vision of political leadership, as symbolized by the figures of the revolutionary generation, to whom politics was a duty and not a profession, and for whom personal wealth was an adjunct to the political process, a prerequisite for power, rather than a result of successful office-holding. Lacking the wealth but desiring the status, Clinton affected an aristocratic style he could ill afford and loaned his way into relative poverty, placing himself in a position where the income of his offices became crucial to the support of his large family.

Not all those Clinton helped were failures, nor was his assistance confined to cosigning loans. His position on the board of the Manhattan Bank made him a champion of its interests, and a sometimes fierce opponent of other banks seeking charters, as we shall see. But his influence extended well beyond banking. In 1808, his fellow Freemason John Jacob Astor told Clinton about his plans for winning back the fur trade from Canadian traders, who dominated the market. Astor also pressed on President Jefferson the need to establish American control over the fur trade, an aim that Jefferson appears to have endorsed, at least in principle. At the urging of both DeWitt and George Clinton, the state legislature granted a charter to the American Fur Company in 1808. Although the charter was granted partly because of the assertion that the company's mission was beyond the capacity of any individual or unincorporated group, the American Fur Company was a shell covering Astor's various business purposes, and he controlled it absolutely. The company limited his liability, and its status as a corporation (as well as its name) suggested that it was designed to benefit the public rather than Astor.[12]

Another beneficiary of Clinton's aid was Robert Fulton—together with his partner, Robert R. Livingston. In 1807, when their monopoly in steamship navigation was expiring, Clinton helped obtain an extension of it, though he declined Fulton's offer of a share in the consortium's larger enterprises, which included a plan for a monopoly on Mississippi River steam travel. Fulton was active in other areas of invention and navigation, and had devoted considerable attention to the prospects of canals in America. He wrote a paper for Albert Gallatin on the subject in connection with Gallatin's "Report to the Senate on the Subject of Public Roads and Canals." Fulton argued that the increase in property values that came with canal construction made such projects very attractive for the government—which, after all, owned a vast quantity of land away from the coast. In 1811 he joined Clinton as one of the state canal commissioners.[13]

Many less successful inventors also turned to Clinton for help. One had devised a method of propelling ships "without steam nor animals." Another had built a "Key'd Harp" in the Empire style, which cost him a thousand dollars to make, and which he wanted to sell to Clinton at cost. A third offered a new telescope of "infinite" power. Clinton was circumspect about reaping personal gain from such schemes, although he was not so wary of incurring losses. But his main interest was in securing the increased prosperity and prominence of his city and state, and he was pleased that Fulton's steamboats and Astor's fur trade contributed to New York's emergence as the nation's leading metropolis.[14]

Eager to encourage the city's rising prosperity, DeWitt Clinton had very specific and detailed ideas on how some of that new wealth should be spent.

Five

o   o   o

CLINTONIAN CULTURE

For clinton and his circle (John Pintard, David Hosack, Samuel Latham Mitchill) the real measure of New York's success was not the affluence of its citizens but the richness of its cultural life. The first was more a necessary precondition for the second than an end in itself. The notion of culture that Clinton embraced was unabashedly elitist, and the standard against which New York would be judged was ultimately set in London and Paris. Had he known that the spare furniture made by the Shakers around New Lebanon, New York, would one day be held in higher esteem than the work of the artists of his acquaintance, he would have been surprised. And he would have been baffled by present-day scholars[1] who have scoffed at the elite nature of the cultural establishment he tried to create, belittling his achievements and those of other early American aspirants to European-style cultural distinction.

In Clinton's time, culture and class had not yet formed into the congealed layers that the historian Lawrence Levine and others see later in the century. But even if Levine is right in perceiving a basic unity in American culture in the early nineteenth century, a "rich shared public culture," that is not the way it looked to Clinton. It was not the unity that was missing but, rather, the culture. Culture was the domain of the social elite, whose responsibility it was, under a kind of trickle-down theory of taste, to offer the blessings of culture to all the rest in the name of general advancement. "The more elevated the tree of knowledge," Clinton told the legislature in 1827, "the more expanded its branches, and the greater will be the trunk and the deeper the roots." The arts and education were the tools, in Clinton's conception, by which a mass electorate could be made capable of exercising the franchise "responsibly." And this, in turn, depended on having an economy sufficiently robust to support the arts and education.[2]

For Clinton, commerce and culture marched together, rather than being antagonistic, as American intellectuals long before Henry Adams and Henry James have argued. But Clinton's cultural agenda was often frustrated. The notion of patrician stewardship of "culture" was undermined by the rise of political democracy, a chronic threat to public support of anything that seemed to interest only a small band of dilettantes; it was marginalized by growing professionalization in the sciences; and it was made to seem anachronistic by the new spirit of romanticism, whose images, no longer those of classical antiquity, now emphasized the unmediated responses of the individual to his own world, and especially to nature. Clinton's concept of cultural stewardship was rooted in the Enlightenment—an era the world he actually lived in was already leaving behind.

The cultural life of New York City at the beginning of the nineteenth century was not exactly flourishing. The departure of the Tories with the British evacuation in 1783 had removed many of those sufficiently educated and wealthy to function as patrons of the arts. But patrons need something more than money; they need artists to support, and the city did not have a lot of cultural talent. An exception appears to have been the visual arts. Painting, fortunately for artists, was an art in which the traditional forms of patronage could easily be modified to suit republican principles. Rather than portraying kings and courtiers, artists could paint republican statesmen, and they found a willing market not just in the homes of the wealthy but also in the halls of public buildings. The visual arts were called into service by a country in need of icons of its own. Americans needed symbols, heroes—an instant past to help provide a cohesive force within and among the states. While some artists may have anticipated the potential market, the desire for new symbols did not have to be contrived—it was there and needed only to be satisfied.

But what of the other arts, particularly literature? How should science be encouraged and advanced? What was needed to elevate American achievement to levels that Europeans would have to acknowledge? Condescension stood in for science in the elaborate efforts of such savants as Buffon to explain why North America produced less beautiful flowers, less noble beasts, and less intelligent people than other parts of the world. The need to refute such claims complemented the need to develop a national mythology, an indigenous tradition. For DeWitt Clinton, it was a critical aspect of nation-building. Without aristocratic patronage, the most frequent form of support was private institutions created to promote art, culture, and education. During his mayoralty and after, Clinton was instrumental in founding or leading several such organizations, and much of his intellectual capital was invested in their success. He also wrote his most important works under their aegis, or for their benefit. And when the resources of these organizations were not equal to their ambitions, Clinton sought, and often procured, government assistance.

Clinton had helped to reopen King's College as Columbia in 1784, when he was only fifteen, and throughout his life he steadfastly supported his alma mater, whether through his own literary efforts or by exerting his influence as mayor or governor to assist the college. Most city aid to Columbia was indirect: assigning city marshals to patrol Columbia's commencement, closing city streets to prevent traffic from interfering with ceremonies, granting rooms in City Hall for meetings of the college's trustees. City officials lent their prestige to the college—and received some from it—

by attending ceremonies there, as Congress had in the 1780s, when New York was the national capital. DeWitt Clinton played "a considerable part," according to Kenneth Nodyne, in getting city aid for Columbia.[3]

The college sought help from the state as well as the city, and in 1815 the state gave the college the land occupied by Dr. Hosack's botanical garden, valued by the state at $75,000. When Columbia sold the land in 1985, it received $400 million—Hosack's garden had since become the site of Rockefeller Center.[4]

In 1827, speaking to a Columbia College audience, Clinton stressed the institution's good fortune in being in a rising commercial city:

> Situated at the confluence of all the great navigable communications of the State, from the shores of the Atlantic to the northern and western lakes, [New York City] presents every facility of economical and rapid access. Placed in the very focus of all the great moneyed and commercial operations of America, where agriculture pours forth her stores of plenty, where manufactures transmit their fabrics, where internal trade and foreign commerce delight to dwell and accumulate riches, where, in short, every man that wishes to buy or sell to advantage, will naturally resort, what site can furnish a stronger invitation to participation in education? Here, too, you will have the most distinguished divines, the most able jurists, the most skilful physicians. Here will men of science and ingenious artists fix their abode,—and also talented men who will devote themselves to vernacular literature. Whoever wealth can tempt, knowledge allure, or the delights of polished and refined society attract, will occasionally visit or permanently reside in this great emporium.[5]

Noting Clinton's emphasis on the connectedness of commerce and culture, Thomas Bender makes his own connection with New York's loss of the national capital, concluding that New York, no longer a seat of government, was forced to define "a version of cultural improvement that was distinctly local and civic rather than general and national." Because New York lacked the authority that a city derives from being a national capital, Bender goes on, its "cultural leadership cannot be assumed, it must be proclaimed."[6]

Bender's picture is plausible as far as it goes, though it closes off much of the complexity in the interrelatedness of urban centers, political power, commerce, and nourishment for things of the mind and spirit in civilized life anywhere. A more comprehensive formulation can be found in Stanley Elkins and Eric McKitrick's history of the early republic, *The Age of Federalism*. Examining the implications of removing the capital from New York to the Potomac, these writers discern an extended series of consequences not simply for New York City but for the entire nation and its political and cultural future—consequences embracing among other things the outlook and attitudes of public officials as well as the position cities themselves came to occupy in the American system of values. Members of Congress, as Elkins and McKitrick put it, were denied the sort of metropolitan vantage "from which the people's chosen representatives might return home wider in sense and spirit than when they came." Without such a capital, and with the choice of a deserted stretch of the Potomac as the home of the nation's government, "a quasi-official benediction was in effect laid upon a set of values which had no real place in them for cities."[7] It may not be too much to say that a Jeffersonian repulsion from cities in general has undermined the intellectual life and the political and social health of the United States for at least two centuries.

DeWitt Clinton, whatever his pretensions, certainly had more than just an inkling of such connections and implications. He took for granted that art and intellect flourished not in bucolic surroundings but in bustling cities; that although there were no American princes and nobles to patronize art, there were merchant princes who might find deep satisfaction in promoting institutions for its furtherance; that the agencies of government had a concurrent responsibility for its support; and that artistic expression would draw its greatest resources of subject and inspiration from the intricately tangled currents of life in a great metropolitan center. Indeed, Nathaniel Hawthorne a generation later would deplore the very absence of this tangled intricacy, with its gradations of light and shadow, of depravity and virtue, for *his* art. How, Hawthorne asked in 1860, could a novelist practice his trade in a land with "no antiquity, no mystery, no picturesque and gloomy wrong, nor anything but a commonplace prosperity, in broad and simple daylight, as is happily the case in my dear native land."[8]

SOCIETIES AND ACADEMIES

Clinton, in his own time, was less preoccupied with "local and civic" rivalry than with the condescension of Europe toward anything America had yet produced in the way of culture. His exertions to overcome this were touchingly earnest. The same argument Clinton made for the logic of situating Columbia in New York City applied as well to other kinds of cultural organizations. He himself took a hand in establishing three such organizations—the New-York Historical Society, the American Academy of the Arts, and the Literary and Philosophical Society—and he served as president of all three.

The earliest of them, the American Academy, actually owed its origins more to the Livingstons than to Clinton. In 1801 Robert R. Livingston began raising money to purchase paintings and sculpture—mostly copies of renowned masterpieces like the Apollo Belvedere and the Laocoön—to be brought to New York to provide artists with proper models for their work. While Livingston was in France conducting the negotiations that led to the Louisiana Purchase, his brother Edward, then mayor, oversaw the establishment of the New York Academy of the Arts, which was renamed the American Academy of the Arts in 1804. Robert R. Livingston, on his return from France that year, succeeded him as president. Although Clinton's early role was a minor one, he did draft the organization's bylaws and in 1807 was able to persuade the state legislature to grant the organization a charter.[9]

With Livingston's death, in 1813, Clinton became president of the academy, and in 1816 he addressed the academy at a City Hall gathering that marked the opening of its quarters in the old Almshouse, renamed the New York Institution. (The ceremony included eulogies of both Livingston and Robert Fulton, who, an amateur artist himself, had been a member of the academy until his death in 1815.) The speech was another expression of Clinton's views on the arts and on government's role in nurturing artistic endeavors. He noted that the works on display should "give elevation to this city, and reflect honour on our country." Much of the discourse was devoted to explaining why the United States was a natural home for creative artists. (Pay no attention to what Europe says about us.) His ideas for subjects embrace both the romantic sensibility of the time in which he was speaking and the neoclassical vision that had suffused the era in which he had been raised. Consider the American landscape: "This wild, romantic and awful scenery, is calculated to produce a correspondent impression on the imagination—to elevate all the faculties of the mind, and to exalt all the feelings of the heart." But the depiction of heroes of the republic is also a fit subject: "The portrait collection of this city, by comprising many of the principal heroes of the country, is entitled to great praise in its tendency to stimulate noble deeds, and to encourage the Fine Arts."[10]

To celebrate America, moreover, was to serve the cause of republicanism in the world. "A republican government," Clinton said, "instead of being unfriendly to the growth of the fine arts, is the appropriate soil for their cultivation." Monarchies, by contrast, "create a barrier against the ascent of genius to the highest stations, and they cast the most distinguished talents and the most exalted endowments in the back ground of society." The proof lay in the achievements of the Athenians. The Acropolis, he declared, is "the most interesting place on the globe" and demonstrates "the immortal honour, which a small republic has acquired, by the cultivation of the arts." A large republic could do the same, and America's cultural achievements should proclaim to the world the capacities and the refinement of its citizens as well as the superiority of republican government.[11]

The relationship between the arts and the citizenry was an important theme, as Clinton drew out the analogy with Athens. If "even the herb women of Athens, could criticise the phraseology of Demosthenes, and the meanest artisan could pronounce judgment on the works of Apelles and Phidias," he asked, "what might not be expected from the well directed efforts of that wonderful nation?" Whether or not DeWitt Clinton would have welcomed suggested improvements in his own phraseology from herb women or anyone else in New York, he nevertheless found something admirable in the principle and hoped the American Academy could spread such blessings here. He undoubtedly believed in his own sincerity as he declared that the wellsprings of art were in "the fertile soil that produces all good . . . the great body of the people."[12]

Government, as always in Clinton's conception of republican society, could play a direct role in nurturing the arts. For the American Academy, the New-York Historical Society, and the Literary and Philosophical Society, the city had provided quarters in the old Almshouse. For its own quarters, Clinton asserted, the city had initiated a "revolution in our taste" in architecture, erecting "a building which, for magnificence of design, and elegance of execution, transcends every public edifice in America." Clinton's claim for City Hall—begun in 1803, the year he became mayor, and completed in 1812, the year he ran for president—remains credible today. (Clinton had probably forgotten that when he first met with John McComb, Jr., the architect who supervised construction, he—as McComb noted in his diary—"took no notice of any of us concerned about the Building.") He now compared New York with the Athenian model, saying that the great monuments of Athens "were erected during the administration of one great man."[13]

The city itself commissioned portraits of leading citizens and war heroes from prominent artists. Its art collection was begun in 1790, when John Trumbull was asked to paint portraits of George Washington and George Clinton. Fourteen years later, Trumbull was asked to paint Hamilton, John Jay, and the mayors from the revolution forward—James Duane, Edward Livingston, Richard Varick, and Marinus Willett. He later added portraits of governors Lewis and Tompkins. In 1813 John Wesley Jarvis, Thomas Sully, and Samuel Waldo were engaged to paint such heroes of the War of 1812 as Oliver Hazard Perry (hero of the Battle of Lake Erie) and Isaac Hull (vanquisher of the HMS *Guerrière*). John Vanderlyn received commissions to paint Monroe and Jackson, and in 1824 Samuel F. B. Morse executed his marvelous full-length portrait of Lafayette, who was then on his triumphal tour of the nation. In 1827 the Common Council authorized the purchase of a portrait by George Catlin of DeWitt Clinton. (Morse also did Clinton: His version hangs in the Metropolitan Museum of Art.) Such patronage was accepted in New York City as a proper use of public funds.[14]

Clinton's address to the American Academy, coming in the fall of 1816, should be read with the Erie Canal in mind, since 1816 was the year he and his allies succeeded in marshalling public opinion decisively in favor of the canal. Like the City Hall building, the canal would prove a great success, and early doubters abandoned or tried to conceal their reservations. Even so, the state was not the city. Clinton never succeeded in persuading the legislature, or the people of New York State, that their taxes should go to raining "beneficence, like the dew of heaven" on artists, or turning DeWitt Clinton into an American Pericles.[15]

Two other organizations that Clinton served as president of received much attention from him—the New-York Historical Society, founded in 1804, and the Literary and Philosophical Society, founded in 1811. For both organizations Clinton obtained government assistance, gave money, and delivered scholarly addresses that both enhanced his own reputation and bestowed the prestige of his offices on the organizations. The New-York Historical Society is the only one of these institutions that survived him by more than a few years—the American Academy expired in 1834, the Literary and Philosophical Society in 1841.[16]

The death blow for the American Academy and the Literary and Philosophical Society came when the city stopped providing free space in the Almshouse. Advocates of the city subsidy in the Common Council had noted that "such a constellation of Science will illuminate our hemisphere" and had also stressed the public amenities that would be gained—a "general reading room," a "School for painting," an observatory "with suitable apparatus for public lectures." But, as the city (and city government) expanded, the space devoted to these activities became more valuable, and the rise of working-class political activity undercut the use of public funds for what seemed to be largely private ends. Clinton's close association with these institutions made them an attractive target for his political enemies. At the same time, scientific inquiry was beginning to be concentrated in academic institutions, and the gentleman scientist, who had flourished in the eighteenth century, was nearing extinction. Men like Clinton who championed the tradition, and carried it on, were also dying out. In 1831, just three years after Clinton's death, the cultural organizations were evicted from the Almshouse.[17]

Thomas Bender calls that eviction the "first formal challenge to elite cultural hegemony." It might also be seen as a step along the road to the division of American culture into the "high and low" categories that Lawrence Levine views as having solidified in mid-century. The activities of Clinton and his cohorts, their patrician prejudices, and the kind of literature and art encouraged by their organizations have been set down as efforts to impose the cultural values of an elite on the entire city. These men are dismissed for their pretensions and for their failure to appreciate "the competing artisanal culture."[18]

Still, there may be a more sympathetic way of viewing them and what they tried to do. It is probably true that they would not have known what to make of "artisanal culture" even if they had heard the phrase. It is also true that the cultural achievements of New York in this period do not embody the hopes so floridly proclaimed before the Common Council in 1815. But the notion that they were aiming for "social control" or "cultural hegemony" does not cover the case, either. Indeed, the picture of an artisan class with a body of cultural values that are at odds with those of the elite, and that the elite is bent on displacing, strikes one as being itself a somewhat fanciful twentieth-century construct. Whatever designs Clinton and his friends had with regard to the artisans were limited to enriching their minds, even in the awareness that their own minds, and everyone else's, were more impoverished than they liked. But the principal aims of Clinton's circle were much higher—and proved in the end unattainable. It was less a matter of power than of glory. They wanted a cultural community that might prove to Europe and the world that intellectual distinction *could* flourish in an American setting and under republican government. Republican government, not sufficiently interested, failed them, and it was not until after the Civil War that commercial wealth, the other factor in their equation of support, fully moved to take its place.

And the very foundation of such a cultural community—the basic element of the grand equation—was hopelessly beyond them: the resources, human or material, were simply not yet there. The case may have been put most succinctly by Gouverneur Morris, the old cynic, in 1811. David Hosack, excusing himself for arriving late for a dinner he was giving at his home, told Morris and his other guests, "I have been detained with some friends, who together this evening have founded a Philosophical Society." "Well, well, that's no difficult matter," Morris replied, "but pray, Doctor, where are the philosophers?"[19]

FREE SCHOOL SOCIETY

Part of the cultural program, and of the larger social and political agenda, was education for New York children who were not receiving any. Clinton sought ways to extend education beyond private, denominational, and charity schools, which reached only a fraction of the poor.

Clinton's concern for educating the poor has been dismissed as being motivated by a wish for docile workers and voters, and he has been twitted for an excessive fondness for cultural organizations that catered to privileged amateurs of the arts and sciences. Actually, his educational efforts included some—women, African Americans, the handicapped—for whom education was considered superfluous or even dangerous by many of his contemporaries. True, we would not speak today of "the diffusion of useful knowledge . . . amongst the lower order of the people," but we could, with the purest of motives, say nearly the same thing in different words. And when we hear DeWitt Clinton remark, with obvious complacency, "Of the many thousands who have been instructed in our free schools in the city of New York, *there is not a single known instance of anyone having been convicted of a crime,"* we could think of him as being more concerned with social peace than with enlightenment. Or we could wish that the same thing were true of our own time, and consider why it is not.[20]

In 1800, education in the city was provided either in private schools for those who could afford them or in charity schools that were generally run by churches. What attention the state had given to education was devoted mainly to colleges. The creation of the Board of Regents of the University of the State of New York in 1784 marked the beginning of this involvement. There was some interest in elementary education, and in 1795 the legislature passed an act devoting $250,000 over five years to promote elementary schools, with the requirement that counties wishing a portion of this aid should match half the amount offered by the state. But the appropriation was not renewed in 1800. Then, in 1805, two measures transformed primary education in New York. The first was the allotment by the legislature of 500,000 acres of state lands and three thousand shares of bank stock for the benefit of public schools. The second was the establishment of the New York Free School Society, whose president, from its inception until his death, was DeWitt Clinton.[21]

The impetus for its founding came from three Quakers, Thomas Eddy, John Murray, Jr., and Matthew Franklin. The original plan was for the Quakers to finance a school for poor children who were not Quakers, but Eddy argued that to achieve their ends they would have to seek broader support, outside the Society of Friends. So a public meeting was held to raise funds and seek legislative aid, and in the first round of fund-raising Clinton gave the largest amount. He also solicited contributions in the First Ward. And it was he who procured a charter for the society and led the successful efforts to obtain state and city support for the Free School Society—which changed its name to the Public School Society in 1825 and was absorbed into the city's Board of Education when the board was created in 1853.[22]

Clinton's hopes for the society were expressed in a speech he gave to mark the dedication of a new school building in December 1809. In it he was eager to relate educational goals to social consequences and create a rationale for public education that would appeal to both altruism and self-interest. Typically, Clinton pointed across the Atlantic for inspiration and for examples of the vices of the old world that could be corrected in the new. He found both in the writings of John Locke, whose educational works he admired except for the fact that "his treatise is professedly intended for the children of gentlemen." Here was the "fundamental error of Europe"—educating only the wealthy, "while the humble and depressed have been . . . sedulously excluded." One reason for this exclusion was the unfortunate belief that education would breed political dissent and irreligion. "That knowledge is the parent of sedition and insurrection, and that in proportion as the public mind is illuminated, the principles of anarchy are disseminated," he said, "is a proposition that can never admit of debate, at least in this country."[23]

In fact, Clinton argued, the danger to society came not from disseminating education but from limiting it—a danger made more acute by the growth of cities. In contrast to the genial view of cities he would paint in his address at Columbia, when the subject was educating poor children the view he presented was closer to Thomas Jefferson's fearsome portrait of urban life. (Jefferson professed to welcome the yellow-fever epidemics because they would "discourage the growth of great cities in our nation & I view great cities as pestilential to the morals, the health and the liberties of man.") Clinton was aware of urbanization's darker side. "Great cities," he told the Free School Society in 1809, "are at all times the nurseries and hot-beds of crime. . . . And the dreadful examples of vice, which are presented to youth . . . connected with a spirit of extravagance and luxury . . . cannot fail of augmenting the mass of moral depravity." In a passage similar to recent arguments about the "underclass," Clinton declared that the "mendicant parent bequeaths his squalid poverty to his offspring, and the hardened thief transmits a legacy of infamy to his unfortunate and depraved descendants." Since the city's charity schools were designed to serve the poor children of a particular denomination, the children who could most benefit from schooling were left out, owing to "the irreligion of their parents."[24]

Having made the case for public education, Clinton confronted the question of funding it. Here he thought the solution was to be found in the educational theories of Joseph Lancaster, an Englishman who had developed the "monitorial" system of instruction for London's poor. The origins of this system were simple: Lancaster started a school for the poor in Southwark, and the number of students soon grew beyond his ability to manage them. He could not afford to hire assistants, so he hit upon the idea of using the more advanced students to teach the less advanced, and in 1803 he elaborated his system in *Improvements in Education As It Respects the Industrious Classes of the Community*. Clinton embraced the Lancastrian approach with the enthusiasm of a politician who feels he has found a cheap solution to an expensive problem. The Free School Society's first school, opened in 1806, was the first Lancastrian school in the United States.[25]

But if using students as teachers was an economical system, it was not a flawless one. For one thing, the education of those students recruited as instructors stalled once they were responsible for passing their knowledge on to younger and slower pupils. Besides, there still had to be a qualified master in the school, and no ready source of such masters existed. During his terms as governor Clinton would stress the need for teachers, and would expand and deepen his argument about the social importance of education in order to encourage greater legislative support for it.

Clinton's intense devotion to education and the diversity of groups it embraced—girls, refugees, deaf and dumb children, blacks—has to be seen as one of the more impressive chapters of his life. His involvement with educational societies was remarkable; the number of causes he worked for seems nearly infinite. He was president of the Economical School Society, a Lancastrian school established for the children of refugees from the Napoleonic wars. He helped found the Orphan Asylum Society, which sought to provide education for orphaned and abandoned children. Impressed by the importance of early childhood education, he encouraged the creation of kindergartens to enrich the education of children while allowing "indigent parents" to "devote themselves to labor." He was a supporter of the African Free School. He was president of the New York Institution for the Deaf and Dumb. He lent his aid to the Mechanic and Scientific Institute, an early effort at vocational training. He pursued educational approaches to the problem of juvenile delinquency. He shepherded the union of Columbia's medical school with the College of Physicians and Surgeons. He was president of the American Bible Society. Although the closeness of his involvement varied from one to another, he worked for all of them and was obviously the most important person in the development of education in New York State in the first half of the nineteenth century. As the historian of education Edwin Fitzpatrick wrote in 1911, Clinton would have been even more renowned for his work for schools if his other achievements had not overshadowed it. "He did for New York," Fitzpatrick concluded, "what [Horace] Mann did for Massachusetts and [Henry] Barnard did for Connecticut."[26]

While Free Schools for poor children meant a great advance over the haphazard collection of charity schools present in 1800, there was still a separate and unequal educational system (as there is today). Children of prosperous parents could attend private academies, while the poor attended separate, and generally inferior, institutions. As the system expanded through the 1820s, this disparity was recognized, and in 1826 Clinton approved an agreement establishing a new relationship between the society and the City of New York, under which the Free Schools would become public schools, open to rich and poor alike. (A requirement that wealthier students pay a nominal fee was also instituted at this time, but never caught on and was eliminated in 1832.) Clinton praised the *"annihilation of factitious distinctions"* and predicted that the presence of rich and poor in the same schools would "be a strong incentive for the display of talents and a felicitous accommodation to the genius of republican government."[27]

He wanted education to be one of the great triumphs of the republican nation then creating itself, and for geniuses of world renown to emerge from the democratic masses. But he also wanted education to help regulate those masses, to teach wisdom and reason, and lead to a responsible exercise of the right to vote. In a frugal society in which the cost of a decent educational system could seem prohibitive, Clinton advanced the Lancastrian method as the perfect blend of uplift and thrift. And he constantly lobbied to involve the state more directly. True, the organizations he supported tended to be run by philanthropists like himself, and they naturally tried to inculcate those values they thought most salutary. But the alternatives to such societies were few. Only later, as the diversity of the city increased and the burgeoning Catholic population began objecting to the Protestant religious instruction dispensed in the public schools, did the shortcomings of this Protestant paternalism become obvious. But if Clinton's conception of education would become outmoded, and if it tried to impose the values of the elite, the Free School Society and the other organizations Clinton supported established education as a primary responsibility of the state. By the time of Clinton's death, New York State had one of the best school systems in the country—an achievement that allowed it to take advantage of its geographical and other advantages as the market revolution advanced.

Governor George Clinton. By Ezra Ames, ca. 1814. © Collection of the New-York Histor-ical Society.

Gouverneur Morris.
By Ezra Ames, ca. 1815.
© Collection of
the New-York
Historical Society.

Arron Burr.
By John Vanderlyn,
ca. 1802. © Collection of
the New-York
Historical Society.

Dewitt Clinton.
By Charles Cromwell
Ingham, ca. 1824. ©
Collection of the New-
York Historical Society.

Ambrose Spencer.
By John Wesley Jarvis,
ca. 1818. © Collection
of the New-York
Historical Society.

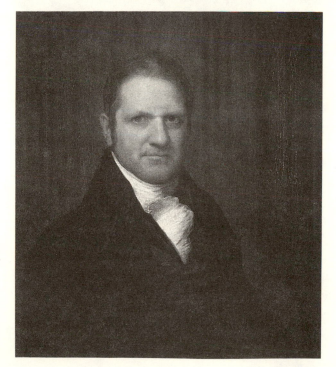

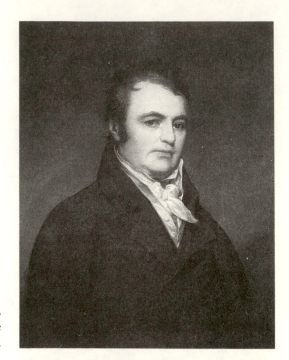

John Pintard. By John Trumbull,
ca. 1817. © Collection of the
New-York Historical Society.

Daniel D. Tompkins.
By John Wesley Jarvis, ca. 1821.
© Collection of the New-York
Historical Society.

Broadway and the City Hall. Engraved by L. Augier. © Collection of the New-York Historical Society.

Canal Aqueduct Crossing a Stream. By George Harvey, ca. 1840s. © Collection of the New-York Historical Society.

Erie Canal, Card—Canal Celebration Ball, November 7, 1825. © Collection of the New-York Historical Society.

Dewitt Clinton. By Samuel F. B. Morse. Courtesy of The Metropolitan Museum of Art, Rogers Fund, 1909. (09.18)

Six

o   o   o

CLINTONIANS AND QUIDS

I T WILL BE RECALLED THAT DeWitt Clinton's first important political task when he became mayor was the destruction of Aaron Burr as a political force in New York State. With the election of Morgan Lewis as governor in 1804, Clinton should have been securely in control. His chosen candidate, a lesser light of the Livingston faction, was installed in Albany; Clinton controlled the Council of Appointment; he reigned as mayor of the City of New York; and throughout 1804 and 1805 he had been actively engaged in establishing the Historical Society and the Free School Society, and in strengthening the American Academy. The Napoleonic wars had brought prosperity to the city's shipping and export trades, and as of March 4, 1805, his uncle George was vice president of the United States. Jefferson had reason to be grateful to DeWitt Clinton for his scourging of Burr, and Federalism was in retreat. With the liberalization of voting requirements and the introduction of the secret ballot in the 1804 municipal elections, the Republicans had gained a majority in the Common Council.

But into all such political Edens the serpent quickly slithers, and it was indeed with almost biblical disgust that Clinton found his hoped-for puppet governor, Morgan Lewis, forsaking him to advance his own and the Livingston interests. The son of Francis Lewis, a New York merchant and a signer of the Declaration of Independence, Morgan Lewis had served in the Continental Army as a quartermaster and as chief of staff to Horatio Gates at the Battle of Saratoga; during the war he had married a daughter of Robert R. Livingston. Before becoming governor, he had been the state attorney general, a state supreme court justice, and then chief justice.[1]

On assuming office, Lewis ejected his enemies and appointed his family and friends in their places. Peter B. Porter, the Ontario County clerk and a Burrite, was dismissed. Maturin Livingston, Lewis's son-in-law, was appointed recorder of the City of New York. Clinton opposed Porter's removal, reasoning that, with Burr out of the picture, Porter, an influential figure in western New York, would have to return to the party's mainstream. It was not patronage, however, but bank politics that caused the split between Clinton and Lewis. Although New York City's economy was diversifying and growing more sophisticated by the year, the financial resources of the city remained meager. In 1802 there were only two banks, the Federalist-run Bank of New York and the Manhattan Company. In 1803 another Federalist bank was started, the Merchants' Bank, but the legislature refused to grant a charter, and just before adjourning in 1804 it banned companies from undertaking banking activities without a charter and ordered the Merchants' Bank and a bank in Albany to close by May 1805. Clinton opposed the Merchants' Bank, not only because of its Federalist connections but also because he now had effective control over the Manhattan Company and was unwilling to see his influence diluted by an expansion of banking facilities in New York.[2]

Lewis, however, felt that it would be unfair to deprive the two banks of their livelihoods just because they were not in compliance with a law passed after they went into business. He backed an effort by the Merchants' Bank in 1805 to get a state charter, an effort marked by accusations of wholesale bribery. Licit and illicit ties between banks and politics were then, as now, widespread. Moreover, in New York City, according to Frederic Cople Jaher, "one-fourth of the 283 federal, state, and city officeholders between 1778 and 1815 were bank directors." In this case, the chief culprit was Ebenezer Purdy, a state senator, who led the senate floor fight in behalf of the charter. He was accused both of accepting a bribe himself and of trying to buy votes in the senate and the assembly. For whatever reasons, the Merchants' Bank got its charter, and the Council of Revision confirmed the bill with the votes of the Federalist Chancellor James Kent, Governor Lewis, and Lewis's wife's cousin Brockholst Livingston. Clinton then went on the offensive. He assembled a slate of antibank candidates for the April 1805 legislative elections and was himself elected to the state senate. Early in 1806, having tightened his control of the Council of Appointment, he removed Lewis's appointees and replaced them with loyal Clintonians. The Clinton-Livingston alliance was shattered, and DeWitt Clinton thought he could now control the state. On March 15, 1806, he introduced a resolution charging Purdy with bribery and calling for his expulsion from the senate. A few days later Purdy resigned, citing ill health. John Pintard wrote in his dairy, "This is tantamount in public opinion to pleading guilty to the charge."[3]

Clinton's actions have baffled political historians. Hammond wonders why Clinton proceeded "without cause . . . to excommunicate Gov. Lewis from the republican church." D. S. Alexander judged that this schism with the Livingstons was both unnecessary and harmful. He wrote that the Livingstons were "not long to continue in New York politics," and that Clinton's moves "condemned him to a career of almost unbroken opposition for the rest of his life; it made precedents that lived to curse him; and it compelled alliances that weakened him." Clinton could hardly have thought the Merchants' Bank a great threat to his power, or believed that the creation of new banks in the city and state could be indefinitely postponed. So why did he act? With George Clinton in virtual retirement as vice president, DeWitt in 1804 was obliged to wield power in New York on his own, without the useful aegis of his uncle. If he saw the Livingstons as dangerous, he was probably right. Alexander assumes that because the Livingstons soon passed from the scene Clinton need not have turned against them, yet in all likelihood it was Clinton's actions that caused their downfall. Actually, even with Clinton's push, their downfall was hardly complete: Chancellor Robert R. Livingston remained a power in the state until his death in 1813; Brockholst Livingston became a United States Supreme Court Justice; and Edward Livingston, DeWitt's predecessor as mayor, would eventually return from his New Orleans exile to Washington, having been elected by his fellow Louisianans to the House and the Senate and then chosen by Andrew Jackson to be secretary of state. Moreover, various other Livingston relations—John Armstrong, Thomas Tillotson, and Morgan Lewis himself—would remain influential in New York for some time to come. Jabez Hammond scolds Clinton for isolating Lewis as a way of advancing his own career, rather than founding his opposition to Lewis on substantial differences in policy.[4]

In fact, it would have been unusual if Clinton had not been plotting his own rise at about this time. When he backed Lewis for the governorship the year before, the Livingston-Clinton alliance was still cemented by fear and hatred of Aaron Burr. But by the spring of 1805 Burr was heading west from Washington through Pennsylvania and Ohio on the way to his western adventures, George Clinton was in Washington, John Jay had retired to his Bedford farm, and Hamilton was buried in Trinity churchyard. The four most powerful figures in New York politics over the previous decade were gone from the scene, and DeWitt Clinton felt that his time at center stage had come. He also seems to have had a plan for getting there.

EMBRACING THE BURRITES

If the attack on Lewis was motivated solely by ambition, there was at least the pretense of a principled difference—the charter for the Merchants' Bank. Clinton and his allies could fulminate in the best republican tradition (and with justice, in view of the bank's corrupt practices) about the money power, luxury, and corruption. But the move that branded him as a political opportunist, an unprincipled seeker of power, was his attempt to bring Burr's now leaderless followers into his camp.

Clinton's actions were later exposed in some detail by two pamphleteers, "Marcus" and "Philo-Cato," who painted a portrait of a corrupt opportunist abandoning classical republican principles for the sake of self-aggrandizement. Both pamphleteers were loyal Burrites. "Marcus" was Matthew L. Davis, and "Philo-Cato" may have been William P. Van Ness. The chronology and the terms of the attempted alliance were laid out in the "Letters of Marcus," written by Davis and addressed to "DeWitt Clinton, Esq." The accusations of "Philo-Cato" concentrate on Clinton's unwillingness to bring his allegations of libel before a court of law.[5]

Around Christmas 1805, Levi McKeen, of Poughkeepsie, a follower of Burr's, came to New York and told his fellow Burrites that he had received overtures from leading

Clintonians, including General Theodorus Bailey, about forming an alliance. He encouraged John Swartwout to meet with General Bailey and explore the grounds for such a reconciliation. Between January 7 and 11, 1806, there were almost daily meetings between Bailey and Swartwout. Other Clintonians involved were Richard Riker (Clinton's second in the Swartwout duel), whom "Marcus" described as bearing the same relation to Clinton "as the *pilot-fish* to the *shark,*" and Pierre C. Van Wyck, "a very incompetent judge of measures of policy," according to the same source. On January 11 a deal was struck with five main points. First, Burr should be accepted as a Republican. Second, Cheetham should stop attacking Burrites in the *American Citizen*. Third, Burrites should be eligible for "offices of honour or profit throughout the state" on "the same footing as the most favoured Clintonians." Fourth, Burrites should receive at least a third of the seats in the legislature from the City and County of New York. And, fifth, Burrites should be granted loans by the Manhattan Bank, which had been denying their applications.[6]

The Burrites demanded that as proof of Clintonian good faith the last of these provisos be satisfied before the union was sealed, and on January 13 the bank loaned John Swartwout nine thousand dollars and advanced an equal sum on the sixteenth. Smaller loans were made to other Burrites. On the eighteenth, Clinton urged Republican members of the legislature to seek a union with the Burrites—a move that "Marcus" denounced as "Consummate duplicity!" because the deal had already been made. On January 24, Clinton gave his personal approval to the rapprochement, volunteering to secure the election or appointment of Burrites to city and state offices and giving the impression that he would pursue policies "flattering to Col. Burr." To celebrate this new alliance, a dinner was held in Manhattan at Dyde's Tavern on February 20, 1806, the so-called "Union Supper," at which Burr was toasted in absentia. But even before the dinner, word of the alliance leaked out, and many Clintonians and other Republicans were appalled. Benjamin Romaine asked whether, after months of denouncing the Burrites as "scoundrells—Traitors—intriguers," the Clintonians really thought they could now effect such a reconciliation: "Will the public mind be thus trifled with?" And James Fairlie, writing on the day of the dinner, warned that for each vote gained by the union "there will be five lost."[7]

The sparks of indignation became a firestorm on February 25, when a meeting was held at Martling's Long Room, another Manhattan tavern, to protest the alliance and to denounce Clinton's role in it. The meeting was called by Burrites unhappy with the new order of things, and their numbers were swelled by supporters of Governor Lewis who, like Clinton, saw the chance of gaining as allies Burr's small but effective band of political operatives. Many Clintonians who opposed the reconciliation were there, too. From this meeting forward, Clinton's opponents in the Republican party were called "Martling Men."[8]

Clinton did not attend the meeting, of course, but his sources were quick to report. James Fairlie related that a large crowd had attended ("The yard & house were crowded, and hundreds around the door"), and that "the reunion met the most decided disapprobation. . . . I was apprehensive that the meeting might have a tendency to disturb the harmony of the Republicans here, but I believe it will not." Fairlie's eyewitness report was presumably more helpful than his analysis; the latter was certainly wrong. Another correspondent, Nathan Sanford, wrote that things had been going well, with Federalists well-disposed toward Clinton, and Lewis's power waning, until the "ill-judged" reconciliation with the Burrites. "Though the immediate irritation produced by the supper and the toasts has considerably subsided," he wrote on February 27, "yet it has excited a spirit of jealousy and suspicion among some of our best friends."[9]

With anger over the reconciliation growing daily, Clinton acted quickly but—one fears—basely. In a public letter to Theodorus Bailey (quoted by "Marcus"), he pretended to have no knowledge of the truce, sententiously declaring that while he would find Burrite support *"universally agreeable,"* it should not be obtained with promises of office. Bailey himself was made to serve as Clinton's sacrificial victim, censured for imprudence. Any allegations that jobs were promised were *"infamous falsehoods."* To clear up matters, Clinton helpfully suggested, "perhaps the most proper mode would be, to require frank and explicit declarations from gentlemen of the Burr party."[10]

The exact agreement reached between Clinton's representatives and the Burrites may be obscure, but there is no reason to doubt that negotiations were attempted, and that some understanding was arrived at. Clinton's denials are thunderous but vague, while the accusations of "Marcus" and "Philo-Cato" are detailed, and contain many allegations that could have been disproved had Clinton been in a position to disprove them. The books of the Manhattan Bank, for instance, could have shown whether Swartwout and other Burrites received loans in January 1806. Statements of the dates and places of meetings could have been refuted by alibis had the persons mentioned been elsewhere. And although Clinton claimed in 1807, after the first "Marcus" letters, that "I have directed prosecutions to be immediately instituted against the authors and publishers," he subsequently let the matter drop, in spite of efforts by Matthew Davis to bring it before the courts. In short, Clinton's efforts to exculpate himself do not seem very persuasive. He lied, because he had blundered. He had miscalculated the effect such a negotiation was likely to have on his reputation. He had worked to banish the Burrites from power, fought one duel, barely avoided a second, and seen one supporter wounded and one killed in other duels arising from the struggle; he had directed the winning campaign against Burr in 1804; and he had seen to it that James Cheetham continued to spread accusations against the Burrites during the preceding fall. Clinton could not reverse course without appearing two-faced. The public mind, as Benjamin Romaine had put it, was not to be "thus trifled with."[11]

At the same time that Clintonians and Burrites were parleying in New York, the legislature in Albany was selecting a new Council of Appointment. In a break from previous practice, the nominations were made by a Republican caucus including the entire state, rather than by caucuses for each of the four senatorial districts represented on the council. The Lewisites, or Quids, as they were dubbed by their opponents, protested this change, claiming that it had been made to secure the election of Clinton to the council, an election he could not win if it was limited to the votes of the Republican legislators from the Southern District. But Clinton had the votes, and the new council swept Lewisites from office and substituted Clintonians. The practice of removals from office as part of the developing spoils system was still, in the view of many, of dubious propriety. In 1801 Clinton's housecleaning had at least been limited to removing Federalists from office, but now, in 1806, he was using the same approach to remove men whose sole crime was loyalty to another faction of the Republican party. Combined with his unprincipled conduct with regard to the Burrites, his sweeping use of patronage leaves the impression, indelible to this day, of a vindictive and scheming politician. True, such conduct would shortly become common practice; it might in time even be indispensable to governing under a party system. But in DeWitt Clinton's case it would haunt him for the rest of his career.[12]

In the April elections of 1806, Clinton lost control of the legislature, and when the new members convened in January 1807, the Quids turned Clinton's methods against him. On February 16, as the first item of business before the new Council of Appointment, Clinton was removed as mayor of New York.

THE FARMER'S BOY

Clinton's removal from the mayor's office would help drive Morgan Lewis out of the governor's office in 1807, but for the time being Clinton was on his own (although he continued in office as a state senator, a post he held until 1811), with a growing family and without the handsome mayoral income. DeWitt and Maria Clinton's fifth son, named George after his great-uncle, was born in 1807, and for Clinton the expense of raising children and maintaining a home in New York City, a summer house on Long Island, and lodgings in Albany during the legislative sessions, as well as entertaining guests, was daunting. And Clinton's position as the leader of so many cultural and charitable organizations put him under obligation to contribute money as well as time to their well-being. His prominence also brought him many entreaties for aid from private citizens; the dowry Maria had brought with her had been compromised many times by Clinton's ill-advised cosigning of loans for entrepreneurial Republicans in the city. As the Burrite pamphlet "Plain Truth" had pointed out in 1804, the Clinton family (and the Livingstons) derived a considerable income from public office. If politics had not yet become professionalized, there were already many professional politicians, in the sense that they depended on political office for part of their livelihoods. Clinton may have affected the airs of a patrician, and acquired patrician debts, but he was also in that sense a professional.[13]

How these matters weighed on him can be seen in his diary, that usually bloodless enumeration of dinner companions and daily temperatures. Soon after his return to New York following the adjournment of the legislature he began for the first time to record grocery prices—oysters, eggs, and so forth. On July 25, for newborn George, he noted the purchase of a "Hat for Baby 2 Dollars." Although he was not given to emotional expression, there are frequent notes about his children and about their outings; on December 7, 1807, for example, he took them to see the "African Panther" then on exhibit in the city.[14]

But a quiet retirement at the age of thirty-eight was not to be Clinton's destiny. Although the attempted reconciliation with the Burrites had done him little good, and it seemed unlikely that he could win election as governor in his own right in 1807, he was not prepared to allow Morgan Lewis to continue in office. At first, the most promising course appeared to be that of rousing up George Clinton once again for the good of republicanism. But the vice president absolutely refused. Once more, as in 1804, the Clintonians sought a surrogate. They found him in Daniel D. Tompkins, whose name was to be linked with Clinton's, as both ally and adversary, for most of the next two decades.[15]

Tompkins was born in 1774 in Westchester County, and his rural origins later paid political dividends in the nickname "the Farmer's Boy," which stayed with him throughout his career. Yet his background and upbringing were as privileged as Clinton's. Tompkins's father was politically prominent, serving as town supervisor of Scarsdale, as a county judge, and in the state legislature. Like DeWitt Clinton, Tompkins attended Columbia College, where he questioned the emphasis on Greek and Latin, and thought that the students' time could be better spent learning to master English. In his own attempts to do so, he wrote essays advocating the end of slavery, favoring better treatment for Indians, and opposing capital punishment. Here, too, both his subjects and his views were congruent with Clinton's. He gave the valedictory address at Columbia's commencement exercises in 1795. He was admitted to the bar in 1797, worked for Jefferson's election in 1800, and soon received an appointment as a federal bankruptcy commissioner. In 1801 he was elected to the constitutional convention that passed Clinton's desired clarification of the right of members of the Council of Appointment to nominate candidates. Tompkins opposed the measure. In 1802 he was elected to the legislature, and in 1804 received an appointment as a New York Supreme Court justice and was elected to the House of Representatives. He declined to serve in Congress, as he declined a federal judgeship the following year, explaining to James Madison that his decision to keep his state post "arises from its tenure being the same, from its emolument being more, and from the greater tendency of its duties to preserve my health." So, again like Clinton, he quickly rose to prominence, while evidently preferring the political and physical climate of New York to that of Washington.[16]

Tompkins's appointment to the state supreme court had come early in Lewis's term, before the Merchants' Bank struggle had estranged Lewis and Clinton. But as that split widened, Republicans had to declare their allegiance. Most decided that the Clintonians would prevail. It appears to have been a simple decision, because on the evening of February 16, 1807—the day Clinton was stripped of the mayoralty—the Republican caucus in the legislature nominated the Clintonian candidate for governor, Daniel D. Tompkins. Clinton wrote the document by which it was done. For Clinton, Tompkins was a handy choice. His duties as a judge had brought him into contact with many prominent New Yorkers; indeed, Jabez Hammond was speaking of

Tompkins when he declared, "There is no position in social life so favorable to acquiring the esteem and confidence of the people as that of a circuit judge of the supreme court, if his manners are fascinating and agreeable." And Tompkins had great personal charm. Even Clinton's biographer James Renwick, who deprecated Tompkins's intellectual gifts, allowed, "He had the faculty, which is invaluable to him who seeks for popular honours, of never forgetting the name or face of any person with whom he had once conversed . . . and of securing, by his affability and amiable address, the good opinion of the female sex, who, although possessed of no vote, often exercise a powerful direct influence."[17]

Tompkins possessed an additional asset: Clinton did not see him as a threat. Personally popular, he was not so distinguished as to command a great following, and his family, if locally influential in Westchester County, was not, like the Livingstons and the Clintons, a power in the state. Nor, Clinton seems to have concluded, was Tompkins sufficiently skilled to mount a serious challenge to his control of the state. The campaign scheme of attacking Lewis as an agent of the oligarchic Livingston family would work better if no member of the oligarchic Clintons was opposing him. One might wonder how DeWitt Clinton could have made the same mistake twice: Tompkins would, like Lewis, desert him and become a powerful opponent. In 1807, however, Clinton had no choice but to seek a stand-in, and Tompkins fit the bill. Clinton certainly could not have expected blind obedience; Tompkins's vote in the 1801 convention had shown independence even in his earliest political activities. Nor should we see the splits between Clinton and Lewis, and Clinton and Tompkins, as betrayals of Clinton, however he himself may have seen them. Clinton took disagreement as disobedience, and criticism as an assault. A less imperious man might have postponed the conflict and remained in harmony longer. But ultimately there could be only one governor, and only one man could lead the Republican party in the state. Clinton intended to be that man, and he could not realistically expect others to attain the state's highest office and then serve as his puppets; yet that is just what he did expect.

While Republicans in the legislature rallied to Clinton and Tompkins's side, Lewis developed support of his own among Federalists and Burrites. That support developed—at least in part—from his own shortcomings. Morgan Lewis possessed the Livingston family's disposition to nepotism. He nominated his son-in-law, Maturin Livingston—whom the Clintonian Council of Appointment had removed as city recorder the year before—to the state supreme court seat made vacant when his cousin Brockholst Livingston was appointed to the United States Supreme Court. Lewis bungled the attempt, and in the end the Council of Appointment gave the seat to William W. Van Ness (cousin of "Aristides," William P. Van Ness), a Federalist from Columbia County. Lewis's nepotism, the Clintonians charged, had cost the Republican cause an important office. Federalists, however, were naturally pleased at the outcome, whatever they may have thought of Lewis's handling of it, and they saw opportunities for more crumbs from the patronage table if Lewis was reelected with their aid. Judge Van Ness encouraged an alliance between Lewis and the Federalists, although it would have to be kept quiet to avoid alienating Lewis's remaining Republican supporters.[18]

The 1807 race was a clash of factions, not of principles. Tompkins was scarcely mentioned in the campaign literature, which portrayed the battle as being between Clintonians and Livingstonians (with the latter tarred as quasi-Federalists). Lewis got help from John Lansing, who now publicized his reasons for declining the 1804 gubernatorial nomination. According to Lansing, George Clinton had tried to extract a pledge from him to follow Clinton's direction, which Lansing refused to do. A week later, after George Clinton denied Lansing's charge, Lansing expanded it. Governor Clinton, he said, had also hinted that DeWitt Clinton should be appointed chancellor if Lansing was elected governor. George Clinton, feeling much put upon, told his nephew that Lansing's words and actions "discovered a depravity of heart & weakness of mind beyond any thing I could have expected." The thunder of the Lewisites was directed against the Clintons rather than against Tompkins, and the replies were aimed at the entire Livingston family, as the "oligarchical enemies of our republican government" and possible agents of Britain.[19]

NEW YORK NATIVISM

The charge of British sympathies (the 1800s equivalent of the Cold War era's accusation of being "soft on communism") was the flip side of a campaign strategy being developed by the Federalists, one that would return, in various forms, many times in the future. The Christmas riots a few months earlier, which Clinton's timely appearance at St. Peter's Church had helped to put down, were only the most dramatic evidence of growing tension between Irish immigrants and Protestant New Yorkers of native stock. That riot had been directed against Irish Catholics, and, indeed, they were the target of the most intense hostility, but many of New York's Irish at this time were Protestants, and they, too, were stereotyped as drunken louts. Clinton's own Irish (Protestant) heritage had inclined him toward both groups of immigrants, and he had, as noted earlier, championed liberal immigration laws while a member of the United States Senate. The Federalists presented their slate under the title of the "American Ticket" and denounced Clinton's allies as "the Gallico-Hibernico-Tom-Clintonians," thus implying French sympathies, Irish support, and the malign imprint of Rome and the Catholic church. The struggle between Burrites and Clintonians had been carried out in pamphlets; the one between Clintonians and Livingstons was waged in the newspapers, and the principal voice of the Livingston family was the *Morning Chronicle*. After Clintonians prevailed in New York City in the April 1806 elections for state office, the *Chronicle* began a drumbeat of criticism of Clinton himself and vilification of his Irish supporters. The election in the city had gone Clinton's way, the paper suggested on May 3, 1806, because two thousand voters were "dependent for their subsistence upon the favor" of Clinton, and that he could also depend on support from "eight or nine hundred newly imported *American patriots.*"[20]

Assaults on the Irish grew ever more crude. On May 19 the paper published an "authentic account" of a conversation between two Clintonians, named Paddy and Murphy:

PADDY (gnawing a huge rib). Arrah, and be me shoul, Murphy, isn't it a rare thing to be a Hambletonian, and get plenty of swate whiskey, and dilicate bull bafe for nothing at all, and less too?

MURPHY (a mug of whiskey in his left hand, and the jaw bone of the ox in his right). Oh! be the powers, you tief, and ye're a Hambletonian then, are ye? [Then Daggerman and Tuny Trincum enter, and clear up the confusion, leading to Paddy's statement] I did mane Clintonian, and I ax pardon with the shoul of me.[21]

As the 1807 election approached, however, the tactic of identifying Clintonians as closet Hamiltonians became less attractive, since Lewis was seeking Federalist support. So the *Morning Chronicle* concentrated on Clinton's Irish supporters, at the same time picturing Clinton as being under French influence. By April, the paper was in paroxysms. On the twenty-fifth it implied that Clinton beat his wife, and on the twenty-seventh it ran an extract from the *"Log Book of the Ship* AMERICAN, [Captain] *Lewis,"* which reported sighting the "ship *Clinton,* bound from *Port Republican* to *Peak Ambition,* deeply laden, with a full cargo of *Irish and Gallic American anarchy."* When the polls opened the next day, there was an announcement in the paper that the election would determine whether the state would be run by "persons under foreign influence," together with the following "Communication":

> What nation stocks our state prison with convicts? The Irish.
> What class of people disturb the public peace with riots and murder our watchmen? The Irish.
> Who are the characters who are almost always concerned in private quarrels and battles? The Irish.
> Who are the men who we constantly witness staggering about our streets, brutalized with liquor? The Irish.
> Who has fostered that class of men by extending to them the favours of government, by licensing them as cartmen, to the exclusion of respectable and industrious Americans, and by making them marshals to the annoyance of the poorer classes of citizens? De Witt Clinton.
> How are these favours repaid? By becoming brawling partizans . . . by quarreling with, and abusing every American who differs with them in opinion.[22]

The Livingstons did not invent anti-Irish prejudice, but their baiting of Irish Catholics certainly contributed to ethnic tensions in the city. At the same time, DeWitt Clinton may well deserve the distinction of being the first big-city mayor in the United States to recognize the electoral potential of Irish immigrants, and to use patronage and policy to enlist their support. To Clinton's place in political history as an inventor of the spoils system we should add this early embrace of the voting potential of the Irish.

The Clintonian press was no less abandoned than the Livingstonian, charging Federalists with being in league with England. According to one writer, the "American Ticket" was almost correct: "One hitch more and it will be right—the Tory ticket—then with great propriety they might put a King on it." The "King" in question was Rufus King, the once and future United States senator and minister to Great Britain, who was a Federalist candidate for the state assembly from New York City. In April

1807, King figured in a series of articles in the Clintonian *American Citizen,* in which he was charged with being a royalist; this was proved by his objections to a British plan to send "Irish state prisoners" to America, objections that, obviously, betrayed King's opposition to increasing the number of true republicans living in America.[23]

Amidst all this, Judge Tompkins could well assume that posture of disinterested, detached acquiescence which should be the attitude of a good republican candidate for public office. When the *Morning Chronicle* first mentioned Tompkins's nomination, the worst it could say was that "by accepting the Clintonian nomination, [he] has assumed the responsibility of that party." When the election was over, the Gallico-Hibernican candidate had beaten Lewis by 4,085 votes out of more than 76,000 cast, and on July 1, 1807, Daniel D. Tompkins became governor of the state of New York, only the fourth man to hold the office since it was established, in 1777.[24]

Seven

o   o   o

NEW YORK AND THE NATION

T HE APRIL 1807 elections put DeWitt Clinton back in command of New York
State politics. Before Tompkins's victory, Clinton had declined President Jefferson's offer of the governorship of the new Mississippi Territory. Jefferson was no
doubt following the Virginia practice of seeking to neutralize the most powerful Republican in New York State, something that had earlier been accomplished by placing
Burr and then George Clinton in the impotent office of vice president. Jefferson
doubtless wanted to maintain cordial relations with the Clintons. But at the same
time, he did not wish to see DeWitt Clinton and his uncle grow more powerful than
they already were.[1]

For his part, DeWitt Clinton appears to have been undercutting Jefferson in private for at least a year. In March 1806, Morgan Lewis wrote to John Smith, then a
United States senator from New York, to report that he had been present at a dinner
where DeWitt Clinton had attacked Jefferson's policy concerning the acquisition of
East Florida and had advocated a more aggressive stand on that issue. (At about the
same time, James Fairlie was writing to Clinton—perhaps in reply to a request for
suggestions—that the behavior of HMS *Leander* off New York might offer good material with which to "traduce" Jefferson.) Lewis told Smith he feared that "too many
Eyes are cast towards the Presidency, and too many wish to supplant the Man whose
guidance has conducted us to a state of unexampled Prosperity." Lewis asked Smith
for news from Washington, remarking that "if you experience as much Intrigue in
the general Government as we do here in that of the State, I pity Mr. Jefferson from
my soul." At the time he wrote, Lewis was seeing his friends removed from office and
branded as Quids by the Clintonians, who had just regained control of the Council of
Appointment.[2]

Personal ambitions were crucial to the disruption of the New York-Virginia electoral alliance, but sectional tensions were now coming into play as well. New York,

the leading American port, was a natural locus of naval activity, and Clinton's efforts as mayor to keep British and French ships under some sort of control and to protect American lives and property have already been mentioned. To the extent that Jefferson was unable to prevent harm to American shipping and commercial interests, he was certain to attract criticism in New York. But when Jefferson tried a new response to British and French depredations, grumbling turned into active protest.

THE EMBARGO

Upset by the affront to American pride, as well as by the actual harm done to American ships and sailors, Jefferson and his secretary of state, James Madison, were certainly not indifferent to the suffering of the ports. But their solution, rooted in weakness, only increased the suffering. And the military weakness that underlay the policy was not its cause so much as a consequence of the same considerations that had led to the Embargo itself. Jefferson and Madison were determined to prevent the creation in America of a powerful military establishment that could threaten individual liberties and state sovereignty. They had reacted quickly, and with suspicion, to military adventures undertaken or even contemplated by the Federalists. America, the Virginians reasoned, could make its power felt through trade policies rather than armies and navies; Europe bought grain and other staples from America, while the trade in this direction was, in their view, largely in luxurious fripperies. Americans could do without lace and fine woolens, but Europe could not do without bread. For New York, which was a major grain-exporting state as well as the port of entry for many fripperies, the consequences of this view would be dire, and have lasting political consequences.[3]

American diplomacy had striven to avoid European entanglements, hoping to preserve American neutrality and profit from the opportunities war offered to a neutral maritime nation. But after Nelson's decisive victory over the French and Spanish fleets at Trafalgar on October 21, 1805, and Napoleon's triumph over the Russian and Austrian armies at Austerlitz on December 2, Britain and France both recognized the crucial role of neutral shipping. Britain proclaimed a blockade of Continental Europe, and Napoleon declared that any ships complying with British requirements were fair game for French customs officers. For the United States, there seemed to be no solution except war or humiliation. Madison, however, thought he saw a way out, through commercial coercion, and he championed the Embargo Act through the cabinet and Congress, which passed the bill on December 22, 1807. By restricting American ships to port (with various exceptions, which proved an invitation to evasion) and banning imports, the Embargo would bring Britain to its knees.[4]

In New York, the effects were immediate and severe. On January 8, 1808—barely two weeks after the bill passed Congress and was signed by Jefferson—a notice in the *Daily Advertiser* asked seamen, addressed as "FELLOW SUFFERERS," to attend a meeting to demand aid from the city government. By March, tax receipts were falling as the crippling of trade hit businesses. In April, the British traveler John Lambert, who had commented on the city's prosperous bustle on his way through in November 1807, wrote that "every thing presented a melancholy appearance. The streets near the water-side were almost deserted, the *grass had begun to grow upon the wharfs.*"[5]

Clinton at first opposed the Embargo, and James Cheetham duly served up anti-Embargo morsels in the *American Citizen*. But public opinion against the Embargo moderated—it was seen as a temporary measure that would either work or give more time to prepare for war—and Clinton hastily reversed course. On January 18, according to his diary, he "Attended General Meeting of Republicans as Chairman" and recanted. Eight days later, Governor Daniel D. Tompkins, in his address to the legislature, endorsed the administration's policy as a lesser evil than war and called for "a magnanimous confidence in the efforts of our national councils." Clinton may even have had a hand in this language, since Tompkins had sent a draft to him a few days before the speech and told Clinton to edit it "with as much freedom as you would amend a Composition of your own."[6]

Clinton's acceptance of the party line on the Embargo no doubt eased his return to the mayoralty—the Council of Appointment returned him to office in February, in time for him to begin worrying about the declining tax receipts reported in March. And his acquiescence was surely encouraged by Jefferson's threat to withhold patronage from any Republican leader who broke with the administration on the Embargo. But Clinton's doubts about the Embargo continued. If it was merely buying time to prepare for war, why were there no preparations? The previous fall, when revulsion over the attack on the *Chesapeake* had fanned war fever in the country, Congress appropriated a paltry $2 million to strengthen harbor defenses and equip some of the lumbering gunboats that Jefferson, with his amateur's ignorance, had decided were a match for the frigates of the Royal Navy. George Clinton, in a letter in February, mocked the gunboats, and said that Jefferson's notion of an army was fatally modeled on the Virginia militia, which merely provides "a force about sufficient to keep their slaves in awe & prevent their cutting their Masters throats." It was George's son-in-law Edmond Charles Genet who led the Clintonian attack on the Embargo, denouncing it as being motivated by Virginia jealousy of the rising prosperity and influence of the commercial states, especially New York. His writings were published in 1808 as *Communications on the Next Election for President of the United States, and on the Late Measures of the Federal Administration*. Genet was advancing a favorite scheme of the Clinton family—placing George Clinton in the White House.[7]

GEORGE CLINTON FOR PRESIDENT, 1808

The belief that George Clinton was not of presidential caliber was, of course, axiomatic among the Virginians, but it had currency elsewhere as well: Senator William Plumer of New Hampshire commented that he had "no mind—no intellect—no memory." In fact, few thought Clinton was a serious alternative to Madison as successor to Jefferson. But with Virginia having claimed the presidency for sixteen of the office's twenty years, sentiment was building that it was time to give another state a chance. Genet's pamphlet fanned the flames of sectional tension. Separating republicanism from "embargoism," Genet tried to show that the latter was harmful to New York, Pennsylvania, and other places connected with the "vivifying auxiliary of commerce," and was designed to "perpetuate the Presidency in the hands of Virginia and . . . consolidate an order of things highly gratifying to the jealousy which the rapid prosperity of New York and of the other commercial states has raised in the indolent slave holders of that state."[8]

Indeed, that jealousy had proceeded far enough so that some Virginians thought that New York should be divided into two states. George Clinton told his nephew that Jefferson had turned to him at dinner and said, "Mr. Vice President I hear it is proposed to divide your state & make the Genesee Country a separate state." George Clinton said he had heard nothing of it, whereupon Jefferson "seemed surprized & as if he had mentioned what he might have better concealed from me."[9]

Meanwhile, George Clinton appeared to many to be the logical choice as the nation's next chief executive. He was, after all, vice president, as Jefferson had been under Adams, and Adams under Washington. He was a hero of the revolution and a man of unquestioned Republican rectitude, which made him an appealing candidate for those Republicans who felt that the Jefferson administration (under the sway of Madison, the Federalist of 1787–88) had drifted from the course of righteousness into what John Randolph called Madison's "cool and insidious moderation."[10]

But those rock-ribbed Republicans of 1808 already had another candidate—James Monroe, who was also a Virginian. Monroe was John Randolph's candidate. In spite of his Old Dominion roots and affiliation with Jefferson, Monroe had been stung by the rejection of the supposedly ineffectual treaty he and William Pinkney had negotiated with Britain concerning neutral rights and other issues, and was encouraged in his pique by Randolph, who claimed that the real reason Jefferson had sent the treaty back for revision was to keep Monroe out of the country and thus ease Madison's path to the White House. Randolph was willing to put Monroe in the second spot on the ticket if it would achieve the goal of blocking Madison, and the combination of Clinton and Monroe—revolutionary heroes, firm Republicans, with the first office going to a non-Virginian—might have been a potent one. But Madison's support in Congress was too much for either Clinton or Monroe, and he was nominated by a Republican caucus on January 23, although the meeting was boycotted by most of the New York delegation and by those southern members in Randolph's camp.[11]

New York had attempted a last-minute compromise with Madison's supporters to get Clinton on the ticket—DeWitt Clinton, who thus would become a leading contender for the presidency after Madison. The suggestion, Genet wrote, "was treated with contempt by Mr. Madison's friends." The caucus then nominated for vice president George Clinton, who also responded with contempt. He had, understandably, little interest in presiding over the Senate, and he did it poorly. He was disgusted with the impotent foreign policy pursued by Jefferson and Madison, and angry at being excluded from meetings at which diplomacy was discussed. He had had little opportunity to express his opposition to the Embargo within the administration, and his stand on it gave him a foreign-policy argument to supplement the central rationale for his candidacy—that he was not a Virginian. But although Clintonians and others denounced the caucus nomination of Madison, and Genet poured forth reasons to support the vice president, George Clinton merely remained in curmudgeonly isolation in his Washington lodgings, eager to return to New York for the summer. Cheetham and Genet continued their campaign for Clinton throughout the spring and attempted to paint Madison as ineffectual. They revived old accusations against him, and Genet claimed that Madison had accepted the gift of French citizenship while Genet was minister to the United States. Both Clintons announced that Cheetham did not represent their views. But as the year progressed George Clinton's prospects faded and the opposition to Madison, such as it was, coalesced around the Federalist candidate, Charles Cotesworth Pinckney, and his running mate, Rufus King. Clinton did receive six electoral votes from his home state, but Madison easily carried the general election by 122 electoral votes to Pinckney's 47. George Clinton was left in possession of the vice presidency, which he valued little.[12]

George Clinton's six votes from New York had been given at the insistence of DeWitt Clinton, and against the entreaties of Governor Daniel D. Tompkins, who pointed out that the action was futile and would only serve to publicize and exacerbate the split in the Republican ranks. The fissures in New York between Tompkins's supporters and Clinton's would not widen for some time, but now the cracks were there.[13]

MAYOR CLINTON PREPARES

DeWitt Clinton harbored an ambition for the presidency from an early age. Perhaps it was born during New York's brief time as the national capital, but after the 1808 efforts to place him second on a Madison ticket his ambitions moved from yearning to acting, and much of what he did from 1808 onward was calculated to advance his candidacy in 1812. Any successful campaign against a Virginia candidate would have to include some accommodation with the Federalists. Clinton would have no hope of winning a three-way race outright—Madison would take the South, a Federalist would do well in New England, and there would not have been enough votes left to put Clinton in office. He might hope to force the decision into the House of Representatives and win Federalist support there, but Clinton did not have Madison's Washington connections, and the outcome of the Republican caucus in 1808 had shown that Madison could count on his party's support in Congress. There was a precedent for an alliance between the Federalists and the Clintonians. Federalists meeting secretly in New York City in August 1808 had considered supporting George Clinton for president that year (although few thought the vice president would accept such a coalition—he had, after all, been a national leader of anti-Federalism). DeWitt Clinton's hope, as foreshadowed by Genet's work for George Clinton in 1808, was to turn the complaints about too many Virginia presidents into a real issue by emphasizing the issues that divided the nation along sectional lines. As mayor of New York, Clinton might have attacked the Embargo to unite northern states against

Madison, but his erratic response to the Embargo at its inception made this a flawed tactic. His best course would be to develop his ties to leading Federalists and await his opportunities. At the same time, he had to keep his footing in the ever-shifting sands of New York politics.[14]

With Governor Tompkins, he had to be vigilant. Tompkins had been steadfast in his support of Jefferson and the Embargo, and as a reward had been granted significant federal patronage. Clinton, however, remained strong, supported by the patronage he could bestow through the mayoralty and the state Council of Appointment, and shining with the reflected revolutionary glory of his uncle the vice president. His brother-in-law and chief collaborator, Ambrose Spencer, had placed his son John in the sensitive post of governor's secretary. Clinton could suppose he had that flank covered—at least, for a time.[15]

The Federalists, meanwhile, presented problems. Clinton had pleased them with his early criticism of the Embargo, although they saw his hasty retreat from that position as cowardice. At the same time, the devastation the Embargo visited on New York City transformed politics for a time, and the Federalists emerged ready to take power again in the state. As Dixon Ryan Fox noted, and David Hackett Fischer later confirmed, the Federalists had realized that in the new politics of the nineteenth century victory would not come to a party that relied on deference at election time. To survive, the Federalists would have to adopt the methods of their opponents. In New York, a rival to the Tammany Society was created, which wrapped itself in the mantle of the first president by calling itself the Washington Benevolent Society. One of the leading forces behind the society was a young Federalist named Gulian C. Verplanck, the son of a prosperous merchant. Verplanck was born on Wall Street, and every fiber of his heritage joined him to the Federalist cause. But he understood that new measures were needed to revive the party, and though the Washington Society's secret rituals and public rallies were insufficient to turn back the democratic tide, they did help restrain it for a time. In a Fourth of July oration in 1809, Verplanck assailed the Jeffersonians, saying they had "dismantled" the navy and left the nation's commerce "to the mercy of every petty pirate." He also leveled the traditional republican diatribe against "executive corruption and unconstitutional influence."[16]

In April 1809, the Federalists won control of the state legislature for the first time in a decade. Clinton was most unlikely to receive favor from the new majority. In January 1809, he had defended the Embargo in the state senate and condemned the Federalists, saying that they, like Milton's Satan, would rather "reign in Hell, than serve in Heaven." When the new Council of Appointment was chosen in 1810, Clinton was again stripped of his most prestigious and lucrative office.[17]

Clinton had seen the problem coming and had tried to reach a reconciliation with his opponents within the Republican party in the summer of 1809. Part of the price Clinton's Tammany Hall counterparts had demanded was the abandonment of James Cheetham, and the testy editor was quickly jettisoned. The hope of Tammany was that the lucrative state printing contracts that Clinton controlled would then go to the Tammany organ in New York City, the *Public Advertiser*. If the previous decade had shown anything in the state's political life, it was the importance of newspapers. Political meetings were announced in them, and the results of those meetings reported according to the paper's political bias. Gatherings of rivals were reported to be thinly attended, while those of the paper's favorites were invariably "numerous and respectable." Disruption at meetings was seen as free speech if the disrupters were of the paper's faction, and as hooliganism if they were from the opposition. The life-blood of these papers, as of today's, was advertising, and a paper with a lucrative government contract could fill an entire page or more with legal notices of various sorts. DeWitt Clinton may have sympathized with Tammany's desires, but he did not respect them. That fall a new Clintonian organ, the *New York Columbian,* was established, nourished by state money and dedicated to the upward progress of DeWitt Clinton.[18]

Although the Federalists had stripped Clinton of the mayoralty, he remained a state senator and an ally of Governor Tompkins. In 1810, he wrote the document placing Tompkins before the electorate for reelection. The *Columbian* praised Tompkins, printed articles exhorting Irish immigrants to vote, and denounced the Federalists. Yet, as we shall see, Clinton himself was also cooperating with those he had condemned in Miltonic cadences just a short time before. His emergence as a champion of the Erie Canal owed much to Federalists, and particularly to Jonas Platt, who was the Federalist candidate for governor against Tompkins in 1810. The party had not run a candidate since the 1801 race, but resentment of the Embargo gave Federalists hope they could regain the governorship, just as they had taken control of the legislature and installed the Federalist Jacob Radcliff as mayor of New York City. The Republicans in Congress were hardly blind to the unpopularity of the Embargo and in 1809 had replaced it with the Non-Intercourse Act, which allowed American vessels to sail again, although not (legally) to Britain or France. While Tompkins was balanced in his criticism of both British violations of American neutrality and Napoleon's violations of international law, Platt denounced the French and defended the British (going so far as to praise the tepid British apology for the attack on the *Chesapeake*). Platt's sympathy for England allowed the Republicans to trot out all the old accusations of Toryism and tales of British and Indian massacres during the Revolutionary War. Tompkins defeated Platt easily. In 1811, Clinton regained control of the Council of Appointment, returned himself to the lucrative office of mayor, and began to give shape to his candidacy for president.[19]

PRESIDENTIAL TIMBER?

Clinton's candidacy for president seems almost incredible today. He had served briefly as a United States senator, but his principal office, mayor of New York, was appointive, and his other elective offices had been solely in the state legislature. He had no military record, except service as a militia officer in the 1790s, and his vacillation over the Embargo had left him with a blotted record in foreign relations. His prominence was seen as the result of his uncle's nepotism, and his reputation was as a party manager, not a statesman. As we have seen, he would have to carry New England to win the White House, but had condemned the Federalists in ringing terms in 1809, and had carried the denunciations into the 1810 gubernatorial campaign. So why was he a plausible candidate for president?

One reason was the reverse side of the nepotism that formed part of the case against him. At a time when Europe still functioned under the civil and military administration of aristocracies, and when many Americans felt that the Jeffersonian notion of human equality was overstated and had led to a tendency toward mob rule, Clinton's family heritage was an asset. The distinction achieved by his father and his uncle were taken as evidence of what he might achieve. Clinton, moreover, lived in New York, which in 1810 had passed Virginia to become the most populous state. The size and electoral power of New York made a candidate from there particularly attractive as an opponent to Madison (just as it had made—and would continue to make—the state an attractive source of vice presidents for the Virginia Dynasty). And New York's power was strategic, since it lay both geographically and politically in the center of the nation. The remaining Federalist stronghold of New England could hope for a share of national power only if the Middle Atlantic states—particularly New York and Pennsylvania—could be separated from Virginia (both states went for Jefferson twice and had supported Madison in 1808).[20] New York had been the crucial state in the election of 1800 (as it would be again in the other race decided by Congress, that of 1824). To many, it seemed the key to the 1812 race, and DeWitt Clinton was both the leading figure in the state and a willing opponent of Madison.

Other aspects of Clinton's candidacy, however, grew out of his own actions, some of which he had cause to regret. Although his denunciation of the Federalists and his belated embrace of the Embargo made it difficult to appeal to Federalist voters, he had qualities that appealed to them. Unlike his uncle in 1808, he was willing to include the Federalists in his coalition. He had worked closely with Federalist leaders like Platt and Gouverneur Morris on the Erie Canal, and with other Federalist leaders on his cultural and philanthropic activities in New York City. Moreover, the circle of the powerful in the nation was small, and its members were fairly well acquainted. A person of DeWitt Clinton's mayoral achievements, with a reputation as an adroit political tactician who had managed to stay in control of New York State for most of the past decade, would be recognized by his peers as a leading political figure, even though he had not held the sort of offices that would be expected of a presidential candidate today.

In 1811 and 1812 Clinton tried to attract Federalist support while remaining inside the Republican camp. To do so, he took advantage of two offices: the mayoralty, to which he was returned that February, and the lieutenant governorship, which had fallen vacant after the death of John Broome. Clinton needed to be in Albany, because the state legislature still controlled the choice of presidential electors, and state legislative caucuses were a useful means of putting a candidate's name forward and launching a campaign. (According to the rituals of the time, a candidate was required to adopt a guise of lofty indifference to his own advancement, even as he schemed and manipulated to win election. There were, to be sure, politicians who were sincerely indifferent to attaining public office and served only from a sense of duty; DeWitt Clinton was not one of them.) A seat in the state legislature would have been at least as useful as the position of lieutenant governor, but Clinton's hopes for that were blocked by Tammany Hall, which backed the popular Nathan Sanford for the senate seat Clinton had held. Jabez Hammond thinks this assault on Clinton must have been approved in Washington, pointing out that Sanford held a federal appointment worth thirty thousand dollars a year, and was a "prudent" man, and would not have agreed to run without Madison's tacit support. In any event, Clinton's power upstate was greater than in the city, where by now he had made numerous enemies in both his own and the Federalist party; he received the endorsement of the legislative caucus for lieutenant governor and was elected in April 1811. With George Clinton still installed as vice president, and DeWitt Clinton now lieutenant governor, the family was specializing in second place.[21]

But DeWitt Clinton was aiming higher, and on a national stage. And now he would have an opportunity to enlarge his Federalist base by defending Columbia College, whose faculty and administration were predominantly Federalist. Mayor Clinton, in his capacity as the city's chief magistrate sitting in the Court of Sessions, could strike a blow for order by bringing to justice the instigators of the Columbia Commencement Riot of 1811.

Some of Clinton's minutes for cases in the Court of Sessions survive in ledger books at the New-York Historical Society, and they give some context for the treatment of the Columbia rioters. Most of the cases brought before him involved petty crimes and were disposed of quickly. Often, two or three cases of larceny, assault and battery, or perjury were recorded on a single page. Many of the accused were slaves, and they were frequently accused of stealing from their masters. (Slavery would not end in New York State until 1827.) Sentences were often severe. A "Yellow girl" (mulatto) named Fanny got four years in prison for stealing items worth fifteen dollars, and the same sentence was given to a mulatto named Maria Brown for taking a silver watch. One slave, named Lucy, was sentenced to three years in prison for putting ground glass in a pot pie and serving it to her mistress. Clinton was particularly harsh on recidivists, noting in one case that the defendant "is a great villain—suspected to have been guilty of many crimes," and in another that the accused "is an old offender." There were many cases of domestic violence, and wives had a difficult time getting justice from Mayor Clinton, unless fines as low as five cents are seen as retribution. In certain ways, however, Clintonian justice was blind in a good sense. In one case where a white man and a black man were in league, both received the same penalty. Mere suspicion was not sufficient to win a conviction, even when the victim was a member of the elite; a man accused of setting fire to a building belonging to Clinton's friend Robert Fulton was acquitted. Justice was not only blind but at times also deaf: Some cases against slaves were thrown out of court because the only witnesses against them were also slaves, whose testimony was not permitted.[22]

That Clinton saw the Columbia riot case as important is shown by the nearly thirty pages of notes he kept on the trial. That he was more sympathetic to the prosecution is clear from the greater attention he gave to the testimony of the prosecution witnesses than to those for the defense.

The Commencement Riot was in fact little more than a shouting match between aggrieved students and insulted faculty members at the college's graduation exercises held at Trinity Church on August 6, 1811. The grievance arose from the treatment of John B. Stevenson, who, like other graduating students, was to make a brief oration, and had chosen as his subject the duty of an elected representative to obey the wishes of his constituents. Some time before the ceremony, Stevenson had given his text to Peter Wilson, a professor at the college, who found it objectionable and proposed some corrections. Stevenson was an ardent Republican, and he gave the speech he had written, without Wilson's changes; while he was speaking, Wilson approached John M. Mason, the provost, and informed him that the speech lacked the required corrections.[23]

As a result, Stevenson was told he would not receive his degree at the ceremony, "but that if he called the next day, it might be settled." Stevenson was unwilling to accept such a public humiliation and went on stage three times to ask for his degree. Then Hugh Maxwell, a relative of Stevenson's and a Columbia alumnus, took the stage to denounce the faculty's actions; he was followed by Gulian C. Verplanck, who denounced the professors as "oppressive" and urged the audience to cheer Maxwell for his defense of Stevenson. President William Harris was by now so fearful that he fled the stage, believing "he would have been shoved off" the stage had he not left. Witnesses testified that the "tone & manner" of the protesters were "objectionable," and that their goal "was to criminate the professors."[24]

The difficulty for the prosecution was that there really had not been much of a riot. People had shouted, fists had been waved, there had been some jostling, one person had been struck, but that was about all. The lawyers for the defense, including Peter A. Jay, a son of John Jay, pressed their case on this ground. Another eminent defense attorney, David B. Ogden (like Jay a Federalist), added that the charge of unlawful assembly was invalid since the assembly had been convened by the college, not the so-called rioters. Therefore, what ensued could be only an "affray," not a riot, and Ogden cited precedents. Verplanck and Maxwell, speaking in their own defense, argued the same point.[25]

Clinton, however, was both unimpressed and impatient. There was a distinction between the original meeting and "a portion of the meeting that drew off in church for riotous purposes." The crime, he insisted, "commences at Stevenson's ascent of the stage and when two or more concurred. This is the first act of illegal resistance." The actual legal content of the protesters' actions mattered little to Clinton. The fracas had so thoroughly interrupted the exercises that, according to President Harris's sorrowful testimony, "the valedictory was not pronounced nor was the ceremony concluded by prayers." Clinton's condemnation of the defendants was blistering: "We have no hesitation in declaring," he said from the bench, "that the disturbance which took place on the occasion alluded to, is the most disgraceful, the most unprecedented, the most unjustifiable, the most outrageous, that ever came within the knowledge of the court." That such disorder should have taken place in "a house dedicated to the worship of God" left Clinton nearly speechless: "I hardly know how to express my opinion of the character of the transaction."[26]

The jury returned guilty verdicts against all the defendants but one, and Judge

Clinton fined Verplanck and Maxwell two hundred dollars each, with lesser fines for the six others who were found guilty. He then indulged himself in a final outburst. Verplanck was "a graduate of the same university—a counsellor of law—an aspirant after literary fame—and of respectable family," and he should have known better. These words, together with "such unprecedented arrogance in a young man," could well have applied, in earlier days, to DeWitt Clinton himself.[27]

There is much to be said for this trial as evidence of Clinton's effort to set himself right with the Federalist party. Soon after the verdict, Ambrose Spencer was reporting, "You have become extremely popular with the federalists for your charge & sentence on the rioters at the late commencement of Columbia College." But the Federalist party was hardly monolithic; Verplanck himself and the defense attorneys Jay and Ogden were staunch Federalists. Whatever the political effect, there may have been something more immediate behind Clinton's words and actions on this occasion—something more visceral, less calculating, and having little to do with his political ambitions. Columbia was *his* college; he himself had been the first student admitted on its reopening after the revolution; he had identified himself in many ways with its well-being; and he viewed its achievement and promise as among the chief measurements of New York's, and indeed the nation's, cultural future. This disorderly outbreak, then, was more than a matter of law and order. It was a rude challenge not only to his college but to *him*.[28]

THE $6 MILLION BANK

Clinton had burned his bridges to the Livingstons over the Merchants' Bank in 1805. In 1811 and 1812, as he was trying to build bridges to the Federalists, he was trapped in the legislative struggle for a huge new bank, which applied for a charter to begin operations with $6 million in capital under the name of the Bank of America. The name was evocative of the Bank of the United States, which expired in 1811, when a renewal of its twenty-year federal charter was defeated by the casting vote of Vice President Clinton. George Clinton delivered a short speech (which Henry Clay helped him write) explaining his vote and denouncing the bank. The Madison administration, led by Albert Gallatin, the secretary of the treasury, supported the recharter, although there was much Republican opposition. Vice President Clinton's vote irritated Madison's contingent, but it also angered Federalists, who were still champions of (and investors in) the institution.[29]

But out of adversity comes opportunity, and the dissolution of the Bank of the United States left large sums of banking capital looking for a new home. New York, emerging as the nation's commercial and financial center, was a logical site for a major institution, and shareholders of the Bank of the United States sought to incorporate the Bank of America in New York under a state charter. This put DeWitt Clinton in an awkward position. Having fought against the Merchants' Bank in 1805 on the basis of party considerations (another Federalist bank would harm the Republican cause in the state), and having a personal interest in blocking any bank in competition with the Manhattan Company, Clinton opposed the Bank of America. But, eager to win Federalist support in the 1812 election, he was quiet in his opposition, since his political prospects depended on not alienating either side. Ambrose Spencer told Jabez Hammond that Clinton indicated he would vote against the bank if he had to (which would happen only if the vote in the senate was tied), but that, in Hammond's words, "he should, on no account, be drawn into a quarrel with the supporters of that measure." He also proclaimed that the matter was one to be decided according to the views of individual members, and not made a party question.[30]

The picture that emerges from Clinton's surviving correspondence differs at least in shading from Spencer's account. In a series of letters to Henry Remsen, president of the Manhattan Company, Clinton portrayed himself as an unwavering opponent of the bank. "I have done all I can," he wrote in March 1812, "consistent with my official station to prevent an augmentation of banks; and this one I especially deplore as a great Leviathan that will eventually swallow up the small ones." Ten days later, he told Remsen he would welcome the opportunity to block the bank charter himself: "I shall esteem it a great favor if it comes to a casting vote, whereby I may have an opportunity of giving a decided opinion against the augmentation of banking capital."[31]

If these were his views, he was in a tight spot. Not only were the Federalists in favor of the bank; so were many of his own followers. The Bank of America's most tireless advocates in Albany were both prominent Clintonians: Solomon Southwick, editor of the *Albany Register,* and David Thomas, who had been appointed state treasurer in February 1812. But at the same time Ambrose Spencer, who had been Clinton's most effective ally for more than a decade and who was the widower of Clinton's sister Mary and the husband of his sister Catherine, was adamantly opposed. He even founded a newspaper that year, the *Albany Republican,* to counter Southwick's probank articles in the *Register.* (Spencer's opposition to the bank may have owed something to his own financial stake in existing banks in New York and Albany.) Spencer and Clinton parted ways over the bank and remained for some years bitter enemies. It is likely that Spencer's alienation arose as much from a cold assessment of where Clinton's political path was tending as from any outraged sense of fiscal propriety. Spencer may simply have decided that it was time to seek new allies among the friends of Mr. Madison.[32]

It is possible, of course, that Clinton was just telling Remsen what he wanted to hear—that Clinton was working to block the charter of a giant competitor for Remsen's bank. But the vehemence of Clinton's letters seems to indicate that he was expressing his true views. Alas for his troubled conscience, he could not act forthrightly in defense of his beliefs without betraying his own hopes for the presidency. Clinton the republican statesman wished to block the irresponsible expansion of banking capital; Clinton the friend of the Manhattan Company wanted to protect existing banks; Clinton the political manager wanted to keep the issue from dividing his party; and Clinton the candidate wanted to please potential Federalist supporters. Probably the most advantageous course he could have taken was the one he did choose, to oppose the bank quietly while making sure it did not become a test of party loyalty and thus sharpen divisions he needed to blur in his quest for the White House.

His situation was made worse by the intensity of the lobbying efforts for and against the Bank of America. Clinton told Remsen that he had argued strenuously against the charter but "that *no reasoning can convince corruption*—that there is such is suspected by many although I sincerely hope there is none." Both Southwick and Thomas were later indicted for bribery in the matter, and although they were acquitted, one of their agents was convicted and sent to jail. Before the bank question could be resolved in the legislature, Governor Tompkins stepped in. On March 27, he prorogued the legislature until May 21, managing with one bold move both to block the bank and to dismiss the legislature before it had a chance to endorse DeWitt Clinton for president.[33]

The governor's stated reason for doing so was the evidence of corruption concerning the chartering of the bank. But the more timely reason may have been a desire to serve Madison by delaying any legislative endorsement of Clinton for president. (The bank's advocates, too, had blocked moves for a nominating caucus in New York, hoping to use the issue as a bargaining chip.) The power of prorogation was a remnant of the colonial era, when royal governors used it to put off uppity provincial assemblies. Although it had been retained in the state constitution of 1777, its use was loudly denounced as a vestige of despotic power. But denunciation could not alter existing law, and on May 18, three days before the New York legislature came back into session, Madison received the endorsement of the Republican caucus in Washington. Eleven days later, Clinton received the backing of the New York legislative caucus, and his candidacy became, in a sense, official.[34]

CANDIDATE CLINTON

The choice of Clinton by the Republicans of the New York legislature was nearly unanimous, but not easy. Opposing a sitting president of one's own party is not done lightly. Madison had the backing of the congressional caucus, and he had already been endorsed by Republican caucuses in Virginia and Pennsylvania. In the midst of the deliberations in Albany, Pierre Van Cortlandt, Jr., and other congressmen arrived from Washington to urge Clinton's nomination. Van Cortlandt's father had been lieutenant governor many times under George Clinton, and the son had attended Vice President Clinton during his last days—he died on April 20—and paid his medical bills. Van Cortlandt and his associates brought a letter from Gideon Granger, the postmaster general, advocating Clinton's nomination in strong terms. Granger said that few in Congress, particularly among those from the North, really wanted Madison to remain president. And, while many also opposed war with Britain, such a war appeared likely, and it would be better, if war came, to have an able executive like Clinton than the cautious and indecisive Madison.[35]

Ninety of ninety-five Republicans in the state legislature voted to nominate Clinton, but there was significant opposition to a Clinton candidacy within New York, and uncertain chances outside. In the state, of course, the Martling Men, Tompkins,

Spencer, the Livingstons-Lewisites, and various others whom Clinton had offended or not sufficiently courted supported Madison. In the nation, Clinton's hopes depended on carrying New England and then gaining enough support in the states between New York and North Carolina to offset Madison's strength in the South and the West. When, on June 19, the United States declared war on Great Britain, Clinton's position was made additionally difficult. How could he oppose a president in wartime without appearing unpatriotic? The Alien and Sedition Acts had shown the tenuousness of political opposition to an administration when war loomed in a country that still had not developed a strong concept of "legitimate opposition," and Jefferson had shown a similar confusion about the difference between dissent and treason during the Embargo. Yet the arrival of hostilities in 1812 also gave the country some evidence of Madison's shortcomings as a war leader, and General William Hull's failure to defend Detroit and his surrender on August 19 provided a discouraging example of military blundering.[36]

This was a subject a candidate had to treat gently or risk seeming disloyal. But there were other themes Clinton's supporters could sound. Articles in the *New York Columbian* emphasized that the mayor had a mind "enlightened by extensive erudition" while being "committed to no particular system, either in diplomacy or administration." This was a rather blatant way of trying to be all things to all voters. (And the emphasis on Clinton's "Herculean mind" might have worked better had his opponent not been James Madison, whose intellect may have been less broad than Clinton's but was far deeper.) Another theme was the public disorder occasioned by the war. The *Columbian* reported regularly on attacks on Federalists around the nation, in particular the bloody assault in Baltimore at the end of July that left one Federalist dead and another, "Lighthorse Harry" Lee, the Revolutionary War general and father of Robert E. Lee, crippled for the short remainder of his life. When some rioters attempted to pull down the home of a Federalist on Jones Street in June, the *Columbian* praised the "characteristic vigilance and promptitude of the mayor" in suppressing the disorder and characterized the one-year jail terms Clinton imposed as the judge in the case as "A LESSON FOR RIOTERS."[37]

The key to Clinton's chances, however, would have to be found less in outside events than in his own ability to form a coalition strong enough to profit from whatever opportunities arose. And the coalition had to have solid support from the Federalists. In spite of his growing association with Federalists in New York, and his pro-development policies with regard to canals and other improvements, Clinton remained an unlikely ally. He was the nephew and protégé of the most prominent anti-Federalist of 1787–78; he had tormented and humiliated John Jay in 1801 over the Council of Appointment, and the former governor and chief justice was still held by Federalists in reverent esteem. Clinton had worked hard to prostrate their party in his state, and only two years earlier, when Federalists had taken control of the Council of Appointment, he had been thrown out of office. Nor could Federalists easily forget his likening them to Milton's Satan. Clinton's verbal barbs remained under his victims' skins for years, and so often did he part ways with former allies that he could scarcely enter a public room in New York or Albany without seeing someone he had offended. Yet, for all this, Clinton ruled in New York, and the Federalists knew they had no hope nationally without carrying the state.

If the Federalists could find a candidate who might appeal to New England and also challenge Madison in Virginia and North Carolina, there was still the possibility of winning. There was one Federalist of national stature who might do that—Chief Justice John Marshall. When he was approached, he seemed to endorse the idea of a fusion candidacy like Clinton's. On the other hand, as chief justice, Marshall was the firmest bulwark of Federalism in the national government, and it would be a risk to jeopardize that influence for an uncertain shot at the presidency. What to do?

Late in July, William Coleman, editor of the *New York Evening Post,* approached Rufus King about the desire of local Federalists for a peace meeting and raised the issue of Federalist support for Clinton. They discussed the matter of a Marshall candidacy, with either Clinton or King as vice president; the Federalists, it seems, were pondering the possibility of adopting the Jeffersonian strategy of combining Virginia and New York on a national ticket. Whatever the risks to Marshall's position on the court, such a move had the additional liability of perpetuating Virginia's hold on the White House—and thus squandering one of the clearest and easiest issues that Madison's opposition could use. Not only New York but sixteen other states might well feel slighted by Virginia's continued domination. Four days later, John M. Mason, the Columbia provost who had played a central role in the Commencement Riot the year before, came to see King and reported that Clinton would like to "confer with any reputable man of the fed. party in order to effect the Union of the State of NYK, &c."[38]

King told Mason he would have to confer with other Federalist leaders, and on August 3 he met with John Jay, General Matthew Clarkson, and Gouverneur Morris at Morris's family estate, Morrisania (in what is now the southwest Bronx). They drafted a statement of principles for Clinton to endorse, and on the following day (while Clinton was attending Columbia's 1812 commencement, doubtless eager to remind all present of his role in punishing those who had disrupted the ceremony a year earlier) other Federalists came to review the document; Clinton was invited to meet with them on the fifth. He came in the afternoon after presiding in Mayor's Court. The Federalists were finishing their lunch, and King peevishly noted that Clinton joined them at table even though he had already eaten. Clinton agreed to the substance of the Federalist requirements, but wanted the contemplated peace meeting postponed for some weeks to allow antiwar sentiment to build. He also urged that their cooperation be kept quiet for the time, being still unsure of how to use this Federalist support without alienating Republicans. King disliked the entire plan. He saw Clinton as an unreliable ally, and questioned whether a Republican who was now opposed by many of the leading figures of his own party in his own state— Tompkins, Armstrong, and Ambrose Spencer among them—would be much help to the Federalists.[39]

During the rest of August, as General Hull lost Detroit and the national government's lack of preparation for the war became increasingly evident, Clinton's campaign remained sluggish. His supporters published an "Address to the People of the United States" on August 17 that was the closest approach they made to a platform. The first part of it denounced the caucus nomination of Madison, diverting attention from questions about the legitimacy of Clinton's nomination by the Republican caucus of his own state legislature. The argument was that the Constitution vested the choice of a president not in Congress but in the states through the Electoral College; thus the initiative to nominate came more properly from the states than from a caucus in the national legislature; that a suitable prominence should be accorded to leading state figures; and that the principle of rotation among the states ought to have due weight in the outcome. The not-very-subtle implication was, among other things, that Virginia had already had more than its share of turns.[40]

The address criticized both Madison's preparation for the war and his conduct of it. With an exposed northern frontier, seaports unfortified, the Great Lakes without a naval force, and land forces hopelessly underequipped, destruction threatened. True, they would not wish to carry this line too far: James Madison, the patriot, had served his country long and honorably. (Besides, he was a Republican—though it might have been just as awkward if he had been a Federalist, in view of the support the Clintonians were reaching for.) He deserved his country's gratitude. But not— regrettably—to the point of deserving another term in office. It was time, suggested the New York "Committee of Correspondence" that signed the address, to place the nation's destiny in younger and stronger hands. DeWitt Clinton, from both experience and position, was perfectly situated to assess the coming danger. He had looked out all too many times over his city's inadequately protected harbor, and he did not need to be told that his state had a more extended and vulnerable frontier than any of the others. How would he act? (This, too, was awkward: Republicans wanted a stronger prosecution of the war; Federalists, very decidedly, wanted peace.) He would display "vigor in war, and a determined character in the relations of peace."[41]

No event discloses more cruelly the central flaw of Clinton's strategy than the secret meeting of Federalists in New York City on September 15–17, 1812. Their secrecy, as Samuel Eliot Morison put it, "shielded the deliberations from vulgar scrutiny" of voters from whom "neither authority nor advice was asked." Federalists debated whom to support against Madison, and what form their support should take. Rufus King noted in his diary that it was judged unwise to nominate Federalist candidates, but that many Federalists, most emphatically King himself, were unwilling to embrace Clinton. The Massachusetts Federalist Harrison Gray Otis, on the other hand, felt that the crucial thing was to oust Madison, and that Clinton had the best chance of doing so. But sufficient opposition existed that on the third day, as King recorded, the best the convention could agree on was to vote to "support such candidates for P. & V.P. as would be likely to pursue a diff. course of measures from that of the now Presidt." When King in disgust proposed to amend this equivocation to "express what it means, namely to support Mr. D. Clinton," his suggestion was rejected on the ground that such an endorsement was "likely to prove injurious to Mr. C." As it did. News of the conclave leaked out and was used without mercy against Clinton in the key state of Pennsylvania.[42]

If the meeting was not an unqualified success, it nevertheless helped establish an important tradition in American politics—the national nominating convention. Caucus nominations were becoming unpopular (or so Clinton's supporters claimed), and the Federalist meeting demonstrated a new way in which a party could select a candidate. Among the effects of the convention system was a lessening of the control over the political process then exercised by Congress and the state legislatures, and a broadening of representation within parties by providing a way that districts in which the opposition party was dominant could still influence the selection of candidates for national and statewide office.

Madison, as was thought seemly, took almost no role in securing his reelection. Aside from letters to the New Jersey convention and the South Carolina legislature, his participation was minimal, while the presentation of his case was left to the Republican press and to his supporters in the several states. Madison's long record of service and his clear status as Jefferson's political heir were the main strengths of his campaign.

Different states had different electoral rules. Some chose electors by popular vote; in others the legislature decided; some gave all the state's votes to the winner, others divided them. The choice of running mates was shaped by the goal of swaying important states. Madison's partner on the ticket was Elbridge Gerry of Massachusetts, whose age, sixty-seven, made him an unlikely presidential candidate four years on. Massachusetts, with twenty-two electoral votes, trailed only New York (with twenty-nine) and Virginia and Pennsylvania (with twenty-five each) in total representation. Republican candidates had grown stronger in Massachusetts since the turn of the century, and Gerry had won election as governor in 1811, losing reelection only narrowly in 1812 as war fever rose and opposition to administration policies increased. If Madison could take Massachusetts, Clinton's chances would be slim.[43]

The crucial state for Clinton was Pennsylvania. On August 26 a Clintonian meeting named Jared Ingersoll, the state attorney general and a Federalist, to be Clinton's running mate. Since the war had more support in Pennsylvania than in states to the north and east, Clintonian propaganda made much of military mismanagement and Hull's defeat, and dwelled on caucus nominations and the merits of rotation in office. Madison's defenders maintained that minimal preparation for war was natural in a republic, and that the alternative was a standing army and the loss of individual and states' rights. The military misfortunes gave the Clintonians hope that they could bring Pennsylvania in, but in the end the state's predominantly Republican electorate went strongly for Madison and provided the critical margin. Madison won 128 electoral votes to Clinton's 89. It was "the most sectionally oriented presidential election prior to 1860," according to Norman Risjord; in the part of the nation northeast of the Delaware River only Vermont's electors supported the president; and Clinton's only support to the south came in Maryland and Delaware. Madison swept the western states.[44]

DeWitt Clinton's candidacy for president was in many ways like George Clinton's anti-Federalist crusade a quarter-century earlier—the reasons for supporting him were too different, and his adherents were too disparate in their aims to coexist.

Some wanted peace, others a more vigorous war effort; some called for a more active national government, while others felt that Madison was violating state sovereignty; some wanted a non-Virginian as president, though others felt simply that Madison was not up to it. In all logic, the shaky state of the Madison administration ought to have inspired the exertions and given grounds for the success of any determined opposition candidate. But not a candidate with the liabilities DeWitt Clinton staggered under. His contortions to juggle them, and to make them balance, evoked the contempt of Henry Adams, who called this the most discreditable campaign for president in American history.

The election of 1812 was nonetheless an important one in the development of American party politics. Richard McCormick has listed its most notable features: "It was the first wartime election. It was the first to have a major state-sponsored candidate in the person of Clinton. It occasioned the first public statements by a candidate, bland though Madison's letters were. It involved the first attempt at the formation of a fusion party—the Peace party. It produced a rudimentary form of party platform, represented by the 'Address' of the New York Clintonians." But "most of all, it exemplified the perils of the Virginia game."[45]

DECLINE AND FALL

Clinton had entered the campaign convinced of his superiority to Madison, and he could not have been unaware of the difficulties his candidacy would face. But the answer to how he would have governed, after election by the support of incompatible factions, seems to have escaped him. He had now severed his ties with the man who had been his closest political associate for a decade, Ambrose Spencer, and his ambition had deepened his differences with Daniel D. Tompkins, who had refused the role of puppet marked out for him in 1807 and had emerged as the most popular politician in the state. Clinton's flirtation with the Federalists, undertaken in secret but widely known, further cemented his reputation as an unprincipled seeker of power, and disillusioned those few charitable Republicans who had accepted his account of the attempted reconciliation with the Burrites six years earlier. His achievements as mayor, his personal and family reputation, and his talents at political management assured him a continuing place in the state's public life. But what that role would be was now very much in question.

The fractured condition of the Republican party in the state had given the Federalists control of the assembly in the April 1812 elections, and when the legislature met in Albany the following January a Federalist Council of Appointment was elected. The last time the Federalists had controlled the council, in 1810, Clinton had been ejected from the mayor's office. By 1813 the case was somewhat altered. Although the Federalist leader Peter Radcliff wanted to return his brother Jacob to the office he had held in 1810–11, Jonas Platt and other Federalists felt that it would ill become them to remove from the mayoralty for party reasons the man they had supported for president. Many of them admired his energetic efforts to improve the city's defenses in wartime and gain financial assistance for it from Albany and Washington. Clinton's appointment as mayor was renewed.[46]

But his chances to remain in charge of the Republican party in the state had dropped to zero. He had broken with the party's national leader and had lost, in the process alienating most of the party's leading figures. In 1813 his ablest remaining ally, Martin Van Buren, would abandon him as well.

And events in New York continued to drive him farther into the political wilderness. On March 4, 1813, the term of United States senator John Smith expired (this was the man to whom both Clinton and Morgan Lewis had poured out their denunciations of each other), and the Republicans nominated James W. Wilkin, a state senator who had presided at the caucus at which Clinton received New York's nomination for president. Although the Federalists controlled the assembly, the New York legislature elected United States senators by a joint ballot of both houses; the Republican majority in the state senate was large, so Wilkin ought to have won, but the victory went narrowly to the Federalist candidate, Rufus King. Cries of "bargain and corruption" rang out, but in the wrong direction. Clinton, it was charged, had repaid the Federalists for their support of him the year before. Yet it hardly seems likely that Rufus King—who had steadfastly opposed Clinton in 1812, whose "knees trembled under him" at the Federalist convention when he denounced Clinton's nomination, who had declared that substituting Clinton for Madison would only put a "Borgia" in Madison's place—would receive Clinton's endorsement. It seems to have been the Bank of America's influence, not Clinton's, that secured King's election. According to Hammond, when the Federalists agreed to support the bank in 1812 they were promised that the bank's agents would see that a Federalist replaced Smith in 1813. And, indeed, a letter to Hammond from James W. Wilkin in 1817 stated Wilkin's own belief that his defeat in 1813 was caused by the bank's adherents.[47]

From 1813 until the conclusion of the war, in 1815, Clinton as mayor directed his energy toward meeting the British threat. In 1812, Clinton had requested an army commission based on his militia service, and the Council of Appointment granted him one at the rank of major general. But when he sought an active command, Governor Tompkins both ignored the request and tried to keep it quiet. Neither his purposes nor Madison's would be served by having Clinton out there as a military hero. Tompkins was less kind to Stephen Van Rensselaer, the patroon, who in 1812 was expected to be Tompkins's opponent for governor the next year. Tompkins appointed the patroon to command the state's troops at the outset of the war, when preparation was so poor that Napoleon himself would have been hard put to organize a successful march, let alone fight a battle. Van Rensselaer tried to lead his men in an invasion of Canada, but as was characteristic of militia troops from colonial times forward, most of them refused to cross the border because their stated mission was the defense of the state of New York. Those who did follow Van Rensselaer were routed. Conceivably Tompkins might have made the appointment with such an outcome in view.[48]

The gubernatorial election of 1813 would pit Tompkins against Van Rensselaer, but the second place on the Republican ticket went to John Taylor over Clinton, by a margin of two to one. Ambrose Spencer was particularly adamant about denying

Clinton the office of lieutenant governor. During the campaign a number of Clinton's Republican friends published a letter denouncing Tompkins and Taylor as tools of the Madison administration and urging support for the Federalist ticket. But Tompkins's popularity and Van Rensselaer's military fiasco were enough to give the election to the Republicans, who also took three of the four senatorial districts. The Federalists, however, managed to retain control of the assembly. In the course of the campaign, the efforts of Solomon Southwick to defeat Tompkins made it evident that a new Republican paper was needed in the state capital, and the *Albany Argus,* destined to be the voice of opposition to Clinton for the next fifteen years, was founded, under the editorship of Jesse Buel.[49]

When the Council of Appointment met early in 1814, it remained under the control of the Federalists and the Clintonians, but their grip on power was nearing its end. As 1814 moved forward, hatred of the British displaced disgust over the management of the war. American naval victories had dampened criticism of the administration, and Governor Tompkins's efforts to aid the national effort had increased his popularity and that of his adherents. Republicans won a commanding majority in the April 1814 state elections. The Hartford Convention, held in the autumn to express the dissatisfaction of the New England states with the union (and containing the latent possibility of secession), brought the very patriotism of the Federalists into question, and after Andrew Jackson's astonishing victory at New Orleans in January 1815, the Federalist party was alive only by galvanic action. The life force was spent, and in another decade the party would be defunct, even in New England. For DeWitt Clinton, the April 1814 elections might have been sufficient to seal his doom, but the subsequent harrowing of the Federalists seemed to make it final. When the new Council of Appointment met, Clinton's removal was only a matter of time. In March 1815, the blow fell, and for the first time since 1797 DeWitt was without public office, except for one unsalaried post. It says something for his untiring resourcefulness that he was able to make of that single position the foundation for a political revival that would make him once again the dominant political power in New York State. That one remaining position was as a member of the state Canal Commission.

Eight

o   o   o

LAUNCHING THE CANAL

A FAVORITE THEME OF historians is the way the actions of individuals and of nations have unintended consequences. But in the case of the Erie Canal, and DeWitt Clinton's promotion of the project, the story is largely one of intended consequences. The backers of the canal saw an opportunity for New York to lead the way in the expansion of the American economy, and they took advantage of it. DeWitt Clinton saw a chance to repair his political fortunes, and he seized it.

The meeting called in New York City at the end of 1815 to rally support for the canal plan initiated the final phase of the battle, and by writing a memorial to the state legislature expressing the sense of that meeting, Clinton made the cause his own. But the history of the canal long predates that occasion, and DeWitt Clinton was not the first champion of a waterway from the Hudson to the Great Lakes, although he was the most successful.

The route had been first exploited by the Iroquois, who settled in the Mohawk Valley and traded along the river. With the coming of European settlers, the river helped traders carry furs and other commodities down to the trading post at Fort Orange (Albany) and the port at New Amsterdam, as well as to bring trade goods back upriver.

The first public document to discuss improving the route was written in 1724 by Cadwallader Colden, who was then the surveyor general of New York and would later become a lieutenant governor of the province. By 1724 the Netherlands had long since lost her North American colonies, and the great rivalry between British and French interests in North America was in the middle of the "Half-Century of Conflict" chronicled by Francis Parkman. Colden's memorial to Governor William Burnet of New York discussed ways by which the British could gain a larger share of the fur trade and curtail the ambitions of the French. Colden enumerated the disadvantages of the St. Lawrence route to the sea, noting that even though the river was "in many places very wide," the navigable part was "at the same time narrow and crooked," with a strong current against anyone trying to go inland, and a hazardous bay waiting at the end for those heading toward the sea.[1]

By now, Colden continued, the route from the Hudson to the Mohawk was already well worn. "From Albany the Indian traders commonly carry their goods sixteen miles over land, to the Mohawk River at Schenectady," he wrote, and from there "they carry them in canoes up the Mohawk River, to the carrying place between the Mohawk River and the river which runs into the Oneida Lake. . . . From thence they go with the current down the Onondaga [Oswego] River to Lake Ontario." This route became an early favorite for the proposed canal, because it was the easiest and shortest river route from the Hudson to the Great Lakes. But there were the further advantages to New York of the river that "comes from the country of the Senecas [the Seneca River], and falls into the Onondaga [Oswego/Oneida] River, by which we have an easy carriage into that country, without going near Lake Ontario. The head of this river goes near to Lake Erie, and probably may give a very near passage into that Lake, much more advantageous than the way the French are obliged to take by the great fall of Niagara."[2]

Just 101 years after Colden wrote this, the Erie Canal opened along a very similar route. But it was as a canal, not as a series of interconnecting rivers.

As the eighteenth century progressed and both French and British colonization moved farther inland, the Mohawk Valley route between Albany and Lake Ontario gained increasing importance in time of war. In King William's War (1689–97) and Queen Anne's War (1702–13), the fighting was concentrated near the coasts, but following the latter both powers began fortifying positions along Lake Ontario, and during the French and Indian War (1754–63) two major British expeditions were directed up the Mohawk Valley toward French positions in Canada. The military importance of this route continued to increase, and the military advantages of a canal—particularly of one that avoided Lake Ontario—became a significant part of the case for construction of such a canal.[3]

One military man who saw at first hand the potential of the route was George Washington, who in 1783 followed the course of the Mohawk west to Wood Creek, and reported to the Marquis of Chastellux that he was struck by "the goodness of that Providence which has dealt his favours to us with so profuse a hand. Would to God we may have the wisdom enough to improve them." In fact, Washington's interest in revising the Articles of Confederation grew in part from the obstacles to internal improvements which he saw arising from that vexed charter.[4]

Two years later, Christopher Colles, an Irish engineer who had undertaken improvements to navigation on the Shannon and had come to America to pursue his profession, stressed both the economic and the military benefits of the canal, pointing to its advantages for the country's internal trade, and to how "in time of war, provisions and military stores may be moved with facility in sufficient quantity to answer any emergency."[5]

PUBLIC WEAL, PRIVATE ENTERPRISE

The real beginning of the Erie Canal came in 1792 with the incorporation, by the New York State legislature, of the Western and Northern Inland Lock Navigation companies, which were charged respectively with creating a usable waterway west from Albany to Lake Ontario and one north between the Hudson and Lake Champlain. The inspiration for these enterprises came from George Washington and Gouverneur Morris, but they took legal form and effect because of the efforts of two other men, Elkanah Watson and Philip Schuyler. Watson, who would later achieve modest fame as the father of the county fair, took up the cause of canals after a visit with Washington at Mount Vernon soon after Washington's trip through New York in 1783. Schuyler was inspired by Morris's vision of a canal system and its potential—a vision Morris had described to Schuyler during the long Saratoga campaign of 1777. Morgan Lewis happened to be present the evening Morris broached the subject with Schuyler, and his memory of the discussion was still vivid fifty years later. He recalled Morris "describing in the most animated and glowing terms, the rapid march of the useful arts through our country, when once freed from a foreign yoke," and outlining the ease with which the country's rivers "might be made to communicate." Then, Lewis went on, Morris "announced in language highly poetic, and to which I cannot do justice, that at no very distant day, the waters of the great inland seas, would, by the aid of man, break through their barriers and mingle with those of the Hudson."[6]

Schuyler's interest in canals had actually been awakened some years before. On a visit to England in 1761 he had seen the pioneering canals designed and built by James Brindley (1716–72), and had come away much impressed. Schuyler subsequently joined forces with Elkanah Watson, who was writing articles publicizing his own ideas, and brought the case for a canal before the legislature, of which he was an influential Federalist member.[7]

The leading role of the Federalist Schuyler provoked DeWitt Clinton's first recorded statement on the canal. Schuyler had appointed himself the chief engineer of the Western Inland Lock Navigation Company, a position for which his sole qualification was the trip he had taken to England thirty years before. Clinton blasted Schuyler in the *New York Journal and Patriotic Register* as a "mechanic empiric" who was "wasting the property of the stockholders." Clinton's interest was not exclusively political; he himself was one of those stockholders. (He owned one share.)[8]

Actually Clinton's interest in canals, if his early biographers may be trusted, went back to his days as a student at Columbia College. David Hosack, who had become a friend of Clinton's when they were students together in the 1780s, pointed to the role of Professor John Kemp, a Scottish émigré who taught mathematics and who favored his students with "many lectures" on the subject of canals and locks. James Renwick's 1840 biography of Clinton likewise cited Kemp and his insistence on "the necessity of abandoning all attempts to improve the navigation of small rivers . . . [and] illustrating his position by the celebrated saying of Bradley [Brindley], that such streams 'were intended by the Almighty for feeding canals.'"[9]

Clinton also had a family tradition in hydraulic engineering to draw on. His father's most notable exploit as a Revolutionary War general had come when he was in command at Lake Otsego in 1779. With more than two hundred bateaux full of supplies afloat on the lake (which was not yet the site of Cooperstown), General Clinton was supposed to proceed down the Susquehanna to join the ill-supplied troops under Major General John Sullivan for a punitive expedition against Britain's Indian allies in western New York. To provide sufficient water in the stream to float his vessels, James Clinton dammed the outlet of the lake into the Susquehanna and raised the lake's level; then when the word came from Sullivan to advance, he ordered the dam burst and floated his bateaux downriver. A plaque on the bridge across the Susquehanna in Cooperstown commemorates this achievement, and DeWitt Clinton must have heard the story more than once in his youth.[10]

Yet whatever general interest Clinton may have taken in the subject, canal navigation does not seem to have been a central concern during his early career. It was only when the efforts of the Western Inland Lock Navigation Company proved inadequate to their object that Clinton emerged as a champion of the canal.

The Western company, launched in 1792, had been given generous support by the state. A grant of $12,500 received with its charter supplemented the money raised by selling shares and the tolls collected as improvements were completed. In 1795 the state purchased 200 shares at fifty dollars a share, making it the company's largest single stockholder. The following year the company received a state loan for $37,500. But the shareholders were obliged to make further contributions as their original purchases of shares proved inadequate to provide the capital needed. By 1801 they had endured nine further assessments, and of the 743 shares sold between 1792 and 1795, 240 were later forfeited. The company's support was bipartisan. When the charter was issued, Governor George Clinton urged that the state legislature give the company "every fostering aid and patronage," because the state would so clearly benefit in having it succeed.[11]

Little progress was made in canal construction during the first decade of the new century. Although the Western company was by then working to improve navigation as far west as Seneca Lake, it proved unable to solve the problem of getting around Cohoes Falls, between Albany and Schenectady. Nor could it manage to effect improvements west of Lake Oneida toward Lake Ontario, and in 1808 it relinquished its right to do so. Private enterprise, even when subsidized by the state, was unequal to the task. But who then could undertake it?[12]

Perhaps the answer lay in Washington. President Jefferson indicated somewhat vaguely in 1805 that some of the nation's growing revenues might be devoted to internal improvements, though only in peacetime, and after the national debt was retired and a constitutional amendment could be passed making such expenditures legal. Three years later Albert Gallatin gave more positive form to these thoughts in his famous *Report of the Secretary of the Treasury on the Subject of Roads and Canals*. New Yorkers in particular could take heart from Gallatin's reference to the Mohawk Valley-Lake Ontario route as a prime choice for a canal.[13]

Newly encouraged, in April 1808 the New York legislature passed a bill introduced by the Federalist members Joshua Forman and Benjamin Wright, appropriating six hundred dollars for a survey of possible canal routes. Another reason for this revival of legislative interest was the propaganda efforts of Jesse Hawley. Hawley was a merchant in Geneva, New York, who had done business in freight forwarding but without much interest in public affairs or much luck in his own. At some point an inspiration struck him. A canal! Many years later Hawley described how he had taken up the canal's cause: "A reverse in my business landed me on the gaol limits of Ontario, in Canandaigua, in August, 1807. Fully persuaded of the practicability of such canal; and having, thus far, lived to but little purpose, I thought I might render myself useful to society by giving publicity to the suggestion." Hawley, as "Hercules," thereupon went to work. In a series of fourteen articles in the *Genesee Messenger* that fall he outlined the tremendous benefits of a canal to the state and the nation. Some of them, such as getting at the state's virgin forests to burn them off and then selling the potash all over the world, may have been overenthusiastic. But he also predicted that the "trade of almost all the lakes in North America . . . would centre at New-York" and that "in a century [that] island would be covered with the buildings and population of its city." Hawley's most important point concerned the canal's location. He advocated routing the canal all the way to Lake Erie rather than taking the shorter Ontario route that had been contemplated by the Western company, by Gallatin, and by most other enthusiasts. Largely as the result of Hawley's urging, the state's six-hundred-dollar survey was specifically required to examine both routes, and the state surveyor, Simeon DeWitt (Clinton's cousin), turned to Joseph Ellicott, a Batavia resident who was the Holland Land Company's agent in the area, for information on the western route.[14]

The Holland Land Company held most of the land in New York west of the Genesee River, land that would increase dramatically in value if a canal was built. Joseph Ellicott understood this, and his reply to Simeon DeWitt stressed the advantages of the inland route over one to Lake Ontario. He also proposed a route across the Holland company's holdings. DeWitt thereupon hired James Geddes to undertake the survey, and Geddes reported with joy that the Erie route was indeed practicable, although he later admitted he did not expect to see it materialize in his lifetime. (Ellicott's influence had been felt even earlier by Hawley, whose own convictions regarding the Erie route were based on earlier surveys undertaken at Ellicott's direction for the Holland Land Company.)[15]

Jefferson's statements in favor of improvements and Gallatin's subsequent report had one immediate effect in New York: the disappearance of all further thought of a canal built through private efforts. By 1810, the Western Inland Lock Navigation Company was again coming to the legislature for funds. On February 21, 1810, the company reported that although its work had greatly benefited the state, "a debt yet remains against the company of ten thousand dollars," and the state was now asked to "relinquish . . . all dividends that may be due on the shares held by the state, and further to relieve the stockholders in such manner as the legislature in their wisdom may deem just and reasonable." Without such relief western New York's trade would inevitably flow to Canada and down the St. Lawrence. The legislature's response was fated to bring a train of momentous consequences, the least of which was the Western company's demise, and these consequences would reach far into the future.[16]

The legislature's immediate action was to appoint a commission to make a journey to examine the route in detail and then report its findings. Jonas Platt, the Federalist senator and gubernatorial candidate, had been appealed to on the company's behalf by its treasurer, Thomas Eddy, but Platt was now absorbed with a grander plan for a canal, like that proposed by Hawley, between the Hudson and Lake Erie. "I also expressed to him," Platt later wrote, "my decided conviction, that no private corporation was adequate to, or ought to be entrusted with, the power and control over such an important object." Platt knew that such an important object would need bipartisan support to succeed, and he thought the enlistment of DeWitt Clinton would be "of primary importance" to it. Including Clinton on the commission would guarantee its not being perceived as an exclusively Federalist measure. Clinton assented, and on March 13, 1810, Platt introduced a motion in the senate for the appointment of a decidedly bipartisan Canal Commission: Gouverneur Morris, Stephen Van Rensselaer, William North, and Thomas Eddy were Federalists; DeWitt Clinton and Simeon DeWitt were Republicans; and Peter B. Porter, though also a Republican, was an anti-Clintonian "Martling Man."[17]

The composition of the commission reflected the Federalists' success in the spring elections in 1809, when disaffection with the Embargo helped to give them control of the assembly and the Council of Appointment. Of the three Republicans, Simeon DeWitt, who would hold his office as surveyor general under various political parties for more than fifty years, was scarcely partisan. DeWitt Clinton's cultural and philanthropic interests had allied him closely with many leading Federalists, and as mayor of New York he had to be concerned both with the effects of the Embargo and with the future well-being of the port. Peter Porter, though allied with Tammany, was a major landowner and businessman in western New York, and his own economic and political future was to be tied up with the canal. An elite tone in the commission appeared with such aristocratic figures as Morris and Van Rensselaer, the patroon of Renssalaerswyck and the state's largest individual landowner.[18]

CLINTON'S CANAL JOURNAL, 1810

For the biographer of DeWitt Clinton the most delightful relic of this 1810 commission's work is the journal that Clinton kept of the journey. It shows Clinton's continuing fascination with a range of subjects that competed for his attention throughout his career. His comments range from observations of local flora and fauna to analyses of the local political scene, and from speculations on the probable success of new industries and businesses that were springing up in the state to hypotheses on the land's Indian past. There are even glimpses of a lurking sense of humor, scarcely evident in the balance of his papers.

Much of the journal is concerned with the daily tribulations of travel, including glimpses of what the gentlemen commissioners expected in the way of deference in their progress, and what they actually got from those they encountered. Clinton left New York City with Thomas Eddy on June 30 to meet the other commissioners in Albany on July 2. Accompanying the two commissioners were Eddy's son, John Hartshorne Eddy, and Samuel and Walter Osgood, the son and the nephew of Clinton's stepfather-in-law. John Eddy kept a diary of the trip as well, providing both corroboration for many of Clinton's observations and occasional contrasts to Clinton's perceptions.[19]

Clinton, who had just been ousted for the second time as mayor of New York, almost missed his boat. "A servant by the name of Thomas Smyth whom I had engaged to attend me, and to whom I had paid a month's wages in advance, disappointed me," he wrote, "and in waiting for him I had nearly lost my passage."[20]

This sort of disappointment followed the commissioners throughout their journey. Clinton recorded his distaste at the Fourth of July celebrations in Schenectady, which were marred by the presence of "crowds of drunken, quarrelsome people." The town itself gave him little pleasure: "Imagine yourself in a large country village, without any particular acquaintance, and destitute of books, and you will appreciate our situation." A few days later, as their boat was being poled along the Mohawk, their appearance seemed to displease some agricultural laborers, one of whom threw a pitchfork at them, nearly hitting a member of the crew. At that, the crew made for shore, alighted, and chased the farmhands, who, fleeing, left their tools behind. The "enraged boatmen," Clinton noted, "took their revenge in breaking them."[21]

In this incident the passengers and crew were as one, but the relations between them soon deteriorated. On July 21 Clinton recorded that the crew "evinced a mutinous spirit yesterday, and threatened to leave us, complaining that they were pushed too hard. On being treated with proper spirit, they took wisdom for their counsellor, and behaved well to-day." But two days later at Seneca Falls they were dismissed, and a new crew was engaged for the journey to Geneva. This one drew protests for its inability to steer a straight course, which left the commissioners veering from one side of the river to the other. One crewman replied that they did it "to give the Commissioners the most ample opportunity of exploring and examining the river." From Geneva, they proceeded on by wagon.[22]

Clinton's interest in what would then have been called "natural philosophy" is evident throughout the journal. About sixteen miles west of Schenectady he reported finding "[i]n dried mullen stalks . . . young bees in a chrysalis state" and the "shell of the common fresh water muscle." At Rome, he catalogued the attendant birds: "wood-ducks, gulls, sheldrakes, bob-linklins, king-birds, crows, kildares, small snipe, woodpeckers, woodcock, wrens, yellow birds, phebes, blue jays, high-holes, thrushes, and larks." He judged the quality of the water in different lakes: at Cayuga, the "miasmatic exhalation" of the lake and its marshes was nauseating; to ascertain why the water of Oneida Lake was unhealthful he looked at it through a microscope, but "could come to no conclusion"; the water of Lake Erie, at least, was "green, transparent, and fit to drink." It also contained a multiplicity of fish, which he duly listed.[23]

The development of manufacturing was another interest, and Clinton recorded such evidence of it as the advertisements in a Schenectady tavern of two new ma-chines for preparing and carding wool and cotton. Just outside Utica, he visited the proprietor of a large cheese factory whose product "is equal to the best English cheese that is imported." A little farther west they came to a water-powered spinning works for cotton owned by the Oneida Manufacturing Society. "It employs forty hands," he noted, "chiefly young girls, who have an unhealthy appearance." Proceeding west-ward, he had the clear feeling that despite the agricultural surroundings the future of the land lay in the direction of manufacturing, commerce, and speculation, not the subsistence farming of an earlier day. In the village of Buffalo, there were "five lawyers and no church."[24]

Religion, however, was evident everywhere else, and Clinton remarked on Quaker efforts to improve the conditions of the Indian tribes and commented on a "camp-meeting of Methodists" that the expedition visited in late July. The flames of revival-ism that were to make western New York the "burned-over district" fifteen years later were already flickering in 1810.[25]

In his complaints about accommodations along the way Clinton seems almost approachable, an ordinary carping traveler rather than Magnus Apollo. On July 7 he wrote, "We relished our breakfast but very indifferently. The swarms of flies which as-sailed the food, were very disgusting; and custards which were brought on the table, *mal apropos* exhibited the marks of that insect as a substitute for the grating of nut-meg." A week later the hardships were even greater. "No sooner were we lodged," Clinton recorded of one stopping-place, "than our noses were assailed by a thousand villainous smells, meeting our olfactory nerves in all directions, the most potent aris-ing from boiled pork, which was left close to our heads. Our ears were invaded by a commingled noise of drunken people in an adjacent room, of crickets in the hearth, of rats in the walls, of dogs under the beds, by the whizzing of musquitoes about our heads, and the flying of bats about the room." Efforts to get to sleep in this Tartarus were defeated by "an army of bed-bugs, aided by a light infantry in the shape of fleas, and a regiment of musquito cavalry." The recourse was to get dressed and go out to smoke a cigar. It was not always that bad. On the following morning they set out early, and after seven miles stopped for breakfast, which consisted of: "common bread, Oswego bread and biscuit; coffee and tea, without milk, butter, perch, salmon, and Oswego bass; fried pork, ham, boiled pork and Bologna sausages, old and new cheese, wood-duck, teal and dipper." The flea-bitten commissioner ate a hearty breakfast.[26]

Throughout, such practical matters are accompanied by observations on the rela-tive strength of Federalists and Republicans in each village, the kinds of newspapers being printed, the intentions of the people of Canada toward the United States, and of course, the proper route for the proposed canal. At one point, summarizing his views of the Mohawk River, he writes, "The river is good only as a feeder." He had evidently retained John Kemp's Columbia lessons.[27]

In both Clinton's account and John Eddy's, the trip seems a kind of gentlemen's adventure, with just enough discomfort to assure them that they were traveling into the wilderness, but enough servants and supplies so that at the end of the day they could smoke a "segar"—Eddy was in charge of these and of the company's library, which filled a large trunk—and refresh the tissues with the supply of "wine both red & white, Porter, shrub & c," which was under the Osgoods' stewardship.[28]

Absent from both accounts is any sense of tension among the commissioners, or any mention of debate about the canal's practicability. While differences existed, they were of detail, not of aim, and this small band of influential men took their findings and prepared to advance the project from speculation into reality.

STATE ACTION, FEDERAL INACTION

The commissioners' report was put into writing by Gouverneur Morris and presented to the legislature the following year. Their first observation was that "experience has long since exploded in Europe the idea of using the beds of rivers for internal navigation, where canals are practicable." The report recommended the construction of a canal by the western route to Lake Erie, declaring that the work should be undertaken by the public, and not by a private company. This last point was crucial, and the commissioners entered their "feeble protest" against a grant to private persons or companies:

> Too great a national interest is at stake. It must not become the subject of a job, or a fund for speculation. Among many other objections there is one insuperable: That it would defeat the contemplated cheapness of transportation. . . . Moreover, such large expenditures can be more economically made under public authority, than by the care and vigilance of any company.

They left open the matter of what portion of the cost should be borne by the nation, and what by the state.[29]

In April the legislature passed a canal law authorizing the commission—to which Robert R. Livingston and Robert Fulton had been added—to seek aid from Congress and from other states, as well as to negotiate the purchase of the assets of the Western Inland Lock Navigation Company. Morris and Clinton were deputed to go to Washington to solicit federal aid. They carried a written application to Congress from the commissioners proclaiming that the project would "encourage agriculture, promote commerce and manufactures, facilitate a free and general intercourse between different parts of the United States, tend to the aggrandizement and prosperity of the country, and consolidate and strengthen the Union."[30]

But the national government was not enthusiastic, and in reporting on their efforts Morris and Clinton were forced to admit defeat. Calling on President Madison on December 23, 1811, they found that "although he expressed himself to be an enthusiast as to the advantages of interior navigation, by means of canals," he was "embarrassed by scruples derived from his interpretation of the constitution." The New Yorkers were skeptical about this objection, since federal aid had already been given to roads. And there was "another idea operating with baleful effect," which was jealousy of New York and fear that the benefits such a canal brought would work to the detriment of other states.[31]

The New Yorkers had been told that their plan would have a better chance if it was linked to a national program of improvements, but efforts in that direction were scuttled both by jealousy of New York and by the threat of approaching war, which provided an easy excuse for inaction. The same arguments that helped win friends for the canal within New York—that it would greatly stimulate the growth of the state and of the City of New York—created opposition elsewhere. New York State was already leaving its competition behind. "Between 1790 and 1810," according to Charles Sellers, "as land-hungry Yankees flooded the Champlain country and Mohawk valley, the population of New York grew 182 percent, compared with 86 percent for Philadelphia's Pennsylvania, 25 percent for Boston's Massachusetts, and 11 percent for Baltimore's Maryland." By 1812, New York had clearly passed Philadelphia to become the nation's largest city, and between 1800 and 1810 New York State had passed Virginia and Pennsylvania to become the most populous state. To Virginians like James Madison, the growing power of this northern rival was a serious threat.[32]

Although sectional jealousies obviously had a great deal to do with this unfavorable climate, there were many who simply could not believe that such an undertaking was within the country's capacity at the time. Thomas Jefferson thought the canal was a good idea, one that might be undertaken in another hundred years. In 1808, he told Joshua Forman bluntly that his "talk of making a canal 350 miles through the wilderness" was "little short of madness . . . at this day." As late as 1822 Jefferson, writing to DeWitt Clinton, still felt that "New-York has anticipated, by a full century, the normal process of improvement." The existing state of the canal art certainly gave grounds for such skepticism. At the time Clinton and Morris were pleading for federal aid, "the world had only one canal more than a tenth as long, and the United States only three canals more than two miles long, the longest twenty-seven miles and none profitable."[33]

In 1812 the New York legislature took a very long and, it might even be said, courageous step. The legislature passed, and Governor Tompkins signed, a measure that gave the canal commissioners authority to borrow $5 million and to undertake further surveys.[34]

There was certainly opposition within the state, just as there had been outside it. Such an effort would entail heavy expense and burdensome taxes, and would encounter tremendous technological obstacles. And while the canal had bipartisan support, the Tammany contingent saw it as little more than a vehicle for DeWitt Clinton's ambition and viewed Clinton's journey with Morris to Washington as "having been undertaken by him for electioneering purposes." James A. Bayard, a Federalist senator from Delaware, agreed: "It is rather supposed that they mean to open a road to the presidency than a Canal from the lakes." The Martling Men derided the canal as "so visionary and absurd that no rational man for one moment, could seriously entertain it." Nevertheless, optimism was enough to outweigh doubts, and the bill passed. The commissioners were exploring the possibility of a European loan when war broke out.[35]

THE WAR OF 1812 AND THE CANAL

The immediate effect of the war's outbreak on the canal plan was disastrous. Any remaining hope of federal aid was, of course, abandoned, and in 1814 the state legislature, by then burdened with war debts, revoked the authority of the canal commissioners to borrow. Clinton's defeat in the presidential campaign of 1812 damaged his career and weakened his power, and the repercussions from the Hartford Convention left the Federalist party, whose adherents had been in the forefront of the canal crusade for two decades, in ruins.

But the war itself was both a result and a harbinger of changes in the national political mood that would culminate in an expansive burst of government promotion of economic growth after the war's conclusion. The "War Hawks" of the Twelfth Congress, led by Henry Clay and John C. Calhoun, pushed the nation from the wistful economic warfare of Jefferson and Madison into the bloody collisions of armies and navies. Both Clay and Calhoun were also economic nationalists and, after the war, would lead the crusade for an active government role in promotion of the nation's material growth. In the congressional session of 1816–17, Calhoun proposed that part of the government's proceeds from chartering the Second Bank of the United States (the first bank had expired in 1811) be devoted to internal improvements, so as "to bind the Republic together with a perfect system of roads and canals."[36]

Perhaps the greatest argument for internal improvements came out of the conduct of the war itself. Britain's fleets could range up and down the coast with ease, while the Americans had to struggle over roads that in many cases were no better than they had been during the revolution. And since the revolution, the expansion of the United States and Canada had broadened the potential theater of war, making trans-Appalachian supply lines a vital concern. Commodore Perry's forces on Lake Erie could be supplied only overland at great cost, and after the war New York congressman James Tallmadge claimed that the cost of transporting a cannon to Lake Erie from Washington cost four or five times as much as the cannon itself.[37]

Following the war, feelings between the United States and Canada remained mutually suspicious, and this, too, favored a canal. Without one, much of the produce of western New York (and perhaps, as they grew, of Ohio, Michigan, and other northwestern states and territories) would proceed across Lake Ontario, through Montreal, and down the St. Lawrence. Since shipping on Lake Ontario was potentially subject to hostile naval action, the inland route to Lake Erie could be justified both economically and militarily. Nor were such apprehensions mere propaganda. In 1815, after the war was over, American ships on the lake were boarded and searched, and at least one vessel was fired on. By the time the Rush-Bagot Treaty, demilitarizing the lakes, was ratified in 1818, the building of the canal was already under way.[38]

CLINTON MAKES IT HIS CANAL

The decline of the Federalist party made it possible for Republican politicians to embrace Federalist programs without seeming to threaten the success of the Jeffersonian "Revolution of 1800." DeWitt Clinton in 1812 had expressed the views of commercial states, which saw Jeffersonian policies as detrimental to those areas of the country that had fully embraced the market economy. "By 1815," Charles Sellers notes, "the combined influence of Federalism and entrepreneurial Republicanism had completed an essential stage of the market revolution by committing the commercial states to the political economy of capitalism." That political economy would give the canal its most powerful ally.[39]

The memorial Clinton wrote to accompany the City Hotel meeting of 1815 left no doubt of where he thought the nation was heading. "If it be important," he wrote,

> that the inhabitants of the same country should be bound together by a community of interests, and a reciprocation of benefits; that agriculture should find a sale for its commodities; manufacturers a vent for their fabrics; and commerce a market for its commodities: it is your incumbent duty, to open, facilitate, and improve internal navigation.

Clinton was now defining human society in terms of market relations; the communitarian values inherent in the world of subsistence agriculture had been abandoned for the contractual relations of the market. At the same time, the interdependencies of agriculture, commerce, and manufacturing would create new "communities of interest" to bind the country together. The ways in which market relations could also dissolve bonds between people were not yet evident; when Clinton saw the young girl laborers at the mill run by the Oneida Manufacturing Society, he did not know he was glimpsing America's immediate future.[40]

At the same time that the market was reaching deeper into the United States both geographically and psychologically, the traditional mercantile assumption that a nation's economic health depended on external markets was eroding, as is evidenced in such writings as those of the Philadelphia economist Matthew Carey. Gordon S. Wood sees this rejection of mercantilism as a watershed change in attitude. "This growing belief that domestic commerce of the United States was 'incalculably more valuable' than its foreign commerce and that 'the home market for productions of the earth and manufactures is of more importance than all foreign ones' represented a momentous reversal of traditional thinking," Wood writes. During the eighteenth century, the term *commerce*

> had usually referred exclusively to international trade. Now it was being equated with all the exchanges taking place within the country, exchanges in which both parties always gained. The Americans, said Fanny Wright in 1819, echoing a phrase heard over and over in these years, were truly forming "a world within themselves."[41]

The Embargo and the war had forced the United States to hasten the development of its own manufacturing, and although the postwar dumping of British goods on the American market threatened domestic manufacturers, it enriched the New York merchants who disposed of those imports through the auction market, and benefited the growing population of the interior who as consumers wanted those goods at lower prices. If American manufacturing could recover from the British challenge, and transportation costs could be lowered, there was a domestic market ready to consume American products. Thus the casting aside of mercantilism led to the espousal of protectionism.

Clinton's embrace of internal markets was of a piece with this altering outlook. In his memorial he claimed that the "prosperity of ancient Egypt, and China, may in a great degree be attributed to their inland navigation," and that in modern times England and Holland, "deprived of their canals, would lose the most prolific source of their prosperity and greatness." New York's potential should therefore be obvious: "If we were to suppose all the rivers and canals in England and Wales, combined into one, and discharging at the ocean at a great city, after passing through the heart of that country, then we can form a distinct idea of the importance of the projected canal." Then there was the looming greatness of the West, and Clinton sketched the promise of the canal for trade with Chicago, Detroit, and Pittsburgh, cities then beginning what would be more than a century of phenomenal growth.[42]

A final argument was the role the canal could play in moderating sectionalism, although the sectionalism Clinton had in mind was not between North and South but rather between Atlantic America and the trans-Appalachian country. This, he thought, was where the "imminent danger" lay. (Aaron Burr's adventurings in the West a decade earlier still stood as a warning.) And the future would indeed show, well after DeWitt Clinton was gone, that opening the way west would not only make any East-West sectional rupture unlikely but would firmly bind the states of the Midwest to New York City and other commercial centers of the Northeast, with significant consequences for the Civil War.[43]

The memorial was Clinton's work, and it made the canal Clinton's project. The part he took would ultimately bring him considerable distinction, though in the short term it hurt the canal. With Daniel Tompkins in the governor's chair, and James Madison in the White House, Clinton—and with him the canal—had powerful enemies. New York City's Martling Men were discovering a new and highly effective form of leadership in state politics under the hand of Martin Van Buren. While Clinton and his allies were successful in arousing public enthusiasm for the canal, the political situation in Albany remained less favorable. Tompkins knew that any canal plan would reflect favorably on Clinton; but he also knew that the canal was becoming very popular. Moreover, if Tompkins supported the western route he would alienate the Tammanyites; but if he supported the Ontario route, he would lose support in the west. He did what he could to dodge the dilemma. "It will rest with the Legislature," he said in his annual address to that body, "whether the prospect of connecting the waters of the Hudson with those of the western lakes and of Champlain is not sufficiently important to demand the appropriation of some part of the revenues of the State to its accomplishment, without imposing too great a burden upon our constitution." There were also, apart from Tompkins's waffling and the reluctance of Clinton's enemies to hand him a victory, some sections of the state that still saw the canal as a threat to their interests. Farmers on Long Island and along the Hudson feared competition from the rich lands to the west, and those in the state's southern tier—the highlands running parallel to the Pennsylvania border—saw themselves paying taxes to enrich their neighbors to the north. Thanks in part to skillful obstruction in the state senate by Van Buren, the best the canal forces could achieve in 1816 was authority for further surveys and another report. Van Buren, to be sure, would eventually support the canal. But he seems to have thought it best for the time being not to let things go too fast.[44]

By the following year, the way was clear for the passage of an act authorizing work on the canal to begin. Daniel Tompkins had been elected vice president and resigned the governorship to take up his duties in Washington. Clinton's advocacy of the canal had revived his political fortunes and he was soon to win election as Tompkins's successor. Sensing the public mood, Van Buren now spoke fervently in favor of the canal in the state senate, during which speech Clinton was in the chamber, and as Van Buren related it, "listened very attentively throughout, and altho' it was only a few weeks after he had obtained the nomination for Governor, which I had so zealously opposed, and our personal intercourse was very reserved, he approached me, when I took my seat, shook hands with me, and expressed his gratification in the strongest terms." On April 15, 1817, the canal bill was passed, and the first paragraph of the law announced that the canal would "promote agriculture, manufactures, and commerce, mitigate the calamities of war, enhance the blessings of peace, consolidate the union, advance the prosperity and elevate the character of the United States." In short, it would provide "signal, extensive, and lasting benefits to the human race." The framers expressed confidence that the federal government, and the governments of "the States equally interested with this state," would contribute to the canal's construction, but such contributions were not made a precondition of the work going forward.[45]

Ten weeks later, DeWitt Clinton was sworn in as governor of the state of New York, and on July 4, 1817, a ceremonial ground-breaking was held at Rome. The namesake of an ancient empire provided the site for the inauguration of a new one.

The market economy was indeed being transformed; so also were the assumptions under which politics and government were conducted. The very forces that helped win support for the canal and brought DeWitt Clinton to the governorship were already building a new kind of politics that would sweep him out of office.

Nine

o   o   o

CLINTONIAN INTELLECT

W HEN DEWITT CLINTON WAS ousted as mayor in 1815, he had been active in political life for twenty-five years and had held appointive or elective office, sometimes both simultaneously, for nearly all of those years. He now withdrew to his farm in Newtown and is said to have taken refuge in alcohol as he brooded over his defeats.[1] His living expenses and his willingness to lend money to friends and acquaintances, together with his charitable contributions, had depleted his family's finances so that, deprived of the income that came with the mayor's office, he was in serious financial straits. Now, with his political foes increasing in influence and number, and his public career seemingly at an end, one would have expected him to retreat into prudent and lucrative employment as a New York lawyer.

CONSOLATIONS OF CULTURE

Perhaps as he pondered his difficulties he found some solace in the life of the mind. Intellectual activity gave balance to Clinton's life, offering a realm of endeavor that did not require political compromises or alliances. His efforts to promote cultural institutions in New York were subject to the contingencies of political life, but his own scientific researches could proceed unhindered. Those researches were a constant feature of his life, and his papers contain scores of letters seeking information about specific subjects and passing his findings on to correspondents in the United States and abroad. He snatched time for his writings where he could—even on the bench while judging cases.[2] The citations that accompany his essays indicate a significant amount of study, and there is nothing to suggest that he had any assistance in this work except the occasional advice of his scientist friends.

One of Clinton's central goals for the cultural organizations he promoted was to secure for America an intellectual life worthy of European notice; this idea underlay much of his own writing, and nowhere is it more evident than in his longest and most important lecture, the *Introductory Discourse Delivered Before the Literary and Philosophical Society of New York*. And it was, appropriately, in the week following the victory of his Republican adversaries in the state elections of 1814 (the victory that spelled the end of Clinton's mayoralty) that he delivered it.

In it, Clinton reviews the case against America as presented by such European denigrators of the New World as the Comte de Buffon and the Scottish historian William Robertson, and offers explanations for why American intellectual life has not equaled that of Europe. He also provides examples of American achievement that he thinks the Old World will soon have to take account of. European condescension toward America had been attacked by others—Jefferson's *Notes on the State of Virginia* had challenged Buffon's statements about the inferiority of North American mammals—but Clinton's counterattacks on Europe give the impression of a man responding to personal insults. He derides the writings of one Prussian observer of North America with the withering comment "As a specimen of his accuracy it is sufficient to state, that he confidently asserts that dogs suffer so much under the deteriorating influence of our climate, that they lose the power of barking."[3]

American climatic conditions, Clinton goes on to argue, are in fact superior: "We have more rain, more evaporation, more sunshine, and a greater number of clear days than they have in Europe: our atmosphere, it is supposed, contains more electrical fluid; and we are exposed to greater extremes of heat and cold." So it is not meteorological factors that explain why "we are far behind our european brethren in the pursuits of literature." (He did have to admit that we were behind.) At the time of America's settlement the European intellectual world "was involved in cimmerian darkness"; many of those who came to America were seeking riches, not knowledge; and there was "something in the nature of provincial government which tends to engender faction, and to prevent the expansion of intellect." (He knew what evils faction could bring and threatening culture was only one of them.) With the early phase of settlement characterized by a "small population, scattered over an extensive country," and with even this small number "composed almost entirely of strangers to literature," cultural development was slow. This was only to be expected.[4]

The winning of independence removed some obstacles and provided stirring subjects for American artists, but there were still hindrances. The difficulty lay not in the great mass of people, who, thanks to common schools and the Lancastrian system, were better educated than their European counterparts. The crucial shortcoming was in the elite: "There is not so much concentrated knowledge in so many individuals as in Europe." To make matters worse, Clinton continued, what intellectual life there was had been too much distracted by factional politics:

> Our ingenuity has been employed, not in cultivating a vernacular literature, or increasing the stock of human knowledge; but in raising up and pulling down the parties which agitate the community. . . . The style of our political writings has assumed a character of rude invective, and unrestrained licentiousness, unparalleled in any other part of the world; and which has greatly tended to injure our national character.

The incompatibility of political conflict and literary achievement seems a novel idea; perhaps he would not have put it that sharply at a different time.[5]

Other obstacles to intellectual life in the United States included a quarreling medical profession, an undistinguished legal tradition, and the fact that "the energies of our country have been more directed to the accumulation of wealth than to the acquisition of knowledge." Nevertheless the logical focus for the flowering of the nation's culture, when it occurs, would obviously be the great City of New York, the fittest location for such institutions as the Literary and Philosophical Society, which he was now addressing. Clinton had great hopes for such societies; meanwhile, he was filled with joy whenever one of their European counterparts recognized the work of an American, as in 1816 when his friend David Hosack was made a Fellow of the Royal Society. He was equally delighted at meeting a Mr. Duncan, an English immigrant preparing to settle near Canandaigua, who, like Hosack, was a Fellow of the Royal Society. He reported his find to John Pintard, crowing that "we will have at least two FRS's in New York."[6]

In his *Discourse* Clinton covered the range of American scientific achievements, including Benjamin Franklin's inventions, Samuel Latham Mitchill's work in chemistry and geology, Hosack's botanical research, Alexander Wilson's ornithological writings, David Rittenhouse's astronomy, and Zebulon Pike's explorations. Their examples should inspire others. "Men of observation and science ought to be employed," he urged, "to explore our country with a view to its geology, mineralogy, botany, zoölogy, and agriculture." Moreover, despite the continent's seemingly limitless resources, he was already concerned with what might need to be done about replenishing the forests, and conserving the fish and game, that might otherwise someday disappear.[7]

AMERICAN LANDS, AMERICAN PEOPLES

Clinton's environmental concerns, impressive for his times, arose in part from his interest in American Indians, a field in which he did the most sustained and original of all his scientific work. Two and a half years before his *Discourse* to the Literary and Philosophical Society, the New-York Historical Society heard a lengthy lecture from him on the subject of "The Iroquois," about whom he knew a great deal. In it he discussed the environmental conflict between Europeans and Indians, observing that "a nation that derives its subsistence, principally, from the forest, cannot live in the vicinity of one that relies on the products of the field." He also noted that the former balance between the Iroquois and their natural domain had been disrupted even before European settlers took over their lands, because from the earliest days of contact the Indians had been encouraged to hunt certain animals, such as beavers, to supply overseas markets, and had thus killed more than they would have had they been hunting only for subsistence.[8]

Within Clinton's own lifetime the Iroquois had gone from being a formidable political, diplomatic, military, and economic force in New York to a much more tenuous existence. The punitive raids led by Clinton's father and General John Sullivan during the Revolutionary War had played a role in the marginalization of New York's Indians, a process completed by the westward expansion that preceded, and then accelerated with, the Erie Canal. While Clinton did not intend to let anything get in the way of his own expansionist visions, even solicitude for the state's Indians, he displayed a greater interest in and respect for their culture and customs than almost any other white person in the state. Indeed, his investigations and theories about the continent's Indian past have been described as possibly "the first archaeological studies ever carried out by an American on an American subject."[9]

Yet, for all the subject's Americanness, Clinton found himself carried away by the possibility of Roman analogies and precedents in North American prehistory. The Iroquois, he thought, might themselves be called "the Romans of this western world," on account of the vast size of the area they controlled, their martial temper, the eloquence of their oratory, and their tendency to amalgamate rather than execute those they conquered.[10]

While it was a common conceit that the Indians of North America were the degenerate remnants of the Lost Tribes of Israel, Clinton rejected the theory in favor of Asiatic origins and a possible link to the ancient Scythians. Citing Herodotus's description of the Scythians' cruelty as warriors, he believed that from them "we may derive the practice of scalping . . . and it is not improbable, considering the maritime skill and distant voyages of the Phoenicians and Carthaginians, that America derives part of its population from that source by water, as it undoubtably has from the northeast parts of Asia by land."[11]

But if scalping originated with the Scythians, Clinton does not hold the Iroquois or other Indians responsible for its practice in America. The Indian's "appetite for blood was sharpened and whetted by European instigation, and his cupidity was enlisted on the side of cruelty by every temptation." Clinton then recounts the history of scalp bounties during the colonial wars between England and France. Although Clinton blamed Europeans for encouraging the use of scalping in America, he did not say that they introduced it, except in the distant sense that it came from the supposed Scythian forebears of the Iroquois.[12]

This preoccupation with the European past, in particular the legacy of Rome, went deeper than analogies to Roman character and possible influences of Scythians, Carthaginians, and Phoenicians on the development of the New World. DeWitt Clinton was so thoroughly steeped in the saga of Rome that he could not help believing that a similar story of a high civilization overwhelmed by invading barbarians had taken place in North America. Nor was he alone in such conceptions; his correspondence is dotted with letters from others pursuing the same theme, and the idea received its fullest and most influential elaboration in the revelations recorded by Joseph Smith as the *Book of Mormon*.[13]

Clinton announces this theme at the end of his address on the Iroquois:

> It would be an unpardonable omission not to mention, while treating on this subject, that there is every reason to believe, that previous to the occupancy of this country by

the progenitors of the present nations of Indians, it was inhabited by a race of men much more populous and much further advanced in civilization. The numerous remains of ancient fortifications which are found in this country, commencing principally near the Onondaga River, and from thence spreading over the Military Tract, the Genesee country, and the lands of the Holland Land Company, over the territory adjoining the Ohio and its tributary streams, the country on Lake Erie, and extending even west of the Mississippi, demonstrate a population far exceeding that of the Indians when this country was first settled.[14]

He has seen several such remains, he declares, in the appropriately Roman-named towns of Pompey, Camillus, and Scipio, among others, and he supports these observations with a footnote that fills half a page in small type. He reviews some possible explanations—that these ancient forts are remnants of early Spanish or French exploration or of the legendary expedition of the Welsh voyager Madoc, whose twelfth-century journey, described in Hakluyt's *Voyages,* had been the subject of a recent epic poem by Robert Southey, the poet laureate of England and one of Clinton's favorite authors.[15]

But he dismisses all such theories of European origin for these ruins and briskly announces that it is "equally clear that they were not the work of the Indians." One bit of evidence for the antiquity of the sites was the great age of trees found growing on the ramparts of one of the forts (Clinton had had a tree cut down and then had counted the rings). Describing two lines of forts running parallel to the southern shore of Lake Erie, he argues that the two lines mark successive shorelines, and that the retreat of the water in the lake could only have happened over centuries. Thus for the oldest line of forts "their origin must be sought in a very remote age." Clinton's theory was that a high civilization had been evolved by peoples who formed the earliest wave of migration from Asia, and that their journeying to the eastern end of North America left them a long time in peace, during which they were at leisure to "devote themselves to the arts of peace, make rapid progress in civilization, and acquire an immense population." Here, then, was the American Rome. Eventually, barbarous migrants arriving from Asia threatened their frontiers, and they were forced to build fortifications:

> At last, they became alarmed by the irruption of a horde of barbarians, who rushed like an overwhelming flood from the North of Asia.
>
> > A multitude, like which the populous North
> > Pour'd never from her frozen loins, to pass
> > *Rhene* or the *Danaw,* when her barbarous Sons
> > Came like a Deluge on the South, and spread
> > Beneath *Gibraltar* to the *Lybian* sands.
>
> The great law of self-preservation compelled them to stand on their defence, to resist these ruthless invaders, and to construct numerous and extensive works for protection. And for a long series of years the scale of victory was suspended in doubt, and they firmly withstood the torrent: but like the Romans, in the decline of their empire, they were finally worn down and destroyed by successive inroads and renewed attacks.

And the fortifications of which we have treated are the only remaining monuments of these ancient and exterminated nations.[16]

Clinton undoubtedly believed—he certainly very much wanted to believe—what he was saying here. He wanted to discover for the New World, if not to invent, some indigenous counterpart of the classical past. And he also saw in the example of Rome a cautionary tale for the nation he was helping to build.

ROMAN REPUBLIC, ROMAN EMPIRE

Historical scholarship on the early American republic over the past generation has done much to illuminate the tradition of classical republicanism that so permeated the political understanding of the revolutionary and postrevolutionary era. The experience of the ancient republics—often those of the Greeks but most of all the Roman republic—was a constant point of reference for Americans in their efforts to envision their own destiny. Yet the Roman tradition, seen in its wholeness, embraced both republic and empire, and for some it was not always easy to keep them separate. Such was the case with DeWitt Clinton. Clinton's archeological efforts, his intellectual aspirations, and his vision of the Erie Canal intimate that hopes for imperial glory might well accompany desires for a virtuous republican citizenry, and that the achievements of the greatest imperial powers of Clinton's time, Great Britain and France, should be examples that might compete with, but also complement, America's own strivings for greatness.

Clinton's canal memorial of 1815, for example, was a testament more in keeping with imperial ambition than with virtuous republican thrift. It bursts with the conviction that the imperial future of his state was not simply a possibility but a solemn obligation:

> Standing on this exalted eminence, with power to prevent a train of the most extensive and afflicting calamities that ever visited the world, (for such a train will inevitably follow a dissolution of the Union,) she [New York State] will be justly considered an enemy to the human race, if she does not exert for this purpose the high faculties which the Almighty has put into her hands.

It would appear only just that New York should come to be called the Empire State.[17]

And yet, almost hidden among Clinton's prophecies of an imperial destiny, a somber note intrudes. America's future as a great civilization is certain: but the time may come when the bill will have to be paid. In his essay on the Iroquois he pointed to the many crimes committed by Europeans and European Americans in the course of settling the continent. They "exterminated millions of red men and entailed upon the sable inhabitants of Africa, endless wars, captivity, slavery and death," and in some distant future retribution might bring calamities upon Americans such as those "we have so wantonly and wickedly inflicted upon others." A "transcendent genius" might then arise in Asia, rally the nations there behind him, and lead an invasion of the United States. Clinton envisioned the contest:

The destinies of the country may then be decided on the waters of the Missouri, or on the banks of Lake Superior. And if Asia shall then revenge upon our posterity the injuries we have inflicted on her sons, a new, a long, and a gloomy night of gothic darkness will set in upon mankind. And when, after the efflux of ages, the returning effulgence of intellectual light shall again gladden the nations, then the wide-spread ruins of our cloud-capp'd towers, of our solemn temples, and of our magnificent cities, will, like the works of which we have treated, become the subject of curious research and elaborate investigation.[18]

America would in the end have achieved a glory equal to that of Greece and Rome, with a civilization future ages might well contemplate with profit. A kind of final moral justice would then be consummated, and the speaker, in predicting it, stands almost transfigured in the thought.

CLINTON'S WORKS AND CLINTON'S AUDIENCE

North American Indians and archaeology occupied a major part, though not the only part, of Clinton's scientific pursuits. He produced various exhortations similar to his address to the American Academy of Arts—a speech to the Phi Beta Kappa Society of Union College in 1823, an address at Columbia in 1827—which held up examples of American genius and recommended that students work hard and add to the nation's knowledge about the continent. He drafted a "Circular Letter" for the Literary and Philosophical Society that sought to collect information about New York's resources from learned men around the state. He contributed scientific papers on fish and birds, and a *Memoir on the Antiquities of the Western Parts of the State of New York,* which elaborated on the evidence concerning higher civilization in North America. And at the same time he carried on an active correspondence with naturalists in other parts of the country and in Britain, while also carrying out his duties as mayor or governor. He told John Pintard that he wrote the *Introductory Discourse* while sitting on the bench in Mayor's Court.[19]

Pintard thought Clinton's scientific and literary work was of the highest quality, and Mitchill and Hosack also had great respect for their amateur friend. Learned societies in the United States and abroad elected Clinton to membership, and at the time of his death he was being considered for election as a Fellow of the Royal Society. Thomas Jefferson carried on a cordial correspondence with him on scientific subjects, suggesting, for example, that Clinton's theories about high civilization in the Americas might receive corroboration if "any of the hard metals could be found, clearly antecedent to the discovery of America," and wishing that the rest of the continent's antiquities could be "described with the care which distinguishes" Clinton's memoir.[20]

Clinton was rarely shy about seeking readers for his work. The *Introductory Discourse* received wide circulation, to judge by the many letters Clinton received from the learned in America and Britain. After delivering his address to the American

Academy of the Arts in 1816, Clinton asked that fifty copies of it be sent to Albany, perhaps hoping they would help advance his campaign for governor.[21]

But Clinton's achievements in this line did not meet universal approbation and were a particular target of the acidulous Gulian C. Verplanck. Clinton could be remarkably pedantic—the *Introductory Discourse,* for example, ran to fewer than forty pages but had more than one hundred pages of notes, including one that simply reprinted his lengthy review of Alexander Wilson's *American Ornithology.* Verplanck's verses mocked Clinton's "curious knowledge of the tails of bears," referring to a lengthy footnote about grizzly bears, whose tails were stated to be shorter than those of common bears. Clinton's suggestion that serious study of Indian languages be undertaken was twitted as an interest in "Tuscarora literature." That there might be something worth studying in Native American cultures was a notion not to be taken seriously.[22]

Clinton, though undoubtedly nettled, could at least suppose himself superior to such jibes as long as he could enjoy the approval of men of science like Hosack and Mitchill. But a more serious blow to his self-esteem came from another side. It was one thing to be mocked as a pedant, but quite another to be dismissed as an amateur, which was what happened toward the end of his career, as the nascent professionalization of science, and of art, began to challenge the authority of the socially prominent elites who assumed that culture fell within their prescriptive domain. In February 1817, a new scientific organization was founded in the city, the Lyceum of Natural History. Clinton's friend Mitchill was the first president. He was also the oldest member; the lyceum's makeup was decidedly younger than that of the Historical Society or the Literary and Philosophical Society, and more weighted toward practicing scientists, predominantly young doctors and medical students. In July of that year Clinton was nominated for honorary membership in the lyceum, but he was not elected. John Pintard wrote immediately to Mitchill angrily protesting that Clinton should not be exposed to such humiliation, particularly since he had not been told his name was being put forward. A few days later, Clinton wrote to Pintard professing to regret that "any excitement should exist in this case." The following year, Mitchill did secure Clinton's election as an honorary member, although the organization does not seem to have attracted much attention from Clinton after that. Political partisanship may have had something to do with his rejection, along with a touch of rivalry between Hosack and Mitchill. Yet the emerging professionalism of American science and a generational split in New York's intellectual vanguard, as described by Thomas Bender, appear to be the most likely causes. These theories also go farthest toward explaining another cultural skirmish of Clinton's later years, which affected the American Academy of the Arts. Younger artists, outraged at the way the academy was run for the convenience of the wealthy merchants who financed its operations, struck out on their own. Clinton had turned the organization's presidency over to John Trumbull, and that venerable recorder of revolutionary battles and heroes was unwilling to make room for younger artists, or to change the academy to accommodate their wishes and needs. A dissident group of artists led by Samuel F. B.

Morse broke away in 1825 and the following year set up the National Academy of Design, which directed its energies toward serving the requirements of artists rather than elevating the city's taste, as Clinton's organization had sought to do.[23]

Clinton's achievements as a scientist may not put him in the same category as the British naturalist Joseph Banks, or even Samuel Latham Mitchill, but he was more than a pompous dabbler in the field of "natural philosophy." His *Introductory Discourse* was an important enough contribution to geology to be republished recently in a series on influential early works in the field, and his work on North American archaeology was original and painstaking. If one sees his scientific achievements as slight beside those of, say, Franklin, one is holding them to a very high standard. Yet it is difficult, except for Franklin, and probably Jefferson, to think of another figure of similar importance in American politics who also made any kind of mark as a scientist.[24]

Yet science was DeWitt Clinton's avocation; politics was his clear vocation. As he stood before the members of the Literary and Philosophical Society on May 4, 1814, to deliver his *Introductory Discourse,* he may have wondered what was to become of him the following year when his enemies would control the Council of Appointment and deprive him of his job as mayor. There was some parallel between this situation and what would happen to him a few years later as a scientist. In politics, as in science, he was a personification of eighteenth-century attitudes. He expected deference to be paid him in both these capacities. But politics, like science, was becoming professionalized, and the new spirit of professionalism in politics was being perfected under Clinton's own eyes, in the state of New York.

Ten

o   o   o

THE GOVERNOR

Τ HE CANAL, AS WE HAVE SEEN, provided the means for Clinton's nearly
miraculous political rebirth. But the obstacles to that reemergence were formidable and were concentrated in two men: Daniel D. Tompkins, whose career Clinton
had launched but who had broken with his patron, and another former Clintonian,
Martin Van Buren.

A gift for conciliation was not among Clinton's qualities, and the conduct of his
presidential campaign had left many individuals and groups estranged from him. His
candidacy managed to sow division in both the Republican and Federalist parties in
New York as well as in the nation. With the triple blows to Federalism that came with
the Treaty of Ghent, the Hartford Convention, and Jackson's victory at New Orleans,
that potential source of support was vastly weakened at precisely the point when
Clinton most needed it. The decline of Federalism had contributed to his removal
from the mayoralty by the Council of Appointment, and the weakness of the Federalist party seemed to preclude any hope for a return to power. But it was the schisms
in his own Republican party that were most troublesome for Clinton, and would remain so until his death.

The sources were many. Some Republicans still resented Clinton's role in defeating Aaron Burr in 1804 and in the punishment of Burrite interests following Burr's
loss and subsequent disgraces. Others had split with Clinton over his cynical attempt
at a reconciliation with the Burrites in 1806. His alliance with the Livingstons had been
sundered by his attacks on Morgan Lewis, a Livingston relation, over the Merchants'
Bank charter in 1805 and by his subsequent opposition to Lewis's reelection as governor in 1807. Still more New Yorkers were offended by his opposition to President
Madison in 1812, either in itself or because it had involved a sub-rosa understanding
with the Federalists. Influential former friends of Clinton's included Lewis, Tompkins,
Van Buren, and Ambrose Spencer. But they were hardly confined to New York. He

was persona non grata among the leaders of the Virginia Dynasty because of his support for his uncle's claims to the presidency in 1808 as well as his own candidacy in 1812.

Theoretically, a purposeful effort could have produced the kind of coalition of entrepreneurial Republicans and former Federalists that eventually became the heart of the Whig party. But circumstances would probably not have allowed such a development this early, and certainly not under the hand of DeWitt Clinton. The ideological baggage he still carried, the suspicions of Federalism that persisted among the voting public, and mistrust of Clinton in what remained of the Federalist party itself—these were all heavy liabilities. Among the Federalists of New York, Rufus King, for one, had made very clear his detestation of Clinton and his policies. Some of the younger Federalists far surpassed King in their hostility to Clinton, and the most vocal of them was Gulian C. Verplanck.

ABIMELECH COODY MEETS A TRAVELLER

After the dressing down and heavy fine imposed on Verplanck by Judge Clinton as a consequence of the Columbia "riot," the young Federalist lawyer was alert to chances for revenge. He became an advocate of Federalist support for the war against Britain, perhaps because Clinton's Federalist support had come largely from those opposed. In 1814 he and his associates organized a ticket of so-called "Washington" or "American" Federalists to run for the state assembly from New York City, but they received a mere handful of votes. Among Verplanck's associates were Hugh Maxwell (who had sided with Verplanck at the commencement fracas) and Jacob and Peter Radcliff (Jacob had been mayor of New York in 1810-11 and had been much annoyed when the Federalists, after regaining control of the Council of Appointment in 1813, had allowed Clinton to remain in office). Ambrose Spencer, who had been a Federalist in the 1790s before becoming a Clintonian, also offered his encouragement. In spite of the poor performance of their ticket, Verplanck and about forty colleagues were that year welcomed into the Tammany Society.[1]

But it was Verplanck's pen, rather than his skills as a political organizer, that commended him to Clinton's opponents. Beginning in 1814 he wrote a series of political satires under the pseudonym "Abimelech Coody." His targets were various Clintonians and Clinton himself, who was described in *A Fable for Statesmen and Politicians* (1815) as "a young Irish greyhound of high mettle and exorbitant pretensions." Verplanck and the other Coodies, as they came to be called, also made sport of Clinton's circle for their cultural exertions. A review in the *Analectic Magazine* in 1814 mocked members of the Historical Society for attaching to their names "a train of titles at the end of them as long as the tail of a comet."[2]

Clinton abruptly retorted with a satire of his own, *An Account of Abimelech Coody, and Other Celebrated Writers of New York* (1815). It was, alas, one of his least attractive outbursts. Under the pseudonym of "A Traveller" he reports making a visit to New York, drawn by the city's great literary reputation, in the hope of meeting Coody, the writer said to be the greatest of all. But he is disillusioned to discover that Coody and all his friends wrote not "for amusement, or for fame," but merely for money. One of them, the editor of the infamous *Analectic Magazine,* was Washington Irving, whose "History," with its "unnatural combination of fiction and history is perfectly disgusting to good taste." Coody himself ("squat and clumsy") was the "head of a political sect called the Coodies, of a hybrid nature, composed of the combined spawn of federalism and jacobitism, and generated in the venomous passions of disappointment and revenge." He had been convicted of disorderly behavior at the college commencement, but "instead of being sent to prison as he ought to have been, he was let off with a fine and a severe reprimand" by the mayor, who, the Traveller learns, was no less a person than DeWitt Clinton. "Mr. Clinton," he adds (unfortunately, since the Traveller's identity shortly leaked out), "among his other great qualifications, is distinguished for a marked devotion to science; few men have read more and few men can claim more various and extensive knowledge; and the bounties of nature have been improved by his persevering and unremitting industry." A "sick lion" (still more unfortunately) "may be kicked even by an ass."[3]

Not long thereafter Verplanck, with his ailing wife, departed for Europe in the hope of restoring her health. But in time he would return, to resume his torments of Mr. Clinton.[4]

FACTION AND PARTY

The lion, even when sick, never lost his high opinion of his own capacities or his vision of honors to come. Clinton continued to picture himself (and so did others) as a possible presidential candidate in the remaining national elections of his lifetime. But the practices and understandings of a former time, which might once have made his candidacy thinkable, were no longer fully at his disposal. The politics of compact elites and personal factions, which had prevailed during his rise to national prominence, was disappearing in the face of a democratic revolution in American politics, a revolution that Clinton both fostered and fought in his career in New York.

Richard Hofstadter has argued that the distinctive contribution of American politics in the early nineteenth century was not so much the presence of competing parties—these had been present in American as well as British politics for some time—as the recognition of opposition parties as not only tolerable but even desirable. Thus emerged "a theory of politics" that accepted the role of a legitimate opposition. Hofstadter credits Martin Van Buren with being its principal developer. And it was in his battles with DeWitt Clinton that Van Buren's political practices were refined and transformed into a new way of thinking as well as of acting.[5]

Clinton, as Hofstadter sees him, was a "transitional figure" who "belonged much more to the old order than the new," an old order built around personal factions rather than organized parties. Crediting Clinton with unusual gifts in the use of patronage, Hofstadter nonetheless finds him unable to innovate as the new politics required.[6]

Yet transitions by their nature involve interpenetrations of the old and the new, and it is not always easy to distinguish between them, especially in accounting for DeWitt Clinton's success after 1815. Hofstadter observes that Clinton "led partly through the force of competence, manifest in his promotion of the Erie Canal, and partly through personal magnetism and brilliance, but never by party good-fellowship." Clinton's notorious hauteur does indeed stand in sharp contrast to Van Buren's soothing ways. Still, his movements during this period sometimes tell us less than they might as to how entrenched in the past he actually was. One writer, Steven Siry, says that Clinton used his strong personal standing to attempt a new political coalition of "practical republicanism"—classical republican values allied with entrepreneurial development—which could unite northern interests against the slaveholding phalanx the Virginia Dynasty spoke for. Yet the (practical republican) Whig party that emerged after Clinton's death, embracing many New York Clintonians and former Federalists, made every effort *not* to present itself as a sectional party. On the other hand, Clinton himself could be said to have fallen in with the nascent Democratic party in national politics even before that party had come fully into being; he was an early and strong backer of Andrew Jackson, whose emergence in the 1820s helped block what remained of Clinton's own presidential hopes. Or his attachment to Jackson could be seen simply as another instance of the intensely personal nature of his approach to politics. The man's career had its depths and perplexities.

A final perplexity is an unsettling correspondence, in personality and actions, with much of what one has seen in politicians from his day to ours. Clinton could be clever and ruthless; he could use, and then discard, Burrites, Lewisites, Federalists, and countless individual supporters. He could abandon an old friend and embrace an old enemy, with few compunctions. He was not without an instinct for the popular mood, and a misstep, as in the case of the Embargo, could be nimbly repaired. He could exploit his opponents' weaknesses, attract new allies, and squeak through close elections without the sort of party apparatus being fashioned by Martin Van Buren. And he was dependent on public office for the support of himself and his family, which completes a still recognizable story.

The energy with which Clinton responded to Gulian Verplanck's satires suggests another aspect of Clinton's political practice that is remarkably modern. He worked very hard to project an image of serious intellect and used this image to win votes. References to his intelligence stud his campaign literature, and his scientific achievements were trotted out regularly to demonstrate his superiority to other candidates. In Clinton's race for governor in 1824, for example, he had a broadside printed that trumpeted Thomas Jefferson's high opinion of him. The first point of his character that Jefferson was said to admire was his "scientific research."[7] Clinton did not have Van Buren's organizational gift and was poor at keeping his alliances in good repair. But he was able to present himself to the world as a man of great intellect and energy, and these qualities were sufficiently appreciated to allow him to continue to win office repeatedly under difficult conditions.

THE LITTLE MAGICIAN

The central fact of Clinton's political life from 1815 until his death was the presence of Martin Van Buren at the head of the state's democratic forces. Van Buren began his political career as an ally of Clinton's, soon became his leading opponent, and at the end of Clinton's life again made a tenuous alliance with him, based on their common support of Andrew Jackson for the presidency in 1828. The fact that Clinton held the governorship for more than eight of his last ten years of life suggests that Van Buren faced an adversary who could keep him busy.

If Clinton was born to the purple, arriving early at political prominence through the influence of his family, Van Buren was a self-made politician. Although he was not exactly poor, Van Buren had a hard upbringing—his father's property, he notes in his *Autobiography,* was originally moderate but "was gradually reduced until he could but illy afford to bestow the necessary means upon the education of his children." According to the son, "It has thro' life been a source of regret" that he had never had the opportunity to get a good education. Clinton, who wore his learning as ostentatiously as any man of his time, may well have awakened, perhaps even played on, a sense in Van Buren of intellectual inferiority. Yet it was the insufficiently educated Van Buren who left both an entertaining autobiography and the *Origin and Course of Political Parties in the United States,* which are still read, while Clinton's scientific efforts, some of them quite respectable, receive faint attention.[8]

It was Clinton who encouraged Van Buren to run for the New York State Senate in 1812. Van Buren had originally dismissed such a thought, considering himself too young and being busily occupied in a career as a lawyer. He changed his mind and he won, although to do so he had had to defeat Edward P. Livingston. Clinton was no doubt gratified at the possibility this provided of thwarting his influential former allies. Once in the New York Senate, Van Buren joined with his Republican colleagues in supporting Clinton's candidacy for president, although in his memoirs he characterized this support as "a great error" on the part of the legislature. He believed that Clinton should have refused the nomination once war broke out.[9]

The rupture between them came the following year. The occasion for it, according to Van Buren, was the election of the Federalist Rufus King as United States senator despite a Republican majority in the state senate. Numerous Clintonians had voted for King, and the suspicion that their votes were a quid pro quo for Federalist support for Clinton in 1812 was widespread. When Van Buren confronted Clinton with these suspicions, Clinton professed his innocence but Van Buren was unpersuaded. (As mentioned earlier, King's election appears to have been related to deals made in connection with the charter of the Bank of America, not Clinton's presidential candidacy, which King opposed.) When the time came to select the nominees for governor and lieutenant governor, Van Buren nonetheless urged the renomination of Clinton for second place on the ticket, but the anti-Clintonians secured the nomination for Judge John Taylor instead. When Van Buren offered his strong support to the ticket, including a role as one of its chief propagandists—he subsequently wrote the address to the voters—Clinton was miffed. Van Buren, for his part, certainly felt that he had reasons to complain of Clinton's treatment of him. He had been led to believe, for instance, that Clinton was going to secure his appointment as state attorney general, but instead Thomas Addis Emmett got the job. Van Buren thereupon inferred, as he tersely put it, that "Mr. Clinton had changed his views." Dashed hopes, together with the election of King, undoubtedly encouraged Van Buren's defection from the Clintonian ranks. (Years later, he discovered that the appointment had been Tompkins's doing and confessed that he had nursed an unjustified resentment against Clinton.)[10]

Van Buren's story of his support of Clinton for lieutenant governor, in spite of his disappointment about the attorney generalship, seems to omit—perhaps characteristically—a certain something. He concedes some inconsistency between his attempt to get Clinton renominated as lieutenant governor and his suspicions of Clinton's dealings with King, but claims he was influenced by "lingering attachments and the dread of being supposed capable of abandoning an old friend."[11]

If Van Buren was for practical purposes the leader of the opposition to Clinton from this time forward, the figurehead of the anti-Clintonians was Governor Tompkins. As we have seen, Tompkins, like Van Buren, received early political encouragement from Clinton, who chose him to run for governor in 1807 after Morgan Lewis had shown his independence of Clinton. Tompkins's allegiance to the Virginia Dynasty, first in his support of the unpopular Embargo and later in his energetic prosecution of the war, had made him a favorite in Washington, just as Clinton's opposition had made him anathema to the Virginians. Ironically, it was Tompkins's ties to the Virginians that gave Clinton his chance at the governorship.

CLINTON'S RETURN TO POLITICS

Clinton's continuance as mayor had depended on Federalist support in the Council of Appointment. In 1813, antiwar sentiment had insured a Federalist majority in the assembly, and Clinton remained in office because of a trade in the council whereby the Republican member of the council, Henry A. Townsend, gave his support to Jonas Platt's nomination to a judgeship in return for Federalist support for Clinton's reappointment as mayor. But the Republican victory in the spring of 1814 signaled that Clinton's days as mayor were numbered, and soon after the legislature convened in January 1815, he was stripped of his office by the Council of Appointment.

The situation of Mr. Clinton, Jabez Hammond narrates,

> was now deplorable, and his prospects were painfully gloomy. To all appearance his political expectations were entirely blasted. He was no longer in fellowship with the republican party. There was no reasonable ground to believe that the federalists would regain an ascendancy either in the state or nation, and if they should, there was little probability that they would bestow on him any marks of distinction or favor. From youth up he had devoted himself to politics, and had never followed any business or profession. He had a large family dependent on him for education and support, and al-

though he was neither a speculator nor profuse in his expenses, by reason of responsibilities he had improvidently assumed for others, and a want of system in his domestic
economy, he was insolvent for many thousands of dollars.[12]

There may have been a trickle of consolation in the letters that came to him from
prominent figures in the Anglo-American intellectual community, thanking him for
copies of his *Introductory Discourse*. There was one from Gouverneur Morris, who also
complained about the way his own efforts to introduce European pheasants and cultivate oyster beds had failed before the guns and rakes of the "idle poor." Another
from Thomas Jefferson congratulated Clinton on the "fast advancing" state of culture in New York. From Philadelphia, the editor of the *Port Folio* requested a copy of
the *Discourse* for review, which Clinton promptly sent him. More thanks poured in
from such prominent men in Britain as the Earl of Buchan and Sir Joseph Banks.[13]

Political consolations were present as well. On the eve of St. Patrick's Day 1815, just
after his removal as mayor was announced, he received a memorial from "Natural-
ized Citizens of Irish Birth" praising his many efforts on their behalf. Various other
correspondents decried his removal and praised his leadership. In March 1816, Clinton
was being urged by Gideon Granger to "allow yourself to be held up for the Presidency of the Nation."[14]

Although by this time Clinton's advocacy of the Erie Canal was already repairing
his political career in New York, he was not likely to receive substantial national support in 1816. But in Albany Daniel D. Tompkins was hoping to convert his longstand-
ing loyalty to the Virginia Dynasty into a chance at succeeding Madison as president.
Jabez Hammond, who was in Congress at the time, records that nearly all the Republican members of the New York delegation were in favor of a Tompkins candidacy.
But congressmen from the South opposed Tompkins, claiming that, never having
held national office, he was unknown to their constituents. Hammond and others
then looked for ways to secure the nomination for William H. Crawford, of Georgia,
the Secretary of War. Tompkins understandably thought they were giving up on him
too quickly. Clinton came out for Monroe; Van Buren stayed on the sidelines; and
Tompkins, following the vice presidential precedent of Aaron Burr and George Clinton, was nominated to serve as the New York backup for a new Virginia president.[15]

Tompkins's claim to national office was based largely on his performance as governor during the War of 1812, when his vigorous support of the Madison administration's war efforts earned him a reputation as a patriot to go along with what was
known of him as a personable politician. His differences with Clinton had grown
more pronounced with the years, and by 1816 he was happy to put whatever obstacles
he could in the way of Clinton's canal project.

The victory of the Monroe-Tompkins ticket, against the feeble Federalist opposition headed by Rufus King, meant that New York would need a new governor. Since
the success of the Republican ticket had never been in doubt, the maneuvering over
a successor to Tompkins had begun soon after he had been nominated. Clinton's
canal work had placed him prominently in the public eye less than a year after his

seemingly final retreat. He had made sure that his works were before the public by writing three articles as "Atticus" that pointed out the virtues of the canal plan while modestly (but accurately) affirming that "no individual, of any political party, can be considered the original projector of the canal."[16]

The impending departure of Tompkins also reshaped alliances within the Republican party in the state. Ambrose Spencer, who had broken with Clinton in 1812, was now ready to patch up their quarrel. Jabez Hammond believed their reconciliation was the work of Spencer's wife, who was Clinton's sister and wanted to restore family harmony. D. S. Alexander thought Spencer perceived that against the power of Tompkins and Van Buren he needed a powerful ally, and that Clinton was, after all, the likeliest one in sight. According to Van Buren, Spencer felt his power in the state "dropping from his hand," and decided, "as no man but himself would have thought of doing," to resurrect his alliance with Clinton. None of these explanations need be wrong. In any event, a dinner was arranged to effect the reconciliation between the brothers-in-law at the Beekman Street residence of Jacob Barker, a New York banker. Van Buren, who was present, says that neither spoke to the other during the meal but "talked at each other through the rest of us in subdued and conciliatory terms," and by the time the evening was over had reconciled. Spencer's son John was decidedly against any such reunion, but his father told him he had better accept it, since "Clinton's nomination as Governor is certain." Besides, "he has been punished eno'."[17]

Van Buren claimed that it would be a pleasure to welcome Clinton back into the party's good graces, so long as it was done gradually enough to preserve the party's integrity. He then determined to block Clinton from becoming governor and considered three different ways of doing it. One was to persuade Tompkins to go on serving as governor while also sitting as vice president, but Tompkins did not care much for that idea. Another was to have Lieutenant Governor Taylor serve the remainder of Tompkins's term (until 1819), but such an arrangement appeared to violate the state constitution. The only remaining course was to find a candidate to run against Clinton for the Republican nomination, but there was an obstacle here as well. Since Spencer controlled the Council of Appointment, "those who sought office knew well whose nomination for governor" they should support. Recognizing the difficulty of obtaining the nomination through the legislative caucus, Spencer and the Clintonian leaders dwelt on the unfairness of that method, which disenfranchised Republican voters in counties that had Federalist representatives. The caucus method had in fact become increasingly unpopular—particularly after the Crawford forces had nearly snatched the Republican caucus nomination for president away from Monroe the year before. The Clintonians were accordingly able to bring about a switch to a convention. Since the Republicans of those counties with Federalist representatives were generally favorable to Clinton, he ended up winning the nomination by a margin of two to one over his fellow canal commissioner Peter B. Porter. In the general election the Federalists offered no candidate, and Porter refused to cooperate with a Tammany scheme to run him in opposition to Clinton. Clinton was elected, with 97 percent of the vote.[18]

GOVERNOR CLINTON

Upon his inauguration as governor on July 1, 1817, DeWitt Clinton might well have relished the thought of how far he had come since his ouster as New York City's mayor just two years before. His thirst for self-congratulation was not easily slaked, nor had his gifts for conciliation and compromise been much enhanced by two years in the political wilderness. And just as the surface calm of the Era of Good Feelings masked the fragmentation of Jefferson's political coalition, so the surface unanimity of DeWitt Clinton's election camouflaged the emergence of a large, well-organized, and brilliantly led opposition. This was the subsequently famous contingent of Bucktails, so called, under the management of Martin Van Buren.[19]

Jabez Hammond, elected to the state senate that year, was a supporter of Clinton. He also had great respect for Van Buren and supposed he would have no trouble voting for bills on their merits, with the various Republican factions working together for the good of the state. "A very few days residence in Albany, and attendance in the senate," he wrote, "convinced me of my error. I found, on one hand, that the governor was cold, if not vindictive, towards Mr. Van Buren and others, who had opposed his elevation, and on the other, a determination to excite prejudices and jealousies against the governor, to render him unpopular . . . and thwart him in his measures."[20]

Measures Clinton had in abundance, and his first address to the legislature laid out a sweeping program of government action that foreshadows President John Quincy Adams's famous inaugural message along similar lines eight years later. Clinton's address called for expanded state aid to support public education as well as subsidies and organizations to further the arts, both useful and fine. It proposed a board of agriculture, "composed of the most experienced and best informed agriculturalists," to help diffuse knowledge, and a "professorship of agriculture" to guide such efforts. But it was not enough, Clinton argued, to improve agriculture if there were not ample outlets for it. Foreign markets had become undependable; the end of the Napoleonic wars had diminished European reliance on American grain and resulted in lower prices. Therefore "we must rely principally on our own internal consumption for the stable and permanent support of agriculture. But this can only be effected by the excitement of other kinds of industry, and the creation of a great manufacturing interest." The end of the wars in Europe had led to a boom in imported goods that contributed to the "prostration of our manufactories," and although the principal responsibility for a cure rested with the federal government, which ought to enact high tariffs, "much may be done by the state government by liberal accommodations, by judicious exemptions."[21]

Another set of recommendations pertained to education, and the Lancastrian system, for which the governor had unbounded expectations. "For if by this means one teacher can perform the functions of ten," he told the legislature, "and if a pupil can learn in one week as much as he would in one month in the common way, it is evident that more wealth, more labor, more time and more industry, can be devoted to the ordinary occupations of life without interfering with the dispensations of knowledge." The state should therefore sponsor a program in which "intelligent young men" would come to New York City to learn their trade at Lancastrian schools already established there, and then would be dispatched across the state to spread enlightenment. Subsidies to academies and colleges should be increased, as "there can be no prodigality in the application of the public treasure" to education. Medical education, too, must be encouraged (for each "well educated physician becomes not only a conservator of health, but a missionary of science"). It must also be reformed; medical students should be required to attend lectures and study for four years before beginning to practice.[22]

Education was just part of Clinton's agenda. The militia, too, should be reformed, and better supplied. (Its early misfortunes in the War of 1812, together with the continued presence of the British Empire on the state's northern border, should stand as a warning.) Governor Clinton heaped renewed praise on the canal, as might be expected. He called attention to the condition of state roads and urged further improvements. He was determined that "all the beneficial objects of society" should be provided for.[23]

But Clinton had more in mind than lavishing the state's resources on every worthy object he could devise; he was also looking for ways to save money, and to spend it more productively. The state debt should be refinanced in order to take advantage of lower interest rates. Auction duties recently removed by the federal government should be replaced by state duties on foreign goods, which would both protect local manufacturers and provide money for state projects. Like his successors today, he attacked the poor laws. They had been based on English models, and "the experience of that country as well as our own, shows that pauperism increases with the augmentation of the funds applied to its relief." In place of relief there should be a "system of coercive labor." He also proposed to end imprisonment for debt, or failing that, to require the creditor to pay the cost of the imprisonment. To protect lenders, however, he wanted stronger laws against fraud.[24]

Although the bulk of the governor's suggestions would increase the scope of state government, Clinton continued to employ the rhetoric of old-fashioned republicanism. Something should be done about the tendency of small country banks to issue far more notes than they could back up, bringing confusion and harm to the state's economic growth. And in ringing republican terms (which echo his "Countryman" letters of thirty years earlier) the governor denounced lawyers who were speculating and buying up notes, the consequence being "excessive consumption of foreign commodities and the introduction of wide-spreading luxury and wide wasting extravagance."[25]

Finally, there was the condition of the Indian tribes in New York State, who, the governor believed, wanted to find new lands, far from any white settlements. At the same time, whites wanted *their* lands in the state. There were thus good reasons to encourage the Indians to move. But any move, Clinton warned, "ought to be free and voluntary on their part, and whenever it takes place, it is our duty to see that they receive an ample compensation for their territory."[26]

Such was the design, brimming with great and worthy aims, that Governor DeWitt Clinton presented in his first address to the legislature.

But what the legislature would do with it, or with the governor himself, was another matter. At least half the trouble lay with the governor. Time and again the combination of Bucktail opposition and Clintonian arrogance brought matters to a standstill. Jabez Hammond had a clear appreciation of the obstacles Clinton faced, and as one of the governor's closest advisers did his best to suggest ways around them. One of those obstacles was the presence of dubious or treacherous allies: Van Buren had managed to arrange for the selection of a Council of Appointment that initially appeared Clintonian but was in fact opposed to him. Henry Yates, from the Eastern District, was the duplicitous member. Similarly the senate, which appeared to be controlled by Clinton, was actually in the hands of his enemies. When Hammond revealed this information to the governor, "he affected to treat [the matter] with great indifference, and urged that I was mistaken in the canvass I had made." Perceiving a rift between Van Buren and Samuel Young, the assembly speaker, Hammond got Young's agreement to an alliance with Clinton—but Clinton rejected it. "From that moment," wrote Hammond, "my confidence in Gov. Clinton, as a good practical politician, in a popular government, was gone. I have never regained it. However noble and magnificent were his ends, he failed in providing the means for their accomplishment."[27]

Clinton was without doubt faced with formidable difficulties. He needed to bring the Federalists, present and former, into his party without seeming to abandon republicanism and without alarming Republican voters or their representatives. But the Federalists wanted offices in return. Clinton managed to give them too few to satisfy them but enough to alarm his fellow Republicans. When he finally determined to use Federalist support openly, in defiance of the Republican party, the result, in Hammond's view, was the Clintonians' "ruin as a party."[28]

The crisis came with the election of the assembly speaker in 1819. Clinton and Spencer wanted Obadiah German, who had been a strenuous critic of the War of 1812, and who for that and other reasons was to Van Buren and his friends "the most obnoxious man in the Clintonian ranks." Owing to careless management by the Clintonians, the Bucktails had a majority at the Republican nominating caucus. All the Bucktails attended the meeting, but seventeen Clintonians were absent. So the Bucktail candidate, William Thompson, was endorsed by the caucus. But the choosing of a speaker required the votes of the entire assembly, so Clinton then enlisted Federalist support for German, who was thereupon elected. Clinton's abandonment of the Republican party's nominee and his use of Federalist votes to thwart the party's choice inflamed partisan Republicans all over the state. With this step, Van Buren later wrote, "the Rubicon was passed by the Clintonians and a speedy separation of the party made certain."[29]

Clinton still had a trump card in his support for the canal. The Bucktails had made opposition to the canal a keystone of their policy. But with the canal moving forward, they perceived that it might be prudent to reverse themselves, which they did. This turnabout removed the most prominent policy dispute between the Clintonians and the Bucktails, and the Bucktails had no scruples about turning their conversion to their own advantage. Their mouthpiece, the *Albany Argus,* portrayed a

Clintonian proposal to let out canal contracts in smaller sections—to get tighter control over costs—as evidence of the governor's halfhearted support of the canal. The Clintonians were naturally outraged by the way in which Mordecai Noah and other Bucktail propagandists tried to present Van Buren as a champion of the canal and Clinton as an enemy of it. Finally, in 1819 Hammond warned the governor that Van Buren's forces were moving to take control of the canal commission. Clinton, he recorded, "laughed at my fears." The joke, however, was on Clinton. The future of the Federalist party was clearly limited, and its members were beginning to seek homes for themselves in the Republican party, some allying with Clinton, but others, who came to be called the "high-minded Federalists," joining with the Bucktails. It was this remnant that assisted Van Buren in electing the Bucktail candidate Henry Seymour to the Canal Commission. The commission was now firmly under Bucktail control, where it remained. "Thus," wrote Hammond, "the political influence which Mr. Clinton had labored [for] . . . was henceforth and until the day of his death used to annoy and to prostrate him." The *Albany Argus* crowed that canal contractors would no longer have to support Clinton to be awarded work; the message was, of course, that they would have to declare themselves in favor of the Bucktails.[30]

Clinton's first term was also a time of personal tragedy. There was at the start some good news—a victory in a legal battle concerning Clinton's real-estate holdings that repaired to some extent his personal fortunes. That year, 1817, also saw the birth of his tenth child, Julia Catherine, and there were now seven surviving children to provide for. But Maria Franklin Clinton sickened after the delivery and never recovered. She died on July 30, 1818. That night Clinton wrote in his diary, "She retired to another & better world with characteristic fortitude, leaving an immedicabile vulnus in my heart, which will be felt with the continuance of life." With characteristic exactitude he recorded her age—forty-two years, eight months, twenty-two days. It is also characteristic that he gave no further expression to his feelings, even to his diary.[31]

Shortly before his wife's death, he had fractured a leg in a fall while riding. The accident left him lame, and without his accustomed exercise he put on weight, and his own health began slowly to deteriorate. As James Renwick wrote of his late friend in 1840, "To this change in habits, from active to sedentary, may be ascribed the gradual approach of that disease, which carried him off in the zenith of his faculties."[32]

Clinton was in many ways a reserved and even cold man, but to his children he was a loving and devoted father. After his wife's death, a certain Mrs. Ingraham had offered to take care of his baby daughter Julia. Declining, but with many thanks, he wrote to her, "You know that parental fondness, is one of the weak points of my character—I cannot part with her—the dear child without understanding her irreparable loss, clings to me with increased assiduity & watches my motions as if she were apprehensive that I should also leave her." When his son Walter died, in 1810, his diary merely noted, "Poor Walter died this morning at 1/2 after 4." But many years later David Hosack, in a memorial address after Clinton's own death, revealed the pain that was contained in those few words. Months after his son's death, Clinton, "when passing through the street, and accidentally observing a lad so resembling in dress, person, and appearance, his departed son . . . eagerly rushed forward in pursuit of his supposed child, calling him to his embrace by the beloved name of his 'Walter!—Walter!'"[33]

DeWitt Clinton remarried within a year of his wife's death—on April 1, 1819—and thus provided his seven children with a new mother. She was Catherine Jones, daughter of Thomas Jones, a New York doctor. Unlike Maria Franklin Clinton, to whom her husband once wrote fondly, "You are not much of a politician," Catherine Jones Clinton enjoyed the political intrigues and social perquisites that went with being the governor's wife.[34]

THE RACE FOR GOVERNOR, 1820

Even the most admiring biographers of DeWitt Clinton have conceded that he was a difficult man to be around. Jabez Hammond, whose portrait of Clinton is sympathetic but not uncritical, tells the story of a farmer who had tried repeatedly to have his imprisoned son pardoned. Twice he had visited Governor Tompkins to ask for a pardon, and twice he was denied. Then he went to Clinton. "The governor was so good as to ask me to breakfast and promptly pardoned my son," the farmer recalled, "but . . . I must say that, although I have seen Gov. Tompkins but twice, and although each time he positively refused to grant me the favor I desired, and Gov. Clinton has granted me that very favor upon the first time of asking, I like Gov. Tompkins better than I like or can like Gov. Clinton—I can not tell the reason why."[35]

Daniel D. Tompkins's political career was built on this very geniality that Clinton lacked. He had added to this advantage by following orthodox Jeffersonian politics and by trusting his fortunes to Van Buren's Bucktails. The "Farmer's Boy" was generally liked, and when the Bucktails looked for a candidate to unseat Clinton in 1820, they turned again to Tompkins.

The contest had national overtones arising from the debate over the extension of slavery that was ignited by the Tallmadge Amendment of 1819 and not resolved by the Missouri Compromise until 1821.[36] New Yorkers played leading roles in this assault on slave institutions. Representative James Tallmadge was from New York, as was the antislavery Speaker of the House, John W. Taylor; Rufus King was a leader of the antislavery forces in the United States Senate. Southerners and their allies charged that Clintonians and Federalists were forming a northern party that would threaten southern interests. Clinton himself was suspected of having been behind the entire conspiracy. But these southern fears were ill-founded. Tallmadge's letters in this period complain of how Clinton had treated him poorly—"Mr. Clinton has found it consistent with his ideas of friendship & fidelity to assail & persecute me"—while Rufus King never relaxed his strenuous dislike for the governor. Clinton showed no great interest in the issue, according to Taylor, until he saw its popularity in New York, at which time he became a vocal supporter of the antislavery initiative. Rufus

King would not support Clinton, but neither could he bring himself to endorse Tompkins in the 1820 gubernatorial race because of Tompkins's "unsoundness" on the extension of slavery.[37]

We have earlier noted the unlikelihood today of anyone's wanting to leave the United States Senate, as DeWitt Clinton did in 1803, to be mayor. It is almost as unlikely that a sitting vice president would present himself for the governorship of any state, even New York. Yet that is what Tompkins did in 1820. He was persuaded to do so by Van Buren, on the ground that only he would have a chance to defeat Clinton. Tompkins did, to be sure, have certain liabilities. One was his deserved reputation as an enemy of the canal project. James Renwick some years later surmised that the election of Tompkins in 1820 "would in all probability have been followed by the cessation of all work upon it, and the withdrawal of the funds appropriated." Renwick may have exaggerated—Bucktail policy had already lined up behind the canal, and Tompkins could probably not have stopped work even if he had wanted to. But his past words and actions were on the record, and there were those who would not be disposed to forget them.[38]

The other difficulty was somewhat larger. During the War of 1812, Tompkins had resorted to a creative intermingling of personal and government finances to continue state support for the war, particularly after the Federalist legislature elected in 1813 did everything possible to thwart Madison's war policies. Throughout much of Tompkins's term as vice president there had been wrangling back home over his accounts, an audit having revealed them short by more than $100,000. Probably few supposed that Tompkins had pocketed the money himself, but the disorder of his finances and the possibility of corruption would do his campaign no good.[39]

But Clinton, too, had his liabilities. For good Republicans, the suspicion that he was in league with the Federalists remained deep, and it had gained in credibility following the actions of the Clintonian Council of Appointment in 1819. Having achieved firm control over the council that winter, Clinton had moved to clean the stables. One of the victims was his former friend Richard Riker, who had split with Clinton in 1814, when Jonas Platt received Clinton's support for appointment to the supreme court. Appointed in 1815 to the job of recorder of the City of New York by the same Council of Appointment that had stripped Clinton of the mayoralty, Riker was removed from office in 1819 and replaced by Peter Jay, who like his father was a staunch Federalist. Then Van Buren was ousted as attorney general and replaced by Thomas J. Oakley, also a Federalist.[40]

It was particularly worrisome that the most vehement denunciations of Clinton's supposed lack of principles should come from a group of "High-minded Federalists" led by the sons of Alexander Hamilton and Rufus King and employing the talents of Gulian C. Verplanck. (John A. King resented the role Clinton had played in blocking his father's reelection to the United States Senate in 1819, when Clinton had supported his nephew John C. Spencer and Van Buren backed Samuel Young. Neither side was able to elect its candidate, and in 1820 Rufus King allied himself with the Bucktails and was elected.) These "Bucktail Bards," as they were known, hastened to denounce Clinton's Federalist allies as being like the Swiss, "whose only thought is pay." Declaring the Federalist party defunct, they enlisted on the side of the Buck-tails, and fifty of them issued a call to the state's Federalists to renounce Clinton. It appears that few heeded the call. Hammond declared that never in the state's history did such an impressive group of men gather "for the accomplishment of a single po-litical object" yet carry "so few of the rank and file men with them, as did these fifty high minded federalists."[41]

But if these High-minded Federalists did not lead a political host, they could cer-tainly jump into print. Their barbs, to the haughty and equally high-minded Clinton, must have been maddening. Being attacked as an unprincipled politician was bad enough. But when these wretches held up to ridicule his picture of himself as a man of science and crusader for culture, they were striking at him where his self-esteem was thickest and his armor thinnest. One of the Bards, "Pindar Puff," versified:

> Of Clinton will I sing, and what sage Pell
> Hath told in pompous prose, in Verse I'll tell;
> His martial deeds upon Hoboken's shore
> His skill in conch-shells, and his Indian lore
> his wond'rous wisdom in our state affairs,
> His curious knowledge of the tails of bears;
> Tell, how the learned all his works review,
> In China, Lapland, Hayti, and Peru;
> How in yon hall, to science dear, and fame,
> Clinton and Newton equal honors claim.[42]

Clinton may have drawn a touch of wan comfort from another piece of doggerel sent him in the mail by a stubborn defender:

> Destin'd to bear a Patriot's honor'd name,
> Each coming day renews thy well earn'd fame,
> Where e'er our limits reach from shore to shore,
> In thee our friend and Patron we implore.
> 'Tis thine each Art and Science to unfold,
> 'Tis thine *Columbia's* honor to uphold.
> *Clinton* proceed, thy steady course pursue
> Let others practice what in thee we view,
> In vain shall Envy raise her sicken'd head
> No factious clamour need'st thou ever dred;
> True to thy country, lov'd, rever'd and blest,
> On this firm basis thou 'lt securely rest,
> Number'd amongst the wisest and the best.[43]

On the other hand, attacks from some Federalists on the heels of attacks from elsewhere for courting other Federalists may have had the inconclusive effect of tak-ing some of the wind out of all such charges. Moreover, the fact that Clinton's most virulent critics called themselves Federalists served to blunt charges of his own com-plicity with the Federalists. And the fact that the national government had, in the wake of the War of 1812, adopted such Federalist policies as a Bank of the United States and a protective tariff also vitiated the force of traditional party enmities, as did the virtual evaporation of the Federalist party itself. In any case the campaign of 1820 was closely fought, with Tompkins assisted by Tammany support in New York City. The *Albany Argus* told its readers that Clintonian meetings were "thinly attended," and a few days before the election claimed to have discovered evidence of a Clintonian attempt to bribe a Rockland County official to manipulate the vote. Tompkins also had some success in playing on the dissatisfaction of those parts of the state, notably the southern tier, which felt bypassed by the bounty now flowing to the areas along the canal route. Clinton's side again stressed his intellect and reminded Irish voters of his long-standing concern for them and of Tammany's tradition of contempt for immigrants. In the end Clinton prevailed, though by the narrow margin of 1,457 votes out of more than 90,000 cast. The Bucktails carried both houses of the legislature, leaving Clinton in office but powerless to achieve very many of his grand objectives.[44]

Yet Clinton could see only his own victory, and it emboldened him to take the high ground in his plans in the state and the nation. On November 11, six months after the election, he wrote to Henry Post that the "Bucktails have risen to fall like Lucifer never to rise again," and a week later he asked Post to gather "authenticated evidence of the interference of the National Gov't in our Elections. Our friends must be up & doing on this subject—It is all important." He also wrote to members of Congress in Washington, "I will thank you for a Statement under oath of your Interview with the Post Master General relative to the removal of certain post masters in this state on the application of Mr. Van Buren."[45]

Clinton, in effect, was declaring war on President James Monroe. He had supported Monroe in 1816, and Monroe had initially favored Clintonians with federal jobs in New York, but he soon began directing the bulk of patronage to Bucktails. The message was made unmistakable in 1820, when two Clintonian postmasters were dismissed and replaced by Bucktails shortly before the state elections. On November 7, Clinton sent a message to the legislature accusing the Monroe administration of interfering in the state elections, whereupon the legislature demanded that the governor back up his claims with evidence. (This was what provoked Clinton's letters to Post and the congressmen, though he might have done better to collect the evidence first.) He did so on January 18, 1821, sending the legislature a packet of documents in a green bag, with a communication that came to be known as the "Green Bag Message." Although there was ample evidence of electoral activities by federal appointees, the Bucktail-controlled legislature saw no need to take any action. Along with a detailed rebuttal to many of Clinton's charges, the reply essentially was that, whether the Governor liked it or not, no law had been broken. Clinton had crowed, "Washington is in terror and confusion." But the sad fact was that the Green Bag held nothing for him.[46]

REFORM AND RETREAT

Although the Bucktails may not have prevented Clinton's reelection, they were certainly not finished with him. They now prepared to drive him from office by rewriting the state's constitution. The constitution of 1777 had already been revised once: in the convention of 1801 DeWitt Clinton had managed to get his own way regarding the Council of Appointment in his struggle with John Jay. But otherwise the old charter remained largely intact, and the relics of aristocracy that remained embedded in it—in particular, the Council of Appointment and the Council of Revision— had through years of abuse become highly unpopular symbols of what was wrong with New York politics. Nearly everyone claimed to favor a revised constitution, but in matters of timing and scope there were considerable differences.

The Clintonians wanted the entire process of revision delayed until the results of the 1820 census could be reflected in the state's electoral districts. The westward movement that construction of the canal had accelerated had brought thousands of new settlers to the western part of the state, and it was now grossly underrepresented in the legislature. It was also strongly Clintonian, as the 1820 election had shown. But delay appeared no longer possible when the Bucktails insisted on making the issue a primary imperative, and on calling a convention immediately—as they did, with great fanfare, at a Tammany Hall meeting on August 25, 1820. Clinton then tried to have the convention's powers limited to certain questions, mainly to abolishing the councils and expanding the suffrage, so that the Bucktails, in what was clearly going to be a Bucktail gathering, would not be free simply to remake the state to their own advantage. He particularly wanted to prevent an assault on the judiciary, which remained a center of Federalist influence. But the various stratagems of Clinton and others to limit the convention failed, and on August 28, 1821, the convention met.[47]

New York's constitutional convention of 1821 was one of the last occasions in American history where a forthright defense of property qualifications for voting was offered by men in power. Chancellor James Kent in particular is remembered for his insistence on defending the rights of property against the leveling tendencies of mass rule. But in the years since the 1801 convention, democratic equality, once seen as a threat, had come to be more or less commonly assumed. At the 1821 convention, property qualifications were for the most part abolished; even attempts to retain a property qualification for those in public office were voted down. A few restrictions on white male voters remained, though these, too, would be removed by law four years later. But on the few African-American voters, who had earlier stood with the Federalists and were now largely Clintonian, was imposed a property qualification exceedingly difficult to meet. They would be disfranchised altogether in the state constitutional convention of 1846.[48]

The results of the convention, as Clinton had rightly feared, amounted to a virtual sweep for the Bucktails. The judiciary was remade, the Council of Appointment and the Council of Revision were abolished, and the expansion of suffrage for white males was nearly complete. The governor was given appointive powers, with the senate having a veto over nominees for the more important positions. Greater power was granted to local governments, and the soldiers of the militia were granted the right to elect all but their general officers. And, with an eye on the incumbent, the term of the governor was reduced to two years and the date of the election moved forward from April to November, so that Clinton's term would end on January 1, 1823.[49]

For once, DeWitt Clinton saw the handwriting on the wall. Deprived of allies by his own intransigence and by the threats and cajoleries of his opponents, with the canal so widely supported that his role as its champion seemed no longer vital, he decided not to run again. At the beginning of 1823 he was back in private life—now, it seemed, for good.

Eleven

o　o　o

RESURRECTION

Cᴏᴍᴘᴀʀᴇᴅ ᴡɪᴛʜ ᴄʟɪɴᴛᴏɴ's prostration in 1815, that of 1823 appeared even more likely to be final. The new state constitution seemed to insure that the reins of state power would remain firmly in the grasp of the Bucktails. Clinton's most potent issue had lost its salience: everyone now favored the canal. The Federalist party, whose remnants had helped Clinton win and exercise the governorship, had dissolved, and many Federalists had cast their lot with Van Buren's men, who controlled patronage and, unlike the erratic Clinton, made a point of rewarding faithful adherents. But, as in 1815, Clinton would manage to associate himself with a political issue that swept all before it, and two years after being driven from office he was again inaugurated as governor. This time he owed his revival to the presidential race of 1824, which brought a divisive end to the brief Era of Good Feelings, and to his own good fortune in being the victim of one of the most misbegotten acts of partisanship in the nation's history.

ON THE SIDELINES

Political defeat always made Clinton worry about money. His ouster from the mayoralty in 1807 had left him in charge of the family purse. After the Federalist victory in the legislative elections of 1809, he became more aggressive in trying to collect sums owed him. In October 1821 a proposal was drawn up to sell shares in his library, which was valued at $20,000. (One of the subscribers was William James of Albany, grandfather of William and Henry James.) Early in 1822 he wrote Jabez Hammond and asked to borrow $1,000. He was often in debt, and he was said to have renewed a loan at the Franklin Bank so many times that by 1827 he owed $200,000.[1]

Yet whatever flaws Clinton may have had, lack of faith in his own powers was not among them, nor was a tendency to mope, and he relentlessly explored ways to place himself once more in public office. Remaining in the public eye was one strategy, and the year 1823 brought a splendid opportunity to remind the voters of his services on the Canal Commission. On October 8, the ceremony opening the link between the completed sections of the canal and the Hudson River was held, and Clinton, having planned the festivities himself, was much in evidence. He was the featured speaker at the ceremonies, and the first boat to pass from the canal to the Hudson was named the *De Witt Clinton*.[2]

Clinton also continued to refresh his image as a man of serious intellect. The opportunity to address the Phi Beta Kappa Society of Union College, in Schenectady, brought forth an oration on the importance of learning to the proper governance of a republic. "Knowledge," he told his listeners, "is the cause as well as the effect of good government." In Europe, he told the Union students, "a corps of literary men in the cities" of even the most despotic regimes "have exercised an influence over public opinion almost irresistible." Even the harshest rulers must bend to "public opinion." Public opinion, he might have added hopefully, would vindicate good rulers who had been turned from power.[3]

PRESIDENTIAL RABIES

Clinton had watched with a bilious eye the 1822 race to succeed him, which was in reality no race at all. It pitted Joseph C. Yates, the Bucktail choice, against Solomon Southwick, a former state printer. Southwick's sanguine personality was such that, Jabez Hammond remarked, "He was in daily expectation that the next mail would bring him news that he had won the highest prize in a lottery." The same Micawberish spirit permeated his campaign for governor. He had the luck to enlist a promising young propagandist (and fellow printer) named Thurlow Weed for his campaign, and Southwick's perpetual confidence clouded the judgment of DeWitt Clinton, who in January 1822 told Henry Post that "Yates and Van Buren are both prostrate & the latter particularly so." In August he wrote that "Yates is unpopular," and in September that "Yates is despised and talked against openly." Yates won in November with 131,403 votes to Southwick's 2,910. Undaunted by the landslide, Clinton declared to Cadwallader Colden early in 1823, "If I had been a candidate, I would have been reelected governor."[4]

Such imaginings carried over onto the national scene as well. Whatever his difficulties with Van Buren and his followers in New York, Clinton's national reputation was enhanced by the already apparent success of the Erie Canal. He could be seen as a man who knew how to get things done; he could also exemplify the case for a more active national government. Although the Republicans in 1816 had appropriated such Federalist objects as a tariff and a national bank, any substantial progress on internal improvements had so far been thwarted by presidents with a narrow interpretation of what the Constitution allowed the federal government to do.

Clinton was all too ready to interpret the slightest favorable-looking ripple as evidence of a rising national tide that would lift him to the presidency. In April 1822, he was sure that all the candidates—Crawford, Calhoun, Adams, and Clay—had "outraged public sentiment." By October these candidates, now joined by Andrew Jackson, appeared to be in even worse straits: "The prostration of Crawford. Jackson and Clay will not get up. Calhoun and Adams are now *hors de combat.*" In December he was looking for copies of writings by John and John Quincy Adams that might be used to brand the son a monarchist, as the Jeffersonians had branded the father a quarter century earlier. Clinton saw Jefferson himself as an avid supporter. In his diary in 1823 he recorded a somewhat unlikely "Story of Jefferson pumped by his neighbors said the President ought to be the greatest man in America—afterwards asked who was, he said DWC."[5]

Clinton recorded in his diary every optimistic scrap, more and more convinced that 1824 might be his year. "Judge Van Ness thinks that the division at Washington would bring in C." (In his diary, Clinton refers to himself as "C.") On October 24, "[Mordecai] Noah told Vanderburgh that the Tammany Party would still support Clinton." Five days later, "The President's Secretary told Dr. Hosack that he believed Clinton would prevail," and the day after that, "Crawford speaks highly of C." And the following day: "Dreams—Can we command our dreams?" Early the next month he has heard that Van Buren told "a young lawyer in Albany that in 10 days I would be nominated at Washington."[6]

Meanwhile, the other contenders' prospects grow ever more desperate. Calhoun is breaking with Adams; "Crawford as great a debauchee as Clay"; Crawford has the backing of politicians and editors but "has failed in getting the people"; "Adams falling off to the west."[7]

Clinton did not personally promote his own cause. One well-wisher was telling him "to be still is to rise" and advising Clinton's other friends "to be silent—every thing will come." As late as March 1824, in spite of various signs, Clinton continued to hope: "I think that Crawford is *hors de combat.* Calhoun never had force, and Clay is equally out of the question. Pennsylvania has made Jackson strong. As for Adams, he can only succeed by the imbecility of his opponents, not by his own strength. In this crisis *may not some other person bear away the palm?*"[8]

END OF GOOD FEELINGS

In 1824 James Monroe's presence in the White House meant that Virginia had supplied the president in all but four of the country's thirty-five years under the Constitution. Now, no Virginia resident was in line to replace him. And the non-Virginian contenders were a remarkably talented and ambitious group. Meanwhile, although DeWitt Clinton was a candidate for president only in his own imaginings and those of his most devoted followers, the presidential contest would have profound consequences for the governor's race in New York; and New York would in turn have a decisive effect on the outcome of the race for the presidency.

Prominent among the presidential contestants was William H. Crawford of Georgia; he had been born in Virginia and was the favorite candidate of the Old Dominion.

Crawford had served in the United States Senate before becoming minister to France under Madison, and then for a time in 1815 secretary of war. Since 1816 he had been secretary of the treasury and was now a favorite candidate of the Old Republicans, those even more fundamentalist in their insistence on republican purity than Madison and Monroe. On St. Valentine's Day 1824, the Republican caucus in Washington nominated Crawford for president, with Albert Gallatin as his running mate. Crawford now had two heavy burdens. One was the caucus nomination; the other was a paralytic stroke he had suffered in the fall of 1823.[9]

The other southern candidate, Calhoun, withdrew from the race in March after the Pennsylvania convention nominated Jackson for president and himself for vice president. He accepted his own nomination, but in the election declined to support any presidential candidate. Both Crawford and John Quincy Adams thought they had earlier assurances from Calhoun that he would not interfere with their campaigns by running in 1824 at all, and each had interpreted this pledge as a sign of support for himself. Both felt betrayed, first by Calhoun's candidacy for president and then by his retiring from the field in a manner that aided Jackson.[10]

The candidate with the greatest enthusiasm for internal improvements was Kentucky's Henry Clay. Clay had tried without success to supplant Tompkins as vice president in 1820; he now had grander ideas, and by 1822 was already angling for the support of state caucuses and conventions. His "American System" of protective tariffs and internal improvements offered benefits to both eastern manufacturers and western agriculturalists. Clay saw the opportunity to advance his candidacy by building a coalition between these two interests, and New York was crucial to his plan. But with Crawford having secured the backing of Van Buren and his organization, Clay received little support in the state outside the westernmost regions, where he picked up the support of such prominent leaders (and anti-Clintonians) as Peter B. Porter and William B. Rochester.[11]

Clay's strategy was foiled not in New York but in the western states of which he had felt so sure when he was planning it. When General Jackson, the hero of New Orleans, was nominated by a legislative caucus in Tennessee in July 1822, Clay dismissed it as no more than a gesture of respect for the old soldier. But Jackson's candidacy was too contagious to be so easily discounted, and his selection by the Pennsylvania convention in March 1824 turned it into a serious challenge. Jackson would eventually receive Clinton's support and had publicly expressed his admiration for Clinton as early as 1819. On a visit to New York that year Jackson rose to respond to a series of toasts at a Tammany Hall banquet in his honor, not quite realizing that the hall was by that time less of a benevolent fraternal club, as in earlier days, than a headquarters for anti-Clinton Republicans in New York City. Jackson raised his glass and declaimed: "DeWitt Clinton, the enlightened statesman, Governor of the great and patriotic State of New York." The commotion that followed was greeted with glee in the local press. Fitz-Greene Halleck sent the *Evening Post* some lines of verse:

The songs were good, for Mead and Hawkins sung 'em,
The wine went round, 'twas laughter all and joke;

When crack! the General sprung a mine among 'em,
And beat a safe retreat amid the smoke.

It is unlikely that this misstep affected Jackson's chances of getting Bucktail support in 1824, Van Buren's chief concern being to rebuild the alliance between "the plain re-publicans of the North and the planters of the South." But it certainly raised Clin-ton's opinion of Old Hickory.[12]

The last of the candidates, John Quincy Adams, was probably the most acceptable one in New York State, although his favor there was rooted in sectional preference, not popular affection. Adams's cold, aloof manner alienated even more potential al-lies than did Clinton's hauteur. But Adams was a man of the North, not the South or the West, and his promotion of internal improvements and cultural progress was much like Clinton's. Such similarities lead as often to rivalry as to alliance, and so it was with Adams and Clinton. "The truth is," one insider wrote, Clinton "hates Mr. Adams." Clinton saw Adams as a threat to his own base of support, and in 1824 many anti-Clintonians supported Adams, partly for that reason.[13]

It was Jackson's emergence, however, that finally put an end to Clinton's presi-dential ambitions for 1824, and the latter's attention turned once more to New York State.

THE PEOPLE'S PARTY

In the 1824 presidential election, the decisive battleground in New York was, as it had always been, the state legislature. Presidential electors were chosen by a legislative, rather than a popular, vote. Once the Twelfth Amendment had removed the possi-bility of intrigues, such as those that had attended the election of 1800, this method had not caused any serious problems—that is, so long as the candidates came from opposing parties. But when all the candidates claimed to represent the Republican interest, legislative choice of electors became fiercely controversial. With William Crawford having secured the allegiance of Van Buren and his followers, the choice in New York seemed a foregone conclusion. But the same democratic spirit that was rendering caucus nominations for president unacceptable was also making the leg-islative choice of presidential electors extremely unpopular. By the 1824 election, eighteen of the twenty-four states chose presidential electors directly. Crawford's op-ponents in New York seized on this issue, which was both damaging to Crawford and embarrassing to the proclaimed democratic principles of Van Buren's forces, now being dubbed the Albany Regency by opponents. This term managed to associate the Bucktails with the unsavory political practices of the British Regency of the previous decade while serving to remind voters that the Bucktails in Albany were acting on the instructions of their now-absent sovereign, Martin Van Buren, who since 1821 had been a United States senator. Those opposed to Crawford and the caucus nomination took the name the People's party, and while the People's movement gathered steam, the Regency sought a way to stop it. The Regency wanted to link the People's Party with Clintonianism, but in doing so succeeded not in defeating the People's party but in returning DeWitt Clinton to the governorship.[14]

By April 1823 the issue of popular choice of presidential electors was being advanced in an organized way, and it was soon dividing the New York Republicans. Rufus King ended his curious alliance with Van Buren over it; Van Buren, predictably, was unwilling to allow democratic principles to obstruct Crawford's election. The legislature expressed its support for the nomination of a presidential candidate by congressional caucus, the method most favorable to Crawford; the poor attendance at that caucus in Washington the following February was the first clear sign that the old New York-Virginia coalition was facing trouble.[15]

The electoral issue was dominating state politics in New York. Governor Yates had been erratic in his support for Van Buren's view; in consequence, he had lost backing within his own party. The bill to allow popular choice of electors was introduced in January 1824, and the Regency leader Azariah C. Flagg directed the floor fight against it. The overwhelming public support for the bill made it impossible to oppose directly, so the Regency forces put forward a variety of plans that would ostensibly deliver the presidential choice to the people but were in fact designed to postpone any decision until after the 1824 election. Since Governor Yates was already hors de combat (as Clinton would have put it), Van Buren turned to Samuel Young, who had successfully positioned himself as a supporter of electoral reform, to be the Regency candidate for governor.[16]

THE REGENCY BLUNDERS

So far, Clinton had remained on the sidelines, and the Regency remained busy. Since the People's party favored conventions over caucus nominations, the Regency denounced conventions, trying to link all conventions with the treasonous Hartford Convention in the minds of voters. The People's party was led by James Tallmadge, Henry Wheaton (a journalist and former judge who had entered the state assembly in 1824), and Thurlow Weed, all staunch Adams men. And since Tallmadge, as the leader of the People's party, was generally expected to be its candidate for governor, the destruction of Tallmadge became the key to the Regency's plans. If the Regency greatly exaggerated the Clintonian influence upon the People's party, it was nonetheless true that the People's candidate for governor could not hope to win without Clintonian support. It was to deprive Tallmadge of Clintonian votes (and to try to make support of Adams synonymous with Clintonianism) that the Regency hatched its boldest plan—and made its biggest mistake. Hours before the adjournment of the legislature on April 12, 1824, the Regency introduced a resolution calling for Clinton's dismissal as a canal commissioner.[17]

William L. Stone, the editor of the Clintonian *New York Commercial Advertiser* at the time of Clinton's removal, described the Regency plot succinctly: "Availing themselves of the supposed unpopularity of Mr. Clinton at that moment, they hoped at once to extinguish all clamour upon the subject of the electoral law, and ruin the cause of Mr. Adams, by identifying the friends of this measure and this candidate, with what they were pleased to consider the broken fortunes of the illustrious individual then suffering the pains of political banishment." Since the resolution was offered by Crawford's backers, the Regency apparently expected all those opposed to Crawford to oppose Clinton's removal, and thus open themselves to accusations of embracing Clinton. But many legislators who opposed Crawford had little affection for Clinton, either, and the measure was carried overwhelmingly in the senate (where only three of twenty-four opposed Clinton's removal) and in the assembly, where the vote for removal was 64 to 31. One of those voting with the Regency was James Tallmadge. Thurlow Weed had urged Tallmadge to avoid "the trap baited for him" and oppose the measure, "assuring him solemnly that if he voted for that resolution he could not receive the nomination for governor." Weed was right.[18]

Dixon Ryan Fox called Clinton's removal from the Canal Commission "the one capital blunder of the Regency." Clinton had served on the commission for fourteen years, refusing to accept the salary that went with the position. He was clearly the guiding force behind the Erie Canal. The canal had proved so popular that no political gain could come from opposing it except in areas that were bypassed, such as the state's southern tier. In the many parts of the state already profiting from the canal trade, the response to Clinton's removal was disbelief followed by outrage. Meetings hastily called by Clinton's supporters in Albany and New York were well attended. One of those at the New York meeting recalled it three decades later as "the far-famed meeting of the tens of thousands opposed to the meanness of party strife." Thurlow Weed recorded that after the vote Tallmadge returned to his Albany hotel, which was "filled with citizens, whose rebukes were loudly heard as he passed through the hall to his apartment."[19]

Tallmadge's blunder was Clinton's rebirth. Public outrage at the legislature's action joined with resentment over the stalled progress of electoral reform, and the logic of making DeWitt Clinton the People's party candidate for governor became irresistible. Tallmadge, who had done so much to advance the People's party, had to accept nomination as lieutenant governor at the party's convention in Utica on September 22. There were other results of the removal vote whose consequences were not so soon apparent; William Seward, then a young attorney, abandoned the Regency for a career that would strengthen first the Whig party and then the Republican party.[20]

Clinton's mail was filled with sympathetic letters from friends and resolutions and petitions of support from outraged residents all over the state. Nor was outrage limited to Clintonians. Van Buren, for one, was furious at his subordinates for having blundered so foolishly. He berated Judge Roger Skinner, who had plotted the removal: "I hope, Judge, you are now satisfied that there is such a thing in politics as *killing a man too dead!*"[21]

The Regency had other internal problems. Governor Yates had given up a secure seat on the state supreme court to run for the governorship two years earlier, and he resented being replaced as the Regency candidate by Samuel Young. Following the removal vote in April, Yates saw that the People's party was split between those favoring Clinton and those for Tallmadge or some other candidate. He decided that he could become the champion of electoral reform and thus emerge as the People's party candidate. So on June 2, claiming that his previous unconcern with electoral reform had been owing to his expectation that federal legislation would deal with the issue, he called a special session of the legislature to consider electoral reform. There was no serious consideration of Yates by the People's party, but Yates did have the satisfaction of seeing his former allies in the Regency embarrassed. The session passed no legislation, but it offered Tallmadge a forum for his considerable oratorical gifts and allowed the People's party to make much of the Regency's democratic inconsistencies. When the session adjourned, the People's party had grown even stronger.[22]

Yates's difficulty was not that he misunderstood the divisions within the People's party but that he was not the man to exploit them. The principal split was between the Clintonians and the members loyal to Tallmadge. Following Clinton's nomination on September 22, some People's party delegates walked out proclaiming their opposition to both Clinton and Samuel Young. They did pledge to support Tallmadge for lieutenant governor. But with nowhere to go in the gubernatorial election, they may, according to Hammond, actually have helped the ticket by "banishing any suspicion of a secret understanding between the Clintonians and the people's party."[23]

The campaign between Clinton and Young was bitter. Their political quarrels had personal antecedents going back to the Canal Commission. In 1819, Young had written a scorching letter to Clinton demanding that he state clearly his view of charges of corruption against Young that Young had heard about from James Geddes. Furious that Clinton had not rejected the charges or done anything to prevent their circulation, Young demanded an investigation, sarcastically observing that no wrongdoing on his part "could elude your vigilance" and complaining that the Clintonian papers had been attacking him "in the most abusive manner." Clinton's response was "a very long angry letter," and Young responded with an even longer and angrier one, accusing Clinton of publishing an anonymous attack on him in the *Albany Register.* "I do not expect that you will 'condescend' under your proper signature to bestow upon me further notice," he wrote to Clinton, "but I know all too well the suavity of your disposition, not to anticipate many anonymous favors at your hands." With the precision of formal sentiment that is one of the delights of early-nineteenth-century correspondence, Young concludes his letter "With due respect."[24]

The campaign in 1824, however, dwelled not on the charges against Young but on the presidential contest, the electoral law change, and Clinton's removal from the Canal Commission. Clinton had the popular side of the last two issues, and Regency counterattacks served only to draw the battle lines more clearly and to its own disadvantage. For instance, the fact that Clinton had never accepted a salary for his work on the commission made his dismissal seem particularly objectionable. The *Albany Argus,* the leading Regency paper in the state, attempted to obscure this perception by publishing an estimate that Clinton had been paid more than $160,000 in salary for all the other state offices he had held since 1797; this mainly served to remind voters of the length and diversity of his public service. The *Argus* reminded voters of Clinton's presidential alliance with the Federalists in 1812 and of his vote against the state constitutional convention of 1821; Clinton's forces responded with broadsides refuting the charge about the convention and proclaiming Thomas Jefferson's admiration for Clinton. Young's attempts to portray himself as the true friend of electoral reform failed because he was the Regency candidate: The Regency was opposed to the electoral change, Young was their candidate, so he must oppose it as well. That, at least, was the opinion of the voters, who gave Clinton a majority of nearly seventeen thousand votes. The victory of the People's party statewide was even more remarkable. Tallmadge defeated his opponent for lieutenant governor, Erastus Root, by more than thirty-two thousand votes, while People's party and Clintonian candidates won three-quarters of the legislature. As Jabez Hammond declared, "It was a complete tornado."[25]

PRESIDENTIAL FACTIONS IN NEW YORK

It would be convenient if national and state allegiances lined up cleanly, so that one could equate Regency with Crawfordite and Clintonian with Jacksonian. But matters were more complex. Nor is there great clarity as to which allegiance—state or national—was more important to politicians and voters in New York. But since the state of New York cast the decisive vote in the 1824 presidential election, the Byzantine complexities of New York State politics had a profound outcome on that contest.

That effect was necessarily indirect. In spite of the lopsided victories of Clinton and the People's party in November, the choice of presidential electors remained in the hands of the existing legislature, which was dominated by Van Buren and his men. (At the People's party convention in Utica that September, one delegate had dismissed the presidential contest, commenting that "it would be idle and preposterous to recommend candidates to disfranchised men.") In the state senate, the Crawford ticket received seventeen votes—from the seventeen senators who had voted to delay electoral law reform. Clay and Adams received seven votes each there. But Crawford was less popular in the assembly, where Adams led on the first ballot with fifty votes to Crawford's forty-three and thirty-two for Clay.

A deal between the Clay and Adams forces was struck, and a joint vote of the assembly and the senate chose twenty-five Adams electors and seven for Clay. But a closely divided legislature and three blank ballots left four electors unchosen. On the next ballot, the remaining electors went to Crawford. Those four electoral votes were crucial—they allowed Crawford to take third place away from Clay in the electoral college. Since none of the candidates had managed a majority, only the top three finishers could be considered by the House of Representatives. Those were the rules under the Twelfth Amendment, which Clinton himself had drafted. Clay's greatest hope had been the manipulation of the election in the House, where he was popular and attuned to every political nuance. Failing to make the final cut, he gave his support to Adams.[26]

In the House, the crucial vote for president would come from New York, whose deciding vote would be cast by Stephen Van Rensselaer. Clinton used his influence with the patroon, which was not inconsiderable, in behalf of Jackson. On December 7 Van Rensselaer had written to Clinton requesting that the governor-elect appoint William Paterson Van Rensselaer, his son, to a post as an aide. In the same letter, he reported that Clay could decide the contest, and "my impression is that Jackson will be elected." On December 11 Clinton wrote back to say the job was William's and, describing the "universal zeal and fervor in favor of Jackson in New York," concluded, "I presume that his success may be considered certain." Van Rensselaer replied on the eighteenth that "if our assembly should express an opinion in favor of Jackson it would have an effect here" in Washington. He also said he would try to prevent the state's delegation from casting a tie (and therefore ineffectual) vote on the first ballot. The day Clinton took office again—New Year's Day 1825—he appointed William P. Van Rensselaer his assistant. Ten days later, the patroon wrote that he thought the delegation would support Jackson, although Adams supporters are "very busy," and "this may be uncharitable but I find many are looking out for themselves."[27]

From then until February 9, when the House would at last decide, Van Rensselaer had a wretched time, as vote solicitors from various factions tried to win his favor. But his final decision was made in a way neither Clinton with his favors nor Washington operatives with their pressures could have foreseen. Martin Van Buren is the source for the dramatic story of the patroon's agonized vote. Van Buren had been confident that Van Rensselaer would support Crawford. When the patroon arrived at the Capitol to vote, however, he was waylaid by Clay and Daniel Webster, who browbeat him about the danger to the nation that would arise from a lengthy period of uncertainty about the election's outcome. They reminded him that his large estates in New York gave him a high stake in preserving order and urged him to vote for Adams. Although shaken, "He took his seat fully resolved to vote for Mr. Crawford, but, before the box reached him," according to the story Van Buren says the patroon told him a few days later, "he dropped his head upon the edge of his desk and made a brief appeal to his Maker for guidance in the matter . . . and when he removed his hand from his eyes he saw on the floor directly below him a ticket bearing the name of John Quincy Adams." Taking it as a sign from Heaven, he voted for Adams, assuring his election as sixth president of the United States.[28]

CLINTON BACK IN POWER

Soon after his inauguration as president, John Quincy Adams offered Clinton the post of minister to Britain. Clinton would undoubtedly have relished the opportunity to mingle with all those British scientists, philosophers, and writers whose esteem he so valued; the fact that he declined says something about his preoccupation at that time with New York politics. Clinton was not fond of Adams, but he refused for a different reason. Jabez Hammond had been in Washington during the period between the presidential vote in November and the resolution of the election in the House in February. Clinton, still hoping for a Jackson victory, had asked Hammond to convey to Jackson his preference for remaining in New York; he had heard rumors that he would be Jackson's choice for secretary of state. When the offer came from Adams, Hammond and other friends of Clinton urged him to accept, but he was adamant. Hammond thought that Clinton probably feared what might happen to his political position in New York if he did not stay at home to defend it. It may have been as well that he declined, since he was "ill calculated to act a subordinate part to any man." Clinton in his reply to Adams said that it would be wrong for him, so soon after having been elected governor by the people of New York, to leave and accept other duties.[29]

Back in New York his address to the new legislature was full of Clintonian projects. He wanted further expansion of the canal system, and called for legislation to enact popular choice of presidential electors and to end the few restrictions on white male suffrage left after approval of the 1821 constitution. But despite the Regency's defeat, Clinton still faced a hostile legislature. The People's men elected generally backed Adams (and more strongly so now that he was in the White House), and Clinton remained unrepentantly Jacksonian. When his allies urged him to build a coalition with the People's men in the legislature, Clinton declined.[30]

CLINTON'S MOMENT

Although Clinton had helped invent the spoils system, he displayed at the same time an eighteenth-century contempt for political organization and the compromises of party politics. He wanted to play the statesman, and it was his insensitivity to the political requirements of that role that limited his capacity to influence the course of politics and government in New York and the nation.

But his one great accomplishment, the Erie Canal, proved that it was still possible to achieve something by eighteenth-century means. The canal, begun three days into Clinton's first term as governor, was completed in 1825, as he returned to office. Whereas the linking of finished portions with the Hudson in 1823 had certainly been marked by celebrations of Clinton and his role in the project, the ceremonies marking the completion of the entire canal were practically a beatification.

The grand occasion began in earnest at 10:00 A.M. on Wednesday, October 26, when the canal boat *Seneca Chief* began its journey east from Buffalo with Governor Clinton, Lieutenant Governor Tallmadge, and Thurlow Weed heading the list of passengers. The cabin was graced by a portrait of Clinton in a Roman toga, painted by George Catlin. The journey began with a cannon salute, but no ordinary one. Guns lined the entire route from Buffalo to New York City, each placed within earshot of the those on either side. The salute boomed down to New York and back to Buffalo in three hours and twenty minutes. Thurlow Weed had seen to it that sufficient artillery was available, and Clinton had written to James Renwick ahead of time to propose that this battery might provide a way of measuring the speed of sound. Renwick worked out a plan to set up chronometers along the route, though nothing came of it.[31]

Other boats followed, with other dignitaries, along with samples of the natural wonders, curiosities, and the marketable produce of the West. A boat called *Noah's Ark* "carried an assortment of birds, fish, insects, two young bears, and two Seneca boys." At each significant port the procession stopped for speeches, musical tributes, fireworks, and banners and transparencies honoring the republic, the canal, and Governor Clinton. A large ceremony at Albany included speeches at the Capitol, where the assembly chamber was decorated with portraits of George Washington, George Clinton, and DeWitt Clinton.[32]

But these were only the prelude to the greatest celebration of all, which came on November 4, 1825, when the *Seneca Chief* and its accompanying fleet arrived at New York. At sunrise, a New York City deputation aboard the steamboat *Washington* met Clinton's flotilla on the Hudson; the captain of the *Washington* hailed the lead boat and asked where she was from, and what was her destination. The reply: "From Lake Erie, and bound for Sandy Hook." The deputation presented an elaborate address to Clinton and the other dignitaries, which, like other addresses along the way, stressed the brilliant conception behind the canal, the difficulties of its construction, and the benefits it would bring. The canal would "extend and multiply the advantages of external and international commerce" as well as serve "the essential interests of agriculture and the mechanic arts." It would also "render the chain of our Union stronger and brighter." Clinton's reply paid tribute to "Republican Government" and the Union, but he gave particular attention to the canal's effects on the city itself. "The valley of the Mississippi will soon pour its treasures into this great emporium, through the channels now formed and forming," Clinton said, "and wherever wealth is to be acquired, or enterprise can be attempted, the power and capacity of your City will be felt, and its propitious influence on human happiness, will be acknowledged."[33]

When the boats reached the Atlantic at Sandy Hook, the climax of the ceremonies, the "Wedding of the Waters," took place. On board the *Seneca Chief* were two kegs, painted green and with gilded hoops, that were filled with water from Lake Erie. A portion of one of the kegs was poured into the sea, and the rest was saved to fill commemorative vials that would be sent to distinguished men, including Lafayette. The *Seneca Chief* also carried some bird's-eye maple and cedar to make boxes to hold the vials and the commemorative medals struck in honor of the day. Clinton's remarks at Sandy Hook were brief. He said merely that the ceremony was intended to mark the completion of the work linking "our Mediterranean Seas and the Atlantic Ocean," attributed the work to the "wisdom, public spirit, and energy of the State of New York," and asked God's blessing on it. Following Clinton, Professor Samuel Latham Mitchill poured waters from various rivers—the Elbe, the Seine, the Thames, and the Tagus—into the sea, and then delivered what one of those present indulgently described as a "long and interesting discourse."[34]

The fleet then proceeded into port, where the festivities continued into the night. There were parades, bands, illuminations at City Hall, and more speeches. Artisans marched together carrying banners and mottoes; bakers and tailors, fancy-chair makers and firemen, house painters and stone cutters followed one another all in procession. The contingent from Columbia College carried a banner covered with Tritons, Naiads, a Water God, the God of the Lake, and a succession of locks. "The attention of the several Deities," said the official record of the celebration, "appeared to be arrested by the coming of Neptune, who . . . was pointing to a scene of Minerva, who, having laid aside her aegis, supported in her left hand a Medallion of Clinton, while, with the right, she pointed to a distant view of Columbia College." This magnificent flag was followed by the college's junior and senior classes, and behind them marched the medical students, the militia, and the Freemasons. It was three days before the election, and state law prohibited "the assembling of armed men within ten days before any state elections," so the militia marched without arms.[35]

All agreed that it was a great occasion, both on account of the ceremonies, but, even more, on account of the work they celebrated. But how far did the canal satisfy the prognostications of great wealth, a more perfect Union, and eternal fame that its celebrants issued that November day in 1825? To what extent, that is, did the Erie Canal succeed, and why? How did it change the fortunes of the City of New York, of the state, and of the nation?

Twelve

o o o

THE CANAL AND ITS
CONSEQUENCES

Tʜᴇ ʙᴜɪʟᴅɪɴɢ ᴏғ ᴛʜᴇ Erie Canal was one of the transforming events of the nineteenth century in the United States. It was certainly the most important American public-works project of the century.[1] The fact that the canal was built, when it was built, by the state government of New York left a lasting mark on the nation's economic development, its attitude toward government intervention in the economy, sectional politics, social attitudes, and cultural values. Many of these changes were the very ones hoped for by the canal's progenitors. But the effects of the canal resonated far beyond even those ambitious plans.

In New York State, it was the canal's physical presence that was easiest to understand. The Erie Canal was, in essence, a trench forty feet wide, four feet deep, and 363 miles long. Because Lake Erie was nearly 600 feet higher in elevation than the Hudson River at Albany, the waterway had to rise through eighty-three locks, including a five-tiered set of double locks at Lockport (near Buffalo) that Thurlow Weed proclaimed "will probably remain for ages as a monument of American Genius and American patriotism." To carry the canal across the Genesee River an aqueduct 802 feet long was raised, spanning the river on stone arches. The engineers in charge of work had limited experience, and their need for more trained help was one of the motives that led to the founding of Rensselaer Polytechnic Institute in 1824, the nation's first school dedicated to civil engineering.[2]

The locks and aqueducts drew admiring visitors from America and abroad, and the work the canal offered also attracted many foreigners, particularly new immigrants from Ireland. Most of the work on the canal did not involve spectacular structures. It was ditch digging, only on a grand scale. Men shoveled dirt into wheelbarrows, teams of oxen helped drag away boulders and trees, all amid heat, rain, wind, and mosquitoes. Fifty cents a day was the common wage for laborers, who were hired by the small contractors who bid for work on sections as small as a quarter of a mile

158

in length. And it was in such small increments, through backbreaking, boring labor, that the canal was built.[3]

CLINTON'S BIG DITCH?

No individual reaped greater immediate benefits from the canal than DeWitt Clinton, although the question of who could claim paternity for the canal was a heated one in his day. It is, ultimately, a false question—no single individual or group could claim credit for an achievement that was predicated on favorable geographical circumstances and pursued, with greater or lesser effort, for decades before the celebrations of 1825. But at the same time the mere fact of favorable topography was not sufficient to create a canal, and it is worth remembering that this colossal effort, which began to seem inevitable even as it was being built, was viewed as visionary by some of the most visionary people of the age (including Thomas Jefferson) and was begun at a most unpropitious time. That others conceived the canal and nurtured it in its early years as a private project, and that thousands of people worked to bring it to completion are all fair points. But it was Clinton who revived the canal when it seemed dead, pushed it forward when federal aid was denied, and championed it in public and private forums until it was completed.

Vital roles were played by Jesse Hawley, who was the first to propose the Erie route; by Gouverneur Morris, whose prominence helped carry the plans forward; by Martin Van Buren, whose crucial change of heart in 1817 insured the passage of the bill in the New York legislature; and by James Kent, whose vote in the Council of Revision allowed the bill to become law. But being indispensable to the enactment of the law is not the same as being responsible for it, and it was clearly the opinion of the citizens of New York, as expressed in the election of Clinton in 1817 and his return to office in 1825, that he was the person responsible for the canal. His Bucktail enemies, by heaping disdain on "Clinton's Big Ditch" during the first years of its construction, merely ratified this attribution of responsibility.[4]

There remains the issue of geographic determinism—this easiest path to the continent's interior from the Atlantic coast would certainly have been taken advantage of eventually. But it is the timing of the canal that made it such a historically important event, and it is timing that makes Clinton's advocacy of it so significant. The inevitability of the canal was far from apparent in 1817. The canals that had been built in England connected areas that had already been developed, so the traffic was guaranteed; and in England private enterprise was able to accomplish the task. Conditions in New York were far different. There was, for example, much less private capital. In 1817, the estimated cost of the project, $6 million, was equal to nearly a third of all the banking and insurance capital in the state. As Julius Rubin noted in his 1961 study of this issue, "The 1817 decision to build the Erie Canal was . . . an unlikely choice among several alternatives; it was an investment of vast funds in an unlikely enterprise; and it was an example of long-range planning in a democracy."[5]

The timing of the legislation was even more remarkable in view of the changed expectations of New Yorkers concerning national aid for the canal. By the early 1800s, the failure of the Western Inland Lock Navigation Company to achieve its goals was becoming clear, but no great flurry of state intervention appeared. The canal's prospects were revived by Thomas Jefferson's remarks on improvements in his second Inaugural Address, and the promise of federal aid fortified the hopes of canal advocates until 1817. Federal assistance seemed imminent when the "Bonus Bill" sponsored by John C. Calhoun passed Congress in 1817. On March 3, 1817, however, the day before leaving office, James Madison vetoed the bill and New York's hopes for outside aid were dashed.[6]

Yet within weeks the canal bill passed the state legislature, and New York set out to build the project supported only by the state's own resources. It was Clinton's memorial, backed by the thousands of signatures obtained throughout the state, that ultimately pushed the project through. Speaking in the state senate that spring, Van Buren noted that "our tables have groaned with the petitions of the people" and argued that the senate had the responsibility to follow the assembly's lead and pass the bill. Although much of Van Buren's party remained hostile to the bill, Clinton had created such a surge of support that Van Buren—the Red Fox of Kinderhook—knew the time had come to enact the bill.[7]

A CHANGED LANDSCAPE

One of the sources of opposition to the canal was the perception that an undertaking supported by the entire state would confer benefits unequally within it—that areas along the route would prosper while others would suffer, either by being left out of the state's transportation network (the dominant concern among inhabitants of the southern tier) or by becoming a victim of competition within that network. Farmers left the hardscrabble hills of New England for the rich soil of the Genesee Valley, and those along the Hudson and on Long Island were forced to change their crops and lower their prices. With the coming of the canal, farmers in western New York gained easy access to domestic and foreign markets, and landowners in the west, such as the Holland Land Company, were finally able to realize the profits that they had anticipated for decades. But growth there meant stagnant, or even declining, populations in counties, such as Otsego and Columbia, that were not situated to benefit from the opening of the New York west.[8]

Perhaps even more important than the expansion of farming was the rise of new cities along the canal route that served as markets for the farmers' produce and as sources of manufactured items. Rochester's growth was remarkable: In 1820, before the canal had reached the town, the census recorded 1,502 residents; by 1850, it had 36,403. In the same period, Buffalo grew from 2,095 to 42,261 inhabitants. As Richard Wade has noted, the story of western movement is not only, or even mainly, a story of farmlands; it is also the story of the "urban frontier." And, as we shall see, the canal cities had a reputation for violent amusement that rivals the later reputations of Dodge City and the gold-rush towns.[9]

Even before the canal was completed, the lands through which it passed had changed dramatically from the sparsely settled domain Clinton and his fellow commissioners had visited in 1810. Upon arriving in Buffalo, Clinton had noted in his diary that the town had "five lawyers and no church." Lafayette, on his visit there in 1825, was impressed with "the appearance of prosperity and business in the harbour," particularly since the town had been nearly leveled by the British in the War of 1812. The few scattered factories that made cheese or wove cloth, which Clinton had carefully recorded in 1810, had multiplied and become commonplace two decades later. "The number of people engaged in manufacturing in the western part of the state," Ronald Shaw notes, "increased by 262 percent between 1820 and 1840, and the number of those employed in commerce and navigation increased tenfold."[10]

TO MARKET

Of course, it was not just the presence of a navigable waterway that impelled this growth; it was the fact that the waters led to market, so that the goods produced in western New York, Ohio, and points even farther west could be transported economically to points where buyers for those goods could be found. If New York City was the center of the market for products traveling along the canal, cities like Rochester, Buffalo, and Cleveland, which grew explosively because of the canal boom, soon became major markets in themselves. Access to markets meant more to farmers than just an outlet for their surpluses. With New York City (or Rochester) merchants offering cash for wheat, western farmers had a reason to increase the amount of land they worked, so that they quickly converted from subsistence farming to cash crops.[11]

The conversion to cash crops also solved a traditional problem of frontier life—a shortage of cash. With cash, farmers could more easily purchase the supplies, as well as the luxuries, that were produced in canal towns or shipped west from New York City. (They were also better able to pay taxes.) The greater demand for shoes, furniture, printed matter, and other manufactures of eastern cities led to greater investment in productive capacity in those cities, fueling the growth of the cities and thereby insuring an expanding market for western commodities. Part of the process of converting from a subsistence to a market economy is the decline of household manufactures, and they fell rapidly in western New York after 1820.[12]

For the first few decades of the canal's operation, the bulk of the produce flowing eastward originated in western New York. But the development of the canal systems of Ohio and other states of the Old Northwest linked the Erie Canal to an entire rich region that was expanding at mid-century. By 1847 freight from states to the west began to exceed New York-made products moving eastward along the canal. Four years later, the ratio was two to one. Of course, the farmers of Ohio, Indiana, Michigan, and Illinois were not limited to the Erie route. With the invention of the steamboat, the great waterways of the Mississippi and its major tributaries had become a two-way street for commerce. But the Erie and its associated canals succeeded in drawing the bulk of products of the Old Northwest to the East Coast. In 1835, before many of the feeder canals to the west were completed, only 23.7 percent of the commodities from that region were shipped to the Northeast, while 62.2 percent headed down the Mississippi and the remainder took the Pennsylvania Mainline, the Pittsburgh Turnpike, or the Cumberland Road. By 1853, as the canal era was peaking and the railroads were emerging as the chief means of transporting freight, the Northeast was garnering 62.2 percent of this trade, while the South retained just 28.9 percent.[13]

The Erie Canal's greatest advantage over the Mississippi River route was that it led to New York City, the principal port for both the coasting trade and international shipments. New York had the capital to purchase the products sent east, the facilities for marketing them, and the market information from elsewhere in America and from abroad to make a profit. It was also, simply in itself, a much larger market than New Orleans—which had the additional disadvantage of the hazardous Gulf route to major American and European markets. (It cost more to insure a trip from New York to New Orleans than one from New York to England or France.) Merchants in the American interior had other reasons to prefer the Erie route. One firm in Nashville in 1833 indicated that the greater expense of receiving goods via the canal system was offset by the fact that goods arrived ten to twelve days faster. And canal rates were frequently reduced in those years, so by 1852 tobacco dealers in Cincinnati found the Erie route both faster and cheaper.[14]

The Erie Canal and the complementary canals that followed it helped give birth to a national market. The availability of staple crops from inland allowed specialization of agriculture in other areas, and the growth of a cash economy facilitated exchange among individuals in different trades, as well as between different regions. The concentration of industry and specialization that the "transportation revolution" made possible, the historian George Rogers Taylor noted, also increased sectional differences. Alfred Chandler pointed out in *The Visible Hand* that the Erie Canal spawned "still another string of middlemen," and it was middlemen like these, involved in distribution rather than in production, who swelled the ranks of middle management in American business. The huge size of the American market as it developed in the nineteenth century made it the "seed-bed of managerial capitalism," in Chandler's phrase, and the Erie Canal provided fertile soil for its early growth.[15]

It was also a hospitable climate for innovation. In a fascinating study based on patent records, Kenneth L. Sokoloff has offered compelling evidence that "inventive activity was quite responsive to market demand," and that there was a "strong relationship between patenting and proximity to navigable inland waterways." Specifically, he finds that "the completion of the Erie Canal in 1825 seems to have sparked . . . a sharp rise in patenting along its route."[16]

CAPITAL MARKETS

The cash that farmers received for their commodities, or inventors for their inventions, fits into a larger story of western development: the greater availability of investment capital. This process began with the construction of canals, which not only brought cash payrolls to residents of canal counties in the west but also brought deposits to local banks to cover payrolls. These deposits increased the ability of banks to lend. And this ability to lend was sorely needed, since the canal was having the effect that supporters had hoped for since at least 1792—it was driving up real-estate prices. Lots near Buffalo that had sold for $250 in 1815 went for $20,000 by 1835.[17]

While the increased trade along the Erie Canal favored the growth of private capital, it was a public project, and soon surpluses from tolls left the canal commissioners with a large supply of public capital to manage. As early as 1825, tolls from the canal were exceeding the amount needed for debt service by $100,000. The canal-fund surplus grew rapidly, and by the mid-1830s it was being used for a host of purposes. When the great fire of 1835 devastated New York City, destroying 650 buildings in lower Manhattan, the canal fund helped finance the recovery.[18] A year earlier, when Nicholas Biddle was attempting to overturn President Jackson's bank veto by disastrously contracting the money supply, the canal commissioners undermined Biddle by resuming a policy of lending to the banks, instead of continuing to use the surplus to buy up existing canal securities. When the Panic of 1837 threatened the credit of New York merchants abroad, the canal commissioners intervened to support the merchants' credit.[19]

The confidence that foreign investors had in the canal's securities was important both to the canal's success and to the growth of foreign investment in the United States. In the early years of the canal, foreign investors were leery of it, so most of the financing of its early loans came from small investors in the United States. One large institutional subscriber was the Bank for Savings, which was founded to serve working people; their many small deposits were combined to buy canal debt. The trustees of the bank, who included Clinton's friends and canal allies John Pintard and Thomas Eddy, risked these funds early on, but committed their own savings only after the canal proved a solid investment. English speculators were even more prudent, and it was not until the spring of 1822, according to Nathan Miller, that they entered the market on a big scale. Positive predictions from the London *Times* (which said that the Erie Canal would make New York City the "London of the New World") and from British observers in America stirred enthusiasm among British investors. By 1823, the Baring Brothers bank was purchasing canal paper, and soon a majority of the canal debt was owned by overseas investors. In 1824 Clinton told the economist Matthew Carey that although he could not give a precise figure on how much canal stock was held by foreigners, an estimate of two-thirds seemed about right. The canal project paid off for those investors and identified the United States as a promising "emerging market," as it would be called today on Wall Street. The canal financings of the 1820s not only opened America to foreign capital but led ultimately to greater sophistication in capital markets here, so that those bankers who handled canal loans in the 1820s prepared the way for underwriting railroad investments in the 1840s, financing the Civil War in the 1860s, and backing corporate issues in the great stock boom of 1898–1903. The Erie Canal served as the thin edge of the wedge that opened the United States to advanced capital markets.[20]

SOCIAL TRANSFORMATION

In less than a generation, settlers in western New York went from a life based on sub-sistence farming, in which the family was the crucial unit of economic life, to a market economy with cash as the chief medium of exchange. The region emerged from relative isolation to integration into, and dependence on, the Atlantic economy. This fundamental historical change had been going on for decades and would continue for decades more throughout the nation. What was different about western New York was the speed with which the change occurred over a large area, and the fantastic intensity and variety of the region's responses. As people confronted a world in which traditional economic principles, family roles, gender relations, and political practices were rapidly shifting and changing, they turned to religion, reform, and political revolt to confront an altered universe and seek new verities in place of ones that had been left in tatters.

There were not many people residing in western New York when the canal got under way. In spite of the ease of river travel and the richness of the soil, significant white settlement there had been foreclosed for nearly two centuries by the presence of the Six Nations of the Iroquois—the Seneca, Cayuga, Oneida, Onondaga, Mohawk, and Tuscarora. This highly developed confederation had combined relatively sophisticated agriculture with formidable military abilities and skillful diplomacy; it had been a crucial part of the military balance between the British and French colonies and, later, between Britain and the United States during the Revolutionary War. The 1779 campaign against the Indians of western New York and Pennsylvania headed by John Sullivan and James Clinton had been launched in response to petitions from the non-Tory settlers of those areas, and Sullivan and Clinton had been instructed by Washington that the territory of the Six Nations should be not "merely *overrun* but *destroyed.*" The expedition had weakened the Iroquois tribes, and after the revolution they were slowly pushed off most of their lands. When DeWitt Clinton traveled west in 1810, he commented on the new habits of the Indians: "Some driving a wagon, and the women milking and churning,—all the indications of incipient civilization." The decades of effort to convert the tribes had had some success—if success meant that the Oneidas, as Clinton recorded, had split into "Christian and Pagan parties." To him, however, it appeared that the "morals of the Pagans are better than those of the Christians."[21]

The white settlers of the revolutionary era were largely German, Dutch, and Scotch-Irish in origin, but after the revolution a great migration of New Englanders, dominated by Connecticut Yankees, began pouring west along the Mohawk. Other migrants came as well—farmers from tired lands near the Hudson, residents of New York and Brooklyn seeking better commercial opportunities in newborn cities, Pennsylvanians moving north up the Susquehanna—but the character of western New York had a distinctly New England cast, and with it what the historian Whitney Cross described as a peculiar "moral intensity."[22]

That moral intensity flared sporadically after the revolution, as occasional religious revivals appeared in western New York, including the "Great Revival" of the winter of 1799–1800. But the revivals remained short-lived, perhaps in part because the area was still too thinly settled to support any kind of sustained social movement and too poor to finance the travels of itinerant revivalists. In fact, rival denominations sometimes cooperated in building churches and providing ministers.

As the canal was bringing this area within the orbit of the market, the harsh face of that market was apparent along the canal's margins, with the boisterous behavior of the boatmen and the urban morals of new arrivals in the canal towns. Herman Melville testified to this aspect of canal-borne change in "The Town-Ho's Story" chapter of *Moby-Dick,* noting both the canal's vastness and the air of lawlessness along its way:

> For three hundred and sixty miles, gentlemen, through the entire breadth of the state of New York; through numerous populous cities and most thriving villages; through long, dismal, uninhabited swamps, and affluent, cultivated fields, unrivalled for fertility; by billiard-room and bar-room; through the holy-of-holies of great forests; on Roman arches over Indian rivers; through sun and shade; by happy hearts or broken; through all the wide contrasting scenery of those noble Mohawk counties; and especially, by rows of snow-white chapels, whose spires stand almost like milestones, flows one continual stream of Venetianly corrupt and often lawless life. There's your true Ashantee, gentlemen; there howl your pagans; where you ever find them, next door to you; under the long-flung shadow, and the snug patronizing lee of churches. For by some curious fatality, as it is often noted of your metropolitan freebooters that they ever encamp around the halls of justice, so sinners, gentlemen, most abound in holiest vicinities.[23]

When the Rochester Sabbatarians tried to get the state legislature to prohibit canal traffic on Sundays, the legislators turned them down, and asked whether they really wanted canallers marooned in Rochester on the Sabbath seeking liquor and female companionship. In Utica, completion of the canal led to explosive growth in the number of grog shops and brothels there.[24]

Mary Ryan's study of Utica explores the ways the arrival of market relations promoted change in family structure. Before the canal, Uticans were generally part of family economies governed by the male head of household and characterized by family interdependency, child labor, and an important economic role for women. With the coming of the canal, new forms of employment arose, and the family ceased to be the central productive unit. Work life and home life, formerly inseparable, were sundered; women who had often taken part in men's business activities were now expected to devote themselves to explicitly domestic activities. Even such traditional domestic activities as spinning and weaving declined as textiles became a product of the factory rather than of the home. For towns like Utica and Rochester, and for the surrounding farmlands, the Erie Canal not only brought the market but did so at frightening speed. Traditional economic and social relations were dissolving, and the riotous behavior of the canallers furnished a lurid example of the moral cost of progress. The response was one of the great religious phenomena of American history.

THE BURNED-OVER DISTRICT

Melville's observation about the customary propinquity of divinity and iniquity need not be restricted to the canal. The religious fervor that swept western New York probably hit with greater force, and had more lasting consequences, than it did elsewhere in the country. The year of the canal's completion was the "turning point," according to Whitney Cross, that separated "the period of scattered, episodic eccentricities from the era of major, significant enthusiasms."[25]

Four aspects of this spiritual firestorm were of particular significance. The first two—the birth of Mormonism and the revival fever fanned by the travels of Charles Grandison Finney—were explicitly religious in nature. The other two—anti-Masonry and the general rise of reform movements like temperance, Sabbatarianism, and abolitionism—channeled that spiritual impulse into more overtly political courses.

The revelations of Joseph Smith were the most lasting and important manifestation of the widespread belief during the early nineteenth century that a high civilization had been vanquished by the "savage" Indians now inhabiting the continent. But Mormon doctrine proved more particularly relevant to the great preoccupation of New Yorkers in the 1820s, the emergence of market capitalism. Smith's followers adopted a standard of behavior rooted in Christian morality but also remarkably well suited to the requirements of the market. Financial gain was praised (tithes helped the church grow), comfort welcomed, and abundance courted. But these materialistic goals were wedded to a communitarian social order founded on an ethic of individual subordination to the good of the church community. Smith's migration westward moved the center of Mormonism out of New York, but the church continued to win many converts in the burned-over district.[26]

For all its future importance, Mormonism remained a small sect in New York in the heyday of the Second Great Awakening between 1825 and 1837. Many more New Yorkers were touched by the revival wave started by Charles Grandison Finney. Thousands went to hear the former lawyer who had abandoned the bar to become an itinerant preacher in 1824. Finney's efforts were untiring, and he met with particular success in revivals held in the canal towns of Utica (in 1826) and Rochester (in 1831). Finney's revivals in Rochester combined religious fervor with programs of secular reform. His supporters, including the wives of many prosperous merchants and attorneys, were on the leading edge of the market revolution, and were among the first to experience the divergence of the economic and family realms.[27]

ANTI-MASONRY

The hazy boundaries between religious, social, and political realms were seldom less distinct than in the great popular cause of western New York in the late 1820s, the Anti-Masonic movement. Few movements appear more fortuitous. Yet Anti-Masonry helped shape post-Clintonian politics in New York for a generation and played a crucial role in the development of the Whig, and later the Republican, parties. In 1826, a man named William Morgan threatened to publish the "secrets" of the Masonic order. Morgan had joined the Masons in 1823 in Rochester, but when he moved west to Batavia, the lodge there rejected him. Morgan then wrote *Illustrations of Masonry,* which he first offered to Thurlow Weed (who declined to publish it, because his partner was a Mason) and later arranged to have printed by the press of the *Batavia Advocate.* Morgan was then arrested under several pretexts and held in jail in Canandaigua, from which he was released on September 12, 1826. He was gagged and thrown into a yellow carriage for a trip west toward Fort Niagara. He is believed to have been drowned in the Niagara River. The simple fact of Morgan's disappearance hardly seems sufficient to explain the political firestorm that followed, but when the inquiry into his disappearance appeared to be obstructed by influential Masons, and when so many of the state's leading figures (including, of course, DeWitt Clinton) turned out to be Masons, Morgan's fate was seen as part of a vast antidemocratic conspiracy that threatened the very existence of the republic.[28]

Such suspicions fell on fertile soil. The canal boom led all to expect a better, more prosperous life, but some were disappointed. Those hoping to succeed needed to gain admission to the "best circles," and one of the most important of these was the Masonic brotherhood. Morgan himself had hoped that his membership in the Rochester lodge would serve as his entrée into Batavia's elite, but he was rejected. Others, too, wished to join the effective business network the Masons had created. But many were excluded, and there were strong resentments. In a political culture steeped in the conspiratorial rhetoric of republicanism, the Masons, with their elite membership and secret rituals, were all too likely a target for anyone whose worldly status failed to measure up to what he thought himself entitled to.[29]

Thurlow Weed, the Rochester printer who declined to print Morgan's exposé, was soon a leader in the effort to capitalize politically on the Anti-Masonic uproar. In the state election of 1827, the Anti-Masons elected fifteen members to the state assembly, their greatest strength being in the western districts adjoining the Erie Canal. Anti-Masons may have resented special privileges accorded by secret societies, but there was no correspondence with the class alignment that Van Buren and others were hoping to bring to state and national politics, with "aristocrats" on one side and "the people" on the other. Many members of the Regency were Freemasons, as was the emerging leader of the Democracy, Andrew Jackson. John Quincy Adams, on the other hand, made the courageous offer to bare the secrets of the shadowy organization to which he belonged—Phi Beta Kappa.[30]

THE CANAL AND POLITICS, THE POLITICS OF CANALS

The popularity of the canal helped return Clinton to the governor's office in 1824. Beyond the realm of personalities, the Erie Canal was reshaping the political landscape and the common conception of the proper role of government. In fact, it did so twice. The first time, beginning with its clear success in the early 1820s, its example greatly increased support for government-backed improvements at the state level, and not just in New York. The second was when many of the projects inspired by the success of the Erie Canal met with failure and led some states into insolvency following the Panic of 1837.

DeWitt Clinton, the most prominent national advocate of canal construction, was hearing from canal enthusiasts in other states as early as 1818. From Cincinnati, one W. Steele wrote him for advice on a plan to link Lake Erie to the Ohio River. The plan, Steele felt, was sound; except that "this country does not afford a monied capital sufficient for this undertaking," and he wondered about the chances of raising $2 million in New York. With an Ohio canal, east and west would be united "by the strongest ties possible, and the trade the City of New York will draw through it will aid very much in making her the Alexandria of the world." Confidentiality would be best for the time being, since the Ohio canal's boosters wanted to "secure some lands which could not be had if their views were known."[31]

By 1820, the Ohio canal project was being encouraged by Charles Haines, Clinton's personal secretary, who wrote to Ohio's governor Ethan Allen Brown urging the state to move forward on the project. Brown had run on a pro-canal ticket in 1818 and had received assurances from such Clintonian stalwarts as William Bayard and Cadwallader Colden that the Ohio undertaking would find adequate capital in New York.[32]

The success of the Erie Canal encouraged other states to imitate New York's example but also impeded a greater federal role in such internal improvements. Albert Gallatin had understood in 1808 that a national internal improvements program had to be comprehensive to overcome sectional and interstate rivalries and pass Congress. In 1825, President Adams was unable to persuade Congress to enact his development program, and one of the obstacles was the success of the Erie Canal. Once New York had gone it alone, at its own expense, the state's substantial delegation in Congress was unenthusiastic about devoting federal dollars to projects in other states. With such regional jealousies added to constitutional objections about federal improvements, there were never enough votes in Congress to advance the kind of nationalist program envisioned by Adams and Clay.

Within New York, too, the success of the canal had unfortunate effects of another kind. Areas left out of the original scheme wanted in on the canal bonanza or to be granted transportation projects that would benefit them. Residents of the southern tier petitioned for a road from the Hudson to Lake Erie running through their lands. Turned down by the legislature in 1827, they soon were back seeking state support for a railroad. Other districts wanted canals to link them with the Erie. By the time some of these projects were finished—for example, the Black River Canal, completed in 1850—railroads had begun to replace canals as the main artery of commerce, and the expense of the newer projects was often never recouped.[33]

Even greater mistakes were made by other states, believing they had to build canals to keep up with New York but having a less favorable topography. Pennsylvania faced two challenges, the Erie Canal's success and the Appalachian mountains. Afraid that any delay would prove fatal, in 1824 the Pennsylvania legislature authorized the appointment of a canal commission to examine routes for a canal between Philadelphia and Pittsburgh. Plans called for an extension of the canal to Pennsylvania's narrow slice of Lake Erie shoreline, in the hope that the state's milder weather would allow the Pennsylvania canal to open earlier each spring and thus take some of New York's canal trade. The planners in Pennsylvania believed their route had advantages that would make up for the expense of the greater number of locks the Pennsylvania canal would require and for the contemplated four-and-a-half-mile-long tunnel they would have to bore so that boats could cross the Appalachians. Though advocates of railroads were urging that Pennsylvania eschew canals, the canal men were afraid any delay would solidify New York's lead. Accordingly, work began on the Pennsylvania canal on July 4, 1826—nine years after the start of the Erie Canal. To marshal the needed votes in the legislature, branch canals were added to different areas of the state, and the system cost $12 million by the time it was completed in 1834.[34]

Pennsylvania's improvements did not yield a wealth of toll revenues, as the Erie Canal had, and the state refused to raise taxes significantly, so debt soared. The Panic of 1837 and the depression that followed a second financial crisis in 1839 eventually led Pennsylvania and eight other states to default on their bonds in 1841 and 1842. Pennsylvania's failure, and those of other defaulting states, naturally discouraged foreign investment in state bonds and forced "stop and tax" movements in various states. The need to pay taxes now to finance construction projects, rather than relying on the less painful recourse of floating long-term debt, undercut public support for government intervention in the economy and helped set the stage for private ownership of the next and greatest stage of the nineteenth-century transportation revolution, the railroad age.[35]

COMMONWEALTH'S END

The defaulting states were objects of scorn in foreign markets, particularly London. The easy profits that had attracted British investors to Erie Canal stock in the 1820s were forgotten, and American investments became so suspect that for a time the flow of European capital to the United States virtually stopped. In 1842, Charles Dickens visited Philadelphia, staying in a room opposite the white marble temple that had housed the Second Bank of the United States. For him, "It was the Tomb of many fortunes; the Great Catacomb of investment; the memorable United States Bank." William Wordsworth wrote a sonnet, "To the Pennsylvanians," that compared the idealistic days of William Penn with the fallen condition of his successors:

All who revere the memory of Penn
Grieve for the land on whose wild woods his name
Was fondly grafted with virtuous aim,
Renounced, abandoned by degenerate Men
For state-dishonour as black as ever came
To upper air from Mammon's loathesome den.[36]

But it was not the shaming of the Pennsylvanians that changed American life; it was rather that such failures cast the entire notion of the activist state into disrepute and brought to a climax the withdrawal of government from the kind of intervention in the economy that DeWitt Clinton had championed. And as private capital became adequate to undertakings that in earlier decades only government had been able to finance, states revised their constitutions, and new states wrote theirs, so as to prohibit government activism in the economy. Wisconsin's constitution of 1848, for instance, contained a strict provision against state enterprise. Although government intervention in the economy would continue in many forms—tariffs, land-use regulations, taxes, monetary policy—the sort of active government role that the State of New York had played in the Erie Canal would not be endorsed again (except in wartime) until the twentieth century. Then it would be the federal government, not the states, that would lead the way.[37]

After Franklin D. Roosevelt's New Deal gave birth to a more active role for the federal government, historians were inspired to search for a fuller understanding of the relationship of government to the economy in the United States. Scholars had taken it for granted that the nation's development had been characterized by unfettered competition and "laissez-faire" policies. New studies of the period from the revolution to the Civil War discovered a strong tradition of government intervention in the states, of which the Erie Canal was simply the most successful. Oscar and Mary Handlin's 1947 study of Massachusetts, *Commonwealth,* became the banner under which this exploration went forward, and a host of books contributed to the "commonwealth" analysis of government policy. Among them were Milton S. Heath's *The Role of the State in Economic Development in Georgia to 1860,* Harry N. Scheiber's *Ohio Canal Era,* and Louis Hartz's look at Pennsylvania, *Economic Policy and Democratic Thought.*[38]

A more recent study of the antebellum economy explores the retreat from government interventionism in New York after 1837. L. Ray Gunn concurs with earlier essays that stressed the active part played by government before 1837 and the role of the economic crisis beginning that year in undermining public confidence in government activism. At the same time that voters were showing themselves uneasy with the role of the activist state, the important levers of economic power were, largely as the result of judicial activism, moving out of the statehouse and into the hands of judges and government administrators. The broadening of suffrage early in the century was thus countered by a subsequent withdrawal of important matters from the arena where suffrage mattered. Gunn, building on the work of Scheiber and of such legal historians as J. Willard Hurst and Morton Horwitz, notes that judges interpreted the law to facilitate the "release of energy" that accompanied the market revolution and the flowering of capitalism. DeWitt Clinton had managed to win popular consent for aspects of his developmental program for New York State, and with this consent had come a significant degree of popular, or at least public, control. But when state legislatures later arrayed themselves against the "release of energy," that energy simply found other champions.[39]

GOOD TIMING

The Erie Canal helped push settlement west to Buffalo and beyond. It fostered economic growth along its route, in the states of the Old Northwest, and in New York
City. It helped secure for New York City the preeminent position in the national
economy it retains to this day. It hastened the development of a truly national market, and directly contributed to the growth of capital markets in the United States.

So dizzying was the pace of change as to make the people of western New York pe-
culiarly susceptible to an epidemic of religious intensity coinciding with the canal's
spectacular first decades. Traditional economic relations dissolved in the Erie's waters, and those left adrift sought new islands of stability. For women, the separation of
the home from the workplace and the decline of household manufactures necessi-
tated new arrangements and new concepts of the "woman's sphere." The conjunc-
tion of revivalism and reform made the region home to various perfectionist movements and to rising abolitionist sentiment.

The canal was begun at a time of relative sectional calm, but when the Missouri
Compromise—Jefferson's "fire bell in the night"—did much to end it, the Erie Canal
played a crucial role in cementing the ties between the Northeast and the Old Northwest. The pathway nature had provided to serve the new lands, the Mississippi and its
tributaries, was challenged, and eclipsed, by the manmade route of the canal system.
The migration of people west along that route also created family links running
east-west, adding personal loyalties and shared values to a community of economic
interests.

The spectacular success of the Erie Canal encouraged imitators whose less successful record helped bring into disrepute the entire concept of government intervention
in the economy on the state level. Sectional and interstate jealousies, as well as constitutional doubts, had impeded federal efforts since the time of Jefferson and Gallatin, and Jackson's veto of the Maysville Road bill in 1830 appeared to make federal
abdication all but final. Then there were the inhibitions raised by the growth of sectional feeling. Southerners like John Randolph feared that the loose view of the Constitution needed to justify federal support of state roads and canals would permit
Washington to interfere with the institution of slavery, or even to abolish it. John C.
Calhoun, an enthusiastic nationalist at the time the Erie Canal was begun, soon perceived the same threat, and retreated to the ground of state sovereignty.

It is certainly possible to overstate the canal's influence. The canal may have abetted capitalist development, but that development was already taking place; it may
have sharpened sectional divisions, but those divisions already existed; it may have
aided New York City's rise, but the city was already ascendant. There was nevertheless
something about its timing that made for a crucial element in insuring its lasting influence. If geography favored New York with the Mohawk Valley to ease travel westward, this advantage was vastly greater in the age of wagon and flatboat than it would
be in the age of railroads just a quarter-century later. New York's advantage was
short-lived, but that quarter-century was enough. Patterns of trade, patterns of mi-

gration, and political affinities were molded by the Erie so that later development followed. Cities such as Buffalo and Rochester, which had been nurtured by the canal, became natural stops for railroads as they moved west. Pennsylvania learned from its canal-era mistakes and its entrepreneurs aggressively built railroads, but the initiative had clearly passed by then to its northern neighbor.

Just as the Erie Canal shaped but did not determine these events, DeWitt Clinton fostered but did not create the canal. He did not create the historical moment that allowed the Erie Canal to have such profound consequences, but he recognized it, he seized it, and he bound himself to it as tightly as he could. His decision was not inevitable, and had he not given the project all his energies, the moment might have passed and a different America might have emerged.

Thirteen

o   o   o

END OF A CAREER

With the completion of the canal, Clinton's own triumph was complete, but his hold on state politics was tenuous. The disappearance of the Federalist party made his reliance on former Federalists less of a liability than it had been five years earlier, and the success of the canal had raised his stature nationally as well as in New York. His agenda remained unchanged: he proposed educational reforms and developmental projects that would build on the success of the canal and proclaim New York the nation's most important state—and Clinton, by association, a most important person. He quickly secured passage of the electoral reforms that the People's party had made the centerpiece of its platform in 1824.[1]

But after that, Clinton's legislative successes were few. In spite of the enormous success of the People's party in the 1824 elections, the party was united only in its opposition to the Regency, and once the electoral reforms were enacted the party's cohesive force was spent. The party had originated among supporters of John Quincy Adams who feared that a Regency legislature would deliver the state's electoral votes to Crawford. But the party's victorious gubernatorial candidate, DeWitt Clinton, supported Jackson. Others in the coalition liked Clay.

Although Clinton's victory probably owed more to his stature and to the Erie Canal than it did to the People's party, he would undoubtedly have been wise to seek common ground with the adherents of Adams and Clay. These men were, after all, sympathetic to the programs of economic and educational development Clinton hoped to advance. Yet many of them were also furious with Clinton for supporting Jackson. It should be recalled that the new legislature convened a month before the presidential election was decided, so the controversy that separated Clinton from the bulk of the People's party was greatest at the very moment when the tone of his next term was being set.

Some People's party leaders even hoped that a new party could be formed from

173

the coalition that had proved so successful in November 1824. The champion of that happy thought was James Tallmadge, the new lieutenant governor, who hoped to cast the Clintonians into one oblivion, the Regency into another, and preside over a broad and successful center. This plan proved to be folly, but it further reduced Clinton's hopes for success in the legislature. In any case, Clinton would not seek or offer any accommodation. It was his nature, Hammond wrote, to "listen to no pacific overtures until he himself, or his opponent, was completely conquered."[2]

STRANGE BEDFELLOWS

There was at this time one political figure—Martin Van Buren—who appeared to fit the description of a "completely conquered" opponent. Van Buren had staked much on Samuel Young's gubernatorial chances, and even more on William Crawford's presidential hopes. Both had been embarrassing failures. Clinton, on the other hand, had not only been elected governor again; he had also allied himself with Andrew Jackson. Although Jackson had lost the 1824 election, his chances looked bright for 1828: He had won the most popular votes, and charges of "corrupt bargain" had been hurled at Adams and Clay. Van Buren was eager to leave the failed Crawford candidacy behind and to align himself with the national hero, and Clinton offered him the best opportunity.

The first move in their reconciliation was apparently made by the Clinton camp. After Clinton's victory Van Buren took the steamer from Albany to New York on his way to Washington to resume his seat in the Senate, "as completely broken down a politician," he later wrote, "as my bitterest enemies could desire." His only reason for stopping in New York was to make good his losses on various election wagers. Aboard the steamboat he met Mrs. Clinton and her brother James Jones, and Jones said to him, "Now is the time admirably fitted for a settlement of all difficulties between Mr. Clinton and yourself."[3]

For all Van Buren's belittling of himself, he was hardly without resources, and the alliance with Clinton that eventually emerged was based on mutual interest and governed by plans for the future, not by past antagonisms. From Clinton's point of view, there were cogent reasons for a rapprochement with Van Buren: the People's party made poor allies; he and Van Buren now agreed on the central issue of national politics, that Andrew Jackson should be the next president; and, with Van Buren's help, perhaps he could even get something done in the state legislature. But such an alliance would take time to construct. After all, Clintonians and Bucktails were as antipathetic in 1825 as Clintonians and Burrites had been twenty years earlier. And the legislature, divided between pro-Adams People's party men, Clintonians, and those loyal to Van Buren, was rudderless.[4]

Perhaps the clearest example of the dysfunctional nature of the legislature was its inability to elect a successor to Rufus King, who retired from the United States Senate on March 4, 1825. Although the assembly had nominated Ambrose Spencer at the beginning of February by a margin of better than three to two, the state senate was divided among more than a dozen candidates. Against Spencer on his own account and also as Clinton's brother-in-law and ally, the opposition shared long-standing animosities. But no faction had sufficient votes to elect one of its own. So New York was represented in the Senate only by Martin Van Buren for the balance of the year and into the next.[5]

With the state government immobilized, Clinton turned to other concerns. During the visit of Lafayette, he offered advice on arrangements for portraits (he should be painted by "different masters"), and to Henry Remsen he gave suggestions about the Manhattan Company and New York City's water supply (lacking the resources to fulfill its promises, the company should try to redo the arrangement). He wrote letters endorsing canals in other states, and dispatched polite notes to such international luminaries as Simon Bolívar. Perhaps his most interesting correspondence that year was with the engineer John Stevens, who held forth on the practicability of railroads. The governor was skeptical and clearly hesitant to admit the possibility that canals would soon be outmoded, but he showed himself to be well informed about railroad developments in England. He also wrote to John Jacob Astor in Europe, asking him to pick up "three Gilt flower baskets" in Paris for Mrs. Clinton.[6]

GREENER PASTURES

Perhaps with the intention, and certainly with the effect, of making himself better known outside New York, Clinton spent a considerable part of 1825 promoting internal improvements elsewhere. As the Erie Canal neared completion, requests arrived from other states seeking advice, recommendations of qualified engineers, or merely his endorsement of new projects. He had been corresponding with canal enthusiasts in other states for years, but in the spring and summer of 1825 he traveled to Pennsylvania, Ohio, Kentucky, and New Jersey to spread the aqueous gospel. In Pennsylvania, he met with the state canal commission and offered his advice on the proper route and other matters. He also recommended his friend David Thomas for the post of chief civil engineer of the Pennsylvania canal, and then conveyed to Thomas the canal commission's offer of it. After returning to New York, he proceeded to Ohio, where on July 4 he took a ceremonial shovel in hand to inaugurate work on one of that state's many new canals.[7]

Clinton's journal of his travels that summer reveals his interests. He comments on archeological sights: three "ancient fortifications" near the Ohio town of Miami, and burial mounds and fortifications near Circleville. He notes local color ("Boast of a Kentuckian a good rifle, a bear dog and a handsome sister") and folklore ("Beech trees never struck by lightning—hunters go there for safety"). He complacently records an innkeeper's refusal to accept his payment for lodging, and a paper mill named for him at Steubenville. He gives particular attention to the toasts offered at a banquet honoring Henry Clay in Cincinnati on July 13. He lists them all but only transcribes the one to himself: "The first officer of the first state in the union. His fame is founded on the imperishable basis of a public life successfully devoted to the public good."[8]

Naturally, there were insinuations from opponents that this was an electioneering trip. Perhaps it was: Clinton had long professed great admiration for Andrew Jackson; he may even have imagined himself claiming Jackson's mantle if anything should happen to the Old Hero before the 1828 election. Or he may simply have thought of the vice presidency, with an eye to eventual succession.

A TRUCE WITH VAN BUREN

That fall Clinton experienced his apotheosis with the opening of the Erie Canal. It was not a coincidence that the extensive festivities, stretching the length of the state, were scheduled for the period immediately before the state elections. This judicious plan did not, however, bear its intended fruit. The Regency regained control of the assembly and took three of the eight senate seats contested that fall. Van Buren notes that although the Regency (or, as he begins to put it, the "Democratic party") "acted in undisguised opposition to Gov. Clinton," the old enmities were dying, and the way now seemed open to consummate the proposed reconciliation between the two largest factions of New York's old Jeffersonian party. But Van Buren, however much he desired a rapprochement with Clinton, had to move carefully so as not to alienate the bulk of his followers. Informal conferences resulted in an awkward modus vivendi under which Van Buren persuaded his party to assent to some Clintonian appointments, while the governor agreed to give greater consideration to Van Buren's candidates for other offices. Clinton was, as ever, a difficult ally, and his refusal to appoint to a circuit judgeship a Regency opponent of electoral reform (whose opposition had cost him his office) left some followers of Van Buren feeling ill used.[9]

The triumph of the Democrats, as we may perhaps now join with Van Buren in designating his faction of the old Jeffersonian party of New York, owed much to careful organization and planning, but also to the fact that the causes of their defeat a year before had become moot by the time of the election of November 1825. With William Crawford defeated and ill, political passions could no longer be inflamed on his account. The electoral reforms that had united the People's party had been achieved. And anger over Clinton's removal from the Canal Commission could hardly be sustained after he had basked in a fortnight of canal celebrations. So with Clinton back in the familiar position of being governor with a largely hostile legislature, he took the atypical step of cooperating with Van Buren.[10]

The understanding between Clinton and Van Buren helped unclog state politics, or at least the process of appointments. A Clintonian was made chancellor, a Regency candidate, Nathan Sanford, was elected to the seat in the United States Senate that Rufus King had vacated. So far did the spirit of conciliation extend that a Clintonian who in 1824 had denounced those who removed Clinton from the Canal Commission as "utterly unworthy of public confidence" was appointed recorder of Albany in 1826 "without a dissenting vote."[11]

One may understand the priorities of Clintonians and Democrats from the fact that their efforts at cooperation were focused on the distribution of state offices, not on the advancement of legislative programs. Yet the governor continued to present an ambitious agenda. His address to the legislature in January 1826 urged that the state establish seminaries for the training of teachers. He also called for lavish state-sponsored scientific efforts to promote economic expansion: "Experimental and pattern farms; plantations of useful trees for ship-building, architecture and fuel; labor-saving machines; improved seeds and plants of those productions now used; new modes of cultivation; and the whole range of rural economy are subjects deserving your animating support." It is one of the contradictions of the Jeffersonian legacy that such enterprises, presumably so dear to Jefferson's scientific imagination, were left unencouraged by the Jeffersonian abhorrence of energetic government. And where Clinton was relentless in linking the advance of education with the cause of republican government, the Regency was reluctant to spend the money needed, and even less eager to suggest to uneducated voters that the franchise might not be entirely safe in their hands. The legislature was unmoved by Clinton's arguments, and the bill for teacher training died in committee, as did most of his proposals.[12]

The major internal improvement Clinton recommended in 1826 was a road through the southern part of the state. It had been proposed by him the year before, and a commission, of which Jabez Hammond was a member, was appointed to advise on possible routes. The road was to open the southern tier to development as the Erie Canal had done in the north. The legislature eventually tabled the bill, and the debate proceeded along geographic, not ideological or party, lines. Samuel Young opposed the bill, as might be expected, but so did Francis Granger, son of Clinton's old backer Gideon Granger and already one of Clinton's foremost supporters. Hammond called this group the "Erie Canal Party," and recorded that opposition to the road was nearly unanimous among those representing counties benefiting from the canal.[13]

LAST CAMPAIGN

If the state road project was not a triumph for the governor, neither did it exacerbate old party tensions, and Clinton may have had reason to hope that his reconciliation with Van Buren might insure that he could run unopposed. In fact, Clinton was not only opposed but nearly defeated by the Democratic candidate, William B. Rochester. How and why are less than clear.

While Van Buren was happy to acquire Clinton's Jacksonian credentials, he did not want to pay too high a price. Van Buren's own account of his role in the 1826 gubernatorial campaign is—perhaps intentionally—a little blurred. On the one hand, he had no plans for an "amalgamation" of Clintonians and Bucktails; supporting Clinton in the governor's race would have been unpalatable because of Clinton's past associations with Federalism. And Clinton's arrogance had engendered virulent personal enmity among many of Van Buren's closest associates. (Judge Skinner, who had engineered Clinton's removal as canal commissioner, died after Clinton's victory in 1824. Van Buren wrote that his "death was obviously hastened by grief and mortification at Mr. Clinton's success.") Yet Van Buren also claimed to have wanted Clinton to win reelection unopposed in 1826. He cited several reasons: from "feelings of personal kindness" and a desire to erase the blot caused by Clinton's dismissal from the Canal Commission to the more plausible desire to avoid a contest that might prove embarrassing "in the then state of National politics."[14]

The "then state of National politics" for Martin Van Buren was one of opposition to the Adams administration, following a year of "non-committalism." After first hedging his bets on the Adams presidency, Van Buren moved into the enemy camp after Adams delivered his address to Congress on December 6, 1825, which urged a vigorous role for the national government in internal improvements, education, and even scientific research. Adams was proposing for the nation a counterpart of Clinton's ambitious plans for the state of New York. "The party with principles," the historian Robert Remini wrote concerning Van Buren's move into open opposition, "had to challenge the party with the program." Dixon Ryan Fox in 1919 saw a similar distinction between the "party with a program" (the Clintonians and, later, the Whigs) and "the party with a creed" (the Democrats). Well and good; yet Van Buren's political course does not in the broad view appear much less circuitous than Clinton's. Van Buren had principles, but chief among them was the principle that Martin Van Buren should be maintained in power and that his power should be increased whenever possible.[15]

Clinton, too, can be cited for steering something other than a straight course in his affiliations and party alliances. But there is a discernible line of consistency as well. He worked with Aaron Burr, then against him, then sought alliance with his followers and then denounced them; he denounced Federalists in Miltonic terms and then solicited their support for the presidency; he made and lost allies throughout the state—yet during all these phases he consistently advocated internal improvements, sponsored educational reform, promoted state aid to cultural institutions, and championed the rights of immigrants, particularly Irish Catholics.

True, his programs altered somewhat over time as well. National aid to state improvements seemed highly desirable when Clinton and Gouverneur Morris went to Washington in December 1811. But when federal aid was denied and New York built the canal using its own resources, Clinton's old Republican affinity for states' rights, inherited from his uncle George, resurfaced and remained with him to his death. Like Adams, he favored activist government, but while he was governor he judged that activism is best contained within state borders. On the other hand, one may still imagine, had he ever succeeded in becoming president, a renewed adaptability in programs and principles.

However malleable Van Buren's principles were, those of his followers were less pliable. The Little Magician met with his supporters in Albany but found that the party would not allow Clinton to run unopposed. The Democrats were planning to hold their first state nominating convention that summer at Herkimer, and Van Buren's fallback plan was to have the party nominate the pallid William B. Rochester and thus allow Clinton to defeat a weak rival and retain his office. D. S. Alexander even suggests that, when the election proved close, Van Buren manipulated returns to insure a victory for Clinton.[16]

The surprise of the election was that Rochester came very close to winning. The crucial issue was the state road through the southern tier that Clinton was advocating and Rochester opposed. Clinton's margin of victory came from the southern tier, and it was the vote there that Van Buren's forces were suspected of manipulating. The vote was so close that for some time after the election Clinton believed he had lost. Van Buren related how he had learned of Clinton's victory: A steamboat from downriver arrived in Albany not long after the election. Soon after the boat docked, Van Buren observed "a busy friend of Mr. Clinton pass my window in hot haste" toward the governor's residence, and remarked that Clinton must have won and that the matter would be made clear later in church. When Governor and Mrs. Clinton entered and took their seats, "Mrs Clinton had no sooner settled herself in her seat than she turned towards us and favored us with a look which induced Marcy [William L. Marcy, the state comptroller] to whisper to me that the election was indeed lost."[17]

THE ANTI-MASONS

But while Rochester and Clinton were running for governor a new, strong, and utterly unforeseen challenge to the Regency and to Clinton was arising in the form of political Anti-Masonry, set off not only by the fact of William Morgan's disappearance but by the evident complicity in the crime of law-enforcement officers and other prominent men who were Masons.

As a prominent Freemason, Clinton was an obvious target, and his last year in office was dominated by the issue. His correspondence began reflecting the furor less than a month after Morgan's disappearance. On October 7, 1826, he wrote to a committee of concerned citizens in Genesee County—of which Batavia, where Morgan had been living, was the county seat—pledging that the law would be enforced properly and any irregularities in the inquiry investigated. He issued a proclamation offering rewards of hundreds of dollars for information leading to the arrest and conviction of those responsible for Morgan's disappearance. He also sent an order to the local law-enforcement authorities to inquire into reports of "outrages and oppressions" at Batavia. At the end of the month, he wrote to the committee that since Morgan was still missing, "I have thought it advisable to issue the enclosed proclamation offering further rewards, which you will please to see published."[18]

By the beginning of 1827, matters were heating up and Clinton was taking further measures to investigate Morgan's disappearance and to appease outraged Anti-Masons. On January 6, 1827, he wrote to the governor of Lower Canada describing the case, mentioning the possibility that Morgan had been taken into Canada by his abductors, and requesting any help the Canadians could provide. Two days later Clinton informed the head of the Batavia committee of his letter and told him that most Freemasons viewed Morgan's abduction as a "most unjustifiable act repugnant to the principles" of Freemasonry. He also reminded the committee of his prompt response to its complaints the previous October, promised to investigate its allegations of corruption against the sheriffs of Geneva and Niagara counties, and asked for evidence of its charges.[19]

Throughut Clinton's correspondence in 1827 runs a thread of serious desire to resolve the Morgan case, frustration with the casual accusations being bandied about, and readiness to punish the guilty. Clinton was outraged at any suggestion that he might have been involved in the plot, and his actions were plainly intended to solve the mystery and punish those responsible. Although Clinton was the state's most prominent Mason, the voters' outrage was eventually channeled against the Democrats. The Anti-Masons' major disgruntlement was over the all-too-cozy relations between Freemasonry and those holding political office in the state, of whom many were followers of Van Buren. Clinton's friend Francis Granger would become a leader of the Anti-Masonic movement, along with Thurlow Weed and the newly prominent William Henry Seward, and these three would play crucial roles in the birth of the Whig party and then of the Republican party in New York State. But DeWitt Clinton was destined, by premature death, not to be further troubled by either the rise or the eclipse of the Anti-Masonic party.

DEATH

Clinton's health had been declining since his riding accident ten years earlier. By the summer of 1827 his health was so bad that several rumors of his death circulated. On June 22 David Hosack informed Clinton of one such report and advised the governor to take better care of himself. Clinton's son Charles had told Hosack that his father was dieting and "exercising on horseback," and Hosack recommended caution. He thought Clinton's sedentary life had resulted in "an accumulation of blood," mostly in the large vessels, which was not being distributed; he prescribed exercise, warm baths, and bloodletting, and laid out detailed instructions on diet. Clinton should take a bowl of coffee or tea at breakfast, along with an egg or herring, then avoid any beverage until dinner, when he should have meat and vegetables with "a tumbler of brandy and water followed by 2 or 3 glasses of madeira." But no claret or cider, and he should watch out for puddings and sweets. A prompt response from the patient so encouraged the doctor that he was moved to warn his friend against taking "abstinence from animal food . . . too far."[20]

By January 1828, however, Clinton's condition was worsening. John Hone, whose daughter Catherine had married Charles Clinton, wrote to his son-in-law on January 9 with some advice of his own. The ailing governor should "make experiments not in medicine but diet. He now lives as I have understood abstemiously if this dont answer He ought to live *higher* take at his meals a few glasses of good wine and no *small drink.*" But this hearty advice came too late for a fair test.[21]

The day of Clinton's death, February 11, 1828, was clear in the morning, but later in the day it started snowing. His son George, for whom he had bought the two-dollar hat in 1807 after being ousted as mayor, left on a trip to Troy. The governor went for a long ride and later met with the "Militia Committee." He faithfully recorded the temperature in the morning, at noon, and before dusk. That evening, while seated at his desk in his library with two of his sons, Clinton suddenly fell forward in his seat, dead.[22]

We are often tempted in history to see what happened as having been destined to happen. For instance, the exit of DeWitt Clinton soon after the triumphant opening of the Erie Canal appears to be a natural phase in the changing of the guard in American politics, as the champions of elite governance were swept away by the democratic enthusiasms of the Age of Jackson. But Clinton's departure was not the result of any such theoretical inevitabilities. He simply died. Yet it is difficult to contemplate his last years without allowing the knowledge of the sudden and early end of his life to color our sense of his options and his possibilities. In 1825, however, many thought that Clinton's years of greatest influence and achievement still lay before him.

Martin Van Buren reminds us of this view:

> His prospects were never more promising than in the early part of the year 1825. His triumphant election as Governor of the largest state in the Union by [a great] majority . . . produced by a wide spread conviction in the public mind that he had suffered great injustice, required only ordinary tact and discretion on his part to ensure a continuing prosperity. The Erie Canal—the success of which was his source of richest strength in the state—was completed this season. . . . The re-election of Mr. Adams was considered, from his well understood want of popularity, highly improbable; Mr. Clay, by accepting the office of Secretary of State, had for the time put himself out of the line of competitors for the Presidency; Mr. Crawford had been withdrawn from public life by indisposition; the sanguine efforts in behalf of Mr. Calhoun had proved signally abortive, and the leading politicians inclined to the opinion that Gen. Jackson's strength could not stand the test of a four years exposure to the public scrutiny. Under such favoring circumstances it was not surprising that Mr. Clinton and his friends should have regarded his chances for the Presidency as better than those of any other aspirant.[23]

Van Buren exaggerates Clinton's eminence—understandably, in the light of his own maneuvers to regain power in the state. While he is mindful of Clinton's continuing influence, influence is not power, and too many obstacles lay in the way of Clinton's realizing either his personal ambitions or his designs for a more active state. But if the chances of electing a President Clinton in 1828 were smaller than they had been sixteen years before, the possibility of becoming Jackson's running mate was real. Illness and death did not just end Clinton's career, they cut it short.

Learning of Clinton's death, John Hone wrote to console his daughter and son-in-law on the fifteenth; the event, he observed, was not unexpected: "[H]is Friends here [in New York City] were not without fears and considerable alarm since the return of Doctr. Hosack who represented the Governor's situation as very critical."[24]

Clinton's death largely extinguished the hostilities that had marred his life and career, and there were tributes to him from around the state and the nation. Van Buren spoke movingly of him before the Senate of the United States, affirming that while in life he envied Clinton nothing, "now that he is fallen [I] am greatly tempted to envy him his grave with its honours." Dr. Hosack prepared a eulogy that was read at a memorial service and then published, along with a large collection of documents relating to Clinton's career and the building of the Erie Canal. Others praised him in ceremonies in town halls, Masonic lodges, and churches across the state. A volume of obituary tributes was published.[25]

Some of the bad feeling from his life remained. Clinton's honesty as a politician is perhaps best authenticated by the fact that after holding public office in the state over the span of four decades he died so poor that the legislature was asked to pass an act for the relief of his family, and a bill appropriating ten thousand dollars for this purpose was accordingly introduced. But it was not passed without opposition, nor was his grave as much to be envied as Van Buren supposed. He did not even find his final resting place for nearly thirty years, when his body was interred beneath an impressive monument in Brooklyn's Greenwood Cemetery.

The Anti-Masons tried to take advantage of Clinton's death to further their own cause, alleging that Clinton had connived at Morgan's disappearance and then killed himself to escape exposure. In the heat of the gubernatorial race of 1830, with Francis Granger running on the Anti-Masonic and National Republican tickets, Granger wrote to Hammond about this rumor:

> I have read the Daily Adv. of Monday with more indignation than at any thing political I have ever seen. I care nothing about the stand it takes against me, further than the base insinuation it throws out that I was among those even tolerating the idea that Mr. Clinton committed suicide, or had any thing to do in the abduction of Morgan & which is more false & malicious than any thing I have ever seen.[26]

But Clinton's name soon faded from the Anti-Masonic controversy and the political events that followed. Not only was he gone but his style of politics had been so fundamentally anchored in his own person that little could remain without him. The innovations of party politics had left him behind, while the innovations of his own improving spirit, in the Erie Canal and in educational reforms, would continue transforming the state for generations.

CLINTON'S LEGACY

Clinton made great contributions to the life of New York and the nation during his long career, and yet there remains, at the end, a sense of disappointment. At first this seems strange. The Erie Canal alone, with its manifold consequences, would be a sufficient legacy to later generations to win Clinton a measure of the fame he sought. And his role in founding public education in New York City and State, his efforts to foster the arts and sciences, and his political pursuits together add up to a remarkably diverse and rich career. But the picture of achievement is shaded by a sense of missed opportunities, squandered ability, and most disturbing of all, a deficit of principles at the man's core.

He was able to hold high office for much of his adult life, but the price he paid for prominence was also high. There is scarcely a year unmarked by pitched battles against Federalists, or Burrites, or Livingstonians, or the Virginia Dynasty, or the long string of Martling Men, Tammanyites, Bucktails, Regency men, and Democrats. Not only did these battles sap his power but his ever-shifting alliances undermined the reputation for disinterested leadership he so craved to cultivate. In the very personal politics of the time, such maneuverings also cost Clinton many friends.

To a certain extent this history of conflict and betrayal arises from Clinton's haughty and self-righteous temper. Had he been a more courteous and less prickly person, he might have had even greater success, but it is likely that the same lofty manner that so alienated his political associates reflected a personality capable of the sort of aspirations—for himself, and for his state and nation—that made his life and career memorable. Although aloof from the great mass of citizens, he nevertheless tried to improve the entire society, not just one segment of it. Indeed, Clinton's very isolation from others, although it made him a poorer politician, made him less tied to any one interest. His social acquaintances were the literary and financial elite, but his vision of society extended well beyond that circle.

Beyond this aloofness of personality, or perhaps arising from it, was a philosophical aloofness from politics that was a great weakness. He expressed it clearly in his *Introductory Discourse,* when he explained America's intellectual backwardness as resulting in part from the country's diversion of intellectual energies into political struggles. Although politics was his career, Clinton somehow did not believe that it required intellectual application. Instead, he tried to convert serious scientific and cultural achievement into a political asset. Campaign broadsides, the speeches of supporters, and the columns of friendly newspapers repeatedly proclaimed the largeness of Clinton's mind and the breadth of his vision. His recurring success at the polls in the 1820s surely owed something to his stature as one of New York's leading minds. Yet during his adult career he never subjected political life to the sort of exploration he lavished on the natural world. If he had, he might have succeeded better.

His political innovations were arrived at on a piecemeal basis and never fashioned into a system. The spoils system was employed to eject opponents from office and to install friends, but Clinton never thought through the possibilities and risks of the patronage power. The convention system allowed him to win elections when legislative caucuses were opposed to him, but he never followed the implications of this into the construction of a coherent statewide organization.

Foolishly, Clinton divided politics from government. Government, in his view, was a noble career, one that a man of his attainments owed it to the people to pursue. Politics, in contrast, was a tawdry struggle for office, a sacrifice of principles to expediency. It was perhaps because he was so easily led to embrace expedient means that he was so conscious of their malignancy. Martin Van Buren made no such distinction between politics and government. He understood that they were two halves of the same fruit, and he meant to harvest that fruit. He understood that if one wished to have a career in government, it behooved one to pursue a parallel career in politics. Clinton never quite accepted this, in spite of all his politicking.

The revolutionary generation had accepted, and to some extent embodied, an ideal of public service that was elitist but noble, in which the price of power was disinterestedness, and the reward deference. Clinton demanded the deference, but failed to appear disinterested. His goals may have been worthy, but he too clearly required that nobody else be allowed to achieve them.

THE LIMITS OF IDEOLOGY

Clinton's political career began with his "Countryman" letters in 1787 opposing the Constitution, and for the balance of his career he employed the rhetoric of republicanism. He stressed public virtue, the evils of luxury, the danger of expanding bank capital, the importance of states' rights. But it is hard to see this rhetoric as much more than window-dressing, particularly in the later part of his career. His vision of New York City certainly accepted luxury as a welcome part of life, and his opposition to banks flared up only when the bank concerned would be controlled by his political enemies.

Nor was Clinton unique in this cavalier use of republican rhetoric. The revolution had sanctified the terms under which it had been fought, and heaven help the politician who used other words or endorsed other views. Yet the republican ideology that had proved so useful a lens through which to view British oppression and the problems of independence was becoming increasingly irrelevant to the life of a nation that was rapidly expanding, industrializing, and dividing along sectional lines. Republican categories had no easy place in which to consider the problem of the enslavement of African Americans; in fact, it provided the convenient rhetoric of state sovereignty, which served as a shelter for slave institutions. The power that the republican vocabulary retained into the mid nineteenth century helped obscure sectional problems during the very decades in which they were deepening.

If republican ideology left out some important considerations, it also carried with it other ideas that proved serviceable to the expanding nation. Clinton's appropriation of the imperial aspect of the Roman tradition was hardly unique to him, nor was that the only imperial tradition around. The example of Britain, and above all of Napoleon, indicated to many Americans of Clinton's time that the nation's destiny might include not just a virtuous republic but an imperial one. Not that ideology was needed to motivate the western movement of settlement. Population growth and hunger for land were sufficient spurs, and the "mission" of bringing Protestant Christianity to the Indians and Mexicans of the West allowed the United States to conceive of the western part of the continent as empty in spite of its many inhabitants.

Clinton may have understood better than most the harsh lesson of imperial glory—that it contained within its success the seeds of its ultimate failure. His vision of an Asiatic genius leading a great force against the United States, and winning a final victory on the banks of the Missouri, paints a vivid image of the fate of empires. What was remarkable about Clinton was that he was willing to pay that price in order to achieve, if only for a while, imperial glory.

Perhaps Clinton saw in the paradigm of imperial rise and fall a reflection of his own career. Again and again, he saw his ideas transform the world, and then be themselves transformed in ways that he did not anticipate. Political measures he devised were refined and used against him; cultural organizations meant to encourage art and science failed to live up to their promise, while new organizations came along that made no hallowed place for the Magnus Apollo. Even the Erie Canal, his greatest success, contained the germ of the destruction of his notion of active government, although that would not occur until a decade after his death.

Eight years after Clinton's death, the painter Thomas Cole completed his great series of five paintings entitled "The Course of Empire." They show mankind's primitive origins, a pastoral Arcadia, a great city representing the "Consummation of Empire," that same city in decline and conflagration, and finally the overgrown ruins of the great metropolis. Clinton's career began during the Arcadian period of the United States, and he would probably have thought that the opening of the Erie Canal was as close to a "Consummation of Empire" as he could expect to see.

People may differ about how far along Cole's imperial progression the United States stands at the end of the twentieth century. But at the beginning of the nineteenth century DeWitt Clinton did as much as anyone to launch the nation on that perilous course.

NOTES

INTRODUCTION

I would like to thank the following libraries for permission to quote from manuscript materials in their collections: Columbia University, Rare Book and Manuscript Library (hereafter CUL); the New-York Historical Society (NYHS); Manuscript and Archives Division, the New York Public Library, Astor, Lenox, and Tilden Foundation (NYPL); Manuscript and Special Collections, the New York State Library (NYSL).

1. James Renwick, *Life of Dewitt Clinton* (New York: Harper Bros., 1840), pp. 13–14.

2. *New York Evening Post*, December 30, 1815; Jonas Platt to David Hosack, May 3, 1828, printed in Hosack, *Memoir of De Witt Clinton* (New York: J. Seymour, 1829), p. 385.

3. *Dictionary of American Biography* (hereafter *DAB*), s.v. "William Bayard"; *Longworth's American Almanac* (New York: Longworth, 1815), p. 87.

4. Ronald E. Shaw, *Erie Water West: A History of the Erie Canal, 1792–1854* (1966; reprint ed., Lexington: University of Kentucky Press, 1990), pp. 10–11; *Longworth's American Almanac* (1815), pp. 96, 95, 97.

5. Joseph A. Scoville [Walter Barrett], *The Old Merchants of New York*, 5 vols. (New York: Worthington Company, 1889), 5: 344–5; *Longworth's American Almanac* (1815), pp. 95, 97–8; Samuel Knapp, *The Life of Thomas Eddy* (New York: Conner & Cooke, 1834), pp. 87–97.

6. John Pintard, *Letters from John Pintard to his Daughter Eliza Pintard Davidson*, 4 vols. (New York: New-York Historical Society, 1940), 1: xxi, xiii, xviii; Scoville, *The Old Merchants of New York*, 2: 227; *DAB*, s.v. "John Pintard."

7. At the time, New York's highest court was called the state supreme court. Today, to the confusion of all, state supreme court is the trial court for felonies, and New York's highest tribunal is called the court of appeals.

8. Kenneth Nodyne, "The Role of De Witt Clinton and the Municipal Government in the Development of Cultural Organizations in New York City, 1803–1817" (Ph.D. diss., New York University, 1969), pp. 69–70; Jabez D. Hammond, *The History of Political Parties in the State of New-York, from the Ratification of the Federal Constitution to December, 1840*, 2 vols. (Albany, N.Y.: C. Van Benthuysen, 1942), 1: 279; Dixon Ryan Fox, *The Decline of Aristocracy in the Politics of New York, 1801–1840* (1919; revised ed., ed. Robert Remini, New York: Harper & Row, 1965), p. 51; Platt to Hosack, in Hosack, *Memoir of De Witt Clinton*, p. 382.

9. Milton Lomask, *Aaron Burr: The Years from Princeton to Vice President, 1756–1805* (New York: Farrar Straus Giroux, 1979), p. 210; Arthur James Wiese, *The Swartwout Chronicles 1338–1899, and the Ketelhuyn Chronicles, 1451–1899* (New York: Trow Directory, Printing and Bookbinding Co., 1899), pp. 274–82; Scoville, *The Old Merchants of New York*, 4: 248–52; *Longworth's American Almanac* (1815), p. 87.

10. *Longworth's American Almanac* (1815), pp. 95–8, 104; Kenneth Wiggins Porter, *John Jacob Astor, Business Man*, 2 vols. (1931; reprint ed., New York: Russell & Russell, 1966), 2: 1184–5.

11. Hosack, *Memoir of De Witt Clinton*, pp. 35–7; Renwick, *Life of Dewitt Clinton*, pp. 121–5; Jonathan Harris, "De Witt Clinton as Naturalist," *New-York Historical Society Quarterly* 56 (Oct. 1972): 264–84.

12. The fullest description of Clinton is in Hosack's *Memoir of De Witt Clinton*, pp. 120–2; the quotation is from the manuscript journal of Sam S. Griscom, a New Jersey schoolteacher, in the New-York Historical Society.

13. Pintard, *Letters from John Pintard to his Daughter*, 1: xv–xvi.

14. Wiese, *Swartwout Chronicles*, pp. 276—80; Lomask, *Aaron Burr: From Princeton to Vice President*, p. 15.

15. Kenneth T. Jackson, *Crabgrass Frontier: The Suburbanization of the United States* (New York: Oxford, 1985), pp. 14–20.

16. Bayrd Still, *Mirror for Gotham: New York as Seen by Contemporaries from Dutch Days to the Present* (New York: New York University Press, 1956), pp. 58, 65, 70, 78.

17. *New York Evening Post*, Jan. 2, 1816; Hammond, *History of Political Parties*, 1: 445.

18. Even without constitutional changes, the franchise was expanding. Enforcement of the stiffer eligibility requirements for voting for governor, lieutenant governor, and state senator was often lax, and in many places those qualified to vote for assemblymen and congressmen were also permitted to cast ballots for other offices. And the electorate was also expanded by vote fraud. See Harvey Strum, "Property Qualifications and Voting Behavior in New York, 1807–1816," *Journal of the Early Republic* 1 (1981): 347–71.

19. DeWitt Clinton, minutes of canal meeting, in DeWitt Clinton Miscellaneous Manuscripts (hereafter DWC Misc. Mss.), NYHS.

20. Michael Kammen, *Colonial New York: A History* (New York: Charles Scribner's Sons, 1975), pp. 278–9.

21. Robert Greenhalgh Albion, *The Rise of New York Port* (New York: Charles Scribner's Sons, 1939), pp. 390–1.

ONE • POLITICAL APPRENTICE

1. Hosack, *Memoir of De Witt Clinton*, pp. 22–24; Dorothie Bobbé, *De Witt Clinton*, (New York: Minton, Balch, 1933), pp. 3–8; "Extract from the Journal of a relative of the late Dr. Joseph Young," printed in Hosack, *Memoir of De Witt Clinton*, pp. 137–41.

2. Bobbé, *De Witt Clinton*, pp. 11–12; Renwick, *Life of Dewitt Clinton*, p. 22; William W. Campbell, *The Life and Writings of DeWitt Clinton* (New York: Baker and Scribner, 1849), pp. xiv–xvii.

3. "Journal of a relative of Dr. Young," in Hosack, *Memoir of De Witt Clinton*, p. 139; Bobbé, *De Witt Clinton*, p. 9; Patricia Bonomi, *A Factious People: Politics and Society in Colonial New York* (New York: Columbia University Press, 1971), p. 294; E. Wilder Spaulding, *His Excellency George Clinton: Critic of the Constitution* (New York: Macmillan, 1938), p. 6.

4. "George Clinton," in John A. Garraty, ed., *Encyclopedia of American Biography* (New York: Harper & Row, 1974), pp. 206–7; Craig Hanyan, *DeWitt Clinton: Years of Molding, 1769–1807* (New York: Garland Publishing, 1988), p. 7.

5. Bobbé, *De Witt Clinton*, p. 13; Hosack, *Memoir of De Witt Clinton*, p. 26; Spaulding, *George Clinton*, pp. 52, 92–3.

6. Bobbé, *De Witt Clinton*, pp. 15–16; Michael P. Lagana, "DeWitt Clinton, Politician Toward a New Political Order, 1769–1802" (Ph.D. diss., Columbia University, 1972), pp. 12–13.

7. Hanyan, *DeWitt Clinton: Years of Molding*, p. 9; DeWitt Clinton MS Diary (hereafter DWC Diary), NYHS. The notes of the debating society are among the diary pages covering 1824.

8. DWC Diary, NYHS; DeWitt Clinton, "Columbia College Address," in Campbell, *Life and Writings of De Witt Clinton*, p. 7.

9. Clinton, "Columbia College," in Campbell, *Life and Writings of De Witt Clinton*, p. 7.

10. Hanyan, *De Witt Clinton: Years of Molding*, p. 21; Clinton, "Columbia College," pp. 7–8.

11. Clinton, "Columbia College," pp. 9–11; Hosack, *Memoir of De Witt Clinton*, p. 28; Bobbé, *De Witt Clinton*, pp. 30–1; Renwick, *Life of Dewitt Clinton*, pp. 28–33.

12. Clinton, "Columbia College," p. 9; Hosack, *Memoir of De Witt Clinton*, p. 30.

13. Steven Edwin Siry, "De Witt Clinton and the American Political Economy: Sectionalism, Politics, and Republican Ideology, 1787–1828" (Ph.D. diss., University of Cincinnati, 1986), pp. 16–8; Henry F. May, *The Enlightenment in America* (New York: Oxford University Press, 1976), p. 342.

14. "A Dream," Jan. 6, 1789, DeWitt Clinton Papers, Rare Books and Manuscripts Collection, Columbia University Library (hereafter DWC Papers, CUL). This is the largest collection of Clinton papers, and it is available to researchers only on microfilm, organized into reels containing his letter-books (that is, the letters he wrote) and his papers (consisting largely of letters he received). The material is organized chronologically, and I have noted when an item is filed out of order or in another place. This account of his "Dream" is filed among miscellaneous papers at the end of the collection.

15. Alexander Clinton to James Clinton, Feb. 4, 1785, Alexander Clinton Misc. Mss., NYHS; Charles Clinton to James Clinton, n.d., Charles Clinton [b. 1767–d. 1829] Misc. Mss., NYHS; Mary Clinton to DWC, Feb. 22, 1785, DWC Papers, CUL; Mary Clinton to Alexander Clinton, August 15, 1786, in James Clinton Misc. Mss., NYHS.

16. Bobbé, *De Witt Clinton*, pp. 34–5.

17. Lagana, "DeWitt Clinton, Politician," p. 29; Spaulding, *George Clinton*, p. 18; Bobbé, *De Witt Clinton*, p. 37; Hosack, *Memoir of De Witt Clinton*, p. 31; James Clinton to DWC, June 20, 1787, DWC Papers, CUL.

18. Charles Clinton to DWC, Nov. 22, 1787, DWC Papers, CUL.

19. Bobbé, *De Witt Clinton*, p. 47; George Clinton to James Clinton, April 27, 1790, in Clinton Family Papers, Washington's Headquarters Museum, Newburgh, N.Y., quoted in Bobbé, p. 47.

20. Spaulding, *George Clinton*, pp. 142–8, 150–4, 168.

21. *New-York Journal, and Weekly Register*, Dec. 6, 13, 20, 1787, Jan. 10, 1788; George Clinton, Jr., to DWC, [Dec.] 22, 1787, DWC Papers, CUL.

22. "A Countryman" [DeWitt Clinton], *New York Journal*, Dec. 6, 1787; Lagana, "DeWitt Clinton, Politician," pp. 31–2.

23. "A Countryman" [DeWitt Clinton], *New York Journal*, Dec. 6, 1787.

24. Linda Grant De Pauw, however, finds Clinton's letters to be among the best of New York's anti-Federalist writings. Linda Grant De Pauw, *The Eleventh Pillar: New York State and the Federal Constitution* (Ithaca, N.Y.: Cornell University Press, 1966), p. 104; U.S. Constitution, Article I, Section 4; *New York Journal*, Dec. 13, 1787; Lagana, "DeWitt Clinton, Politician," p. 35; Hanyan, *DeWitt Clinton: Years of Molding*, p. 34.

25. Spaulding, *George Clinton*, p. 173, says they were written by George Clinton; Cecilia M. Kenyon merely says they have been attributed to the governor, Kenyon, *The Antifederalists* (1966; reprint ed., Boston: Northeastern University Press, 1985), p. 301; and Bernard Bailyn gives no attribution for the "Cato" essays he reprints in his *Debate on the Constitution*, 2 vols. (New York: Library of America, 1993) 1: 31. In an appendix to her book *The Eleventh Pillar* (pp. 293–302), Linda Grant De Pauw disputes the attribution of the "Cato" letters to George Clinton. She finds that the reasons originally put forward by Paul Leicester Ford to support his attribution do not hold up, and she offers Abraham Yates as "not an improbable guess" to be the author of the "Cato" letters. But the evidence she adduces also sug-

gests another possibility—that DeWitt Clinton might have written them, either on his own or in collaboration with his less fluent uncle. The "Cato" letters appeared in the same newspaper as the "Countryman" letters; they cover much of the same ground—for instance, the "Countryman's" fears of a manipulation of voting places for national elections in order to deprive the common people of a voice is reiterated in the seventh and last "Cato" letter. Perhaps DeWitt found the guise of a rustic critic of the Constitution too confining for his intellectual pretensions (as his citing of Beccaria suggests) and wanted to be able to make the same arguments in the high-flown and learned oratorical style he was then perfecting. Certainly some of DeWitt's favorite intellectual reference points—Montesquieu, Coke, Milton—are sprinkled through the "Cato" letters, and the paranoid style is similar to DeWitt's own letters at the time. Among the contemporary references to "Cato" that De Pauw finds to be authentic is one that refers to him as a "state demagogue," and one calling him "some little State Sovereign." A third refers to "Cato" and "his X-L-N-C" as two different persons. One argument that Ford made to support the attribution to George Clinton was that the letters stop in January 1788, and this showed that once the legislature went into session the governor no longer had time for his literary efforts. De Pauw suggests that this argument would apply even more to a legislator, like Yates. But DeWitt, too, may have been busy performing secretarial duties for his uncle as the legislature convened, and his own "Countryman" letters stopped on January 10, 1788—one week after the last of the "Cato" letters appeared. No proof of this hypothesis can be found in DeWitt Clinton's papers, but perhaps it is fair to say that, like Yates, DeWitt Clinton as "Cato" is "not an improbable guess." In his recent biography of George Clinton, John P. Kaminski concedes that George Clinton's authorship of the letters cannot be proved, but critiques some of DePauw's arguments for Yates's authorship; Kaminski, *George Clinton: Yeoman Politician of the New Republic* (Madison, Wis.: Madison House, 1993), pp. 130–7, 309–10.

26. Kenyon, *The Antifederalists*, p. 301.

27. DWC to Thomas Greenleaf, June 22, June 27, 1788, DWC Papers, CUL; Spaulding, *George Clinton*, p. 179.

28. DWC to Charles Tillinghast, July 18, 1788, DWC Papers, CUL; Spaulding, *George Clinton*, pp. 181–2; Paul Gilje, *The Road to Mobocracy: Popular Disorder in New York City, 1763–1834* (Chapel Hill: University of North Carolina Press, 1987), pp. 97–9.

TWO • POLITICAL JOURNEYMAN

1. Clinton's formal appointment as secretary came in 1790 (Siry, "De Witt Clinton and the American Political Economy," p. 24; Bobbé, *De Witt Clinton*, p. 54), but he appears to have begun serving in that capacity part-time at least as early as February of 1788, when he was signing documents transmitted to the Council of Revision by Governor George Clinton. See George Clinton Papers, Documents of the Council of Revision, Feb. 21, 28, March 17, 1788, NYHS.

2. Spaulding, *George Clinton*, p. 185; Kaminski, *George Clinton*, pp. 164–5.

3. Yates, though a strong opponent of the Constitution during the ratification debates in 1788, had become a supporter of the document by the following year.

4. For Hamilton's financial plan, see Stanley Elkins and Eric McKitrick, *The Age of Federalism: The Early American Republic, 1788–1800* (New York: Oxford University Press, 1993), pp. 114–61.

5. Evan W. Cornog, "To Give a Character to Our City: New York's City Hall," *New York History* 59 (1988): 389–423.

6. DWC to Charles Clinton, July 20, 1790, in John W. Francis, ed., *Old New York Reminiscences*, 13 vols. (New York: Charles Roe, 1865–95), II: 1458; Lagana, "DeWitt Clinton, Politician," pp. 104–5.

7. James Parton, *The Life and Times of Aaron Burr*, 2 vols. (1857; reprint ed., Boston: James R. Osgood, 1876) I: 169; Lomask, *Aaron Burr: From Princeton to Vice President*, pp. 138–40.

8. Lomask, *Aaron Burr: From Princeton to Vice President*, pp. 141–4; Hammond, *History of Political Parties*, I: 50.

9. DeAlva S. Alexander, *A Political History of the State of New York*, 3 vols. (New York: Henry Holt, 1906), 1: 50–5, 62; Leonard White, *The Federalists: A Study in Administrative History* (New York: Macmillan, 1948), p. 256; Howard Lee McBain, *DeWitt Clinton and the Origin of the Spoils System in New York* (New York: Columbia University Press, 1907), p. 79; Spaulding, *George Clinton*, p. 200; Hammond, *History of Political Parties*, 1: 55–8; Lomask, *Aaron Burr: From Princeton to Vice President*, 1: 162–4.

10. Hammond, *History of Political Parties*, 1: 62–70; Spaulding, *George Clinton*, pp. 202–4; Kaminski, *George Clinton*, p. 215; Alan Taylor, *William Cooper's Town: Power and Persuasion on the Frontier of the Early American Republic* (New York: Alfred A. Knopf, 1995), pp. 170–3.

11. Elkins and McKitrick, *Age of Federalism*, p. 330; John C. Miller, *The Federalist Era, 1789–1801* (1960; New York: Harper Torchbooks, 1963), pp. 132–9; Lagana, "DeWitt Clinton, Politician," pp. 139–40; Edmond Charles Genet to Thomas Jefferson, June 1797, Genet Papers, NYHS.

12. Alfred Young, *The Democratic Republicans of New York: The Origins, 1763–1797* (Chapel Hill: University of North Carolina Press, 1967), pp. 394, 395, 412; Lagana, "DeWitt Clinton, Politician," pp. 160–1; J. Ludlow to DWC, March 8, 1794, DWC Papers, CUL.

13. Alexander, *Political History of New York*, 1: 61–2; Charles Z. Lincoln, *Constitutional History of the State of New York*, 5 vols. (Rochester: The Lawyers Cooperative Publishing, 1906), 1: 599; Hammond, *History of Political Parties*, 1: 79–82; Kaminski, *George Clinton*, p. 245. Benson had earlier been one of George Clinton's closest advisors, and personal feelings may have moderated the governor's resistance to his appointment.

14. Jerome Mushkat, *Tammany: The Evolution of a Political Machine, 1789–1865* (Syracuse, N.Y.: Syracuse University Press, 1971), pp. 8–21; Sidney I. Pomerantz, *New York, an American City, 1783–1803: A Study of Urban Life* (1938; reprint ed. Port Washington, N.Y.: Ira J. Friedman, 1965), pp. 470–2; Bobbé, *De Witt Clinton*, p. 55.

15. Erik McKinley Eriksson, "De Witt Clinton, A Great Masonic American," *Grand Lodge Bulletin* [Grand Lodge of Iowa, A. F. & A. M.] 30 (1929): 248; Porter, *John Jacob Astor*, 2: 1084–5; DeWitt Clinton, *An Address Delivered Before the Holland Lodge, December 24, 1793* (New York: Francis Childs and John Swaine, 1794), pp. 15, 4, 8, 9. Clinton's installation as Master of Holland Lodge was apparently the spark for a power struggle within the lodge between Federalists and Republicans. It seems that he had been prepared to resign from the lodge if he was defeated, although whether his attitude stemmed from political rectitude or personal vanity is impossible to determine. See John Ludlow to DWC, March 9, 1794, DWC Papers, CUL; Young, *Democratic Republicans*, p. 399; John Speyer to DWC, Feb. 20, 1795, DWC Papers, CUL.

16. DeWitt Clinton, *An Oration on Benevolence, Delivered Before the Society of Black Friars* (New York: Friar M'Lean, 1795), pp. 10–18; Lagana, "DeWitt Clinton, Politician," pp. 163–166.

17. Lagana, "DeWitt Clinton, Politician," p. 117; Bobbé, *De Witt Clinton*, pp. 60–1; John Speyer to DWC, Feb. 20, 1795, DWC Papers, CUL.

18. Francis Silvester to DWC, Feb. 12, 1788, DWC Papers, CUL; John Speyer to DWC, Feb. 20, 1795, DWC Papers, CUL; Timothy J. Gilfoyle, *City of Eros: New York City, Prostitution, and the Commercialization of Sex, 1790–1920* (New York: Norton, 1992), p. 87.

19. Bobbé, *De Witt Clinton*, pp. 61–2; Cornelia Clinton to DWC, Jan. 15, 1794, DWC Papers, CUL; DWC to Cornelia Clinton, March 9, 1794, Genet Papers, Library of Congress, quoted in Lagana, "DeWitt Clinton, Politician," pp. 182–6; Renwick, *Life of Dewitt Clinton*, p. 47; Hosack, *Memoir of De Witt Clinton*, p. 32; DWC Diary, July 30, 1818, NYHS.

20. Lagana, "DeWitt Clinton, Politician," pp. 176–7, 162; Spaulding, *George Clinton*, p. 213; Edward Livingston to DWC, Mar. 13, 1794, DWC Papers, CUL.

21. Alexander, *Political History of New York*, 1: 65; Bradford Perkins, *The First Rapprochement: England and the United States, 1795–1805* (Berkeley: University of California Press, 1967), p. 33.

22. Alexander, *Political History of New York*, 1: 65; John Beckley to DWC, July 24, Sept. 13, 1795, DWC Papers, CUL; Elkins and McKitrick, *Age of Federalism*, pp. 442–6; Lagana, "DeWitt Clinton, Politician," pp. 195–200.

23. Gilje, *Road to Mobocracy,* pp. 104–7, Lagana, "DeWitt Clinton, Politician," pp. 233–6; Bobbé, *De Witt Clinton,* p. 64.

24. DWC to Oliver Phelps, Oct. 2, 1796, Nov. 13, 1796, and Feb. 23, 1797, DWC Papers, CUL.

25. Lagana, "DeWitt Clinton, Politician," p. 226; DWC to Peter B. Porter, Oct. 5, Dec. 10, 1797, DWC Papers, CUL.

26. DWC to "R.W.B.," April 21, 5799 [1799], DWC Papers, CUL.

27. Elkins and McKitrick, *Age of Federalism,* pp. 569–79; Bobbé, *De Witt Clinton,* p. 73; Renwick, *Life of Dewitt Clinton,* p. 51.

28. Miller, *Federalist Era,* pp. 208–9, 235–6; Elkins and McKitrick, *Age of Federalism,* pp. 710–1; Albert Gallatin to DWC, Jan. 30, 1799, DWC Papers, CUL.

29. Hammond, *History of Political Parties,* 1: 137–9; Lomask, *Aaron Burr: From Princeton to Vice President,* pp. 225–7, 248–9 (quote on 249).

30. Lomask, *Aaron Burr: From Princeton to Vice President,* pp. 240–3; Hammond, *History of Political Parties,* 1: 136–7. The person he characterized as "uncandid" was James Cheetham, Clinton's chief tool in the "pamphlet war" with Burr that began in 1802.

31. Hunloke Woodruff to Isaac Ledyard, April 9, 1800, Woodruff Misc. Mss., NYHS (in a note on this document, Clinton says his son's illness is imperfectly described, but is unclear on what part is deficient); "Grotius" [DeWitt Clinton], *A Vindication of Thomas Jefferson; Against the Charges Contained in A Pamphlet Entitled, "Serious Considerations," &c* (New York: David Denniston, 1800), pp. 7–10; Gordon S. Wood, *The Radicalism of the American Revolution* (New York: Alfred A. Knopf, 1992), p. 330.

32. Elkins and McKitrick, *Age of Federalism,* pp. 282–8; Miller, *Federalist Era,* pp. 89–94; John Howe, Jr., "Republican Thought and the Political Violence of the 1790s," *American Quarterly* 19 (1967): 147–65.

33. Alexander, *Political History of New York,* 1: 92, 100; Lomask, *Aaron Burr: From Princeton to Vice President,* p. 294; Henry Adams, *History of the United States of America during the Administrations of Thomas Jefferson and James Madison* (1889–1891; reprint ed. in 2 vols., New York: Library of America, 1986), 1: 133. Adams included Chief Justice John Marshall in the mutual disadmiration society.

34. Howard Lee McBain, *DeWitt Clinton and the Origin of the Spoils System in New York,* pp. 79, 86.

35. Marinus Willett to DWC, Dec. 22, 1800, DWC Papers, CUL.

36. Charles Z. Lincoln, *Messages from the Governors of the State of New York,* 11 vols. (Albany: J. B. Lyon, 1909), 2: 473; George Clinton to DWC, March 28, 1801, DWC Papers, CUL.

37. Alexander, *Political History of New York,* 1: 107–11; Lincoln, *Constitutional History,* 1: 596–610; McBain, *DeWitt Clinton and the Spoils System,* pp. 91–6.

THREE • CLINTONIANS AND BURRITES

1. Lomask, *Aaron Burr: From Princeton to Vice President,* pp. 293–5; Charles Z. Lincoln, *Constitutional History of New York,* 1: 609.

2. For the tangled story of the 1800 vice-presidential nomination, see Lomask, *Aaron Burr: From Princeton to Vice President,* pp. 247–55; George Clinton to DWC, Dec. 13, 1803, DWC Papers, CUL; statement signed by James Nicholson, dated Dec. 26, 1803, DWC Papers, CUL; Spaulding, *George Clinton,* p. 217; Kaminski, *George Clinton,* pp. 253–5. The accusation about Clinton's role in depriving Burr of the nomination in 1795 was made by "Aristides" [William P. Van Ness] on Burr's behalf.

3. George Clinton to DWC, Jan. 13, 1801, DWC Papers, CUL.

4. *DAB,* s.v. "James Cheetham"; Lomask, *Aaron Burr: From Princeton to Vice President,* pp. 315–6.

5. Alexander, *Political History of New York,* 1: 122–3. "A Citizen of New York," [James Cheetham], *Narrative of the Suppression by Col. Burr of the History of the Administration of John Adams . . .* (New York: Denniston and Cheetham, 1802), pp. 9–10, 40; James Cheetham, *A Letter to a Friend on the Conduct of the Adherents to Mr. Burr* (New York: James Cheetham, 1803), p. 36.

6. *Encyclopædia Britannica,* 11th ed., s.v. "Illuminati"; G. P. Gooch, "Europe and the French

Revolution," in *The Cambridge Modern History*, Vol. 8, *The French Revolution*, ed. by A. W. Ward, G. W. Prothro, and Stanley Leathes, (1904; reprint ed., Cambridge: Cambridge University Press, 1969), pp. 772–4; R. R. Palmer, *The Age of Democratic Revolution*, 2 vols. (Princeton, N.J.: Princeton University Press, 1964), 2: 162–4, 250–1; John Wood, *A Full Exposition of the Clintonian Faction, and the Society of the Columbian Illuminati* (Newark: Printed for the author, 1802), pp. 22, 25, 45, 48–9.

7. Eric Foner, *Tom Paine and Revolutionary America* (New York: Oxford University Press, 1976), pp. 245–7; Wood, *A Full Exposition of the Clintonian Faction*, pp. 11, 13, 15.

8. Fox, *Decline of Aristocracy*, p. 59; Alexander, *Political History of New York*, 1: 124; Clare Brandt, *An American Aristocracy: The Livingstons* (New York: Doubleday, 1986), pp. 132, 146, 154; DWC to Thomas Tillotson, Dec. 20, 1803, DWC Misc. Mss., NYHS. William P. Van Ness should not be confused with Columbia County's William W. Van Ness, a pillar of Federalism in the Hudson Valley.

9. DWC to Thomas Tillotson, Dec. 20, 1803, DWC Misc. Mss., NYHS; Ward & Gould to DWC, Dec. 12, 1803, DWC Papers, CUL.

10. George Clinton to DWC, Dec. 13, 1803, DWC Papers, CUL; "Aristides" [William P. Van Ness] *An Examination of the Various Charges Exhibited Against Aaron Burr . . .* "A new edition, revised and corrected" (New York: Ward & Gould, 1804), pp. 7, 65, 58; Ward & Gould to DWC, Dec. 7, 1804, DWC Papers, CUL; Ward & Gould to DWC, n.d. [1805], DWC Papers, CUL.

11. Lomask, *Aaron Burr: From Princeton to Vice President*, pp. 252, 287; Hammond, *History of Political Parties*, 1: 186; Alexander, *Political History of New York*, 1: 127; Siry, "De Witt Clinton and the American Political Economy," pp. 50–2; Bobbé, *De Witt Clinton*, p. 89.

12. Wiese, *Swartwout Chronicles*, pp. 273–80; Siry, "De Witt Clinton and the American Political Economy," pp. 51–4; Parton, *Aaron Burr*, 1: 324–6; Alexander, *Political History of New York*, 1: 127; Bobbé, *De Witt Clinton*, pp. 88–93.

13. Hammond, *History of Political Parties*, 1: 183–4; John Armstrong to Thomas Tillotson, Dec. 6. 1801, Jan. 25, 1802, Thomas Tillotson Misc. Mss, NYHS; Lomask, *Aaron Burr: From Princeton to Vice President*, p. 299; Hammond, *History of Political Parties*, 1: 186.

14. George Clinton to Thomas Jefferson, Feb. 9, 1802, quoted in Bobbé, *De Witt Clinton*, p. 86; Fox, *Decline of Aristocracy*, p. 62.

15. Siry, "De Witt Clinton and the American Political Economy," p. 69; Fox, *Decline of Aristocracy*, pp. 76–8.

16. DeWitt Clinton, "Mississippi Question," in Campbell, *Life and Writings of De Witt Clinton*, pp. 278–9, 285–6, 288–90, 291, 294.

17. Lomask, *Aaron Burr: From Princeton to Vice President*, pp. 299–307; *DAB*, s.v. "Samuel Osgood." A daughter from Osgood's first marriage, Martha Brandon Osgood, would become Edmond Charles Genet's second wife in 1814. *DAB*, s.v. "Edmond Charles Genet."

18. Richard Hofstadter, *The Idea of a Party System: The Rise of Legitimate Opposition in the United States, 1780–1840* (Berkeley: University of California Press, 1969), p. 139; Richard P. McCormick, *The Presidential Game: The Origins of American Presidential Politics* (New York: Oxford University Press, 1982), pp. 46–9.

19. McCormick, *Presidential Game*, pp. 52–7; Lolabel House, *A Study of the Twelfth Amendment to the Constitution of the United States* (Philadelphia, 1901), pp. 27–9.

20. Herman V. Ames, "The Proposed Amendments to the Constitution of the United States During the First Century of Its History," *Annual Report of the American Historical Association for the Year 1896*, 2 vols. (Washington: GPO, 1897), 2: 77–9; House, *A Study of the Twelfth Amendment*, pp. 39–40, 45.

21. Ames, "Proposed Amendments," p. 79.

22. Siry, "De Witt Clinton and the American Political Economy," pp. 78–80; unsigned and undated note of apology, DWC Papers, CUL (this note is filed with the affidavit referred to below, so it is clearly the note to Dayton).

23. W. C. Nicholas to DWC, October 27, 1803, DWC Papers, CUL; affidavit dated Nov. 20, 1803, signed S. Smith and Robert Wright, DWC Papers, CUL.

24. Parton, *Aaron Burr,* 2: 326; *DAB,* s.v. "William Coleman"; Hammond, *History of Political Parties,* 1: 187–8; [Matthew L. Davis and/or William P. Van Ness?] *Letters of Marcus and Philo-Cato, addressed to De Witt Clinton Esq.* (n.p., 1810), pp. 38, 41.

25. Bobbé, *De Witt Clinton,* p. 99; DWC to P[?] Butler, Nov. 18, 1803, DWC Papers, CUL (filed with letters to him, rather than as part of his letterbooks). Clinton's fellow United States senator from New York in 1803, Theodorus Bailey, resigned his office in 1804 to accept appointment as postmaster of New York City, a position he retained until he died, in 1828. *A Biographical Congressional Directory,* (Washington: GPO, 1913), p. 451; Leonard D. White, *The Jeffersonians: A Study in Administrative History, 1801–1829* (1951; New York: Free Press, 1965), p. 321.

26. Hammond, *History of Political Parties,* 1: 200.

27. George Clinton to DWC, Nov. 16, 1803, DWC Papers, CUL; Henry Adams, *History of the Administrations of Thomas Jefferson,* pp. 416–7.

28. Alexander, *History of Political Parties,*1: 129; Adams, *History of the Administrations of Thomas Jefferson,* p. 418; Thomas Jefferson, "The Anas," in *Writings of Thomas Jefferson,* ed. Merrill D. Peterson (New York: Library of America, 1984), pp. 690–3; Lomask, *Aaron Burr: From Princeton to Vice President,* p. 335.

29. Fox, *Decline of Aristocracy,* p. 62; Henry Adams, *History of the Administrations of Thomas Jefferson,* p. 568; David Hackett Fischer, *The Revolution of American Conservatism: The Federalist Party in the Era of Jeffersonian Democracy* (New York: Harper & Row, 1965), pp. 175–6; Lomask, *Aaron Burr: From Princeton to Vice President,* pp. 340–1.

30. Alexander, *Political History of New York,* 1: 136–7; *DAB,* s.v. "John Lansing"; *DAB,* s.v. "Morgan Lewis"; Hammond, *History of Political Parties,* 1: 205.

31. Alexander, *Political History of New York,* 1: 136–8; Lomask, *Aaron Burr: From Princeton to Vice President,* pp. 337–8; "Genuine Republicans," [campaign broadside, 1804], Early American Imprints, second series, No. 6371.

32. B[rockholst] Livingston to DWC, March 7, 1804, DWC Papers, CUL; "A Clintonian" to DWC, n.d.(but filed between March 12 and March 27, 1804), DWC Papers, CUL; Gid[eo]n Granger to DWC, March 27, 1804, DWC Papers, CUL; M[organ] Lewis to DWC, April 4, 1804, DWC Papers, CUL; George Clinton to DWC, April 14, April 27, 1804, DWC Papers, CUL.

33. Lomask, *Aaron Burr: From Princeton to Vice President,* pp. 353–5; Christine Chapman Robbins, *David Hosack: Citizen of New York* (Philadelphia: American Philosophical Society, 1964), pp. 134–6.

FOUR   •   MAYOR CLINTON

1. Pomerantz, *New York: An American City,* pp. 36–7, 53, 308.

2. Hammond, *History of Political Parties,* 1: 198–9. Hammond's splendid history has served me as both a primary and secondary source, and has been used extensively throughout this biography. Anyone who has read Hammond's work must be impressed with both his sagacity and his objectivity. He was, as Dixon Ryan Fox described him, a "sincere though discriminating admirer" of Clinton, but also "too independent in mind to make a successful party man." Hammond's regard for Clinton makes him a sympathetic observer, but that sympathy seldom clouds his carefully weighed judgments of Clinton's measures and motives. His history is an indispensable resource for anyone attempting to discover the substance and texture of the political world Clinton inhabited. See Fox's life of Hammond in the *DAB.*

3. Raymond Mohl, "Education as Social Control in New York City, 1784–1825," *New York History* 51 (April 1970): 219–37; Thomas Bender, *New York Intellect: A History of Intellectual Life in New York City, from 1750 to the Beginnings of Our Own Time* (New York: Alfred A. Knopf, 1987), pp. 75–7; Hanyan, *DeWitt Clinton: Years of Molding,* in unpaginated section.

4. Pomerantz, *New York: An American City,* pp. 140–5; Hendrik Hartog, *Public Property and Private Power: The Corporation of the City of New York in American Law, 1730–1870* (Ithaca, N.Y.: Cornell University Press, 1983), pp. 135–9. Hartog points out that although the struggle over the suffrage involved differing

claims about the power of the city's charter versus the powers lodged in the legislature, focusing on that issue in this period "hides the deeper consensus that committed the postrevolutionary generation to changing the traditional legal bases for municipal government." In the same way, it is important not to read the struggles of Federalists and Jeffersonians in New York City against the national backdrop. Although the two parties fought bitterly (among themselves as well as with each other), there was an underlying consensus both on New York's destined future greatness and on the importance of commerce and industry to achieving that end. After all, there was little room for true agrarians in the city, and the power of workingmen had not yet been tested as it would be two decades later. See Hartog, *Public Property and Private Power,* p. 139, and Sean Wilentz, *Chants Democratic: New York City & the Rise of the American Working Class, 1788–1850* (New York: Oxford University Press, 1984), pp. 172–216.

5. Bobbé, *De Witt Clinton,* p. 111; Fox, *Decline of Aristocracy,* p. 78; proclamation in DWC's hand, dated Dec. 26, 1806, DWC Papers, CUL (filed with letters to DWC from 1808); Gilje, *The Road to Mobocracy,* pp. 130–2.

6. Pomerantz, *New York: An American City,* pp. 338–50; Robbins, *David Hosack,* pp. 35–42; Siry, "De Witt Clinton and the American Political Economy," p. 92.

7. DWC to Thomas Barclay, Dec. 27, 1803, DWC Papers, CUL; DWC to M. Ascounbel[?], Dec. 26, 1803, DWC Papers, CUL; DWC to Thomas Barclay, June 17, 1804, DWC Papers, CUL; DWC to James Madison, June 19, 1804, DWC Papers, CUL; Madison to DWC, June 25, 1804, DWC Papers, CUL.

8. Siry, "De Witt Clinton and the American Political Economy," p. 101; Marshall Smelser, *The Democratic Republic, 1801–1815* (New York: Harper Torchbooks, 1968), pp. 157–8; Adams, *History of the Administrations of Jefferson and Madison,* 1: 740–1; James Fairlie to DWC, March 6, 1806, DWC Papers, CUL; Henry Rutgers to DWC, March 7, 1806, DWC Papers, CUL; Bradford Perkins, *Prologue to War: England and the United States, 1805–1812* (Berkeley: University of California Press, 1961), p. 107; Diary of John Pintard (typescript copy), April 26, 28, 1806, Pintard Papers, NYHS.

9. James Madison to DWC, May [ ], 1806, DWC Papers, CUL; Henry Whitby to DWC, May 2, 1806, DWC Papers, CUL; Ralph Ketcham, *James Madison: A Biography* (New York: Macmillan, 1971), pp. 452–7.

10. Albion, *The Rise of New York Port,* pp. 213–27; Alexander, *Political History,* 1: 121; *DAB,* s.v. "Samuel Swartwout."

11. Hammond, *History of Political Parties,* 1: 199–200.

12. Porter, *John Jacob Astor,* 1: 164–9; Bobbé, *De Witt Clinton,* pp. 130–1.

13. Bobbé, *De Witt Clinton,* p. 139; Cynthia Owen Philip, *Robert Fulton* (New York: Franklin Watts, 1985), pp. 216, 213–4; Shaw, *Erie Water West,* p. 45.

14. Charles Gobert to DWC, April 27, 1812, DWC Papers, CUL; Joseph C. Guttwatch[?] to DWC, April 22, 1819, DWC Papers, CUL; Thomas Skidmore to DWC, Aug. 22, 1822, DWC Papers, CUL.

FIVE • CLINTONIAN CULTURE

1. Lawrence Levine, *Highbrow/Lowbrow: The Emergence of Cultural Hierarchy in America* (Cambridge, Mass.: Harvard University Press, 1988), pp. 3–9; Bender, *New York Intellect,* pp. 46–88.

2. Levine, *Highbrow/Lowbrow,* p. 9; Charles Z. Lincoln, ed., *Messages from the Governors of the State of New York,* 5: 161.

3. Nodyne, "De Witt Clinton and Cultural Organizations," pp. 51–2, 49, 69–70; Hosack, *Memoir of De Witt Clinton,* pp. 30–1. See also Hanyan, "DeWitt Clinton: Years of Molding," p. 27.

4. Nodyne, "De Witt Clinton and Cultural Organizations," p. 144; *New York Times,* Feb. 6, 1985. Clinton described the site of Hosack's garden in his *Introductory Discourse:* "The view, from the most elevated part, is variegated and extensive; and the soil itself is of that diversified nature as to be particularly adapted to the cultivations of a great variety of vegetable productions." Not content with

this, he then cites the authority of a "british writer, in the London Medical and Physical Journal," who declared that "no region of the earth seems more appropriate to the improvement of botany . . . than that where the Elgin Botanic Garden is seated." Clinton, *An Introductory Discourse Delivered Before the Literary and Philosophical Society of New-York* (1815; reprint ed., New York: Arno Press, 1978), pp. 41–2.

5. DeWitt Clinton, "Columbia College," in Campbell, *Life and Writings of De Witt Clinton*, pp. 14–5.

6. Bender, *New York Intellect*, p. 55.

7. Elkins and McKitrick, *Age of Federalism*, pp. 189, 192.

8. Nathaniel Hawthorne, *The Marble Faun* (1860; reprint ed., New York: New American Library, 1961), p. vi. Henry James was drawn to this passage in his consideration of *Hawthorne* (1879; reprint ed., Ithaca, N.Y.: Great Seal Books/Cornell University Press, 1956), p. 33. In Elkins and McKitrick, *Age of Federalism*, p. 166, James's own catalogue of the "complex social machinery" a novelist depends upon is explored.

9. Nodyne, "De Witt Clinton and Cultural Organizations," pp. 19–20, 24; Ray W. Irwin, *Daniel D. Tompkins: Governor of New York and Vice President of the United States* (New York: The New-York Historical Society, 1968), p. 60.

10. Philip, *Robert Fulton*, pp. 1–2; DeWitt Clinton, *A Discourse Delivered Before the American Academy of the Arts . . . 23rd October, 1816* (New York: T. & W. Mercein, 1816), pp. 4, 16, 17.

11. Clinton, *Discourse Before the American Academy*, pp. 13, 12, 8. The theme of "refinement" has been extensively explored by Richard L. Bushman in *The Refinement of America: Persons, Houses, Cities* (New York: Alfred A. Knopf, 1992).

12. Clinton, *Discourse Before the American Academy*, pp. 9, 11–3.

13. Ibid., pp. 18–9, 6; John McComb, Jr., "Diary of the Proceedings Relative to Building the New City Hall," October 29, 1803, McComb Papers, NYHS; Cornog, "To Give a Character to Our City," p. 410.

14. "On City Hall, In City Hall," catalogue of exhibition, Art Commission of the City of New York (New York, 1984), p. 3; Mary T. Flannelly, "City Hall," typescript, 1975, pp. 80–1. Both Courtesy of the Art Commission of the City of New York.

15. Clinton, *Discourse Before the American Academy*, p. 6.

16. Nodyne, "De Witt Clinton and Cultural Organizations," p. 15.

17. Bender, *New York Intellect*, pp. 75–7; Arthur Everett Peterson, ed., *Minutes of the Common Council of the City of New York, 1784–1831*, 19 vols. (New York: The City of New York, 1917), 8: 235; Nodyne, "De Witt Clinton and Cultural Organizations," pp. 115–9.

18. Bender, *New York Intellect*, p. 77; Levine, *Highbrow/Lowbrow*, pp. 64–8.

19. John W. Francis, *An Inaugural Address Delivered Before the Academy of Medicine* (1848), quoted in Bender, p. 75.

20. Edward A. Fitzpatrick, *The Educational Views and Influence of De Witt Clinton* (New York: Teachers College, Columbia University, 1911), pp. 96, 54; Lincoln, *Messages from the Governors*, 2: 61; DeWitt Clinton, "An Address to the Benefactors and Friends of the Free School Society of New-York, Delivered on the Opening of that Institution, in their New and Spacious Building" (New-York: Collins and Perkins, 1810), pp. 6–11.

21. Fitzpatrick, *Educational Views of De Witt Clinton*, pp. 144, 90–2; David M. Ellis et al., *A Short History of New York State* (Ithaca, N.Y.: Cornell University Press, 1957), p. 199; Knapp, *Life of Thomas Eddy*, pp. 164–5.

22. *DAB*, s.v. "Thomas Eddy," "John Murray, Jr."; Knapp, *Life of Thomas Eddy*, pp. 160–2; Fitzpatrick, *Educational Views of De Witt Clinton*, pp. 91–2.

23. Clinton, "Free School Society," in Campbell, *Life and Writings of De Witt Clinton*, pp. 311, 319.

24. Paul L. Ford, ed., *The Writings of Thomas Jefferson*, 10 vols. (New York, 1892–99), 9: 146–7; Clinton, "Free School Society," pp. 314–6.

25. *Encyclopaedia Britannica*, 15th ed., s.v. "Joseph Lancaster."

26. Fitzpatrick, *Educational Views of De Witt Clinton*, pp. 103–11, 124–37, 154.

27. Fitzpatrick, *Educational Views of De Witt Clinton*, p. 147.

SIX • CLINTONIANS AND QUIDS

1. *DAB*, s.v. "Morgan Lewis."

2. Clare Brandt, *The Livingstons*, pp. 165–6; Bray Hammond, *Banks and Politics in America from the Revolution to the Civil War* (Princeton, N.J.: Princeton University Press, 1957), pp. 158–61; Hammond, *History of Political Parties*, 1: 215–20; Alexander, *Political History*, 1: 149; Fox, *Decline of Aristocracy*, p. 69.

3. Hammond, *History of Political Parties*, 1: 220–6; Frederic Cople Jaher, *The Urban Establishment: Upper Strata in Boston, New York, Charleston, Chicago, and Los Angeles* (Urbana: University of Illinois Press, 1982), p. 210; Alexander, *Political History*, 1: 149–50; Diary of John Pintard, March 21, 24, 1806, Pintard Papers, NYHS.

4. Hammond, *History of Political Parties*, 1: 226; Alexander, *Political History*, 1: 150.

5. "Letters of Marcus and Philo-Cato Addressed to De Witt Clinton, Esq. Mayor of the City of New York" (n.p.: Poughkeepsie, 1810). Matthew L. Davis is identified as "Marcus" by "Philo-Cato" (pp. 24, 61), and by James Parton, *Life of Aaron Burr*, 2: 352. "Philo-Cato," according to the introduction to the compilation of their letters published in 1810, "will never be known," but broad hints are given that he is none other than "Aristides," that is, Van Ness (see pp. 38–42). The *New York Columbian Centinal*, a Clintonian paper, fingered Tunis Wortman as Philo-Cato on Feb. 25, 1811. (Or he, like "Marcus," may have been Davis, as Jabez D. Hammond reports, *History of Political Parties*, 1: 227.)

6. "Letters of Marcus," pp. 3–6; Parton, *Life of Burr*, 2: 347–53.

7. "Letters of Marcus," pp. 7, 9, 11–13; B[en]j[ami]n Romaine to DWC, Feb. 19, 1806, DWC Papers, CUL; Ja[mes] Fairlie to DWC, Feb. 20, 1806, DWC Papers, CUL.

8. Hammond, *History of Political Parties*, 1: 230. The term *Martling Men* held for most of the next decade, until that identity merged with that of Tammany Hall and took the name Bucktails.

9. Ja[mes] Fairlie to DWC, Feb. 26, 1806, DWC Papers, CUL; Nathan Sanford to DWC, Feb. 27, 1806, DWC Papers, CUL.

10. "Letters of Marcus," p. 14. John Pintard noted the appearance of Bailey's letter in his diary for March 31, 1806, the day it appeared in the *American Citizen*. Pintard appears to accept Bailey's unlikely claim that Clinton had no role in the affair and comments that the attempted alliance had "excited indignation on the part of Republicans generally." See typed transcript of Pintard's Diary, March 31, 1806, Pintard Papers, NYHS.

11. Ibid.; James Parton, *Life of Burr*, 2: 352; Benjamin Romaine to DWC, Feb. 19, 1806, DWC Papers, CUL.

12. Hammond, *History of Political Parties*, 1: 233; Alexander, *Political History*, 1: 151.

13. Bobbé, *De Witt Clinton*, p. 125.

14. DWC Diary, June–July, 1807, July 25, Dec. 7, 1807, NYHS.

15. George Clinton to DWC, Jan. 17, 1807, DWC Papers, CUL; *New York Morning Chronicle*, Feb. 21, 1807.

16. Irwin, *Daniel D. Tompkins*, pp. 5, 25–6, 49–50.

17. Hammond, *History of Political Parties*, 1: 239; Renwick, *Life of Dewitt Clinton*, p. 66.

18. Alexander, *Political History*, 1: 153–7; Fox, *Decline of Aristocracy*, pp. 70–4.

19. Hammond, 1: 241–2; George Clinton to DWC, May 9, June 2, 1807, DWC Papers, CUL; Irwin, *Daniel D. Tompkins*, p. 54.

20. *New York Morning Chronicle*, May 3, 1806. See also ibid., May 8, 10, 15, and 16, 1806.

21. *New York Morning Chronicle*, May 19, 1806.

22. *New York Morning Chronicle*, April 25, 27, 28, 29, 30, May 2, 7, 8, 1807.

23. Fox, *Decline of Aristocracy*, pp. 78–83; Charles R. King, ed., *The Life and Correspondence of Rufus King*, 6 vols. (New York: G. P. Putnam's Sons, 1898) 5: 14–23.

24. *New York Morning Chronicle*, Feb. 28, 1807; Irvin, *Daniel D. Tompkins*, p. 55.

SEVEN • NEW YORK AND THE NATION

1. George Clinton to DWC, April 8, 1807, DWC Papers, CUL; Siry, "De Witt Clinton and the American Political Economy," pp. 106, 108.

2. Morgan Lewis to John Smith, March 23, 1806, John Smith of Mastic, L.I., Misc. Mss., NYHS; James Fairlie to DWC, March 6, 1806, DWC Papers, CUL. Smith was also one of Clinton's correspondents, and two years after Lewis's letter to him Smith received one from Clinton calling Lewis a "public defaulter" and his supporters "contemptible" (DWC to Smith, Feb. 20, 1808, John Smith of Mastic, L.I., Misc. Mss., NYHS); Irving Brant, "The Election of 1808," in Arthur M. Schlesinger, ed., *History of American Presidential Elections*, 4 vols. (New York: Chelsea House, 1985), 1: 189–90.

3. For Jefferson's economic ideas and the Embargo, see Elkins and McKitrick, *Age of Federalism*, pp. 130–1, 381–8; Burton Spivak, *Jefferson's English Crisis: Commerce, Embargo, and the Republican Revolution* (Charlottesville: University Press of Virginia, 1979), pp. 1–12, 198–210; Drew R. McCoy, *The Elusive Republic: Political Economy in Jeffersonian America* (New York: W. W. Norton, 1980), pp. 212–23; Lance Banning, *The Jeffersonian Persuasion: Evolution of Party Ideology* (Ithaca, N.Y.: Cornell University Press, 1978), pp. 292–4; J. C. A. Stagg, *Mr. Madison's War: Politics, Diplomacy, and Warfare in the Early American Republic, 1783–1830* (Princeton, N.J.: Princeton University Press, 1983), pp. 20–3.

4. Ketcham, *James Madison*, pp. 442–57; Dumas Malone, *Jefferson and His Time*, 6 vols. (Boston: Little, Brown, 1948–80), 5: 485–90.

5. Cornog, "To Give a Character to Our City," pp. 417–8.

6. Siry, "De Witt Clinton and the American Political Economy," pp. 110–3; DWC Diary, Jan. 18, 1808, NYHS; Hammond, *History of Political Parties*, 1: 260; Alexander, *Political History*, 1: 163–4; Daniel D. Tompkins to DWC, Jan. 24, 1808, DWC Papers, CUL.

7. Alexander, *Political History*, 1: 165; Ketcham, *James Madison*, 456; George Clinton to DWC, Feb. 13, 1808, DWC Papers, CUL; Siry, "De Witt Clinton and the American Political Economy," pp. 114, 119–20; "A Citizen of New-York" [Edmond Charles Genet], *Communications on the Next Election for President of the United States, and on the Late Measures of the Federal Administration* (New York: Printed for the author, 1808), pp. 11–12.

8. Spaulding, *George Clinton*, p. 280; Genet, *Communications on the Next Election*, pp. 11–12; Irving Brant, *The Fourth President: A Life of James Madison* (Indianapolis: Bobbs-Merrill, 1970), p. 389; George Clinton to DWC, Feb. 13, 1808, DWC Papers, CUL.

9. George Clinton to DWC, Feb. 13, 1808, DWC Papers, CUL.

10. Irving Brant, *The Fourth President*, p. 389.

11. Brant, *The Fourth President*, p. 390; Brant, *James Madison*, 6 vols. (Indianapolis: Bobbs-Merrill, 1941–61), 5: 420–8; Harry Ammon, *James Monroe: The Quest for National Identity* (Charlottesville: University Press of Virginia, 1990), pp. 270–7; Malone, *Jefferson and His Time*, 5: 412–3, 547–9; Kaminski, *George Clinton*, pp. 278–82; Spaulding, *George Clinton*, pp. 288–9.

12. Brant, *The Fourth President*, pp. 391–2; Kaminski, *George Clinton*, pp. 282–9; Spaulding, *George Clinton*, pp. 280–92; Malone, *Jefferson and His Time*, 5: 547; Brant, "Election of 1808," in Schlesinger, ed., *American Presidential Elections*, 1: 206–17.

13. Alexander, *Political History*, 1: 166–7.

14. Hammond, *History of Political Parties*, 1: 297–8; Siry, "De Witt Clinton and the American Political Economy," p. 133; Brant, "Election of 1808," in Schlesinger, ed., *American Presidential Elections*, 1: 203, 214–5; Kaminski, *George Clinton*, p. 283.

15. Solomon Nadler, "The Green Bag: James Monroe and the Fall of De Witt Clinton," *New-York Historical Society Quarterly* 59 (1975): 204; Siry, "De Witt Clinton and the American Political Economy," p. 122; Irwin, *Daniel D. Tompkins*, pp. 43, 56.

16. Fox, *Decline of Aristocracy*, pp. 88–94, 109; Fischer, *Revolution of American Conservatism*, p. xvii; Robert W. July, *The Essential New Yorker: Gulian Crommelin Verplanck* (Durham, N.C.: Duke University Press, 1951), pp. 3–7.

17. Bobbé, *De Witt Clinton*, p. 135; Alexander, *Political History*, 1: 168.

18. Gustavus Myers, *The History of Tammany Hall*, 2nd ed. (1917; reprint ed., New York: Dover, 1971), p. 28; Mushkat, *Tammany Hall*, p. 39; *New York Columbian*, Nov. 1, 1809.

19. *New York Columbian*, Jan. 16, 19, Feb. 16, 17, April 14, 1810; Hammond, *History of Political Parties*, 1: 281–5; Fox, *Decline of Aristocracy*, pp. 112–6; Alexander, *Political History*, 1: 173–9.

20. The electoral vote in Pennsylvania had been eight to seven for Jefferson in 1800, and, as we have seen, New York gave six votes to George Clinton in 1808.

21. Alexander, *Political History*, 1: 180–1; *New York Columbian*, March 12, 1811; Hammond, *History of Political Parties*, 1: 291–4; Mushkat, *Tammany Hall*, p. 42.

22. DeWitt Clinton, "Minutes of Cases, Court of Sessions, NYC," BV, NYHS, June 8, Aug. 2, June 11, July 2, Oct. 6, 1808; Feb. 8, 1812.

23. Clinton, "Minutes of Court of Sessions," testimony of Peter Wilson, testimony of John M. Mason. See also July, *Gulian C. Verplanck*, pp. 32–9; Fox, *Decline of Aristocracy*, pp. 162–5; Gilje, *Road to Mobocracy*, pp. 115–6.

24. Clinton, "Minutes of Court of Sessions," testimony of Peter Wilson and John Nitchie, Esq.; July, *Gulian C. Verplanck*, pp. 34–6.

25. Clinton, "Minutes of Court of Sessions"; July, *Gulian C. Verplanck*, p. 36.

26. Clinton, "Minutes of Court of Sessions"; July, *Gulian C. Verplanck*, pp. 36–7; *The Trial of Gulian C. Verplank [sic], Hugh Maxwell, and others . . .* (New York: n.p., 1821), p. 26. Clinton clearly thought to gain politically from this trial; on August 20, the Clintonian paper, the *New York Columbian*, devoted three columns to printing the entirety of the mayor's charge to the jury.

27. Clinton, "Minutes of Court of Sessions"; *The Trial of Gulian C. Verplank*, p. 30; July, *Gulian C. Verplanck*, p. 38.

28. Fox, *Decline of Aristocracy*, p. 164, and Bender, *New York Intellect*, p. 70, portray Clinton's actions at the trial as calculated to win Federalist support; Ambrose Spencer to DWC, Sept. 23, 1811, DWC Papers, CUL; DWC Diary, August 4, 1812, NYHS.

29. Spaulding, *George Clinton*, pp. 297–303; Kaminski, *George Clinton*, p. 290; Bray Hammond, *Banks and Politics*, pp. 162–3. Henry Clay later became a great champion of the Second Bank of the United States, but in 1811, according to Merrill D. Peterson, "retreated to the sanctity of Republican dogma," a decision Peterson finds to be the "most incongruous" of Clay's career. Peterson, *The Great Triumvirate: Webster, Clay, and Calhoun* (New York: Oxford University Press, 1987), p. 17.

30. Hammond, *History of Political Parties*, 1: 307–8.

31. DWC to Henry Remsen, March 3, 13, 1812, DWC Papers, NYPL.

32. Hammond, *History of Political Parties*, 1: 305–10; *DAB*, s.v. "Ambrose Spencer"; Irwin, *Daniel D. Tompkins*, p. 113.

33. DWC to Henry Remsen, March 11, 1812, DWC Papers, NYPL; Bray Hammond, *Banks and Politics*, pp. 162–3; Hammond, *History of Political Parties*, 1: 309. Tompkins himself had no doubts about Clinton's opposition to the bank and wrote in early April that Clinton "has, I really believe, taken greater pains to convince members of the impropriety of voting for it than I have done." Irwin, *Daniel D. Tompkins*, p. 122.

34. Irwin, *Daniel D. Tompkins*, p. 122; Norman K. Risjord, "Election of 1812," in Schlesinger, *American Presidential Elections*, 1: 252–3.

35. Risjord, "Election of 1812," p. 252; Siry, "De Witt Clinton and the American Political Economy," p. 140; Spaulding, *George Clinton*, p. 303.

36. Alexander, *Political History*, 1: 201–2; Risjord, "Election of 1812," p. 253; Fox, *Decline of Aristocracy*, p. 167; Hofstadter, *Idea of a Party System*, pp. 3–8, 221–6; Leonard W. Levy, *Jefferson and Civil Liberties: The Darker Side* (1963; reprint ed., Chicago: Elephant Paperbacks, 1989), pp. 131–4, on Embargo repression; Siry, "De Witt Clinton and the American Political Economy," p. 159.

37. *New York Columbian*, June 13 (reprinting material from the *Albany Advertiser*), July 31, June 30, Aug. 1, 1812.

38. Risjord, "Election of 1812," pp. 253–4; Diary of Rufus King, July 27, July 31, 1812, King Papers, NYHS.

39. Diary of Rufus King, August 3–5, 1812, King Papers, NYHS; Risjord, "Election of 1812," p. 254; Fox, *Decline of Aristocracy*, pp. 168–9.

40. New York Committee of Correspondence, "Address to the People of the United States," August 17, 1812, in Schlesinger, *American Presidential Elections*, 1: 274–8.

41. Ibid., pp. 278–82.

42. Samuel Eliot Morison, *Harrison Gray Otis, 1765–1848: The Urbane Federalist* (Boston: Houghton Mifflin, 1969), pp. 261–3; Diary of Rufus King, Sept. 15–17, 1812, King Papers, NYHS; James M. Banner, Jr., *To the Hartford Convention: The Federalists and the Origins of Party Politics in Massachusetts, 1789–1815* (New York: Alfred A. Knopf, 1970), pp. 311–2; Victor A. Sapio, *Pennsylvania & the War of 1812* (Lexington: University Press of Kentucky, 1970), pp. 178–9.

43. Risjord, "Election of 1812," pp. 256, 262.

44. Risjord, "Election of 1812," pp. 258, 272; Siry, "De Witt Clinton and the American Political Economy," pp. 155–61; Bobbé, *De Witt Clinton*, pp. 185–8; Sapio, *Pennsylvania & the War of 1812*, pp. 172–3.

45. McCormick, *Presidential Game*, p. 103.

46. Hammond, *History of Political Parties*, 1: 311, 343; Fox, *Decline of Aristocracy*, pp. 174–5.

47. Alexander, *Political History*, 1: 211; Fox, *Decline of Aristocracy*, p. 171; Hammond, *History of Political Parties*, 1: 343–4.

48. Bobbé, *De Witt Clinton*, pp. 181–2; Fox, *Decline of Aristocracy*, pp. 172–3.

49. Hammond, *History of Political Parties*, 1: 354–8.

EIGHT • LAUNCHING THE CANAL

1. Fox, *Decline of Aristocracy*, p. 14; Cadwallader Colden, "A Memorial concerning the Fur Trade of the province of New-York," in Hosack, *Memoir of De Witt Clinton*, p. 236.

2. Colden, "Memorial," pp. 238–9.

3. R. Ernest Dupuy and Trevor N. Dupuy, *The Encyclopedia of Military History* (New York: Harper & Row, 1970), p. 660. Military considerations also worked against the canal—or at least an attempt was made to make them do so. In 1817, before leaving for Washington to assume the office of vice president, Governor Daniel D. Tompkins tried to derail Clinton's triumph by getting the Council of Revision to reject the law authorizing canal construction. His argument was that war with Britain remained likely, so funds should be devoted to improving defenses, not to building a canal. See Shaw, *Erie Water West*, p. 76.

4. Washington to Chastellux, from Marshall's *Life of General Washington*, Vol. 9, quoted in Hosack, p. 275; Shaw, *Erie Water West*, pp. 11–2; Elkins and McKitrick, *The Age of Federalism*, p. 43.

5. Shaw, *Erie Water West*, p. 13.

6. Fox, *Decline of Aristocracy*, pp. 150–1; Shaw, *Erie Water West*, pp. 14–5; Morgan Lewis to Harmanus Bleecker, May 26, 1828, in Hosack, *Memoir of De Witt Clinton*, p. 250.

7. Fox, *Decline of Aristocracy*, pp. 150–1; Shaw, *Erie Water West*, pp. 14–5.

8. Nathan Miller, *The Enterprise of a Free People: Aspects of Economic Development in New York State During the Canal Period, 1792–1838* (Ithaca, N.Y.: Cornell University Press, 1962), p. 23–4; the stock certificate is in the DWC Papers, CUL.

9. Hosack, *Memoir of De Witt Clinton*, p. 97; Robbins, *David Hosack*, p. 18; Renwick, *Life of Dewitt Clinton*, pp. 32–3.

10. Renwick, *Life of Dewitt Clinton*, p. 23–4; Christopher Ward, *The War of the Revolution*, 2 vols. (New York: Macmillan, 1952), 2: 639–41; Bobbé, *De Witt Clinton*, p. 151.

11. Shaw, *Erie Water West*, pp. 16–9; Miller, *Enterprise of a Free People*, p. 26; Bobbé, *De Witt Clinton*, p. 154; Spaulding, *George Clinton*, p. 156.

12. Shaw, *Erie Water West*, pp. 17–8; Miller, *Enterprise of a Free People*, p. 29.

13. Thomas Jefferson, Second Inaugural Address, in *Writings*, ed. Merrill D. Peterson (New York: Library of America, 1984), p. 519; Carter Goodrich, *Government Promotion of American Canals and Railroads, 1800–1890* (New York: Columbia University Press, 1960), pp. 28–37.

14. Hosack, *Memoir of De Witt Clinton*, pp. 34–7; "Hercules" [Jesse Hawley], "Observations on Canals," Nos. 5 and 6, in ibid., pp. 321, 323; Shaw, *Erie Water West*, pp. 29–31.

15. Shaw, *Erie Water West*, pp. 33–4; "Hercules" [Jesse Hawley], "Observations on Canals," No. 2, in Hosack, *Memoir of De Witt Clinton*, pp. 312–13.

16. Miller, *Enterprise of a Free People*, p. 31; *Journal of the Senate of the State of New-York* (Albany, N.Y.: Solomon Southwick, 1810), p. 57.

17. Hosack, *Memoir of De Witt Clinton*, pp. 382–3; *Senate Journal*, 1810, pp. 99–100; Shaw, *Erie Water West*, pp. 19, 38–9.

18. *DAB*, s.v. "Simeon DeWitt,"; David M. Ellis, *Landlords and Farmers in the Hudson-Mohawk Region, 1790–1850* (Ithaca, N.Y.: Cornell University Press, 1946), pp. 36, 227.

19. Campbell, *Life and Writings of De Witt Clinton*, p. 29; John Hartshorne Eddy, "Diary describing a tour of inspection of the Commissioners Appointed by Joint Resolution of the Legislature of New York in 1810, to examine the navigation of the western parts of the State of New York between the Hudson River, and Lakes Ontario and Erie," MS Diary (photostat; original in Newberry Library), NYPL, n.p.

20. DeWitt Clinton, "Canal Journal," in Campbell, *Life and Writings of De Witt Clinton*, p. 29.

21. Ibid, pp. 33, 31, 37.

22. Ibid., pp. 90, 99, 102, 104.

23. Ibid., pp. 35, 56, 97, 64, 79, 137–8.

24. Ibid., pp. 34, 52, 137.

25. Ibid., pp. 106, 187.

26. Ibid., pp. 39, 71, 73.

27. Ibid., p. 56.

28. John Eddy, "Canal Diary," p. 19.

29. *Journal of the Senate of the State of New-York* (Albany, 1811), pp. 65–75.

30. New-York Corresponding Association, for the Promotion of Internal Improvements, *Public Documents, Relating to the New-York Canals, which are to Connect the Western and Northern Lakes, with the Atlantic Ocean* (New York: William A. Mercein, 1821), pp. 2–56 (hereafter cited as *Canal Documents*); Shaw, *Erie Water West*, pp. 46–7.

31. *Canal Documents*, pp. 60–64.

32. Charles Sellers, *The Market Revolution: Jacksonian America, 1815–1846* (New York: Oxford University Press, 1991), pp. 40–3, quote pp. 40–1.

33. Hosack, *Memoir of De Witt Clinton*, pp. 347–8; Sellers, *Market Revolution*, p. 42.

34. Shaw, *Erie Water West*, p. 50–1.

35. Hammond, *History of Political Parties*, 1: 302; Bayard to Caesar Rodney, Dec. 22, 1811, quoted in Roger Evan Carp, "The Erie Canal and the Liberal Challenge to Classical Republicanism, 1785–1850" (Ph.D. diss., University of North Carolina, 1986), p. 125, FN 49.

36. Goodrich, *Government Promotion of Canals and Railroads*, p. 37.

37. Miller, *Enterprise of a Free People*, p. 41.

38. Samuel Flagg Bemis, *John Quincy Adams and the Foundations of American Foreign Policy* (New York: Alfred A. Knopf, 1956), pp. 229–30.

39. Siry, "De Witt Clinton and the American Political Economy," pp. 732–65; Sellers, *Market Revolution*, p. 40.

40. Hosack, *Memoir of De Witt Clinton*, p. 407; Sellers, *Market Revolution*, p. 39.

41. Gordon S. Wood, *The Radicalism of the American Revolution* (New York: Alfred A. Knopf, 1992),

pp. 315–6. The United States Constitution is an important exception to Wood's statement that "commerce" meant international trade. Twice in Article I (Sec. 8 [3] and Sec. 9 [6]) commerce among the states is specified. I am grateful to Stanley Elkins for pointing this out.

42. Hosack, *Memoir of De Witt Clinton*, pp. 407–10. Chicago, in fact, was then little more than a few huts near Fort Dearborn and only began to grow in earnest after the Erie Canal opened. The city was not incorporated until 1837. See Harold M. Mayer and Richard C. Wade, *Chicago: Growth of a Metropolis* (Chicago: University of Chicago Press, 1969), pp. 12–4. That ambitious young politician Abraham Lincoln portrayed himself as an expert on internal improvements and a champion of canals in his first political contest in 1832. See Mark E. Neely, Jr., *The Last Best Hope of Earth: Abraham Lincoln and the Promise of America* (Cambridge, Mass.: Harvard University Press, 1993), p. 7.

43. Hosack, *Memoir of De Witt Clinton*, p. 420. By the time of the Civil War, the railroad links were more important than canals, but the trains followed routes originally traced by canals, and in many cases connected cities that had first bloomed because of canal traffic.

44. Shaw, *Erie Water West*, pp. 60–3; Martin Van Buren, *The Autobiography of Martin Van Buren* (1920; reprint ed., New York: Chelsea House, 1983), p. 84; Joseph Ellicott to Clinton, Feb. 21, 1816, DWC Papers, CUL; James W. Stevens to Clinton, Feb. 26, 1816, DWC Papers, CUL.

45. Van Buren, *Autobiography*, p. 85; *Canal Documents*, p. 267.

NINE   •   CLINTONIAN INTELLECT

1. Alexander, *Political History*, 1: 243.

2. Nodyne, "De Witt Clinton and Cultural Organizations," p. 84.

3. De Witt Clinton, *An Introductory Discourse Delivered Before the Literary and Philosophical Society of New-York* (1815; reprint ed., New York: Arno Press, 1978), pp. 3, 39.

4. Ibid., pp. 18, 4, 5, 7.

5. Ibid., pp. 14–5.

6. Ibid., pp. 17, 20–1; Robbins, *David Hosack*, p. 158; DWC to John Pintard, August 18, 1816, DWC Papers, NYPL.

7. Clinton, *Introductory Discourse*, pp. 13, 21–2, 40, 32–4.

8. DeWitt Clinton, "The Iroquois," in Campbell, *The Life and Writings of De Witt Clinton*, pp. 252–3.

9. Jonathan Harris, "De Witt Clinton as Naturalist," *New-York Historical Society Quarterly* 56 (1972): 280.

10. Clinton, "The Iroquois," pp. 210, 216–7.

11. Among those who thought the Indians were descended from the ancient Israelites were William Penn and Roger Williams. See Alden T. Vaughan, "From White Man to Redskin: Changing Anglo-American Perceptions of the American Indian," *American Historical Review* 87 (1982): 926; Clinton, "The Iroquois," pp. 217–22.

12. Clinton, "The Iroquois," pp. 223–4. That Europeans were the instigators, or even the inventors, of scalping is the subject of James Axtell's essay "The Unkindest Cut, or Who Invented Scalping?" Axtell traces the idea that scalping was a European invention to remarks to that effect made by Cornplanter, an Allegany Seneca chieftain, in 1820. Clinton's essay was written nine years earlier, which indicates not that the idea came from Clinton, but only that it did not originate with Cornplanter. See James Axtell, "The Unkindest Cut, or Who Invented Scalping?" in Axtell, *The European and the Indian: Essays in the Ethnohistory of Colonial North America* (New York: Oxford University Press, 1981), pp. 16–35.

13. One of the most intriguing letters Clinton received concerns a Roman coin from the reign of Commodus that was found in Tennessee, "in a ravine, 4 feet below the surface," having been unearthed by a rainstorm. Clinton's informant, Caleb Atwater, wonders whether this coin was deposited there "by the ancient people who erected our forts, mounds, &c?" but concludes that it was probably dropped there by some more recent arrival from Europe. Atwater to DWC, Oct. 4, 1820, DWC Papers, CUL.

14. Clinton, "The Iroquois," pp. 256–7. He expanded on the theme and explored the archeological evidence in greater detail in *A Memoir on the Antiquities of the Western Parts of the State of New-York Read Before the Literary and Philosophical Society of New-York* (Albany, 1818).

15. Ibid.; *Encyclopedia Britannica*, 15th ed., s.v. "Madog"; Robert Southey, *Madoc* (London: Longman, Hurst, Rees, and Orme, 1805), p. viii; Hosack, *Memoir*, p. 38.

16. Clinton, "The Iroquois," p. 265. The verse is taken from Book 1 of *Paradise Lost*, lines 351–5.

17. Clinton, "Memorial of the Citizens of New-York, in Favour of a Canal Navigation," in Hosack, *Memoir of De Witt Clinton*, p. 420.

18. Clinton, "The Iroquois," pp. 252, 266.

19. DeWitt Clinton, "Address to the Alumni of Columbia College," in William W. Campbell, *Life and Writings of De Witt Clinton*, pp. 1–20; idem, "Address Before the Phi Beta Kappa Society of Union College," in Campbell, pp. 329–63; Clinton, "Circular Letter of the Literary and Philosophical Society of New-York, on the Subject of a Statistical Account of the State of New-York," *Transactions of the Literary and Philosophical Society* 1 (1816): 559–65; Clinton, *A Memoir on the Antiquities of the Western Parts of the State of New-York Read Before the Literary and Philosophical Society of New-York*; Typescript of John Pintard's "Notes Respecting the Acquaintance of J. Pintard with the Late Governor Clinton," Pintard Papers, NYHS.

20. Jonathan Harris, "De Witt Clinton as Naturalist," p. 266; Thomas Jefferson to DWC, Oct. 8, 1818, DWC Papers, CUL.

21. Nodyne, "The Role of De Witt Clinton in Cultural Organizations," p. 92.

22. [Gulian C. Verplanck], *The State Triumvirate, A Political Tale: and The Epistles of Brevet Major Pindar Puff* (New York: J. Seymour, 1819), pp. 103–4, 12.

23. Nodyne, "De Witt Clinton and Cultural Organizations," pp. 181–96; DWC to John Pintard, August 7, 1817, DWC Misc. Mss, NYHS; Bobbé, *De Witt Clinton*, p. 197; Bender, *New York Intellect*, pp. 70–2, 124–6.

24. Clinton's scientific interests have survived in remarkable ways. There are two humble wines of the Po valley in Italy that honor him: Clínto, a rough wine made from an American vine called Fragola (strawberry) in Italy, and Clintòn, an even rougher wine made from an American vine named for DeWitt Clinton. According to Mario Soldati, Clínto is "the only wine that is definitely pure, for the simple reason that its cost is so low that it would never be worth the trouble to alter it." Both vines, being American, were immune to the grape phylloxera, an insect (and also an American export) that ravaged native European vines in the mid-nineteenth century. Mario Soldati, *Vino al Vino* (Milan: Mondadori, 1977), p. 138; Burton Anderson, *Vino* (Boston: Atlantic–Little Brown, 1980), pp. 164–5. I am grateful to Shirley Hazzard for this information.

TEN ○ THE GOVERNOR

1. July, *Gulian C. Verplanck*, pp. 43–4; Fox, *Decline of Aristocracy*, p. 203; Gustavus Myers, *History of Tammany Hall*, p. 36.

2. Fox, *Decline of Aristocracy*, pp. 203–4; July, *Gulian C. Verplanck*, pp. 46–7.

3. "A Traveller" [DeWitt Clinton], *An Account of Abimelech Coody, and Other Celebrated Writers of New York* ([New York], 1815), pp. 6, 9, 13, 16, 21–2.

4. July, *Gulian C. Verplanck*, pp. 50–1.

5. Hofstadter, *The Idea of a Party System*, p. xii.

6. Ibid., pp. 219–23.

7. "Thomas Jefferson's Opinion of DeWitt Clinton," 1824 broadside, NYHS.

8. Donald B. Cole, *Martin Van Buren and the American Political System* (Princeton, N.J.: Princeton University Press, 1984), pp. 13–4; Van Buren, *Autobiography*, p. 11.

9. Van Buren, *Autobiography*, pp. 37–8.

10. Cole, *Martin Van Buren*, p. 28; Van Buren, *Autobiography*, pp. 45, 47, 38–9, 96.

11. Van Buren, *Autobiography*, pp. 38–48.

12. Hammond, *History of Political Parties*, 1: 399–400.

13. Gouverneur Morris to DWC, Feb. 19, 1815, DWC Papers, CUL; Thomas Jefferson to DWC, March 15, 1815, DWC Papers, CUL; Earl of Buchan to DWC, Jan. 21, 1816, DWC Papers, CUL; Joseph Banks to DWC, June 12, 1816, DWC Papers, CUL.

14. Robert Walsh, Jr., to DWC, March 28, 1815, DWC Papers, CUL; A. Rodney to DWC, April 22, 1815, DWC Papers, CUL; W. J. MacMenen [?] to DWC, Feb. 27, 1816, DWC Papers, CUL; Gideon Granger to DWC, March 27, 1816, DWC Papers, CUL. Jabez Hammond also urged Clinton to run in 1816. See DWC to Hammond, April 19, 1816, DWC Papers, CUL.

15. Hammond, *History of Political Parties*, 1: 407–12. At the time of the maneuverings Hammond describes, Crawford was still secretary of war; he was soon after appointed secretary of the treasury.

16. "Atticus" [DeWitt Clinton], *Remarks on the Proposed Canal from Lake Erie to the Hudson River* (New York: Samuel Wood, 1816), p. 11.

17. Hammond, *History of Political Parties*, 1: 430; Alexander, *Political History*, 1: 245; Van Buren, *Autobiography*, pp. 74–5; Ambrose Spencer to John C. Spencer, n.d.[ref. No. 14927], NYSL.

18. Hammond, *History of Political Parties*, 1: 432–44; Alexander, *Political History*, 1: 245–51; Fox, *Decline of Aristocracy*, pp. 196–7; Siry, "De Witt Clinton and the American Political Economy," p. 186.

19. The Bucktails got their name from one of the Tammany emblems, the tail of a buck worn on a hat.

20. Hammond, *History of Political Parties*, 1: 449.

21. Fox, *Decline of Aristocracy*, pp. 197, 215–7; Lincoln, *Messages of the Governors*, 2: 898–9.

22. Lincoln, *Messages of the Governors*, 2: 903–5.

23. Ibid., 2: 908–11.

24. Ibid., 2: 906–7, 913–5.

25. Ibid., 2: 915–8.

26. Ibid., 2: 916.

27. Hammond, *History of Political Parties*, 1: 458–62.

28. Ibid., 1: 480.

29. Ibid, 1: 478–82; Alexander, *Political History*, 1: 259–60 (he erroneously reports these events as taking place in 1818); Van Buren, *Autobiography*, pp. 89–91.

30. Hammond, *History of Political Parties*, 1: 496–7, Roger Evan Carp, "The Erie Canal and the Liberal Challenge to Classical Republicanism," p. 291; Van Buren, *Autobiography*, p. 91; Alexander, *Political History*, 1: 260–1. Control of the canal patronage allowed Tammany Hall to cultivate the support of recent Irish immigrants who had until then been strong supporters of Clinton. Many of these immigrants were Protestant. As the Catholic presence increased, Tammany turned against the Irish once more before cementing the final alliance that was to shape New York City politics for several generations. See Mushkat, *Tammany Hall*, pp. 59–62, 66.

31. Bobbé, *De Witt Clinton*, pp. 218, 224–6; Hosack, *Memoir of De Witt Clinton*, pp. 119–20.

32. James Renwick, *Life of Dewitt Clinton*, p. 256.

33. DWC to Mrs. Ingraham, August 12, 1818, DWC Papers, CUL; Hosack, *Memoir of De Witt Clinton*, p. 126.

34. DWC to Maria Clinton, March 14, 1813, DWC Papers, NYSL.

35. Hammond, *History of Political Parties*, 2: 271–2.

36. Tallmadge proposed that an amendment be added to the bill admitting Missouri as a state, and specifying that slavery be prohibited in the new state. The Missouri Compromise allowed slavery in Missouri, but barred it in the rest of the Louisiana Purchase north of 36° 30′ and admitted Maine as a free state.

37. George Dangerfield, *The Awakening of American Nationalism, 1815–1828* (New York: Harper & Row, 1965), pp. 119–22; James Tallmadge to John W. Taylor, March 2, 1820, John W. Taylor Papers, NYHS; Irwin, *Daniel D. Tompkins*, p. 261. Taylor was speaker at this time, from Nov. 15, 1820, to March 3, 1821. See *DAB*, s.v. "John W. Taylor."

38. Renwick, *Life of Dewitt Clinton*, p. 237.

39. Alexander, *Political History*, 1: 275–7; Irwin, *Daniel D. Tompkins*, pp. 258–63. The legislature eventually declared the accounts settled as they stood, rejecting both the results of the state audit and Tompkins's own demands.

40. Hammond, *History of Political Parties*, 1: 506–7; Alexander, *Political History*, 1: 273.

41. July, *Gulian C. Verplanck*, p. 66; Fox, *Decline of Aristocracy*, p. 208; Hammond, *History of Political Parties*, 1: 529.

42. Fox, *Decline of Aristocracy*, p. 203; July, *Gulian C. Verplanck*, p. 68; [Verplanck], *The State Triumvirate*, pp. 103-4.

43. R. Messitle [?] to DWC, April 10, 1819, DWC Papers, CUL. The poet has taken care so that the first letters of the lines spell out the subject's name.

44. Hammond, *History of Political Parties*, 1: 532–3; Alexander, *Political History*, 1: 281; *Albany Argus*, April 14, 21, 25, 1820; "To Adopted Citizens," 1820 broadside, NYHS; Irwin, *Daniel D. Tompkins*, p. 259.

45. DWC to Henry Post, Nov. 11, Nov. 19, 1820, Henry Post Papers, NYSL; DWC to Robert Monell and Joseph S. Lyman, Nov. 14, 1820, DWC Papers, CUL.

46. Solomon Nadler, "The Green Bag," *New-York Historical Society Quarterly* 59 (July 1975): 203–25; DWC to Henry Post, Nov. 25, 1820, Henry Post Papers, NYSL.

47. Hammond, *History of Political Parties*, 1: 538–46, 558–71; Alexander, *Political History*, 1: 295–8; Fox, *Decline of Aristocracy*, pp. 234–5.

48. Fox, *Decline of Aristocracy*, 267–9. Although significant property restrictions on white male voters remained in effect until the 1821 constitution was ratified, these qualifications had come to be largely ignored; see Harvey Strum, "Property Qualifications and Voting Behavior in New York, 1807–1816," *Journal of the Early Republic* 1 (1981): 347–71.

49. Hammond, *History of Political Parties*, 2: 1–85; Charles Z. Lincoln, *The Constitutional History of New York*, 1: 743–50; Alexander, *Political History*, 1: 312–5; Fox, *Decline of Aristocracy*, 279–81.

ELEVEN • RESURRECTION

1. DWC to Stephen Ross, May 11, 1809, DWC Papers, CUL; DWC to Humphry Rowland, May 30, 1809, DWC Papers, CUL; "Proposition," Oct., 1821, DWC Misc. Mss., NYHS; DWC to Hammond, Jan. 12, 1822, DWC Papers, NYSL; [Scoville], *Old Merchants of New York*, 5: 73.

2. Shaw, *Erie Water West*, pp. 167–8.

3. DeWitt Clinton, "Annual Address Before the Alpha of the Phi Beta Kappa Society of Union College," July 23, 1823, in Campbell, *The Life and Writings of De Witt Clinton*, pp. 330–2 (hereafter cited as "Phi Beta Kappa Address").

4. Hammond, *History of Political Parties*, 2: 101; DWC to Henry Post, Jan. 10, 1822, Henry Post Papers, NYSL; John Bigelow, "De Witt Clinton as a Politician," *Harper's New Monthly Magazine* 50 (1875): 415; Alexander, *Political History*, 1: 316–20; Fox, *Decline of Aristocracy*, pp. 279–80; DWC to Cadwallader Colden, Jan. 2, 1823, DWC Papers, CUL.

5. Bigelow, "DeWitt Clinton as a Politician," pp. 567–8; DWC Diary, Nov. 18, 1823, NYHS.

6. DWC Diary, Oct. 14, 24, 29, 30, 31, Nov. 3, 1823, NYHS.

7. Ibid., Oct 29, Nov. 2, 9, 13, 1823.

8. DWC Diary, Oct. 30, Nov. 6, 1823, NYHS; Bigelow, "DeWitt Clinton as a Politician," pp. 567–8; DWC to Henry Post, March 4, 1824, Henry Post Papers, NYSL; Bobbé, *De Witt Clinton*, p. 257.

9. Raymond Walters, "William Harris Crawford," in John A. Garraty, ed., *Encyclopedia of American Biography* (New York: Harper & Row, 1974), pp. 238–9; Dangerfield, *The Awakening of American Nationalism*, pp. 30–1, 213–4; James F. Hopkins, "Election of 1824," in Schlesinger, *American Presidential Elections*, 1: 351–2, 370, 367.

10. Dangerfield, *Awakening of American Nationalism*, p. 218; Peterson, *Great Triumvirate*, p. 116.

11. Peterson, *Great Triumvirate*, p. 122.

12. Peterson, *Great Triumvirate*, pp. 122–3; Dangerfield, *Awakening of American Nationalism*, pp. 219–26; Bobbé, *De Witt Clinton*, 230–1; Siry, "De Witt Clinton and the American Political Economy," pp. 262–3.

13. Hammond, *History of Political Parties*, 2: 127; Alfred Conkling to Jabez Hammond, March 13, 1825, Conkling Misc. Mss., NYHS.

14. Hopkins, "Election of 1824," p. 409; Craig Hanyan, "King George, Queen Caroline, and the Albany Regency: The Origins of a Political Term," *New York History* 76 (1995): 349–78. The People's party has received microscopic study in *De Witt Clinton and the Rise of the People's Men*, by Craig Hanyan with Mary L. Hanyan (Montreal & Kingston: McGill-Queen's University Press, 1996).

15. Alexander, *Political History*, 1: 324; Hammond, *History of Political Parties*, 2: 128–32; Fox, *Decline of Aristocracy*, pp. 286–8.

16. Alexander, *Political History*, 1: 325–7; Hanyan, *Clinton and the People's Men*, pp. 160–75. The unfortunate Yates had hoped to be Crawford's running mate. See Hammond, *History of Political Parties*, 2: 154.

17. Alexander, *Political History*, 1: 324, 327; Hammond, *History of Political Parties*, 2: 128–32, 159.

18. William L. Stone to David Hosack, March 25, 1829, printed in Hosack, *Memoir of De Witt Clinton*, pp. 481–7; Alexander, *Political History*, 1: 328; Hanyan, *Clinton and the People's Men*, pp. 184–6; Glyndon G. Van Deusen, *Thurlow Weed: Wizard of the Lobby* (Boston: Little, Brown, and Company, 1947), p. 27.

19. Fox, *Decline of Aristocracy*, p. 292; John W. Francis, *Old New York; or, Reminiscences of the Past Sixty Years* (New York: Charles Roe, 1858), p. 34; Weed, *Autobiography*, p. 113, quoted in Alexander, *Political History*, 1: 329.

20. Hammond, *History of Political Parties*, 2: 165–6; Fox, *Decline of Aristocracy*, p. 293; John M. Taylor, *William Henry Seward: Lincoln's Right Hand* (New York: HarperCollins, 1991), p. 20.

21. For letters of support, see John Pintard to DWC, April 15, 1824, DWC Papers, CUL; Francis Adrian Vanderkemp to Clinton, April 19, 1824, DWC Papers, CUL; memorial of the citizens of Geneva, New York, May 1, 1824, DWC Papers, CUL; memorial of the citizens of Erie County, DWC Papers, CUL, May 10, 1824; Van Buren, *Autobiography*, p. 144.

22. Alexander, *Political History*, 1: 330–1; Hammond, *History of Political Parties*, 2: 166–70.

23. Alexander, *Political History*, 1: 331–2; Hammond, *History of Political Parties*, 2: 173–4.

24. Samuel Young to DeWitt Clinton, Oct. 12, 1819, DWC Papers, CUL; James Geddes to Stephen Van Rensselaer, Nov. 8, 1819, DWC Papers, CUL; Young to Clinton, Dec. 20, 1819, DWC Papers, CUL.

25. *Albany Argus*, Oct. 29, 1824; "Caucus Calumny Refuted," 1824 broadside, NYHS; "Thomas Jefferson's Opinion of De Witt Clinton," 1824 broadside, NYHS; Fox, *Decline of Aristocracy*, p. 296; Hammond, *History of Political Parties*, 2: 174–5.

26. Fox, *Decline of Aristocracy*, pp. 299–300; Van Buren, *Autobiography*, p. 145; Hammond, *History of Political Parties*, 2: 176–7; Alexander, *Political History*, 1: 338–9; Hopkins, "Election of 1824," pp. 372–3.

27. Stephen Van Rensselaer to DWC, Dec. 7, 1824; DWC to Stephen Van Rensselaer, Dec. 11, 1824; Stephen Van Rensselaer to DWC, Dec. 18, 1824; DWC to William P. Van Rensselaer, Jan. 1, 1825; Stephen Van Rensselaer to DWC, Jan. 10, 1825; all in DWC Papers, CUL.

28. Van Buren, *Autobiography*, p. 152. It is possible that Van Rensselaer, guided by his Maker, may have intended to vote for Adams all along. In 1823, John W. Taylor had written to Adams and let him know that "The Postmaster in Albany [Solomon Van Rensselaer] informs me that his kinsman Gen. Van Rensselaer may be calculated upon as a firm friend although he does not choose at this time publicly to express his opinion." John W. Taylor to John Quincy Adams, Aug. 2, 1823, John W. Taylor Papers, NYHS.

29. Hammond, *History of Political Parties*, 2: 188–90, 200; DWC to John Quincy Adams, Feb. 25, 1825, DWC Papers, CUL.

30. Hammond, *History of Political Parties*, 2: 183.

31. Shaw, *Erie Water West*, pp. 184–5; DWC to James Renwick, Oct. 1, 1825; James Renwick to DWC, Oct. 10, 182[5], DWC Papers, CUL.

32. Shaw, *Erie Water West*, pp. 185–7.

33. Cadwallader D. Colden, *Memoir, Prepared at the Request of a Committee of the Common Council of the City*

of New York, and Presented to the Mayor of the City at the Celebration of the Completion of the New York Canals (New York: W. A. Davis, 1825), pp. 177–9.

34. Ibid., pp. 196, 198, 271, 273.

35. Ibid., pp. 256–9.

TWELVE • THE CANAL AND ITS CONSEQUENCES

1. The transcontinental railroads were built with significant governmental assistance, but were not public projects in the same sense, or to the same degree, as the Erie Canal, which was owned and operated by the state.

2. Shaw, *Erie Water West*, pp. 17, 407, 127; Carol Sheriff, *The Artificial River: The Erie Canal and the Paradox of Progress, 1817–1862* (New York: Hill & Wang, 1996), p. 36. Sheriff's book offers a subtle and careful analysis of the many ways the Erie Canal shaped American attitudes in the nineteenth century.

3. Shaw, *Erie Water West*, pp. 90–3.

4. The most useful collection of documents exploring the issue of responsibility for the canal is found in David Hosack's *Memoir of DeWitt Clinton*, published in 1829. The principal modern narrative treatment of the canal's origins, Ronald Shaw's *Erie Water West*, concurs with Hosack (and most other authorities) in giving Clinton the largest single share of the credit.

5. Sellers, *The Market Revolution*, pp. 43–4; Miller, *The Enterprise of a Free People*, pp. 84–5; Julius Rubin, "An Innovating Public Improvement: The Erie Canal," in Carter Goodrich, ed., *Canals and American Economic Development* (1961; reprint ed., Port Washington, N.Y.: Kennikat Press, 1972) p. 16.

6. Thomas Jefferson, *Public and Private Papers* (New York: Vintage Books, 1990), p. 193; Hosack, *Memoir of De Witt Clinton*, pp. 306–7, 344–5; Sellers, *Market Revolution*, p. 79.

7. Rubin, "Erie Canal," p. 63.

8. Ellis, *Landlords and Farmers in the Hudson-Mohawk Region, 1790–1850*, p. 163.

9. Shaw, *Erie Water West*, p. 263; Richard C. Wade, *The Urban Frontier: Pioneer Life in Early Pittsburgh, Cincinnati, Lexington, Louisville, and St. Louis* (Chicago: University of Chicago Press, 1959), p. 1.

10. DWC, "Canal Diary," in Campbell, *Life and Writings of De Witt Clinton*, p. 137; A. Levasseur, *Lafayette in America*, 2 vols. (New York: White, Gallaher & White, et al., 1829), 2: 208; Shaw, *Erie Water West*, p. 264.

11. Harvey H. Segal, "Canals and Economic Development," in Goodrich, *Canals and American Economic Development*, p. 222; Ellis, *Landlords and Farmers*, p. 159.

12. Segal, "Canals and Economic Development," p. 223; Douglass C. North, *The Economic Growth of the United States, 1790–1860* (1961; Norton Library Edition, New York: W. W. Norton, 1966), p. 157.

13. North, *The Economic Growth of the United States*, pp. 104–5; Ellis et. al., *A Short History of New York*, p. 247; Segal, "Canals and Economic Development," p. 231.

14. Albion, *Rise of New York Port*, pp. 106, 119.

15. George Rogers Taylor, *The Transportation Revolution, 1815–1860* (1951; reprint ed., Armonk, N.Y.: M. E. Sharpe, 1977), p. 169; Alfred D. Chandler, *The Visible Hand: The Managerial Revolution in American Business* (Cambridge, Mass.: Harvard University Press, 1977), p. 24.

16. Kenneth L. Sokoloff, "Inventive Activity in Early Industrial America: Evidence from Patent Records, 1790–1846," *Journal of Economic History* 48 (1988): 817, 833–6.

17. Segal, "Canals and Economic Development," p. 224; Shaw, *Erie Water West*, p. 271.

18. *New York City Guide*, American Guide Series (New York: Random House, 1939), p. 68.

19. Miller, *Enterprise of a Free People*, pp. 115–53, 189–91, 161–3, 262–3.

20. Miller, *Enterprise of a Free People*, pp. 86, 88–9, 99–102, 106; Hurst, *Law and the Conditions of Freedom*, p. 61; DWC to Matthew Carey, Oct. 7, Oct. 23, 1824, DWC Papers, CUL; Harry N. Scheiber, *Ohio Canal Era: A Case Study of Government and the Economy, 1820–1861* (1968; second printing, with a new preface by the author, Athens, Ohio: Ohio University Press, 1987), p. 361.

21. Christopher Ward, *The War of the Revolution*, 2: 639; Clinton, "Canal Diary," in Campbell, *Life and Writings of De Witt Clinton*, pp. 186–7.

22. Dixon Ryan Fox, *Yankees and Yorkers* (1940; reprint ed., Port Washington, N.Y.: Ira J. Friedman, 1963), pp. 190, 193–4, 198; Whitney R. Cross, *The Burned-Over District: The Social and Religious History of Enthusiastic Religion in Western New York, 1800–1850* (Ithaca, N.Y.: Cornell University Press, 1950), pp. 4, 6–7.

23. Herman Melville, *Moby-Dick*; in *Novels* (New York: Library of America, 1983) pp. 1059–60.

24. Paul E. Johnson, *A Shopkeeper's Millennium: Society and Revivals in Rochester, New York, 1815–1837* (New York: Hill & Wang, 1978), p. 84; Mary P. Ryan, *Cradle of the Middle Class: The Family in Oneida County, New York, 1790–1865* (Cambridge and New York: Cambridge University Press, 1981), p. 91.

25. Cross, *The Burned-Over District*, p. 55.

26. Ibid, pp. 141–9.

27. Ibid., pp. 151–3; Ryan, *Cradle of the Middle Class*, pp. 92, 84–5.

28. Cross, *Burned-Over District*, pp. 114–15; Van Deusen, *Thurlow Weed*, pp. 38–40; Johnson, *Shopkeeper's Millennium*, pp. 66–7; Paul Goodman, *Towards a Christian Republic: Antimasonry and the Great Transition in New England, 1826–1836* (New York: Oxford University Press, 1988), pp. 3–4.

29. Lee Benson, *The Concept of Jacksonian Democracy: New York as a Test Case* (Princeton, N.J.: Princeton University Press, 1961), pp. 17–20; Johnson, *Shopkeeper's Millennium*, p. 66.

30. Van Deusen, *Thurlow Weed*, pp. 44–6; Benson, *The Concept of Jacksonian Democracy*, p. 26; Cross, *Burned-over District*, pp. 115–6.

31. W. Steele to DeWitt Clinton, June 10, 1818, DWC Papers, CUL.

32. Scheiber, *Ohio Canal Era,* pp. 3–21.

33. Ellis, *Landlords and Farmers*, pp. 166–7.

34. Julius Rubin, "An Imitative Public Improvement: The Pennsylvania Mainline," in Carter Goodrich, ed., *Canals and American Economic Development*, pp. 67–106.

35. Rubin, "The Pennsylvania Mainline," pp. 106–14; Hammond, *Banks and Politics*, p. 512; Peter Temin, *The Jacksonian Economy* (New York: W. W. Norton, 1969), p. 154.

36. Temin, *Jacksonian Economy*, p. 154; Bray Hammond, *Banks and Politics*, p. 526; William Wordsworth, "To the Pennsylvanians," from "Sonnets Dedicated to Liberty and Order," in *Wordsworth: Poetical Works* (Oxford: Oxford University Press, 1936), p. 403.

37. Harry N. Scheiber, "The Transportation Revolution and American Law: Constitutionalism and Public Policy," in *Transportation and the Early Nation: Papers Presented at an Indiana American Revolution Bicentennial Symposium* (Indianapolis: Indiana Historical Society, 1982), p. 20.

38. Oscar Handlin and Mary Flug Handlin, *Commonwealth: A Study of the Role of Government in the American Economy,* (1947; revised ed., Cambridge, Mass.: Harvard University Press, 1969); Milton S. Heath, *The Role of the State in Economic Development in Georgia to 1860* (Cambridge, Mass.: Harvard University Press, 1954); Scheiber, *Ohio Canal Era;* Louis Hartz, *Economic Policy and Democratic Thought: Pennsylvania, 1776–1860* (Cambridge, Mass.: Harvard University Press, 1948). I am indebted to Elizabeth Blackmar for making me aware of a number of issues in this area early in my research.

39. L. Ray Gunn, *The Decline of Authority: Public Policy and Political Development in New York, 1800–1860* (Ithaca, N.Y.: Cornell University Press, 1988), pp. ix–x, 16, 22, 133–4; Scheiber, "The Transportation Revolution and American Law: Constitutionalism and Public Policy," in *Transportation and the Early Nation: Papers Presented at an Indiana American Revolution Bicentennial Symposium* (Indianapolis: Indiana Historical Society, 1982), p. 20.

THIRTEEN • END OF A CAREER

1. Lincoln, *Constitutional History of the State of New York*, 1: 204–5, 222–3.

2. Hammond, *History of Political Parties*, 2: 183.

3. Van Buren, *Autobiography*, p. 149.

4. Hammond, *History of Political Parties*, 2: 184.

5. Hammond, *History of Political Parties*, 2: 185–6, 192–5.

6. DWC to Lafayette, Feb. 16, June 13 and 17, 1825; Remsen to DWC, Feb. 10, 1825; DWC to Remsen,

March 10, 1825; DWC to Alfred [Kelley?][Ohio], Feb. 7, 1825; DWC to John Law [Illinois], Jan. 31, 1825; DWC to John Sergeant, Aug. 17, 1825 [Pennsylvania Canal Board]; John Stevens to DWC, Jan. 19, 1825; DWC to Stevens, Jan. 24, 1825; DWC to Astor, Jan. 8, 1825; all in DWC Papers, CUL.

7. Hammond *History of Political Parties,* 2: 203; Bobbé, *De Witt Clinton,* p. 273; Fox, *Decline of Aristocracy,* p. 314; Siry, "De Witt Clinton and the American Political Economy," p. 282; DWC to David Thomas, June 17, 1825, DWC Papers, CUL.

8. DWC, Diary of 1825 visit to Ohio, July 11, 26, 15, 24, n.d., 8, August 1, July 13, 1825, DWC Misc. Mss., NYHS.

9. Van Buren, *Autobiography,* pp. 157—9.

10. Robert Remini, *Martin Van Buren and the Making of the Democratic Party* (New York: Columbia University Press, 1959), pp. 96—7.

11. Alexander, *Political History,* 1: 347.

12. Fitzpatrick, *Educational Views and Influence of De Witt Clinton,* pp. 62—5; Hammond, *History of Political Parties,* 2: 217.

13. Hammond, *History of Political Parties,* 2: 218—25.

14. Van Buren, *Autobiography,* pp. 145, 159, 145; Bobbé, *De Witt Clinton,* p. 283.

15. Remini, *Martin Van Buren and the Democratic Party,* pp. 96—104, quote on p. 102; Fox, *Decline of Aristocracy,* p. 285.

16. Van Buren, *Autobiography,* p. 161; Hammond, *History of Political Parties,* 2: 232; John Niven, *Martin Van Buren: The Romantic Age of American Politics* (New York: Oxford University Press, 1983), pp. 169—70; Alexander, *Political History,* 1: 350—2. Robert Remini's somewhat picturesque theory is that the ever-subtle Van Buren had hatched a brilliant plot to destroy Clinton. Since Rochester backed Adams, he would attract votes from those Adams men who might normally support Clinton but wanted to make sure that the state had a governor friendly to the president in place for the 1828 elections. "In turn," according to Remini, "the entire body of Adams supporters would desert Clinton after the election, [and] the Governor's party would collapse," thus leaving the state in the hands of the Democrats. Remini's support for this theory rests upon Van Buren's assertion that at this point there was "a more cordial union between the friends of Clinton, Adams and Clay than existed in 1824," and that by nominating Rochester the Regency could "drive a wedge into that union" and thus aid Jackson. But the Little Magician's deftness at covering himself at both ends, and his talent for bemusing contemporaries as well as historians, has already been noted. Clinton was clearly going to support Jackson, and those of his supporters who were partial to Adams had shown no inclination to subordinate their presidential preferences to Clinton's desires. In fact, there really was no Clinton party at this point, and certainly the 1825 legislative session had shown that he could expect little support from the People's party. The elections that year had demonstrated that the People's party was already dissolving, incapable of organized political action across the state. Only Clinton's personal popularity sustained him in power, with the assistance of political allies sufficiently loyal or stubborn to remain in his camp. See Remini, *Martin Van Buren and the Democratic Party,* pp. 120—1; Van Buren, *Autobiography,* p. 162—3.

17. Hammond, *History of Political Parties,* 2: 235; Fox, *Decline of Aristocracy,* p. 313; Alexander, *Political History,* 1: 353; Van Buren, *Autobiography,* pp. 162—3.

18. DWC to Theodore F. Talbert et al., Oct. 6, 1826, and DWC to the "Committee in Behalf of the Citizens of Genesee County," Oct. 26, 1826, DWC Papers, CUL.

19. DWC to the Earl of Dalwinnie, Jan. 6, 1827, DWC Papers, CUL; DWC to Theodore F. Talbot, Jan. 8, 1827, DWC Papers, CUL.

20. Hosack to DWC, June 22, June 29, 1827, DWC Papers, CUL.

21. Bobbé, *De Witt Clinton,* p. 292.

22. DWC Diary, Feb. 11, 1828, NYHS; Bobbé, *De Witt Clinton,* p. 292. The cause of Clinton's death was probably a heart attack.

23. Van Buren, *Autobiography,* p. 157.

24. John Hone to Charles A. Clinton, Feb. 15, 1828, Clinton Family Papers, NYHS. Hosack's frankness was not received gratefully by Charles Clinton, who had to be counseled by Hone to control his anger since Hosack was a powerful man who could harm Charles's career. John Hone to Charles A. Clinton, March 7, 1828, Clinton Family Papers, NYHS.

25. Van Buren, *Autobiography*, p. 167; Hosack, *Memoir of De Witt Clinton, passim;* Cuyler Staats, *Tribute to the Memory of De Witt Clinton* (Albany: Webster and Wood, 1828), *passim.*

26. *Francis Granger to Jabez Hammond, Oct. 21, 1830, Francis Granger Misc. Mss., NYHS.*

BIBLIOGRAPHY

PRIMARY SOURCES

Manuscripts

Albany, New York. New York State Library. DeWitt Clinton Papers.
Albany, New York. New York State Library. Henry Post Papers.
New York. Columbia University Libraries, Rare Book and Manuscript Library. DeWitt Clinton Papers.
New York. New-York Historical Society. David Bruce Miscellaneous Manuscripts.
New York. New-York Historical Society. DeWitt Clinton MS Diary.
New York. New-York Historical Society. DeWitt Clinton Miscellaneous Manuscripts.
New York. New-York Historical Society. Clinton Family Miscellaneous Manuscripts.
New York. New-York Historical Society. George Clinton Miscellaneous Manuscripts.
New York. New-York Historical Society. Alfred Conkling Miscellaneous Manuscripts.
New York. New-York Historical Society. Thomas Eddy Miscellaneous Manuscripts.
New York. New-York Historical Society. Francis Granger Miscellaneous Manuscripts.
New York. New-York Historical Society. Rufus King Papers.
New York. New York Historical Society. Records of the Literary and Philosophical Society of New-York.
New York. New-York Historical Society. Robert R. Livingston Papers.
New York. New-York Historical Society. John Pintard Papers.
New York. New-York Historical Society. John Smith of Mastic, L.I., Miscellaneous Manuscripts.
New York. New-York Historical Society. Ambrose Spencer Miscellaneous Manuscripts.
New York. New-York Historical Society. John W. Taylor Papers.
New York. New-York Historical Society. Thomas Tillotson Miscellaneous Manuscripts.
New York. New-York Historical Society. Francis Adrian Van der Kemp Miscellaneous Manuscripts.
New York. New-York Historical Society. Hunloke Woodruff Miscellaneous Manuscripts.
New York. Manuscripts and Archives Division. New York Public Library. Astor, Lenox and Tilden Foundations. DeWitt Clinton Papers.

New York. Manuscripts and Archives Division. New York Public Library. Astor, Lenox and Tilden
    Foundations. George Clinton Papers.
New York. Manuscripts and Archives Division. New York Public Library. Astor, Lenox and Tilden
    Foundations. John Hartshorne Eddy, Diary.

Published Material

Adams, John Quincy. *The Diary of John Quincy Adams.* Edited by Allan Nevins. New York: Charles Scrib-
    ner's Sons, 1951.
Bailyn, Bernard, ed. *The Debate on the Constitution.* 2 vols. New York: Library of America, 1993.
Burr, Aaron. *Political Correspondence and Public Papers of Aaron Burr.* Edited by Mary Jo Kline et al. 2 vols.
    Princeton, N.J.: Princeton University Press, 1983.
Campbell, William W., comp. *The Life and Writings of De Witt Clinton.* New York: Baker and Scribner,
    1849.
Francis, John W. *Old New York; or, Reminiscences of the Past Sixty Years.* New York: Charles Roe, 1858.
Hamilton, Alexander. *The Papers of Alexander Hamilton.* Edited by Harold C. Syrett et al. 27 vols. New
    York: Macmillan, 1961–81.
Hone, Philip. *The Diary of Philip Hone, 1828–1851.* Edited by Allan Nevins. 2 vols. New York: Dodd, Mead,
    1927.
Jefferson, Thomas. *The Writings of Thomas Jefferson.* Edited by Paul L. Ford. 10 vols. New York: Putnam,
    1892–99.
Journal of the Assembly of the State of New York.
Journal of the Senate of the State of New York.
King, Rufus. *The Life and Correspondence of Rufus King.* Edited by Charles R. King. 6 vols. New York:
    G. P. Putnam's Sons, 1898.
Levasseur, A. *Lafayette in America, in 1824 and 1825; or, Journal of Travels, in the United States.* 2 vols. New York:
    White Gallaher & White et al., 1829.
Lincoln, Charles Z. *The Constitutional History of New York.* 5 vols. Rochester, N.Y.: Lawyers Cooperative
    Publishing Company, 1906.
New York City Directories, 1786–1831.
New York Corresponding Association, for the Promotion of Internal Improvements. *Public Documents,
    Relating to the New-York Canals, Which are to Connect the Western and Northern Lakes, with the Atlantic Ocean.*
    New York: William A Mercein, 1821.
Peterson, A. Everett, ed. *Minutes of the Common Council of the City of New York, 1784–1831.* 19 vols. New York:
    City of New York, 1917.
Pintard, John. *Letters from John Pintard to His Daughter.* Edited by Dorothy C. Barck. 4 vols. New York:
    J. J. Little and Ives, 1941.
Still, Bayrd, ed. *Mirror for Gotham: New York as Seen by Contemporaries from Dutch Days to the Present.* New York:
    New York University Press, 1956.
Van Buren, Martin. *Autobiography.* 1920. Reprint ed. New York: Chelsea House, 1983.
————. *Inquiry into the Origin and Course of Political Parties in the United States.* 1867. Reprint. Reprints of Eco-
    nomic Classics. New York: Augustus M. Kelley, 1967.

Pamphlets

Cheetham, James. *A Narrative of the Suppression by Col. Burr, of the History of the Administration of John Adams.*
    New York: Denniston & Cheetham, 1802.
————. *A View of the Political Conduct of Aaron Burr.* New York: Denniston & Cheetham, 1802.
————. *An Antidote to John Wood's Poison.* New York: Southwick & Crooker, 1802.

————. *A Letter to a Friend on the Conduct of the Adherents to Mr. Burr.* New York: James Cheetham, 1803.

Clinton, DeWitt. *An Address Delivered Before the Holland Lodge, December 24, 1793.* New York: Francis Childs and John Swaine, 1794.

————. *An Oration on Benevolence, Delivered Before the Society of Black Friars.* New York: Friar M'Lean, 1795.

————. ["Grotius"]. *A Vindication of Thomas Jefferson.* New York: David Denniston, 1800.

————. *An Introductory Discourse Delivered Before the Literary and Philosophical Society of New-York.* 1815. Reprint. History of Geology Collection. New York: Arno Press, 1978.

————. *A Discourse Delivered Before the American Academy of the Arts by the Honourable De Witt Clinton, LL.D. (President) 23rd October, 1816.* New York: T. & W. Mercein, 1816.

————. [Atticus]. *Remarks on the Proposed Canal from Lake Erie to the Hudson River.* New York: Samuel Wood, 1816.

————. "Circular Letter of the Literary and Philosophical Society of New-York, on the Subject of a Statistical Account of the State of New-York." In *Transactions of the Literary and Philosophical Society* 1 (1818): 559–65.

————. *A Memoir on the Antiquities of the Western Parts of the State of New-York Read before the Literary and Philosophical Society.* Albany, New York, 1818.

————. *On Certain Phenomena of the Great Lakes of America.* New York, 1818.

————. ["Hibernicus"]. *Letters on the Natural History and Internal Resources of the State of New-York.* New York: E. Bliss & E. White, 1822.

Conkling, Alfred. *A Discourse Commemorative of the Talents, Virtues, and Services of the late De Witt Clinton.* Albany, N.Y.: Websters and Skinners, 1828.

Davis, Matthew L. ["Marcus"]. *Letters of Marcus and Philo-Cato addressed to De Witt Clinton, Esq. Mayor of the City of New-York.* "A new edition, containing one letter of Marcus, and several numbers of Philo-Cato, never published before." 1810.

Genet, Edmond Charles ["A Citizen of New York"]. *Communications on the Next Election for President of the United States.* New York: Printed for the author, 1808.

Genuine Republicans. New York, 1804. Early American Imprints, second series, no. 2021.

Lincoln, Charles Z., ed. *Messages from the Governors.* 11 vols. Albany, N.Y.: J. B. Lyon, 1909.

Pintard, John. *Letters from John Pintard to His Daughter Eliza Pintard Davidson.* 4 vols. New York: New-York Historical Society, 1940–1.

Van Ness, William Peter ["Aristides"]. *An Examination of the Various Charges Exhibited Against Aaron Burr, Esq. Vice-President of the United States.* New York: Ward & Gould, 1803.

Verplanck, Gulian C. *An Anniversary Discourse Delivered Before the New-York Historical Society, December 7, 1818.* New York: E. Bliss & E. White, 1821.

————. *The State Triumvirate: A Political Tale: and The Epistles of Brevet Major Pindar Puff.* New York: J. Seymour, 1819.

Wood, John. *A Full Exposition of the Clintonian Faction, and the Society of the Columbian Illuminati.* Newark, N.J.: Printed for the author, 1802.

Newspapers

Albany Argus
Albany Register
New York American Citizen
New York Columbian
New York Evening Post
New-York Journal, and Weekly Register
New York Morning Chronicle
New York Morning Courier

SECONDARY SOURCES

Books

Adams, Henry. *History of the United States of America during the Administrations of Thomas Jefferson and James Madison.* 9 vols., 1889–91. Reprint (2 vols.). New York: Library of America, 1986.

Albion, Robert Greenhalgh. *The Rise of New York Port, 1815–1860.* New York: Charles Scribner's Sons, 1939.

Alexander, DeAlva Stanwood. *A Political History of the State of New York.* 3 vols. New York: Henry Holt, 1906.

Alexander, Holmes. *The American Talleyrand: The Career and Contemporaries of Martin Van Buren, Eighth President.* 1935. Reprint. New York: Russell & Russell, 1968.

Ames, Herman V. *The Proposed Amendments to the Constitution of the United States During the First Century of Its History.* Published in *Annual Report of the American Historical Association for the Year 1896,* vol. 2. Washington: Government Printing Office, 1897.

Ammon, Harry. *James Monroe: The Quest for National Identity.* Charlottesville, Va.: University Press of Virginia, 1990.

Appleby, Joyce. *Capitalism and a New Social Order: The Republican Vision of the 1790s.* New York: New York University Press, 1984.

Bailyn, Bernard. *The Ideological Origins of the American Revolution.* Cambridge, Mass.: Harvard University Press, 1967.

Banner, James M., Jr. *To the Hartford Convention: The Federalists and the Origins of Party Politics in Massachusetts, 1789–1815.* New York: Alfred A. Knopf, 1970.

Banning, Lance. *The Jeffersonian Persuasion: Evolution of a Party Ideology.* Ithaca, N.Y.: Cornell University Press, 1978.

Becker, Carl Lotus. *History of Political Parties in the Province of New York, 1760–1776.* 1909. Reprint. Madison, Wis.: University of Wisconsin Press, 1966.

Bemis, Samuel Flagg. *John Quincy Adams and the Foundations of American Foreign Policy.* New York: Alfred A. Knopf, 1956.

———. *Jay's Treaty: A Study in Commerce and Diplomacy.* 2nd. rev. ed. New Haven, Conn.: Yale University Press, 1962.

Bender, Thomas. *New York Intellect: A History of Intellectual Life in New York City, From 1750 to the Beginnings of Our Own Time.* New York: Alfred A. Knopf, 1987.

Benson, Lee. *The Concept of Jacksonian Democracy: New York as a Test Case.* Princeton, N.J.: Princeton University Press, 1961.

Blackmar, Elizabeth. *Manhattan for Rent, 1785–1850.* Ithaca, N.Y.: Cornell University Press, 1989.

Bobbé, Dorothie. *De Witt Clinton.* New York: Minton, Balch, 1933.

Bonomi, Patricia. *A Factious People: Politics and Society in Colonial New York.* New York: Columbia University Press, 1971.

Brandt, Clare. *An American Aristocracy: The Livingstons.* Garden City, N.Y.: Doubleday, 1986.

Brant, Irving. *James Madison.* 6 vols. Indianapolis and New York: Bobbs-Merrill, 1941–61.

———. *The Fourth President: A Life of James Madison.* Indianapolis and New York: Bobbs-Merrill, 1970.

Bridges, Amy. *A City in the Republic: Antebellum New York and the Origins of Machine Politics.* Paperback edition, with a new preface. Ithaca, N.Y.: Cornell University Press, 1987.

Buel, Richard, Jr. *Securing the Revolution: Ideology in American Politics, 1789–1815.* Ithaca, N.Y.: Cornell University Press, 1972.

Burnham, Walter Dean. *Critical Elections and the Mainsprings of American Politics.* New York: W. W. Norton, 1970.

Bushman, Richard. *Joseph Smith and the Beginnings of Mormonism.* Urbana and Chicago: University of Illinois Press, 1984.

———. *The Refinement of America: Persons, Houses, Cities.* New York: Alfred A. Knopf, 1992.

Chandler, Alfred D. *The Visible Hand: The Managerial Revolution in American Business.* Cambridge, Mass.: Harvard University Press, 1977.

Cole, Donald B. *Martin Van Buren and the American Political System.* Princeton, N.J.: Princeton University Press, 1984.

Coles, Harry L. *The War of 1812.* The Chicago History of American Civilization. Chicago: University of Chicago Press, 1965.

Cross, Whitney R. *The Burned-Over District: The Social and Religious History of Enthusiastic Religion in Western New York, 1800–1850.* Ithaca, N.Y.: Cornell University Press, 1950.

Dangerfield, George. *The Era of Good Feelings.* New York: Harcourt, Brace & World, 1952.

———. *The Awakening of American Nationalism, 1815–1828.* New York: Harper & Row, 1965.

Davis, Matthew L. *Memoirs of Aaron Burr.* 2 vols. New York: Harper & Brothers, 1837.

De Pauw, Linda Grant. *The Eleventh Pillar: New York State and the Federal Constitution.* Ithaca, N.Y.: Cornell University Press, 1966.

Elkins, Stanley, and Eric McKitrick. *The Age of Federalism.* New York: Oxford University Press, 1993.

Ellis, David Maldwyn. *Landlords and Farmers of the Hudson-Mohawk Region, 1780–1850.* Ithaca, N.Y.: Cornell University Press, 1946.

Ellis, Joseph J. *After the Revolution: Profiles of Early American Culture.* New York: W. W. Norton, 1979.

Fischer, David Hackett. *The Revolution of American Conservatism: The Federalist Party in the Era of Jeffersonian Democracy.* New York: Harper & Row, 1965.

Fitzpatrick, Edward A. *The Educational Views and Influence of De Witt Clinton.* New York: Teachers College, Columbia University, 1911.

Foner, Eric. *Tom Paine and Revolutionary America.* New York: Oxford University Press, 1976.

Formisano, Ronald P. *The Transformation of Political Culture: Massachusetts Parties, 1790s–1840s.* New York: Oxford University Press, 1983.

Fox, Dixon Ryan. *The Decline of Aristocracy in the Politics of New York, 1801–1840.* 1919. Revised edition, edited by Robert V. Remini. New York: Harper & Row, 1965.

———. *Yankees and Yorkers.* Empire State Historical Publication 25. 1940. Reprint. Port Washington, N.Y.: Ira J. Friedman, 1963.

Garraty, John A. *Silas Wright.* Studies in History, Economics, and Public Law, edited by the Faculty of Political Science of Columbia University, No. 552. New York: Columbia University Press, 1949.

Gilfoyle, Timothy J. *City of Eros: New York City, Prostitution, and the Commercialization of Sex, 1790–1920.* New York: W. W. Norton, 1992.

Gilje, Paul. *The Road to Mobocracy: Popular Disorder in New York City, 1763–1834.* Chapel Hill, N.C.: University of North Carolina Press, 1987.

Goodman, Paul. *Towards a Christian Republic: Antimasonry and the Great Transition in New England, 1826–1836.* New York: Oxford University Press, 1988.

Goodrich, Carter, ed. *Government Promotion of American Canals and Railroads, 1800–1890.* New York: Columbia University Press, 1960.

Gunn, L. Ray. *The Decline of Authority: Public Economic Policy and Political Development in New York, 1800–1860.* Ithaca, N.Y.: Cornell University Press, 1988.

Hammond, Bray. *Banks and Politics in America from the Revolution to the Civil War.* Princeton, N.J.: Princeton University Press, 1957.

Hammond, Jabez D. *The History of Political Parties in the State of New-York, from the Ratification of the Federal Constitution to December, 1840.* 2 vols. Albany: C. Van Benthuysen, 1842.

Handlin, Oscar, and Mary Flug Handlin. *Commonwealth: A Study of the Role of Government in the American Economy, Massachusetts, 1774–1861.* Revised ed. Cambridge, Mass.: The Belknap Press of Harvard University Press, 1969.

Hanyan, Craig, with Mary L. Hanyan. *DeWitt Clinton and the Rise of the People's Men.* Montreal & Kingston: McGill-Queen's University Press, 1996.

Hartog, Hendrik. *Public Property and Private Power: The Corporation of the City of New York in American Law, 1730–1870.* Ithaca, N.Y.: Cornell University Press, 1983.

Hartz, Louis. *Economic Policy and Democratic Thought: Pennsylvania, 1776–1860.* Cambridge, Mass.: Harvard University Press, 1948.

Heath, Milton S. *The Role of the State in Economic Development in Georgia to 1860.* Cambridge, Mass.: Harvard University Press, 1954.

Higginbotham, Sanford W. *The Keystone in the Democratic Arch: Pennsylvania Politics, 1800–1816.* Harrisburg, Penn.: Pennsylvania Historical and Museum Commission, 1952.

Hodges, Graham. *The New York City Cartmen, 1667–1850.* The American Social Experience Series. New York: New York University Press, 1986.

Hofstadter, Richard. *The Idea of a Party System: The Rise of Legitimate Opposition in the United States, 1780–1840.* Berkeley: University of California Press, 1969.

Horton, John Theodore. *James Kent: A Study in Conservatism, 1763–1847.* 1939. Reprint. New York: Da Capo Press, 1969.

Horwitz, Morton. *The Transformation of American Law, 1780–1860.* 1977. Reprint. New York: Oxford University Press, 1992.

Hosack, David. *Memoir of De Witt Clinton: with an Appendix, containing Numerous Documents, illustrative of the Principal Events of his Life.* New York: J. Seymour, 1829.

House, Lolabel. *A Study of the Twelfth Amendment to the Constitution of the United States.* Philadelphia, 1901.

Hurst, James Willard. *Law and the Conditions of Freedom in the Nineteenth-Century United States.* Madison: University of Wisconsin Press, 1956.

Irwin, Ray W. *Daniel D. Tompkins: Governor of New York and Vice President of the United States.* New York: The New-York Historical Society, 1968.

Jackson, Kenneth T. *Crabgrass Frontier: The Suburbanization of the United States.* New York: Oxford University Press, 1985.

Jaher, Frederic Cople. *The Urban Establishment: Upper Strata in Boston, New York, Charleston, Chicago, and Los Angeles.* Urbana: University of Illinois Press, 1982.

Johnson, Paul E. *A Shopkeeper's Millennium: Society and Revivals in Rochester, New York, 1815–1837.* New York: Hill and Wang, 1978.

Kaminski, John P. *George Clinton: Yeoman Politician of the New Republic.* Madison, Wis.: Madison House, 1993.

Kammen, Michael. *Colonial New York: A History.* New York: Charles Scribner's Sons, 1975.

Kass, Alvin. *Politics in New York State, 1800–1830.* Syracuse, N.Y.: Syracuse University Press, 1865.

Kenyon, Cecilia M., ed. *The Antifederalists.* 1966. Reprint. Boston: Northeastern University Press, 1985.

Kerber, Linda K. *Federalists in Dissent: Imagery and Ideology in Jeffersonian America.* 1970. Paperback edition, with a new preface. Ithaca, N.Y.: Cornell University Press, 1980.

Ketcham, Ralph. *James Madison: A Biography.* New York: Macmillan, 1971.

Knapp, Samuel L. *The Life of Thomas Eddy.* New York: Conner & Cooke, 1834.

Levine, Lawrence W. *Highbrow/Lowbrow: The Emergence of Cultural Hierarchy in America.* Cambridge, Mass.: Harvard University Press, 1988.

Lincoln, Charles Z. *The Constitutional History of New York.* 5 vols. Rochester, N.Y.: The Lawyers Cooperative Publishing Company, 1906.

Lipson, Dorothy Ann. *Freemasonry in Federalist Connecticut.* Princeton:, N.J.: Princeton University Press, 1977.

Lomask, Milton. *Aaron Burr.* 2 vols. New York: Farrar Straus Giroux, 1979–82.

McBain, Howard Lee. *DeWitt Clinton and the Origin of the Spoils System in New York.* Studies in History, Economics and Public Law edited by the Faculty of Political Science of Columbia University, vol. 28, no. 1. New York: Columbia University Press, 1907.

McCormick, Richard L. *The Party Period and Public Policy: American Politics from the Age of Jackson to the Progressive Era.* New York: Oxford University Press, 1986.

McCormick, Richard P. *The Presidential Game: The Origins of American Presidential Politics.* New York: Oxford University Press, 1982.

McCoy, Drew R. *The Last of the Fathers: James Madison and the Republican Legacy.* Cambridge and New York: Cambridge University Press, 1989.

Miller, John C. *The Federalist Era, 1789–1801.* New York: Harper & Row, 1960.

Miller, Nathan. *The Enterprise of a Free People: Aspects of Economic Development in New York State During the Canal Period, 1792–1838.* Ithaca, N.Y.: Cornell University Press, 1962.

Mohl, Raymond A. *Poverty in New York, 1783–1825.* The Urban Life in America Series. New York: Oxford University Press, 1971.

Morison, Samuel Eliot. *Harrison Gray Otis, 1765–1848: The Urbane Federalist.* Boston: Houghton Mifflin Company, 1969.

Mushkat, Jerome. *Tammany: The Evolution of a Political Machine, 1789–1865.* Syracuse, N.Y.: Syracuse University Press, 1971.

Myers, Gustavus. *The History of Tammany Hall.* 2nd ed. Reprint. New York: Dover, 1971.

Niven, John. *Martin Van Buren: The Romantic Age of American Politics.* New York: Oxford University Press, 1983.

Nye, Russel Blaine. *The Cultural Life of the New Nation, 1776–1830.* The New American Nation Series. New York: Harper & Row, 1960.

Parton, James. *The Life and Times of Aaron Burr.* 2 vols. Enlarged edition. Boston: James R. Osgood, 1876.

Perkins, Bradford. *The First Rapprochement: England and the United States, 1795–1805.* Berkeley: University of California Press, 1967.

————. *Prologue to War: England and the United States, 1805–1812.* Berkeley: University of California Press, 1961.

Peterson, Merrill D. *The Great Triumvirate: Webster, Clay, and Calhoun.* New York: Oxford University Press, 1987.

Philip, Cynthia Owen. *Robert Fulton: A Biography.* New York: Franklin Watts, 1985.

Pierson, George Wilson. *Tocqueville in America.* Garden City, N.Y.: Anchor Books, 1959.

Pomerantz, Sidney I. *New York: An American City, 1783–1803.* 2nd edition. Port Washington, N.Y.: Ira J. Friedman, 1965.

Porter, Kenneth Wiggins. *John Jacob Astor: Business Man.* 2 vols. 1931. Reprint ed. New York: Russell & Russell, 1966.

Pred, Allan R. *Urban Growth and the Circulation of Information: The United States System of Cities, 1790–1840.* Cambridge, Mass.: Harvard University Press, 1973.

Remini, Robert V. *Martin Van Buren and the Making of the Democratic Party.* New York: Columbia University Press, 1959.

Renwick, James. *Life of Dewitt Clinton.* New York: Harper & Bothers, 1840.

Robbins, Christine Chapman. *David Hosack: Citizen of New York.* Philadelphia: American Philosophical Society, 1964.

Rock, Howard P. *Artisans of the New Republic: The Tradesmen of New York City in the Age of Jefferson.* New York: New York University Press, 1979.

Ryan, Mary P. *Cradle of the Middle Class: The Family in Oneida County, New York, 1790–1865.* Interdisciplinary Perspectives on Modern History. New York: Cambridge University Press, 1981.

Sapio, Victor A. *Pennsylvania & the War of 1812.* Lexington: University Press of Kentucky, 1970.

Scheiber, Harry N. *Ohio Canal Era: A Case Study of Government and the Economy, 1820–1861.* 1968. Second printing, with a new preface by the author. Athens, Ohio: Ohio University Press, 1987.

Schlesinger, Arthur M., Jr., ed. *History of American Presidential Elections.* 4 vols. New York: Chelsea House, 1985.

Sellers, Charles. *The Market Revolution: Jacksonian America, 1815–1846.* New York: Oxford University Press, 1991.

Shaw, Ronald E. *Erie Water West: A History of the Erie Canal, 1792–1854.* 1966. Reprint. Lexington: University Press of Kentucky, 1990.

Sheriff, Carol. *The Artificial River: The Erie Canal and the Paradox of Progress, 1817–1862*. New York: Hill & Wang, 1996.

Smelser, Marshall. *The Democratic Republic, 1801–1815*. The New American Nation Series. New York: Harper & Row, 1968.

Spaulding, E. Wilder. *His Excellency George Clinton: Critic of the Constitution*. New York: Macmillan, 1938.

———. *New York in the Critical Period, 1783–1789*. Empire State Historical Publication XIX. 1932. Reprint. Port Washington, N.Y.: Ira J. Friedman, 1963.

Spivak, Burton. *Jefferson's English Crisis: Commerce, Embargo, and the Republican Revolution*. Charlottesville: University Press of Virginia, 1979.

Stagg, J. C. A. *Mr. Madison's War: Politics, Diplomacy, and Warfare in the Early American Republic, 1783–1830*. Princeton, N.J.: Princeton University Press, 1983.

Taylor, Alan. *William Cooper's Town: Power and Persuasion on the Frontier of the Early American Republic*. New York: Alfred A. Knopf, 1995.

Taylor, George Rogers. *The Transportation Revolution, 1815–1860*. The Economic History of the United States, vol. 4. 1951. Reprint. Armonk, N.Y.: M. E. Sharpe, 1977.

Taylor, John M. *William Henry Seward: Lincoln's Right Hand*. New York: HarperCollins, 1991.

Temin, Peter. *The Jacksonian Economy*. New York: W. W. Norton, 1969.

Van der Kemp, Francis Adrian. *An Autobiography, Together with Extracts from His Correspondence*. Edited, with an historical sketch, by Helen Lincklaen Fairchild. New York: G. P. Putnam's Sons, 1903.

Van Deusen, Glyndon G. *Thurlow Weed: Wizard of the Lobby*. Boston: Little, Brown, 1947.

Vaughn, William Preston. *The Antimasonic Party in the United States, 1826–1843*. Lexington: University Press of Kentucky, 1983.

Wallenstein, Peter. *From Slave South to New South: Public Policy in Nineteenth-Century Georgia*. Chapel Hill, N.C.: University of North Carolina Press, 1987.

Way, Peter. *Common Labour: Workers and the Digging of North American Canals, 1780–1860*. New York: Cambridge University Press, 1993.

Weise, Arthur James. *The Swartwout Chronicles, 1338–1899, and the Ketelhuyn Chronicles, 1451–1899*. New York: Trow Directory, 1899.

White, Leonard D. *The Federalists: A Study in Administrative History*. New York: Macmillan, 1948.

———. *The Jeffersonians: A Study in Administrative History, 1801–1829*. 1951. Reprint ed. New York: Free Press, 1965.

Wiebe, Robert H. *The Opening of American Society: From the Adoption of the Constitution to the Eve of Disunion*. New York: Alfred A. Knopf, 1984.

Wilentz, Sean. *Chants Democratic: New York City and the Rise of the American Working Class, 1788–1850*. New York: Oxford University Press, 1984.

Wood, Gordon S. *The Creation of the American Republic, 1776–1787*. New York: W. W. Norton, 1969.

———. *The Radicalism of the American Revolution*. New York: Alfred A. Knopf, 1992.

Wyckoff, William. *The Developer's Frontier: The Making of the Western New York Landscape*. New Haven, Conn.: Yale University Press, 1988.

Young, Alfred. *The Democratic Republicans of New York: The Origins, 1763–1797*. Chapel Hill, N.C.: University of North Carolina Press, 1967.

Articles

Appleby, Joyce. "Republicanism in Old and New Contexts." *William and Mary Quarterly*, 3rd ser., 43 (1986): 20–34.

———. "What is Still American in the Political Philosophy of Thomas Jefferson?" *William and Mary Quarterly* 39 (1982): 287–309.

Banning, Lance. "Jeffersonian Ideology Revisited: Liberal and Classical Ideas in the New American Republic." *William and Mary Quarterly*, 3rd ser., 43 (1986): 3–19.

Brant, Irving. "Election of 1808." Vol. 1. In *History of American Presidential Elections, 1789–1968*, pp. 185–221. Edited by Arthur M. Schlesinger, Jr. New York: Chelsea House, 1985.

Cornog, Evan W. "To Give a Character to Our City: New York's City Hall." *New York History* 69 (1988): 389–423.

———. "American Revolution, Democratic Revolution, Market Revolution: A Review Essay." *New York History* 74 (1993): 87–96.

Cress, Lawrence Delbert. "'Cool and Serious Reflection': Federalist Attitudes toward War in 1812." *Journal of the Early Republic* 7 (1987): 123–45.

Ellis, David Maldwyn. "Rise of the Empire State, 1790–1820." *New York History* 56 (1975): 5–27.

Formisano, Ronald P., and Kathleen Smith Kutolowski. "Antimasonry and Masonry: The Genesis of Protest, 1826–1827." *American Quarterly* 29 (1977): 139–65.

Hanyan, Craig. "De Witt Clinton and Partisanship: The Development of Clintonianism from 1811 to 1820." *New-York Historical Society Quarterly* 56 (1972): 109–31.

———. "King George, Queen Caroline, and the Albany Regency: The Origins of a Political Term." *New York History* 76 (1985): 349–78.

Harris, Jonathan. "De Witt Clinton as Naturalist." *New-York Historical Society Quarterly* 56 (1972): 264–84.

Henretta, James A. "The Transition to Capitalism in America." In *The Transformation of Early American History: Society, Authority, and Ideology*, pp. 218-38. Edited by James Henretta, Michael Kammen, and Stanley N.Katz. New York: Alfred A. Knopf, 1991.

Hopkins, Vivian C. "The Empire State: De Witt Clinton's Laboratory." *New-York Historical Society Quarterly* 59 (1975): 6–44.

Howe, Daniel Walker. "European Sources of Political Ideas in Jeffersonian America." *Reviews in American History* 10 (1982): 28–44.

Howe, John R., Jr. "Republican Thought and the Political Violence of the 1790s." *American Quarterly* 19 (1967): 147–65.

Hunter, Gregory S. "The Manhattan Company: Managing a Multi-Unit Corporation in New York, 1799–1842." In *New York and the Rise of American Capitalism: Economic Development and Political History of an American State, 1780–1870*, pp. 124–46. Edited by William Pencak and Conrad Edick Wright. New York: The New-York Historical Society, 1989.

Nadler, Solomon. "The Green Bag: James Monroe and the Fall of De Witt Clinton." *New-York Historical Society Quarterly* 59 (1975): 203–25.

Onuf, Peter S. "Reflections on the Founding: Constitutional Historiography in Bicentennial Perspective." *William and Mary Quarterly*, 3rd ser., 46 (1989): 341–75.

Prince, Carl E. "The Passing of the Aristocracy: Jefferson's Removal of the Federalists, 1801–1805." *Journal of American History* 57 (1970): 563–75.

Riesman, Janet A. "Republican Revisions: Political Economy in New York after the Panic of 1819." In *New York and the Rise of American Capitalism: Economic Development and Political History of an American State, 1780–1870*, pp. 1–44. Edited by William Pencak and Conrad Edick Wright. New York: The New-York Historical Society, 1989.

Risjord, Norman K. "Election of 1812." Vol. 1. In *History of American Presidential Elections, 1789–1968*, pp. 249–72. Edited by Arthur M. Schlesinger, Jr. New York: Chelsea House, 1985.

Rupp, Robert. O. "Parties and the Public Good: Political Antimasonry in New York Reconsidered." *Journal of the Early Republic* (1988)8: 253–79.

Scheiber, Harry N. "Government and the Economy: Studies of the 'Commonwealth' Policy in Nineteenth-Century America." *Journal of Interdisciplinary History* 3 (1972): 135–51.

———. "The Transportation Revolution and American Law: Constitutionalism and Public Policy." In *Transportation and the Early Nation: Papers Presented at an Indiana American Revolution Symposium*, pp. 1–29. Indianapolis: Indiana Historical Society, 1982.

Shaw, Ronald E. "Canals in the Early Republic: A Review of Recent Literature." *Journal of the Early Republic* 4 (1984): 117–51.

Sokoloff, Kenneth L. "Inventive Activity in Early Industrial America: Evidence from Patent Records, 1790–1846." *The Journal of Economic History* 48 (1988): 813–47.

———, and Khan, B. Zorina. "The Democratization of Invention During Early Industrialization: Evidence from the United States, 1790–1846." *The Journal of Economic History* 50 (1990): 363–78.

Strum, Harvey. "Property Qualifications and Voting Behavior in New York, 1807–1816." *Journal of the Early Republic* 1 (1981): 347–71.

Turner, Lynn. "Elections of 1816 and 1820." Vol. 1. In *History of American Presidential Elections, 1789–1968,* pp. 299–321. Edited by Arthur M. Schlesinger, Jr. New York: Chelsea House, 1985.

Wallace, Michael. "Changing Concepts of Party in the United States: New York, 1815–28." *American Historical Review* 74 (1968): 453–91.

Dissertations

Carp, Roger Evan. "The Erie Canal and the Liberal Challenge to Classical Republicanism, 1785–1850." Ph.D. dissertation, University of North Carolina, 1986.

Hanyan, Craig. "DeWitt Clinton: Years of Molding, 1769–1807." Ph.D. dissertation, Harvard University, 1964.

Lagana, Michael P. "DeWitt Clinton: Politician Toward a New Political Order, 1769–1802." Ph.D. dissertation, Columbia University, 1972.

Nodyne, Kenneth Robert. "The Role of De Witt Clinton and the Municipal Government in the Development of Cultural Organizations in New York City, 1803–1817." Ph.D. dissertation, New York University, 1969.

Siry, Steven Edwin. "De Witt Clinton and the American Political Economy: Sectionalism, Politics, and Republican Ideology, 1787–1828." Ph.D. dissertation, University of Cincinnati, 1986.

Willis, Edmund P. "Social Origins of Political Leadership in New York City from the Revolution to 1850." Ph.D. dissertation, University of California, Berkeley, 1967.

INDEX